W9-BUN-577

Searching
FOR
Beauty

Also by Cherie Burns

The Great Hurricane: 1938

Stepmotherhood:
How to Survive Without Feeling Frustrated,
Left Out, or Wicked

Searching
FOR
Beauty

THE LIFE OF MILLICENT ROGERS, THE AMERICAN HEIRESS WHO TAUGHT THE WORLD ABOUT STYLE

Cherie Burns

 ST. MARTIN'S GRIFFIN NEW YORK

FRONTISPIECE: Millicent as she was photographed in 1947 at Falcon's Lair, Rudolph Valentino's former villa in Benedict Canyon overlooking Beverly Hills, which she rented during her pursuit of Clark Gable in Hollywood. (*Archives of the Millicent Rogers Museum, Taos, New Mexico*)

SEARCHING FOR BEAUTY. Copyright © 2011 by Cherie Burns. All rights reserved. Printed in the United States of America. For information, address St. Martin's Press, 175 Fifth Avenue, New York, N.Y. 10010.

www.stmartins.com

Design by Meryl Sussman Levavi

The Library of Congress has cataloged the hardcover edition as follows:

Burns, Cherie.
    Searching for beauty : the life of Millicent Rogers / Cherie Burns.—1st ed.
        p. cm.
    Includes bibliographical references and index.
    ISBN 978-0-312-54724-0
    1. Rogers, Millicent, d. 1953.   2. Upper class women—United States—Biography.
    3. Heiresses—United States—Biography.   4. Socialites—United States—Biography.
    5. Philanthropists—United States—Biography.   6. Models (Persons)—United States—
    Biography.   7. Art—Collectors and collecting—United States—Biography   8. Rogers,
    Millicent, d. 1953—Relations with men.   9. Taos (N.M.)—Biography.   10. Taos (N.M.)—
    Intellectual life—20th century.   I. Title.
        CT275.R763B87 2011
        978.9'53054092—dc23
        [B]

                                                                                                    2011019821

ISBN 978-0-312-54725-7 (trade paperback)

First St. Martin's Griffin Edition: October 2012

D 10 9 8 7 6 5 4 3 2

To Taos—real, remembered, and imagined

Contents

Acknowledgments

MILLICENT'S STORY BEGAN TO TAKE SHAPE FOR ME after my friends Jack Smith and Paul Pascarella introduced me to Millicent's son, Arturo Peralta-Ramos, who invited me to lunch. He then spent a number of hours with me in a series of interviews that formed the starting point for my research. While Arturo later chose to support an authorized biography, which did not materialize, I am grateful to him for the time he gave me, and for his fierce interest in his mother's story.

I am also indebted to other members of Millicent's family: Arturo Peralta-Ramos III, Philip Peralta-Ramos, Wiltraud Salm, Antonia Salm, and especially to Christina Lucia Peralta-Ramos for her conscientious help. Fellow authors Annette Tapert, Shelby Tisdale, and Adam Lewis, generously shared information with me. Donald Sturrock navigated time differences between New Mexico and England to provide details about Millicent and Roald Dahl from research for his recent biography of Dahl.

Millicent made headlines during her life from Massachusetts to California, and this book could not have happened without the expertise of research librarians and archivists across the country who helped me follow her trail: Shawn Waldron at Condé Nast, John Cantrell at Hearst, Debra Charpentier at the Millicent Library in Fairhaven, Massachusetts; Mary Cummings at the Southampton Historical Society, the Southampton Public Library, Angie Parks at the Brooklyn Museum, and the incredible Carolyn Waters at the New York Society Library. Also Barbara Hall at the Margaret Herrick Library in Beverly Hills, Ned Comstock and Dace Taube at the Doheny Memorial Library at the University of Southern California, Christina Rice at the Los Angeles Public Library, Katherine Feo at the Harry Ransom Collection at the University of Texas, and Tomas Jaehn at the Fray Angelico Chavez History Library in Santa Fe. Helpful as well were the New-York Historical Society, Planting Fields Arboretum State Historic Park in Oyster Bay, New York; the Southampton Public Library, the Historical Society of Washington, D.C., the District of Columbia Public Library, the New Mexico State Records and Archives, and the Center for Southwest Research at the University of New Mexico in Albuquerque. Closer to home, Fred Peralta, Carmela Quinto, and the staff of the Millicent Rogers Museum in Taos were always supportive. Jina Brenneman at the Harwood Museum of Art lent her enthusiasm and resources to the project.

I am grateful to the Millicent Rogers Museum for granting me access to and permission to quote from Millicent's letters and diary and other materials held in their archives. I am also grateful to Wiltraud and Antonia Salm for permission to quote from *My Dear Peter—Confessions of a Father*, and to the following libraries and institutions for access to and permission to quote from material in their collections: the Center for Southwest Research, University Libraries, University of New Mexico; the Harry Ransom Center at the University of Texas at Austin; the Roald Dahl Museum and Story Centre, Great Missenden, Buckinghamshire, UK; and the Planting Fields Foundation, Oyster Bay, New York.

There is a long list of people in New Mexico who helped me put together those many aspects of Millicent's life that were never recorded on paper or film. Judy Anderson, Benton Bond, Barbara Brenner, Paul "Paco" Castillo, Paulle Clark, Phoebe Cottam, Elizabeth Cunningham, Barbara Duff, Clark Funk, Jean-Vi Lenthe, Tom and Barbara McCarthy, Ouray Meyers, Dollie Mondragon, Dalton Montgomery, Robert Parsons, Joan Pond, Jackie Peralta-Ramos, Steve Petit, Rena Rosequist, Sylvia Rodriguez, Deborah Sherman, Francy Speirs, Bob Tenorio, Olga Torres-Reid, Norbert Vigil, Bill Westbury, Mary Wheeler, Art Wolfe, and Barbara Waters were the Taos locals, some of whom have moved on by now, who directed me to other people and places that would help tell her story. Patricia Ripley, Susan Streeper, and Dori Vinella were often my confessors and guides. Larry Torres, who shared the videotape of his interview with the late Paul Peralta-Ramos, provided me a glimpse of Millicent's son I had come to Taos too late to meet.

Dr. Robert Knudson patiently walked me through the stages of rheumatic fever and treatment during the past century to help me understand the medical menace that stalked Millicent's life.

I will gratefully and long remember sitting by Miranda Masocco Levy's bedside in Santa Fe while she good-naturedly recalled the Millicent she had known seventy years earlier. The late Martha Reed also cheerily shared her wealth of Western fashion experience with me as she moved in and out of hospitals. She lit up like a young girl each time she opened her closet to show me the Western skirts and dresses we discussed.

Susan Dicus Chittim, who sat at Millicent's knee when she first came to Taos and lived in the house now owned by Kathy and Michael Fitzgerald, made that house come alive for me in a different time and era, with Millicent ensconced and smuggling puppies into the front room.

Pat Allen and Rebecca Rodriguez patiently scanned and copied photos and pages for a jittery author with a deadline.

My friend and fellow writer Bonnie Lee Black generously read the manuscript early on and contributed her valuable observations and copyediting.

Lloyd Bolander, Skip Keith Miller, and Bill Westbury helped me chase the phantom of Millicent's reported visit to Tres Ritos, which we could never corroborate or document beyond a photo.

Ernesto Luhan, Kathleen Cornbringer Michaels, Dawn Mirabal, Tony Reyna, Mary Esther Winters, Juanita Marcus Turley, and Santiago Suazo helped me understand Millicent's involvement with Taos Pueblo and its people.

Elizabeth Irvine, Judith Price, Edward Landrigan, Kenneth Jay Lane, and Federico Jimenez guided me to some understanding of the the world of jewelry making. Hamish Bowles, Harold Koda, Jan Reeder, Arnold Scaasi, Babs Simpson, and John Galliano generously shared with me their fashion insights and thoughts on Millicent.

I want to especially thank Louise Grunwald, Leonard Stanley, Daphne Root, Jody Donohue, and Lotsie Holton, who opened their social diaries and address books in order to help. Others tolerantly let me exhume old ghosts of bygone lovers, ex-spouses, gossip, and family matters. Robin Adrian, Louise Balcom, Oatsie Charles, Michael Coe, Paul Gregory, Maria Janis, Rita Kip, Charles Mallory, Bunny Mellon, Payne Middleton, Patricia Munn, the Countesses Jacqueline de Ribes and Sheila de Rochambeau, Warren Sinsheimer, Odette Terrel des Chênes, Thomas R. Vreeland, Hutton Wilkinson, Vanessa Wilcox, Betsy Wright, and Kohle Yohannan contributed their time and recollections.

A personal thanks to David Michaelis for his help and sound advice. I am truly indebted to my agent, Cynthia Cannell, for making this book happen, beginning to end, and to Toby Greenberg, who steered me through the daunting process of choosing a few select images of a woman who was photographed her entire life. And to my editor, Michael Flamini, of St. Martin's Press for his unwavering enthusiasm and big vision, his assistant, Vicki Lame, for helping carry it through, and to my husband, Dick Duncan, for his love, support and expert meddling.

Introduction

FIRST TOOK NOTE OF MILLICENT ROGERS WHEN I VISITED THE museum named after her in Taos, New Mexico, when I came here with my family to ski in the 1990s. I didn't know much about her and the name blurred with Mabel Dodge Luhan, Dorothy Brett, Frieda Lawrence, and Georgia O'Keeffe, other famous women who found their way to New Mexico and left an impression with their bohemian ways, flair, mischief, and artistry. One cannot but wonder at the photos of Frieda Lawrence, D. H.'s wife, who often had a cigarette dangling from her lip; O'Keeffe, the severe artist with her tight kerchiefs; magisterial Mabel; and eccentric Brett. It was not until I came to live in Taos in 2005 that I routinely visited the Millicent Rogers Museum, and Millicent Rogers began to come into focus for me. She was an elegant beauty, mysterious and evocative because less was known publicly about her life. I often took visitors to the adobe museum on the edge of town to show them the regional artistry and New Mexican sensibility on display. Waiting for them in the lobby, I had time to study the likenesses of Millicent on the walls. Her whimsical drawings for her children in the last gallery intrigued me almost more than her fashion shots, and there was much more in between.

The more I looked into her legend and realized that of her fifty-one-year-long life, only six of those years were lived in Taos, the more intrigued I became. Though she is associated in the modern public consciousness with New Mexico, she lived most of her life in New York and Europe, tripping the light fantastic wherever she went. Researching her life story gave me the opportunity to learn more about Taos, and to fill in my dearth of knowledge about the 1930s and 40s, Millicent's heydays, in both fashion and political history.

People have asked me if I could "feel" Millicent as I have researched and written about her. It's a kind of question that is perhaps more frequent in Taos, where unseen connections and omens are common enough topics among seekers of all stripes. Yet the answer is no, at least not in the way I believe the question is asked. I never felt a special connection or channel to Millicent Rogers. I never felt, as fun as it might have been, that I lived, albeit temporarily, in her skin.

At times I have felt certain that I understood her. As I increasingly came to know more about her I began to understand that she was a woman who knew tremendous freedom to act and live on her own terms, yet she was often hampered—caged even—by the very money and status that made her free. She was a sympathetic character. Even her story seemed kept under wraps, hostage to legend, filial possessiveness, and time. Somebody, somewhere, always thought they knew best what was right for Millicent Rogers, and she struggled against that. As her biographer, I came to feel that writing her story was a liberating act that could set her memory free by gathering together all the bits and pieces of her tale into one determined narrative. If she does hover over us somewhere in the ether, having found the place she called "part of the earth," I hope it sets her free.

There never was a man who holding pain within himself had not seen God and known eternity and walked from them alone . . . or else, seeing beauty, thirsted after it as some life-giving force to which he must give his whole abandon.

—MILLICENT ROGERS

Searching FOR *Beauty*

CHAPTER ONE

Farewell to an Heiress

JANUARY 1953

THE PROCESSION OF MOURNERS WOUND ALONG THE RUTTED unpaved road toward a weedy little graveyard next to Indian land. Behind it tolled the bells of Our Lady of Guadalupe Church in town; ahead of it rose Taos Mountain, the Sacred Mountain, all white with its peak hidden in the clouds. Brightly colored plastic flowers, indigenous to Spanish gravesites, bloomed from decorated crosses and gravestones in the high-desert resting place for local Spanish families and anglos. Millicent Rogers, in a manner as improbable yet fitting as so much of her unsettled life, was going home.

Taos, New Mexico, had long captivated artists, bohemians, scamps, and freethinking souls from elsewhere, who settled into its hive of quirky adobe houses at the feet of the Sangre de Cristo Mountains. Millicent Rogers had finally been one of them. She had been one of the most beautiful and richest women in America, perhaps the world. The toast of barons, industrialists, and royalty for almost five decades, she was known and admired in the fashion ateliers of Paris, London, and New York. Her face and fashions had appeared in *Vogue* and

Harper's Bazaar all her life. She had loved a constellation of spectacular men. Now that the grand arc of her life had come to an end she was laid, as she requested, with her head facing Taos Mountain, next to the pueblo village and Indian people whom she had fallen nearly desperately in love with during the last six years of her life.

One mourner, the critic and writer William Goyen, wrote of the day,

> The ceremony was a dreadful small-town ceremony in the graveyard produced by the local funeral home. . . . A sort of Muzak chimed a mawkish hymn. We all gathered round while the priest said his words, and a brilliant game rooster suddenly leapt to a fence just to one side of the grave and crowed. When the brief ceremony was over, Benito, the young Indian who had been in love with Millicent—wild, with flowing black hair to his shoulders, and flowers in his hair, and bedecked with bracelets, necklaces, beads, and drunk—and who had been held back, sullen and grief-stricken until now, rushed from the background and broke through the crowd toward the grave, crying out. But he was caught and held back by other Indians.[1]

Goyen's cosmopolitan eye noted that the funeral was attended by "the rich and celebrated from various parts of the world." One English aristocrat, Dorothy Brett, got her car ahead of the hearse and out of grief or her own haphazard driving habit, zigzagged the whole procession along the road.

Millicent's three sons had come: the eldest, wearing a cutaway suit, was the product of her ill-fated elopement with an Austrian nobleman when she was twenty-one, the other two were sons from her second marriage to an Argentine aristocrat that had also ended in divorce. Millicent's mother, Mary Rogers, a dowager from the East Coast, had arrived after a three-day train trip in her own railroad car, a legacy from a life underwritten by an oil and railroad fortune that had also richly funded her daughter's stylish life. The funeral was postponed for several days to allow for her arrival. Mary had quietly asserted that under these circumstances the rail companies could accommodate her request to make the trip without a train change, and they had.

There was a certain incongruity for the writer Goyen, and perhaps to others on the scene, that these people of pedigree and wealth were gathered together to say their good-byes to a high-flying daughter, mother, friend, and lover as she was lowered into such a humble gravesite. Yet she had toward the end of her life taken refuge, sought peace and beauty, in elemental things. Her quest had led her to Taos. Though true happiness seemed always to elude her, Millicent claimed to her youngest son in a letter months before her death, an event she felt approaching at age fifty, that she was finally at peace. It would offer some comfort to her survivors.

Her life, like her funeral, had been distinctive, even unpredictable. During her time in Taos, she had deliberately befriended the Indians from the pueblo and they came to her funeral in numbers unprecedented to mourn the death of an outsider. Draped in the colorful blankets that they wore against the cold in winter and for celebrations, they appeared to bid her safe journey to the afterlife and farewell, in a rainbow of reds, blues, and yellows, their shiny black hair drawn back into buns and plaits, their heads bowed. They stood respectfully in a riot of color against the wide, Western winter sky.

Millicent was dressed as finely in her mahogany coffin as she had been in life. She wore an Apache-style dress made for her by her designer friend and fashion legend Elsa Schiaparelli. A great silver concho belt was twined at her waist. The large, mostly turquoise, rings that she favored were on her hands and a fine Indian chief blanket was wrapped around her. There was a brief Catholic ceremony. In a late life conversion, Millicent had become a Catholic the week before her death. After Benito's display of grief, most of the mourners looked away or hurried to their cars to leave.

For almost no one who left the Sierra Vista Cemetery on that day, had Millicent Rogers truly been put to rest. Her life and image would be reflected for decades to come through her vast belongings, words, old photographs, and history. She would be reinvented again and again by the fashion world, which she influenced in almost equal parts in life and after death. She cast a long shadow even from the grave on her family, and her three sons would variously strive to uphold, repudiate, and re-create her legend. With each subsequent year, her true self would seem to fade and grow faint, like a photograph exposed to the harsh New Mexican sun, while her heirs continued to retouch it. It would become more and more difficult to separate the truths of her life from the myth, especially because in life Millicent had been a restless soul, one who seldom stayed for long in one place. She was mistress of the grand gesture and exercised a practiced inscrutability, which no doubt accounted for much of her allure.

Her life arched over half a century of American history and across two continents. Born in the Edwardian era, she died just as the first signs of the upheaval of the sixties were visible on Taos's funky horizon. The beginning of her remarkable trajectory, like the origin of so many American sagas of the twentieth century, lay in the crystallization of wealth that produced great fortunes in the late 1800s. Her life and its trappings would have inspired an Edith Wharton heroine. With good looks, plenty of money, and a personal elegance that seemed to transcend both, she sampled life widely, but never fully invested. She was both a debutante and a flapper of the twenties, and she had no sooner come of age than she eloped with a titled European as the most daring daughters of great wealth did after the first World War. There were two more husbands and many more high-profile lovers as she lived the ex-patriot high life of Europe before World War II, and joined into the heady whirl of wartime Washington during the war. When the conflict ended, still recognized as a fashion trendsetter, she joined the new front of American glamour in Hollywood. There was a fling with the movie star Clark Gable, and then her constant quest for beauty in fashion, art, men—all the world around her—led her to Taos, where she found, finally, unexpected fulfillment. It was more than most women dream of, accomplished in five decades. Then at fifty she was dead.

CHAPTER TWO

Fortune and Family

A GLAMOROUS LIFE OF TRAVEL, HIGH FASHION, AND SUperstar social status like the one that Millicent Rogers led required a gusher of money in early twentieth century America. Wealth like that was not drawn from widely held corporations, but from privately won fortunes generated by hard-driven individuals who often had little or no formal training or background in their fields. Millicent Rogers' good fortunes sprang from such a man, her paternal grandfather, who in 1860 was a young grocery clerk contemplating a career in a dying industry, whaling.

Whaling was what most young men aspired to in Fairhaven, Massachusetts, across the harbor from New Bedford. But like his father who had given it a try before he decided to open a grocery store, Henry Huttleston Rogers didn't find whaling his calling. The low wages and three-year voyages had little appeal for "Hen" as the dark and slim young man was known around town. He worked in the family's Union Grocery store, carried newspapers, and delivered groceries with a horse and cart. There was little exceptional about him except for his occasional acting performances at Phoenix Hall, the local theater. He had taken time out of high school after his sophomore year to apprentice himself to an architect, but much to his mother's relief, he returned to school. He didn't particularly like architecture, either. After graduation he worked as a railroad brakeman and baggageman, living at home with his family in order to save money. He had a sweetheart, Abigail Gifford, a classmate and fellow thespian who lived three blocks away, and marriage was the logical next step. But Hen had a restless streak.

Whalers, and those who depended on the whaling industry like the citizens of Fairhaven and New Bedford, had taken note with foreboding in 1854 when petroleum was discovered in western Pennsylvania. The first successful drilling rig was put into use in Titusville, Pennsylvania, in 1859, and within five years the output of one single well exceeded the cumulative oil output of Europe for the previous two hundred years. Kerosene, the principal product of petroleum and natural gas, would soon replace whale oil for lighting in North America.

Whaling had reached its peak in 1857, when Henry was seventeen. He'd heard townspeople, many of whom depended on whaling for their livelihood, talk about the new competition from Scandinavia. Some like Abigail's father, a whaler whose whaling crews and vessels were diverted to assist in blockading the Confederate coastal areas and ports during the Civil War, said that its best days were over. Whaling no longer looked like a good bet for an enterprising young man in New England. Henry, in one of the defining moments of his life (and to some degree, United States economic history), pooled his $600 savings with his friend Charles Ellis and the two of them set out for western Pennsylvania.

Full of trepidation and enthusiasm, the young partners invested in a refinery and gave it a Native American name from home, Wamsutta. When Henry Rogers returned home a year later, the Wamsutta Oil Refinery had made them $30,000, three times what an average three-year whaling voyage would earn back in Fairhaven or New Bedford. In short order he married Abbie Gifford and took her back to the oil fields of Pennsylvania. The future looked promising for the young couple, though Abbie and her husband set up housekeeping in a one-room shack along Oil Creek to be near the Wamsutta Oil Refinery.

Things moved quickly for Ellis and Rogers. The challenges were often sudden and dramatic. They partnered with a man Ellis had sold whale oil to in Fairhaven, Charles Pratt, the owner of a paint and oil company. At first the going was rough and Ellis lost heart, but Rogers persevered. He went to see Pratt, and took responsibility for the debt that he and Ellis had incurred in their contract to provide crude oil to Pratt's business. It was a bold move, and Pratt was impressed enough with his young partner's grit to make Rogers foreman of his Brooklyn refinery. Rogers moved his wife and baby daughter to Brooklyn and in the next few years became indispensable to the Pratt operation. A hard and conscientious worker, Rogers often slept three hours a night rolled up in a blanket by the side of a still.[1] Abbie dutifully slipped in to the refinery to bring him his dinner. Their efforts were rewarded when Pratt made Henry the manager of Pratt's oil refinery. Soon he became a partner in the business.

Meanwhile, a young man in Cleveland, Ohio, was ambitiously learning the shipping business. John D. Rockefeller believed that the real money to be made from the oil industry would not be made from oil itself, but from hauling and refining it. By 1863 the first railroad was completed, reaching into the heart of the oil region, and refineries sprouted up alongside it almost overnight. The Atlantic and Great Western Railroad in Cleveland carried 115 million barrels of petroleum in 1863 and became the principal oil carrier in the country. Rockefeller had started a company, Clark and Rockefeller, with eighteen hundred dollars, a thousand of it borrowed from his father. Seeing the growth in oil, he put an additional four thousand dollars into the business, and never looked back.

An idea to make common cause between the producers of oil and its shippers was beginning to take shape in his mind. If a large refiner could provide a steady high volume of oil to the railroads for shipping, thought Rockefeller and his team, they could corner the market.

Secretly, Rockefeller and his partners convinced other large refiners to join him in a monopoly that would control the oil business in return for stock in the company. It was ruthless business. "... If you don't sell your property to us, it will be valueless and those who refuse will be crushed," John D. Rockefeller told his own brother, Frank.[2]

The Charles Pratt Company was one of the refineries that joined in Rockefeller's clandestine plan to buy up as much of the local competition as possible before their coup was widely recognized. Pratt's involvement was fortuitous for Henry Rogers, who had earlier been noted for his initial efforts *against* Rockefeller's plan to control oil shipping rates. Rockefeller's biographers Peter Collier and David Horowitz, note that Pratt brought to the merger "... the considerable daring of Henry H. Rogers." Both sides operated expediently. Rockefeller saw a cunning and determined talent in the young Henry Rogers. Rogers had resisted Rockefeller's steamrolling of the refiners, but he turned around when he and Charles Pratt extracted terms for their participation in a company that would guarantee them jobs and financial security. Pratt's son became Secretary of Standard Oil and his father's protégé, Rogers, was vice president by 1890.

The Standard Oil Company, as Rockefeller's brainchild became, was the most spectacular success story in business history. It was indisputably the most powerful industrial organization in the nation, and the most visible symbol of growing American might abroad. But the "Standard Oil Gang," as the group became known, was feared and admired. "There is no question about it but these men are smarter than I am a great deal . . . I never came in contact with any class of men as smart and able as they are in their business," William Vanderbilt told a government investigation into railroad rates.[3] Rockefeller believed almost religiously in letting each executive do what he wanted to do and what he could do best. Rogers proved himself an able hatchet man and strategist. In 1899 he bought the Anaconda Copper Mining Company for $39 million in a deal that required the seller to hold back the purchase check long enough to allow him to organize the Amalgamated Copper Company and transfer all the Anaconda mines to it, issuing $75 million worth of shares in the new corporation. He and his fellow executives borrowed money on these shares, offered the stock to the public, and pocketed $36 million on no investment at all. Such lethal maneuvers earned Rogers the name "Hellhound of Wall Street." He, like other robber barons, stonewalled investigations into the secretive dealings of The Standard Oil Trust. "Relentless, ravenous, ruthless as a shark, knowing no law of God or man in the execution of his purpose," the author Thomas W. Lawson said of Rogers in his book *Frenzied Finance: The Crime of Amalgamated*, in 1905. Rogers proudly managed to outsmart the trustbusters of the day in order to keep the profits of Rockefeller's monopoly for himself and other trustees of the company.

He had risen into the rarified society of millionaires who were not only rich enough to live well, but were a class of Americans unto themselves. They thrived on their own business matters and companionship. Walking down the streets in their top hats, chesterfield coats, and freshly shined shoes, they looked even a breed apart. The public both admired their acumen and reviled them for the ruthless tactics and exploitation of the market.

John D. Rockefeller was considered a single-focused business magnate with few other interests and friends outside of his work, but Henry Rogers was distinguished by his duality. The tabloid journalists called him the "Jekyll and Hyde of Wall Street"; on one hand a steely cold businessman, and on the other a generous family man, wit, and raconteur. He and Abbie had five daughters during the first ten years of their marriage, and the growing family continued to move to quarters appropriate to its size and growing wealth in America's Gilded Age. They began on 26 East Fifty-seventh Street, but by the turn of the century had moved to a lavish townhouse at 3 East Eighty-first Street. Rogers also owned a building on East Fifty-seventh Street that served as a garage and stable for his collection of automobiles, horses, and carriages. In 1894 he began building an eighty-five-room mansion on Fourth Street in Fairhaven, where he and his family spent weekends and summers. The house was equipped with its own gas and electric plant, stables, and greenhouses and gardens for Abbie's prized chrysanthemums.

Rogers played his dual role well. He went to church regularly, supported the arts, and was a member of half a dozen social clubs. He often visited his widowed mother in Fairhaven and kept up with old friends, who still called him Hen. He built the Rogers School, a gift to the Fairhaven community school, and put out the town's eyes with a costly Unitarian church and parsonage, in addition to a public library and town hall, the former designed in Italian Renaissance style with granite and terra-cotta, the interior decorated to rival a sumptuous Italian interior with carved scrolls, window pilasters, and copies of Italian bas-reliefs. His charity put him in touch with persons outside his own walk of life, and was responsible for a remarkable and enduring friendship with the writer Mark Twain. Twain had unwisely invested almost his entire worth in an unsuccessful enterprise to construct a typesetting machine—an endeavor that threatened to ruin him financially—until his newfound friend assumed some of his indebtedness and stepped in to rescue the business plan. "I owe more to Henry Rogers than to any other man whom I have known," Twain wrote in a particular tribute to his friend some years later.[4] Twain, in turn, directed Rogers' generosity to Helen Keller and Booker T. Washington. The bonds between Twain and Rogers went beyond financial expediency. Photos of them, two distinguished looking older men with fluffy white mustaches (Twain's punctuated by a cigar), onboard Rogers' steam yacht, *Kanawah*, attests to their friendship. Twain would outlive Rogers and remain a fast friend of Rogers' only son, Henry Huttleston Rogers Jr., born in 1879.[5]

Despite his millions from Standard Oil, Rogers kept his hand in the business world and continued to make money. He always kept an office in New York, where Twain often arrived after lunch to take a nap. Rogers operated as the transportation czar of Staten Island. He was the principal owner of its railroad, traction lines, and ferries. His final enterprise was the building of the remarkable Virginian Railway that ran from the West Virginia coalfields to Norfolk. Ten thousand men were employed to cut its course, much of it through solid rock.[6] In his later years, Rogers seemed equally comfortable in the boardrooms of railroad companies as he was dandling a grandchild on his knee on the lawn of his Fairhaven mansion overlooking New Bedford harbor. He would live to see eight grandchildren. Second among them, his son's first child, was a precocious, pretty little brown-eyed daughter, Millicent, named after his and Abbie's third daughter, who had died at seventeen from heart problems. His $150 million fortune (worth 3,950,000,000 in 2009) would support his family for generations to come. Nothing approaching his genius for moneymaking and managing would be evidenced by his heirs.

Henry Huttleston Rogers Jr., heir to his father's fortune—along with his four sisters—was quite a catch for eligible young girls in New York society. Called Harry to distinguish him from his father, he was the only living Rogers son (another had died in infancy), and a junior at Columbia College when he became engaged to the lively Mary Benjamin, a petite nineteen-year-old with wit and confidence borne of her own well-established lineage.

Theirs was not a great love story, but the mild-mannered pairing of young rich New Yorkers from the same social tribe. They were, as were many society folk and European aristocrats who moved in small tight circles, vaguely related.

The Rogers and Benjamin families seemed destined to be connected. The Benjamins were a prominent New York family with an illustrious history of their own. Their famous forefather, Park Benjamin, had been a leading journalist in Boston and New York in the nineteenth century. Along with Horace Greeley, the legendary newspaper editor and reformer, Benjamin helped establish *The New York Herald Tribune* and was associated with Henry J. Raymond, the founder of *The New York Times*. Benjamin was also a friend of Edgar Allan Poe, Herman Melville, Nathaniel Hawthorne, and Henry Wadsworth Longfellow. H. H. Rogers eldest child, Anne, born when Abbie and Henry Rogers were living in the oil fields of Pennsylvania, married one of Park's sons, William Evarts Benjamin, a bookdealer and publisher who had helped Mark Twain during his financial troubles by purchasing the rights to his ten-volume *Library of American Literature.*

Mary's father, George, was a patent expert and industrial engineer. He had been a practicing physician, a criminologist, and a lawyer, and in his latest incarnation was editor of *The National Cyclopedia of Applied Mechanics,* a respected dictionary of mechanical engineering and arts when such sciences were considered the cornerstones of progress.

Mary Benjamin was rooted in the entitled traditions of propriety, success, and polite society. The women of the family and their friends and in-laws' names often appeared in "What Is Doing in Society," *The New York Times*'s society column at the turn of the century, with descriptions of the balls, teas, and parties that invariably portrayed them graciously entertaining amid arrays of massed palms, ferns, and flowers. Mary, an attractive auburn-haired nineteen-year-old with elfin features, won admirers with her pretty pertness, manners, and a flair for fine clothes. She lacked a higher education, as did most young women of her social station of her day, yet she followed the fine arts and music, and was known for her energy and quick wit. In the tradition of her family, she was a good writer and would develop into a fine painter.

Mark Twain continued to crisscross through the annals of the Rogers' family history. Mary was one of the young women Mark Twain made a member of his Aquarium Club, a collection of bright young women he doted on. Though, like Lewis Carroll's penchant for photographing young ladies during the Victorian era, which raised eyebrows and questions when brought to light in modern times, Twain's devotion to the Angelfish, as he called the members of the Aquarium Club, strains our modern sense of propriety. Yet at the time, the aging author's attentions were considered acceptable. Girls in middies posed adoringly on his arm or at his knee as he postured in academic robes, composing what could have been a charade of vestal virgins and a foppish lecher perhaps. Yet these tableaus were designed to reflect an ideal of the older man of letters with a demure admiring bevy of bright, innocent young women. It was an honor to be one of the creatures—

"pets" to use the quaint social definition—whom Twain singled out for lively conversation and debates and often erudite correspondence while in his sixties and seventies.[7] He was a widower and devoted father to his own daughters, but he enjoyed the stimulus and lilt that the Aquarium provided, and Mary, due to her own writing facility, warmth and cleverness, became a favorite. Twain signed his letters to her "Loving Uncle" and the correspondence between the two was eventually published in a book called *Mark Twain's Letters to Mary*, in which he unabashedly called her, "pulsatingly alive."[8] On a more conventional level, Twain was just as enamored with his friend Henry's young son Harry, whom he called "Electric Spark," for his excess energy. He dedicated his book of travel adventures, *Following the Equator*, to Henry Huttleston Jr. in 1897. Theirs was described as a fellowship between young rogues, though Twain was the age of Harry's father. Appropriately enough, they also shared a passion for playing billiards and could often be found hanging over Twain's pool table, a gift from the elder Rogers.

When Twain learned of the pending marriage between the two, he wrote, addressing Mary as Dear Miss Benjamin, " I feel a deep personal interest in this fortunate marriage because I helped to rear Harry Rogers and make him what he is." There was a note of jest, as when he continued to say he had the idea of sending her a diamond coronet as a present, but couldn't find any fresh diamonds of this year's crop. There was no need for diamonds. When she stood in her parents' home at 46 East Seventy-fourth Street for a ceremony decorated with palms and chrysanthemums on November 7, she wore a collar of diamond and pearls over the nape of her white crepe de chine dress, a present from her bridegroom's father, Henry Huttleston Rogers. Harry, too, had given her a diamond pendant.

At the time of her marriage to Harry Rogers, there was an air of sweetness and promise to her match with a young man who had so far done little to distinguish himself. Not one blemish had yet darkened the carefree prospect that seemed to stretch before them. There were no signs that the benevolent atmosphere surrounding the couple would in time become a rancorous tangle of quarrels, alcohol, and the intense marital battles for power, property, and money that the rich can most masterfully wage. Three days after the wedding the couple sailed on the *Kaiser Wilhelm II* for Gibraltar, Naples, and Genoa. During their nine-month honeymoon they journeyed as far as Egypt, where they were photographed in front of the pyramids. Upon their return they hopped onto her father-in-law's newest proud possession, the steam yacht, *Kanawha*. It was reputed to be "the fastest cruising steam yacht in American waters," according to a mention in *The New York Times*. ". . . with a high sharp clipper bow and a fine sheer," it cruised at a speed of twenty-two knots. Perhaps more to the point, it was considered superior to J. P. Morgan's boat, *Corsair*.

No one was more a-titter over the August cruise up the coast of New England with Henry Rogers, friends, his adult children, and their spouses, than Twain. Their excursion began with the laying of the cornerstone of the Unitarian Church her father-in-law had built in memory of his mother in Fairhaven and continued on to Boothbay and Bar Harbor, Maine, and New Brunswick. If Mary was restless with the horseplay and poker that characterized such trips, or travel-weary after nine months abroad, she apparently didn't let on. She and Twain reportedly had "some kind of spoofing good time at a luncheon party, conspiring against the others by making a game out of using long words which they pretended no one but themselves could understand"[9] Twain enjoyed playing young at heart, as though he and Mary and Harry were conspiring against the old folks.

As usual, Mary was outgoing and a good sport. She was also four months pregnant. Her and Harry's first child would be born the following February. They named their baby girl Mary Millicent Abigail Rogers. Besides being her mother's namesake, the baby was named in memory of her father's sister, Millicent, and her grandmother, Abigail.

CHAPTER THREE

Rich Beginnings

ONE CAN ALMOST HEAR THE RUSTLE OF THE LAYETTE silks and lace that swathed the newborn Mary Millicent Abigail Rogers. The ideal young Gilded Age couple, children of America's new royalty, had produced a princess. It was a momentous event for a household staffed with nannies, cooks, and butlers. Her parents shuttled her between their New York townhouse on Fifty-seventh Street and Madison Avenue, a country home in Tuxedo Park fifty miles up the Hudson River, and the Rogers' family seat in Fairhaven. Dark-haired and evenly featured, by all accounts Millicent was, perhaps predictably, a lovely child. At four she posed solemnly next to her newly christened brother, Henry Huttleston Rogers III, in a studio portrait. She appears to take herself seriously in the photo, but in a few others she exhibits some of the twinkle and zaniness she would become known for, staring bright-eyed with roses and hydrangeas stuck in her hair.

She was doted on, and like most young children of the leisure class, her moods and antics were solemnly noted as personality traits likely to distinguish her in years to come. Some would become self-fullfilling prophecies. Her grandfather wrote to his friend Mark Twain in the fall of 1905 of his son's family visit to Fairhaven, "We baptized Henry Rogers Junior a week ago last Sunday at the church in Fairhaven. Millicent (Harry's little girl) ran through the house before the occasion and told everybody that the baby was to be 'atomized' on Sunday."[1] He clearly delighted in her precociousness and energy.

Visits to the family homestead in Fairhaven were warm occasions for a growing brood of Rogers grandchildren. Rogers' daughter Mai had married William R. Coe and their infant son, William, was slightly younger than Millicent. In a letter to Mark Twain Mary described one of Millicent's antics. She seemed bossily to invoke her slight seniority over her young cousin in social matters. "I heard Millicent say to Billy Coe yesterday, 'Muddie said No, Billy, she would not give me another chocolate, and I will not ask her again, it would be very rude.'" Millicent was assertive and confident from the start, and amusing to her elders. According to her daughter-in-law, Wiltraud von Furstenberg Salm, "She was ridiculous even then." Antonia Salm says that the elder Rogers and Mark Twain benevolently found her flights of fancy amusing.

In 1906, Henry, the proud patriarch, was photographed seated amid his brood of eight grandchildren, posed in front of his grand estate in Fairhaven. Millicent, four years old, stood to his left in a starched white middy and buttoned high-top shoes, with a silken bow tying back a strand of her curls. Already she was arresting as she stared into the camera, ready for the first of the many photo ops that would land her in little more than a decade on the front of newspapers around the world and in the pages of fashion magazines.

Millicent's early childhood was unremarkable but for the life she led as a rich New York princess of the Gilded Age. Her sons portrayed her in conversation as a childhood beauty, at one stage wearing her hair in braids coiled over her ears like a young *fraülein* or in the soft twisted coronets fashionable at the time, as she would appear in *Harper's*

Bazaar in her teens. In early photos her hair is always down, festooned with a bow. Her mother dressed her in the loveliest of the white pinafores and middies that were popular for little girls in the early 1900s. In photos it is the backgrounds and her sober demeanor that are distinctive. Her fingers, already long and large for her age, stand out. Posed on an ornate brocade sofa in front of a leaded glass window in the family's apartment, a sober-faced Millicent, age seven, dangles one dress shoe over the head of a tiger rug on the floor beneath her. From the nursery in her parents elegant East Fifty-seventh Street townhouse, Millicent was bustled about to Central Park and on outings to Tuxedo Park. The best times were summer outings in Fairhaven where she could play with her cousins in the vast gardens surrounding the mansion with views of the sea. From the pillars of the cavernous reception hall to the main staircase with mahogany-topped banisters, it was a suitable palace for the Rogers grandchildren, who didn't know life could be anything else.

Millicent, like all the other grandchildren of Henry Huttleston Rogers, was expected to troop every winter into the office of her grandfather's friend, Dr. Clarence Rice, a successful ear, nose, and throat physician. Rice treated the Italian opera star, Enrico Caruso, and stage stars like Lillian Russell. He administered to her grandfather and Mark Twain, both. In his offices the Rogers grandchildren had their throats cauterized to guard against cold-weather illness.[2] It was not uncommon then, as now, for children to suffer from winter sore throats and colds, but in a world without antibiotics, the threat that these childhood maladies posed was more serious.

In the winter of 1910 a hush fell over the nursery in the Rogers' home when a stealthier infection struck the young Millicent. She came down with a sore throat and was put to bed, but within days her discomfort worsened. A high fever put everyone on alert. It recurred intermittently. Her usual gamboling high spirits, frisky kookiness, and zest gave way to listlessness. Even when her fevers ceased, her recovery seemed slow and her malaise lingered for days, then weeks. Dr. Edward Quintard, the attending physician who paid a house call to the Rogers' home on East Fifty-seventh Street, delivered his prognosis in somber tones. Her unblemished childhood would soon be marred, if not ended, by a much-feared and often fatal disease of the time, rheumatic fever.

Little was known about this illness that most commonly struck five- to fifteen-year-olds. Today it is understood to be an infection developing from strep throat (or any other streptococcal infection), and its spread can be arrested with antibiotics. But the discovery of penicillin was three decades away. Bed rest and the usual cold remedies, plasters and gargles, were the best the medical world at that time could prescribe.

The threat of long-term weakness, even death, was associated with the disease, but the antibody activity that can involve the heart, joints, skin, and brain functions was not well understood in 1910. The stricken parents, Mary and Harry Rogers, were told that Millicent would probably not live beyond age ten. They were also advised that if she survived, she should not try to bear children, which would tax her weakened system. It was soon apparent that her left arm had been affected, the result of circulatory complications during the fever. Yet the Rogers, especially Mary, tackled the challenge with the spirit of determined invincibility that their power and money had fostered. Millicent's sickbed quickly became a schoolroom, cheery and full of distractions for her. Books and drawing paper were supplied to amuse her.

In hindsight, her illness was a hinge in the story of her life. Bedridden for months, Millicent was forced to turn her childhood physical energies to her mind and imagination. Spurred by her parents, she embarked on a path of self-education. She was bound at any rate by her sex and social status to be educated privately, with the emphasis on modern languages and good manners that was standard for young ladies. If her illness somewhat stunted her social development for a time, it strengthened her intellectual confidence and authority. She began a habit that continued till her death of writing in the margins of her books, as if she were conversing with the author, stating her accord or issue with the writer's premise. Precociously, she believed her opinion counted. The Rogers supported her curiosity with the best education that money could buy. When she felt well enough, she was tutored in French and German. She learned to translate Rilke and continued to learn Latin and Greek in order to translate works unavailable in English. It was both a wonderful way to fill her time, and something she seemed to have a knack for. She demonstrated a true facility for languages. She and her brother Henry, two years younger, spoke to each other in Latin, rather than a childhood make-believe language, when they wished to keep their conversation secret from their parents.

Millicent also took a keen interest in art. Her mother had long been a student of painting and an art enthusiast, and energetically encouraged Millicent in both activities. With determination and spirit, her family rallied round their weakened daughter, and together they weathered the blow that could have been fatal.

Illness shaped Millicent's life in unpredictable ways that extended beyond her physical constitution. Cosseted and spared any kind of physical exertion, she developed a languid manner. She was admonished to go about her activities slowly, and then her repose became a habit. It suggested a maturity, true or false, beyond her years. One thinks, for instance, of that favorite heroine of childhood stories, the crippled Clara in the classic, *Heidi*, who accepted her curtailed life and activities until she was convinced she could walk again. Millicent could no longer make an impression with scampering energy, but replaced it with collected calm, even a precocious dignity.

Frail and elongated at age nine, she was already considered beautiful. Her legs were long and her brown almond-shaped eyes had a mandarin slant.[3] Rather than cuteness and bounce, she had the charm of the cygnet about her as a preteen. She was briefly gawky, but soon her height, five foot seven, and her gaunt look would work to her advantage. Then as now, thinness was fashionable. Mary, known for her own fashion sense, passed down her interest in style to Millicent, who seemed to learn quickly what a spell she could cast. She spent long hours dressing for every occasion and took pleasure in putting together her own look. It was almost a hobby, a silent expression of who she was, and much safer than the exertion required for horseback riding and the outdoor sports that other society girls flaunted. Clothes and personal style were an acceptable way for a cloistered adolescent to lay claim to herself.

The restrictions that her fragile health imposed on Millicent shaped her personality in yet other ways. She began to exhibit a marked social reserve. Her granddaughters and daughters-in-law, speaking not from the experience of knowing Millicent during her youth but from the stories shared with them by her sons, explain Millicent as someone who would quietly seat herself at the end of the table rather than jump into chatter and social interaction at a gathering or dinner. She had learned resourcefulness during the long hours of her convalescence. Her world was the books and stories she read for long hours and the clothes that were part of her public persona. As she matured, the clothes, almost like costumes for an actor, functioned both as an attraction and as a shield between her and others. She invariably made an impression, a little intimidating, as though she could be observed but not approached. By all accounts she achieved an unusual amalgam of confidence in her intellect and appearance and shyness, stemming from her lagging social experience and uncertainty following her illness. Those who knew her as a child, like fellow socialite Bunny Mellon, speak of her girlish sweetness. When Bunny was five she and Millicent, twelve years old, played on the beach in Southampton every summer afternoon. Bunny has never forgotten the time Millicent ran after her favorite handkerchief when it blew away in the wind. Despite their age difference, "She was kind and we played games," recalls Mellon.[4]

There were other formative elements fomenting in the young Millicent that we can only guess about. Her daughter-in-law, Jackie Peralta-Ramos, believes it was necessary for Millicent to separate and differentiate herself from her extroverted, willful mother. Mummy Da, as Mary was known, was an exuberant personality, full of energy and bounce, the very attributes that had so attracted Mark Twain to her in her twenties. Years later, a daughter of one of Millicent's close friends would remember "Mary was like the lady in Babar. That perfect. Adorable, slender, and beautiful like Queen Mary in miniature. But she was completely different from Millicent. Mary was very cozy." Millicent wasn't cozy. Mary was more present, open, friendly, and quick to respond. Her daughter was remote and cool. Millicent, for whatever reasons, created a different identity for herself. People invariably described her as composed and elegant, and she seemed actively to polish that image.

Contrary to Doctor Quintard's doleful warning, she did not die before her tenth year. By her teens Millicent had recovered enough robustness to be part of the ice-skating that formed the center of New York society's winter sports scene for young ladies. Her friend Lela Emery, often a partner of Millicent's on the ice at Tuxedo Park, remembered that as girls they did "a lot" of skating. They were out of doors and on the ice so long that one girl's mother had a lead-lined trunk made for their carriage, in order to store a sealskin coat for the coachman whose job it was to wait for the girls during their hours on the ice.[5]

While Millicent convalesced and moved through adolescence, her family's plans and fortunes blazed ahead. Raising or maintaining stature in New York's tightly structured and often ruthless high society required work and great vigilance, even for those as well-established and respected as Mary and Harry Rogers. As Wilbur de Lyon Nichols explained in his 1904 book *The Ultra-Fashionable Peerage of America*, a tome that is hard to take seriously today, but reflected the social mores and aspirations of its time, the correctness of one's every move seemed to matter while establishing a presence in New York society. Nichols, for example, advised the new rich to try mooring a sailboat offshore in Newport before investing in the "cottage" (as those old Newport summer mansions were called) to test the social waters and avoid the embarrassment, should they not be quickly accepted or give parties that were poorly attended. The Rogers were at the forefront of a kind of New York society in the making that had not been seen in the United States before. New York society almost shamelessly emulated European, especially English, aristocracy. "Strange to narrate, in our free, democratic United States, almost within a decade, there has sprung up an exclusive social caste as valid at certain European courts as an hereditary titled aristocracy—a powerful class of ultra-fashionable multi-millionaires, who, at their present ratio of ascendancy, bid fair to patronize royalty itself. Personages these are whom Edward VII well might prefer to his own subjects for dinner companions and intimate week-end house parties . . ." Nichols declared. It is noteworthy that the Rogers family, with all its efforts, was not among the Astors and Twomblys and Vanderbilts and Goelets on the list, created by Mrs. Caroline Astor and Ward McAllister, of the "Famous 400" who counted as ultrafashionable in the United States in the late 1890s. The list's intent was to protect a social elite with old connections and "gentle breeding" from being overtaken by the newly self-made rich, which included the Rogers. Nichols provides a candid window into society's ambitions. "Wealth, then, forms the principal ingredient entering into the composition of this big social trust whose subjective aim is pleasure, and whose objective one is to make a fine art of social life. . . ."[6]

A thunderbolt struck the Rogers family on a morning in May of 1909 when Henry Rogers got up to go to his office, complained of pain in his left arm and nausea, and then keeled over, unconscious. Emilie, Henry's second wife—whom he married in 1894 after Abbie died— called for a doctor but by the time he arrived, Henry was dead of a stroke. The repercussions sped through the family and Wall Street.

The next day, May 20, *The New York Times* announced: "H. H. Rogers, dead, leaving $50,000,000." That was conservative. Some Wall Street estimates suggested his worth at $75 million (about two billion dollars today). The Rogers' vast fortune was stunning. The funeral at Church of the Messiah on Madison Avenue was widely attended by New York power figures, including William Rockefeller, E. H. Harriman, Mark Twain, and Dr. Rice, who served as pallbearers. Rogers would be buried, as he had requested, in Fairhaven. Newspapers snapped photos of Mary, a long black veil covering her face and trailing behind her, leaving the church with Harry. But the elder Rogers could not be separated in the public eye from his money. Even at his memorial seven months later, the *Detroit Free Press* wrote, "The growth of his company was marked by ruthless ruin for thousands. It rests on a foundation of special privilege and stolen extorted rights. . . . On the other hand, the dead king of finance leaves some devoted friends." And so it would go with American's relationship to the Robber Barons, so admired for their capitalist success, yet loathed for their techniques.

Harry Rogers, who had already been given an office in his father's suite at 26 Broadway, the legendary Standard Oil address in Manhattan, became sole owner of the Virginian Railway Company upon his father's death. An absorbing flurry of financial activity, consolidation, and realignment followed Henry's death. Harry, his critics noted,[7] lacked Henry's brilliance for business, but he assumed his father's seat on the board of directors of the Virginian Railway Company, considered his father's final crowning achievement, just the same. The papers noted, "Mr. Rogers' son, however, is only in his thirtieth year. . . . It is not believed that he will undertake single-handed the management of the important projects with which Mr. Rogers individually had been identified."[8] Harry's brother in-law, Urban Broughton, married to Harry's sister, Clara, became president of Virginian Railway, thus further assuring the family stake in the business.

To his second wife, Emilie, Henry left three million dollars. Harry was willed the Fairhaven mansion and all of his father's property in Fairhaven. The other Rogers children, Harry's sisters, were given trust funds with codicils about their claim to the estate, and trustees were appointed in the will for the benefit of Rogers' children and their descendants. Henry Huttleston Rogers had thought through his finances and left nothing to chance. The husbanding of his great fortune seemed to come easily to him, and he assured his descendants bright, prosperous, and secure futures.

Harry waited until his stepmother's death three years later to begin dismantling the Fairhaven mansion. The newspapers chronicled the wrecking of the lavish interior, the sale of the mahogany dining room furniture, the leaded glass window, $7,500 doors and ornate chandeliers. Fairhaven residents mourned the end of the mansion and disapproved of Harry's decisions to wreck it, but Harry, increasingly willful, seemed not to care.[9] Freed of the shadow of his famous father, he was embarking on his own approach to life. Small-town Fairhaven had less appeal than the playgrounds of New York society.

While living primarily in Manhattan, he and Mary had summered and spent weekends mostly in Tuxedo Park, but in 1914 the couple decided to build an estate on 1,800 acres in Southampton, ninety miles away on Long Island. The Hamptons, as West-, Bridge-, East-, and South-Hampton were called, were quickly becoming the primary summer place for New York City's rich and famous. The region was hailed as "the Newport of Long Island" and "truly smart." "It could not be otherwise, for all the wealth and luxury of hundreds of Gothamites center here," rhapsodized a local real estate magazine, thrilling over the "exclusivity, and ultraaristocratic palatial residences surrounded by parklike lawns and beautiful beaches where architects vie to build costly homes." Harry Rogers commissioned the École des Beaux-Arts–trained architects Walker and Gillette to design an oceanfront estate, an Italian-inspired villa, poised on the edge of the Atlantic Ocean. His grand vision included a curved lily pool, ionic columns, stables, and a sweeping hipped roof. The living room would be a forty-four by twenty-nine-foot room with a coffered wood ceiling. The breakfast loggia with a barrel-vaulted ceiling would be adorned with Florentine frescoes. The six upstairs bedrooms were designed with nine-foot ceilings and fireplaces. For Millicent and her younger brother,

Henry Huttleston Rogers III, there was a children's playhouse planned along the inner garden wall, the kind of playful conceit Mary was known for. On the site plan it was titled Villa Del Mar, in keeping with the American rich's yen for European grandeur. "We are buccaneers, perhaps; but though derelict in this compassless present, we have the wit to be in love with the past; and we express ourselves, our curiosity and hunger and passion, like artists," wrote Mary Cass Canfield in her feature on the Rogers' house after its completion in *Harper's Bazaar*. In her evaluation, which was an admiring swoon, the Rogers' had succeeded in transporting the atmosphere of a villa that "might have sunnily and chastely endured through the ages on the slopes of Fiesole, amid the windy dunes of Long Island's south shore." There was no end to the extravagant decorative flourishes borrowed from the Italian Renaissance, juxtaposed with modern details that reflected American sensibility and scale. With its portico, loggia, and urns, so apropo to the style of the coming twenties, soon it would be a perfect backdrop—and stage—for the blooming young beauty who would come of age on its grounds. A marble-curbed lily pool was the centerpiece of the oblong courtyard. The ionic columns flanked the entrance where, at one early lavish party, three hundred guests were admitted for a dinner dance with Spanish singers, South American dancers, and a fortune-teller.

Family dynamics behind the scene also began to shape Millicent's outlook. Despite their full life and prosperity, Mary and Harry Rogers were growing dissatisfied in marriage. Beneath the calm patina of money and luxury, the headstrong and opinionated Mary and hard-living, heavy-drinking Harry created a tumultuous home life for Millicent and her younger brother. The parents' boisterous quarrels and the state of domestic warfare that developed between them are cited by family members as another reason for Millicent's withdrawal at an early age into a world of books and fantasy. "It was just as easy for her to go to her room, even feign that she wasn't feeling well, when her parents were yelling and fighting," says her granddaughter,

Christina, the family member who speaks publicly and candidly about the tempestuous atmosphere in the Rogers family.[10]

By the time she was fifteen, Millicent led quite a normal life for a teenage girl in her social circumstances. She took drawing lessons, went to choir practice, studied natural history, prepared for her confirmation and, in 1917, started a diary in which she detailed her daily life in Tuxedo Park and Manhattan.[11] She wrote of her dreary governess, of the "rippingly funny" play she attended, and the antics of her visiting cousins, the Coes. She had serious problems with spelling and punctuation, and they would plague her correspondence all her life, but her more immediate concern was that she longed to be a better skater. "The ice looks so devine. Why can't I skate!" Already her critical eye and a sense of wit—and some hauteur—colored her observations. She had little patience with her teacher Miss McZoers,[12] who spoke to her charges, "'Now you little girls' must so and so. Oh Lord, why should I curtsie to her, she isn't the Queen of England or New York either." She sputtered when "Mrs. Mc" gave the school a lecture on George Washington. "It's a wonder she didn't compare herself to him," Millicent wrote. Like most teens Millicent found certain persons in her midst "insupportable." She wrote of "tiresome creatures." Her moods were up and down. One day she "went to the zoo and acted childish." The next day she wrote of the "usual boredom." The day after that she wrote, "I'm depressed. I do wish I could be alone for three minutes. This evening Dad and Ma started an argument. . . ." On her fifteenth birthday she recorded, "Germany is getting reckless and threatens to sink our ships. War is all people can speak of. Oh, declare it. Good Lord, hurry up!" Then she checked herself: "Yes, I know it will mean that all our friends will go away and many never come home again. It will mean death and orphaned children." She illustrated the entry with a drawing of a U-boat.

Illness did not preoccupy her any longer, but she did write: "I don't know why it is that regularly every two weeks I get a cold." She stayed back from her lessons and wrote, "Ma presented me with my red fox furs. I'm quite delighted. My perfect day in bed." This, too, she illustrated. She kept a canary called "The Yellow Peril." "The hateful little animal detests me!" she explained when he fluttered out of her reach. She thrilled over outings to the Museum of Natural History in New York City and was stirred by the trunk of an old sequoia tree on exhibit. "What secrets it could tell. The fall of the Roman Empire . . . the time of King Alfred, Columbus discovery of America." History always seemed to intrigue her. She also wrote of boys, some rather swooningly. Once, over a young man named George Rushmore, "Rushy," she wrote: "I'm a goner this time. I feel it . . . He wouldn't look at me, darn him, but when we had gone I turned around and looked back and he did the same."

Rushy, who she learned had gone to St. Marks and was probably twenty-one, was "excuciatingly fun in his boredom of Mr. Woods sermon," she wrote. He turned out to be twenty-five. "I made a fatal error," she chided herself. They talked for hours and hours and she began to outline their conversations and "how topics can run into others." Topics were dogs, sports, parties and houses, walking and fishing. The accounts developed into full-blown dialogue, something like a play. When Rushy joined the military it began,

"I've been conceited enough to think that you will miss me."

"Won't you write me?"

"No."

"Please do."

"I don't think I ought to."

"No I won't."

"Stop, be fair."

Fact or fiction, she had a sense for conversational drama. Her evenings in Tuxedo were filled with dances and the newly popular Tombala, an Italian form of bingo. When summer arrived the family moved to Southampton, where she wrote, "Summer has really begun when we get to Long Island. God, I'm sick of the place. I want to do something for a change." With war breaking out she took a course in home nursing that covered first aid and surgical dressing. "I hate the dressing, they

are so stupid and one has to do them just so, it's horrible in the ex-
tream." Already she had a critical eye for clothes, and while admiring
the iris gardens that she toured in East Hampton, she wrote of the
"lovely ladies. My heavens they were dreadful. Some of the colors and
ways the things were put on." When one matron turned her ankle
and fell into the muddy water, she thought it "awfully funny." She
seemed in her lovely slant handwriting to be a teenage girl to the core.

When it became clear that her father would be stationed in
Washington, D.C., which would require the family to spend the
winter there, she wrote, "HORRIBLE!!"

In 1914, the assassination of Archduke Franz Ferdinand, heir to
the Austro-Hungarian throne, by a Serbian nationalist triggered the
beginning of World War I, and unleashed four years of cataclysmic,
bloody conflict between the great powers of Europe. The United
States did not join the fight until 1917. In Europe, an era of gracious
nobility began to crumble. The Russian and Austro-Hungarian em-
pires collapsed, the Germans were crushed, the French and British
were exhausted, and 117,000 young Americans had died in faraway
trenches. Yet life for rich Americans like the Rogers was largely un-
affected. They continued to model their lives on prewar European
society, building mansions and determinedly booking themselves on
the grand tours to European capitals considered the model of civility
and high culture even as those features waned. Paris had not, after all,
fallen to the Huns. The romance of war, heard in Millicent's adolescent outcry in her diary, echoed her father's military enthusiasm.

Colonel Harry Rogers had long been more interested in military
matters than industry. He had joined the New York National Guard
in 1904 and earned the rank of captain of infantry by 1909. Following
his graduation in 1913 from the United States Army's School of Fire
in Ft. Sill, Oklahoma, he continued to study and observe the usage of
field artillery in Europe. Then in 1916, when there was unrest across
the Mexican border, he commanded an artillery regiment there. After
the entry of the United States into World War I he served in France

with the American Expeditionary Force and took command of the Third Field Artillery Regiment. His expertise extended to logistics and the movement of ammunition, and while he saw action in a number of battles, when he received commendations at the war's end, they particularly mentioned his achievements in getting the right supplies to the right place, on time.[13] He left the military as a colonel, and thereafter he was known, even in civilian life, as Colonel H. H. Rogers, "The Colonel," thus making it easier to distinguish him from his namesake father. These duties obviously reduced the time he had available for parenting.

The army stationed Rogers in Washington, D.C., during World War I and Mary bought a newly built house at 1629 K Street, a fashionable Washington address that neighbored ambassadors and embassies. She and the Colonel continued to straddle the social scenes between D.C., Southampton, and their Park Avenue apartment in Manhattan. In the fall of 1917 Millicent enrolled as a freshman at the Madeira School on Dupont Circle. Madeira prided itself on being one of the earliest college preparatory schools for women, in contrast to the more typical "finishing" schools for girls. Often the physically robust Miss Madeira led walks for the girls along Rock Creek Park, Great Falls Park, and the city's canals. Millicent began her freshman year with credits in English, Latin, and French, with a note on her transcript that she had been privately tutored in New York. But the formalities of school (Deportment and Neatness were required classes) seemed not to appeal to her; or perhaps it was her outsider status that kept her from distinguishing herself. She was a day student among classmates who were mostly boarders. There is no record that she participated in art, music, sports, or service organizations of any kind with her classmates. Her involvement may have been hampered further by an influenza outbreak in the fall of 1918, soon after classes began, when the "day girls" were banned from attending classes until the epidemic ended, the following spring. In the school's records she was not considered a high achiever. She did not return for her junior year in the fall of 1919, the autumn planned for her debut. The end of the war came just in time for the rituals of her social launching and ushered in a social and fashion hedonism in stark contrast to the somber dress and attitudes of sacrifice during wartime. Soon the madcap flapper would take center stage, and Millicent would be poised to join in.

The Rogers returned from Washington to their Southampton estate and its glamour during the following summer months. They kept up social appearances as a couple. At Villa del Mar, variously called Bel Mar and Miramar in the press and eventually dubbed The Beach House by the family, they were building a reputation for extravagant parties, and the social pulse of New York was quickening for Millicent. Her hair, coiled high about the ears, revealed her elegant neck and shoulders. She was photographed in profile wearing a flowing Grecian, nouveau-styled gown of the time, posed as a pensive and demure maiden among the urns and flowering trees on the family portico.

Costume parties seemed all the rage that year, and the Rogers gave a fantasy ball at Bel Mar called "The Masque of Queen Bersabe." A photograph of Millicent as the character "Ahola," in a silky shiny gown with train and a headdress, posed holding a crystal ball, appeared in *Harper's Bazaar*, where she was beginning to assume her role as a trendsetter. She indeed looked the part of a young queen, and as the photo shows, the cygnet *had* become a swan. Her lankiness and long neck had suddenly become assets, giving line to her long and elegant demeanor. She was blessed with a fair, smooth complexion that her admiring family likened to alabaster. Her avoidance of overexertion caused her movements to be deliberate, and coupled with that flash of theatrics that underlies all fashion and style, she was, by all accounts, arresting.

Her coming of age coincided with the Jazz Age, an era that admired extravagant and original behavior, so Millicent fit right in. She began pushing the edge of the envelope as she was coming of age. She would show up at debutante balls wearing creations by the top couturiers of the day, often tweaked to match her own vision of how she should look. In one account handed down in the family, she made a splash when she wore a little black dress and a Chinese headdress bought in Chinatown—and daringly painted her nails bright red—for a debutante ball in New York. While she had the nerve to be outrageous, she was most often noted for achieving a kind of perfection. Younger debutantes remember being awed by her presence at parties or in the back of limousines. "She was wonderful to look at. Her hair and clothes were always perfect," says Payne Middleton, who was among her girlish admirers in Manhattan society. It was one thing to be heralded as the Standard Oil Heiress, a unique label that generated interest by itself, but it was quite another to be bewitching as well. She was creating a trail of admiring fashion notices, even before she left Washington the previous spring. *The Washington Post*'s fashion and society column mentioned her for a dress she wore to a dinner given by Mrs. Larz Anderson for the Washington debutante Jane Story. "Another extremely youthful belle not yet formally presented to society, but participating in a succession of dinners and dances for the younger set is Miss Millicent Rogers . . . who is wearing a fascinating frock of white satin of the radian variety, which is draped or rather hung in very graceful lines suited to its youthful wearer," reported *The Post* in the first of many fashion notices Millicent would inspire that year. By fall, the New York social columnists were licking their lips in anticipation of the social season ahead. "The H. H. Rogerses will see to it that Miss Millicent's debut is attended with all the éclat due a miss of such exalted station," trumpeted *Town Topics* in the same paragraph with the announcement that Cornelia Vanderbilt would, too, have her deb ball in December.

In the November issue of *Town & Country* a full-page photograph of Millicent was the frontispiece. She was listed in the table of contents as "Miss Millicent Rogers." Her name was announcement enough. The next six months were an uninterrupted period of dinners, dances, and debutante occasions that thrust Millicent directly into the public eye. She would never completely escape that exposure. While the press seemed determined to note her every move in public, her family was equally determined to monitor her movements at home.

In terms of its impact on the contemporary social scene, the importance of the young heiress's formal debut in 1919 can hardly be underestimated. It was the culminating event of her upbringing and the announcement that she was now suitable for introduction into society. She could, after her debut, step out into public alone rather than be constantly surrounded by her protective family and chaperones. But her period of relative freedom was to be short-lived by design, since a young woman's debut was the event, like a tribal puberty rite, that declared she was now marriageable and the mating games, played for high stakes in Millicent's world of money and status, were free to begin. Millicent made this passage with much hoopla. She was seventeen.

"Her name is legion and she will continue to pass through the portals of Society, officially and formally, the entire winter," announced "The Week in Society" column in *Town & Country* of November 10. "Miss Rogers is an exceedingly pretty girl, of the frail flower type. Her family, as nearly everyone who reads T & C knows, lives at Southampton in the summer." It was noted that the family was now of New York and Washington, D.C. *Town Topics*, the society bible of the social northeast, noted that the Rogers had generously distributed invitations among their Washington friends for the debut of Millicent at Southampton but that she would be introduced as well "with a fine flourish" in November on K Street. "Miss Millicent will be far and away one of the most important buds of the Washington winter," it predicted.

But the real gala event was on November 24, at the Ritz-Carlton in New York. Two thousand were invited to the debut that *The New York Times* claimed "will probably be the largest ball of the season." There were thirteen hundred acceptances for supper in the ballroom and Crystal Room suite. Such balls were typically preceded by dinners, and Millicent, according to *The Times*, was feted by Mrs. George Baker. Reporters described the unique decorations that created a fall fantasia feeling. The florist Kottmiller had transformed the ballroom of the Ritz with twenty tall, slender oak trees with russet foliage that lined the room and umbrella-shaped trees with tops of chrysanthemums. Pots of mums and ferns banked the walls. Oak boughs cut off the corners of the room and there were ferns and autumnal foliage in the smoking rooms. The decorations extended into the foyer and down the balustrades of the stairways. Australian tree ferns were used in the Crystal room where green orchids made up the centerpieces on the tables. A thirty-piece orchestra played throughout the evening.

Millicent received the guests, who started to arrive at eleven. Old social New York began and partied late. She posed with her mother at the top of a wide stairway leading into the ballroom wearing a dress of plain white brocaded satin shaped over a white satin foundation. The skirt was made with panniers trimmed with white lace. She wore a green satin girdle and a green wreath in her hair. However, in all the gasping over the décor and diplomatic corps who attended, Millicent was hardly mentioned by the reporters who covered the party. The affair was planned to be grand and unrivaled, yet by some accounts, Mary Rogers, its architect, had overreached. The ballroom became too tightly packed to turn around in. The following week on its front page, *Town Topics* reported on the party crashers. "Young people tried to locate the friends with whom they had hoped to flock, but found themselves hedged in by strangers. The magnificent floral decorations were lost completely in such a mob." Mary had difficulty trying to get word to the musicians to play more softly and it was not until the older guests began to leave or go to supper in the adjoining rooms that there was room for dancing. *Town Topics*, as was its wont, went on to preach: "Mrs. Roger has always been generous, very open minded and noted for her amiability, but it would have been a far better plan to give two or three dances for Milly rather than one at which there was such an appalling crush." The reporter then went on to question what H. H. Rogers senior would have thought of "a jamboree of this sort" were he still alive, and pointed out that both he and Mary's father, George Hillard Benjamin, had had simpler tastes. In a final fillip, it was concluded, "Evidently she has other plans for her Milly." And so she did.

CHAPTER FOUR

Coming Out

THOUGH MILLICENT'S DEBUT GRABBED HEADLINES AND marked her ostensible freedom to move about more independently, it was equally momentous for Mary, whose concern for appearances and the good opinion of society were the hallmarks of her traditional, somewhat Victorian, outlook. According to her descendants, she could be imperious and something of a snob (whereas Millicent was not). Though wealthy and established in society, the Rogers weren't bluebloods; they did not breathe the rare social ether at the top with the ultrafashionable old rich families, even though some, notably Brigadier General and Mrs. Cornelius Vanderbilt, had attended Millicent's debutante party. The Rogers' money was too new, their ancestry's toehold among society's rank too fresh. There was still a higher level of social distinction to achieve. In Millicent, a rich young beauty who attracted suitors and attention, Mary had the perfect instrument for advancement to the heights. Marriage was the chief means of advancement for women, and it would have been unusual for a woman of Mary's background and resources *not* to keep her eye on the social game. Marrying well was a sport for New York society. It was even possible to surpass New York society, the pinnacle of American social status, by casting one's sights toward Europe. Toward England, certainly. Perhaps even toward Westminster Abbey.

After all, *The New York Times* had mentioned in its coverage of Millicent's debut that "it will be remembered that the Prince of Wales danced with the debutante at the White Sulphur Springs and also at Mrs. Whitelaw Reid's dance." It was not the first time that Prince Edward's attentions to Millicent would be written about in the papers, which soon became obsessive on the subject.

Millicent's debut into society was nearly overshadowed by her status as a favorite of the young Prince of Wales when he traveled to the United States in 1919, before her debut. His extended visit across the country, complete with photos of himself in an Indian headdress in South Dakota, charmed Americans and nearly exhausted society columnists. The whole Washington-New York social scene seemed to sustain a high-pitched frenzy. "Miss Rogers Favorite of Prince of Wales" was the headline of one Washington column after the young prince chose her for six dances that evening. The paper continued, "Although Miss Mary Millicent Rogers, daughter of Mr. and Mrs. Henry H. Rogers, Jr. was a favorite dancing partner of Edward, Prince of Wales, during the last week of his visit to Washington, White Sulphur Springs, and New York, she has not been formally introduced to society." The writer raised an eyebrow over the fact that Millicent's Washington debut would not be until February, yet already she was gaining notice in the papers. As would often be the case, she had gotten ahead of social conventions.

The Rogers retreated again to White Sulphur Springs, West Virginia, a fashionable resort for political Washington, in the week following Millicent's debut in New York. The Prince's hosts, the wealthy Mrs. Larz Anderson, invited Millicent, her parents, and several other D.C. debs to a luncheon at the Greenbrier for the Prince's amusement. In turn, the Prince entertained the party with a small dinner in his private suite that same evening. Later the same week was the Thanksgiving ball in aid of the Navy Relief society, where it was reported "Miss Millicent Rogers, claimed by both Washington and New York" was among the debutantes who wore smart new gowns even though society matrons made a point of wearing last year's fashions to exhibit their thrift for the war effort. The tone of the story was grudging.

Mary Rogers was quick to join in the royal play and she hosted His Royal Highness the following week. "Mrs. Rogers gave a brilliant tea dance at the Casino from six to eight for the Prince, and, naturally, Millicent was for once sufficiently in the limelight to please her exacting parents, who, it will be admitted, put a great feather in their caps by being thus privileged to entertain royalty."[1] Somewhat more amusing was the report that Millicent had tapped out the rhythm of the music on Edward's shoulder while she danced with him. The carefree gesture was caught by a hawk-eyed reporter for Town Topics, who rose to the occasion with a pompous lecture: "But those who looked on wished Mildred [sic] might have been a little more informed in royal etiquette than to play tunes with the tips of her fingers on the Prince's shoulder while dancing with him. Many a society woman has been barred from the Court of St. James's for a familiarity even less than this."

The papers had a heyday with his royal highness and his attentions to Millicent. It was noted that the Prince began to "sit up and take notice" when he met Millicent Rogers. "His interest in the charming heiress first became apparent at the great ball given for him by Mr. and Mrs. Cornelius Vanderbilt, it was noticed that he simply could not keep away from her. They danced together and HRH showed his pleasure so naively that his several New York hostesses realized that if they wanted to make the prince happy they must be sure to include Miss Rogers in all of their parties. And so . . . wherever Miss Mary Millicent went, the prince, just like Mary's little lamb, was sure to go," trilled The Washington Post.

Was Millicent actually smitten? There is an interesting entry in her diary, coinciding with the Prince's visit, that rhapsodizes over an Englishman named (or nicknamed) "Wig."[2] He is someone she met at a ball given by the British Embassy and is in the British Navy. He even makes it into her list of addresses at the back of her diary with the location entry, Scotland. Her last entry about Wig is May 28, 1919, the same day that the headline "Miss Rogers Favorite of Prince of Wales" made the newspapers. She had quit her daily entries after discovering that Mary was reading them and only returned to writing on May 28, 1919, after being with the Prince at several social occasions that spring.

"God bless his English kisses," she proclaimed. "I miss them, Lord knows, now I don't get them—if he only understood how I missed him. . . . I'm not going to tell you the wonderful times I've had. I can live them over, but I can't put them down, so what is the use of my trying? Wig knows and I know that is enough. But the guess to me now is when will he be able to come back." If Wig was HRH, he did not come back in time. As the world would learn, he had a preference for older women. And Millicent did not seem devastated.

She wrote often in her diary of young men. Several had already proposed to her. She tells of one flirtation after another. There is one suitor who she said "is not quite master of himself" whom she tells "to keep his hands away from me and sit up and stop making a fuss." Of another she says, "I am tired of being crazy about some very beautiful thing who doesn't give a damn for me—or anyone else—it's too hard work." She had one crush after another. "I'm falling again. I spend my time falling it seems to me." She writes of Henry D. Keresy, nicknamed Donn, "He is too devine, I'm perfectly creazy probably but I like him." She continues to describe his "beautiful physic, long lashes and funny way of keeping his eyes half closed gives him a sort of sleepy look. If I could think that he was as far gone on me as I am on him I'd be happy as a lark." She was smitten enough to declare, "I'm going to marry Donn but he doesn't know it."

She is stumped when a married woman asks her to define her ideal of a man. "I couldn't do it because I had never tried to put into words what I wanted." The next day she did, declaring, "I know this it is." The pages that followed were in outline form.

1. *He must be a gentleman,* every inch of him.
   a. mentally mind
   b. morally heart
   c. phisicly (by birth)
2. *He must be a real man "he man"*
   a) physically
   b. at heart
   c. morally
3. *He must have*
   a. perfect manners
   b. be cleaver
   c. have a wonderful education
   d. have a sense of humor and talk well
   e. Some occupation
   f. in which he can rise
   g. have a will of his own
   h. character
   outspoken, generous absolutely upright.
4. *He must love me really and not be the kind who will go off flirting with another woman the minute we are married.*
5. *He must be my superior to a certain extent although not too much.*
   a. mentally
   b. phisically
6. And he must understand me. How to manage me. Our minds must be perfectly in accord.[3]

And so she set the bar high for her ideal man, and joined the timeless multitude of women who wish for everything.

The press hype and speculation about a royal marriage dissipated almost as quickly as it had arisen after Prince Edward traveled on. *The Washington Post* wrote that Millicent had turned down the offer of a place in Court, which would have made her little more than a mistress, but there is no evidence that such a proposal existed, other than in the *Post*'s imagination.

Millicent's grandchildren believe their great grandparents, chiefly Mary, were smitten by the prospect that Millicent might marry the Prince of Wales. Millicent, it seemed, had "come out" just in time. She was nearly bursting out of the silence and anonymity that was appropriate for girls who had not yet been formally introduced to society.

The New York social season was fuller than usual that winter and it was remarked in the papers that it would need to begin earlier and end later, closer to Christmas than usual in order to accommodate the high number of debutante balls and events for the calendar. By December 24, the ball at the Ritz-Carlton for Lela Emery, the daughter of a late Cincinnati real estate tycoon, was already hailed the largest of the season in *Time* magazine. In a December issue, *Town Topics* talked of the "strain of continuous gaiety. A dance and usually a reception every day but Sunday attest the staying powers of the youngsters (debutantes)... And with all else that is going on, they still manage frequent appearances in the parterre at the Opera." The opera was yet another venue where the moves and fashions of society members were duly reported. When Millicent's fellow debutante Louise Schieffelin appeared at the opera, it was also an occasion to mention Millicent. "On the other side of the parterre, Renee Carhart and Milly Rogers, side by side, with Milly's mother (Mrs. H. H. Rogers, who favors black velvet exclusively now, perhaps because she likes to dress the part of duenna correctly) were fresh, lovely and animated as if it were their first appearance of the season."[4] Mary may have been tactfully cautious not to rival or overshadow Millicent during her debut season. Mrs. Vanderbilt and her countess daughter were also in attendance at the opera, ensuring an extra dollop of excitement for the papers. And then, like a smothered candle, the gossip and news came to a halt after the holiday parties as families began to depart for Europe, where the "London season" was about to begin. That year the Rogers postponed going to Europe in order to host another dance for Millicent at the Washington Country Club. That, too, was written about as a great social event. As far north as New Bedford, Massachusetts (across the river from Fairhaven), *The New Bedford Sunday Standard* called the Washington, D.C., bash, "the party of the year and Miss Rogers was the belle of the affair."

It comes as almost a surprise that there was a real live girl beneath all the pomp, circumstance, and management, who had thoughts of her own. As her diary during these years shows,[5] Millicent was beginning to shape her own opinions. Now she was even settling on a beau of her own choosing. She was not one to fall behind expected social conventions and marriage was the next step. The following year she and Lela Emery would both be bridesmaids for their mutual friend Elise Everett, another New York society girl, when she married Paul Abbott. The marriage-go-round was about to begin for her and her contemporaries.

A winter of dinners and "musicales" in Millicent's honor at the Rogers' New York residence was followed by a spring and summer in Southampton that were a blur of parties and gowns.[6] There was a welcome respite from society scrutiny and notices, but one begins to sense an anxiousness in Millicent that she would become better known for later. She did not like life to be at a standstill. Frustrated by enforced inactivity during her convalescent years, she may have felt a need to live fully. In any event, she tended to keep the pot brewing, as if she was afraid of missing something. Intimates and friends at parties in Southampton began to notice that a romance was blossoming between her and Jimmy Thompson. Tall, slender, curly-haired Thompson had been a regular in the Rogers home and at numerous social events on its grounds all summer. The son of the late James M. Thompson and Mrs. C. K. Bispham of Madison Avenue in New York, he was part of the Rogers' social set. His mother was a Baltimore socialite and his stepfather, C. K. Bispham, was a man after Colonel Rogers' heart, an internationally known big game hunter and fisherman. Jimmy, reputed to be a good golfer, tennis player, and swimmer, had been largely under the social radar until the Rogers announced his engagement to Millicent the first week of August. He lived with his mother in Manhattan and had a job in the steel business, just a few blocks north of The Standard Oil Company. The match had the proper hallmarks.

Thompson certainly seemed the smiling All-American good guy—from her world and bound for success—that Millicent could appropriately marry. The sweethearts were photographed seated on the sand at the beach in Southampton, he in a coat and tie and knickers, she under a wide-brim hat covered with flowers, and wearing a suit and ruffled blouse. The *New York Sun* and *Herald* described her as "an exceptionally attractive girl, with very fair skin and dark eyes and hair." In October the papers would snap Thompson and Rogers on the grounds of a lawn tennis tournament in Southampton. Millicent was turned out in tennis apparel, pearls, and a big hat to protect her against the sun. She wore saddle shoes and stood jauntily with her hands on her hips. Jimmy, all smiles, sported white trousers, and a tweed sports jacket over his tennis whites. While the papers crooned that Millicent's mother was a strong advocate of marrying young (she had been nineteen when she married the Colonel) Mary remained publicly silent on her daughter's announcement. Millicent had just turned eighteen. No plans were announced for the wedding as the Rogers were planning to be in Europe for the winter season.

Colonel Rogers threw a dinner party for roughly thirty people in the couple's honor in late October at the Ritz-Carlton where guests sat in the main dining room making toasts to the couple at a large table decorated with roses. After dessert the party moved on to the Century Theatre to attend the play, *Mecca*. Millicent's friend Lela Emery, a Chicago heiress who had also attended her debutante ball and would in many ways shadow Millicent's course in life, was also there. Mary Rogers did not attend. Speculators could not agree whether the cause was illness, disapproval of the match, or being at odds with her husband.

A few days before New Year's 1921, Millicent, the Colonel, and Mary set sail for Europe. Jimmy Thompson went to the pier to see her off. The *New York Herald* ran a photograph of Millicent stylishly bundled in a fur stole and muff on the deck of the White Star Liner's *Olympic*, aboard which the family would spend New Year's Eve celebrating with other society passengers, including Margaret Kahn, daughter of the wealthy financier Otto Kahn. No one—but perhaps the imaginative Millicent herself—could have predicted that the trip ahead would upend all notions about her future.

CHAPTER FIVE

The Grand Tour

As soon as her debuts in Washington and New York were accomplished, the Rogers launched Millicent socially in Europe, where New York's wealthiest families typically went for "the season." Setting out from Southampton or Tuxedo Park, the Rogers routinely stayed in New York at the Ritz-Carlton hotel and readied for their trip. They were newsmakers, and worth chronicling, in much the same way the Europeans watched their royalty. Newspapers dutifully reported which ocean liners they would be traveling on, who was traveling with whom, and which of the city's fine hotels would accommodate them once they arrived. The elite posed proudly at the docks—finely dressed in coats and hats, and often with their dogs on leashes—for eager newspaper photographers.

Castles in Scotland, villas in Italy, and de rigueur stops at the fine hotels in Paris and London were standard on their European itinerary. These were truly grand tours, made with an array of steamer trunks, the family dogs, and staff necessary to attend to wealthy travelers. In one family story that has become part of Mary Rogers' legend, the day before such a sail she was attracted by a shiny new car in a Manhattan showroom. As was her style, she swept into the dealership and said, "I am leaving on the Queen Mary tomorrow. Can you have it on the boat?" she asked, pointing toward the car. The questioning tone was merely rhetorical cover for a command. The salesman on the floor began to stammer that such a thing wasn't possible, that the car she admired must be kept on display, and that there were other impediments to fulfilling her request. "Clearly you're not in charge here," was Mary's response, and she asked him to call Walter Chrysler, with whom she was acquainted. "Walter, I'm in one of your shops . . ." she began when she had him on the phone. The next morning the car was on the Queen Mary when it sailed.[1]

Millicent was an eager traveler, anxious to practice her foreign languages and see the world. The Rogers' European trips, made on White Star ocean liners and typically lasting four to five months, were considered prime opportunities to expose Millicent to prospective suitors beyond America's shores. She was dangled in front of European society, her exposure rationed and controlled to create enough of a stir to build interest in her, but to stay within the bounds of socially acceptable conduct. Her arrival in Europe was duly noted, and well before her presentation as a debutante, the European society columnists dubbed her the new "Dollar Princess." The tabloids loved to speculate about the marriageability of rich American girls and the titled Europeans they were likely to marry. By the end of the World War, when a great number of European aristocrats found their fortunes were ruined even though their titles were intact, such marriages made the headlines. Americans were almost uniformly impressed with the sophistication and status of a noble title, and a number of American heiresses, including Barbara Hutton and Eleanor Green, were swept off their feet into titled European marriages.

European nobility, perhaps a bit more studiously, took great notice of the lovely daughters of capitalism's new tycoons. As the literary critic Leon Edel stated in his praise for Edith Wharton's unfinished novel on the subject, *The Buccaneers*, it was a story of

"American beauties questing for British titles and British titles questing for American dollars." There was no secret about it. The Irish Duke of Leinster candidly admitted in bankruptcy court in London that he had spent $700,000 courting American heiresses. Waistcoats, yachts, and thoroughbreds were essential in competing for a trip to the altar, called a "commercial perambulation" in *The Washington Post.* "Poor Barons Seek Wealth at the Altar," "Glamour of Foreign Titles Often Lures American Girls to Heartbreak," and "They Know How to Please Women by Smooth Manners" were the headlines that followed such marriages.[2] Yet none of these cautionary reports could temper the romantic notion of rich American girls marrying into European nobility.

The Buccaneers addressed the subject and carefully explained the social nuances of the day. The difference between the girls, called Buccaneers in the book, and Millicent Rogers, is that they, though rich from "new money," needed the social boost that marriage to a titled European or Englishman would bring. Millicent, on the contrary, did not. She was already well up on the American society heap, yet there was always a notch or two further to climb.

The Rogers were not unique in their social aspirations for Millicent. Their daughter's marriage (there was no acceptable alternative) was expected to advance her social position and possibly even increase Millicent's wealth. "A marriage outright into the smart set is far and away the surest method of effecting an entrance into it," wrote social chronicler of the time Charles Wilbur de Lyon Nichols for anyone who had not already thought of it.[3] Those were the unspoken rules of the social machinations of the day, akin to the drawing room scenes in the popular novels of the time and rooted in centuries of desire of European nobility and royalty to ensure their continuance through marriage and money.

According to Millicent's grandson, Arturo Peralta-Ramos III, "Her parents tried to get her social position by pushing her into socially acceptable marriages. That's what families like theirs did with their daughters." Millicent was complicit in their efforts, at first. As the Rogers family trips to Europe began to expose Millicent to marriageable Europeans, her list of admirers grew.

If Millicent felt overprogrammed, there is no evidence that she complained or resisted such social managing. To the contrary, she seemed to enjoy the attention. It was a welcome antidote to the long quiet spells required during her convalescence and continuing fragile health. Her family believes she always lived with a certain prescience about death, knowing that she had cheated it early. Instead of feeling the invincibility that most teenagers know, Millicent matured with a sense of her mortality and life's uncertainty. Her response was to see and to experience as much as she could in what time she had left. She plunged into whatever was set before her and eagerly studied the history and language of the countries she visited alongside her parents, who took her as far afield as China. They traveled to the Far East on the ocean liner "Impress of Russia," as Millicent recorded it in white ink on the black pages of her photo album of those years. She and Mary were often in society columns for their attendance at the opera. Millicent loved to dance and was quite good at the formal steps of the time, as her attraction to Prince Edward suggests. Yet the trips to Europe, routine during the "winter season," became more social than exploratory. They variously cast Mary as a managing stage mother, or as a handler worthy of our sympathy for taking such an enchanting creature to Europe in a day when one misstep or rumor could dash a girl's reputation and marriage suitability. For a while, at least, Mary seemed to have things under control. Nothing more scandalous occurred than Millicent pirouetting on the ice rink in St. Moritz the winter following her debut, even though by one report she was studiously admired by a middle-aged Austrian count. She was beginning to cast her spell.

The year after Millicent's debut, the Rogers stayed on into the summer in Europe. Perhaps Mary Rogers hoped for the undoing of Millicent's engagement, if indeed, Jimmy Thompson did not meet with her expectations for Millicent. Or perhaps Millicent, now free of the hectic debutante calendar and the public and familial aspirations surrounding her marriageability, was free to savor some of the European indulgence. Whatever it was, Jimmy Thompson began to fade. Their trip extended for six months, quite long enough to unravel engagements for many young women. They began with several weeks in North Africa and ended with the London season in England where Millicent's brother Henry, a prep school student, joined them. On June 24, the Colonel cabled his friends to say that Millicent and Thompson had ended their engagement. His office, which typically fielded questions about business or family, offered no explanation for the breakup. A taste of European aristocracy apparently eclipsed Jimmy Thompson. Four weeks later it was reported in *The Washington Post*'s society column that the Rogers, the Colonel, Mary, and Millicent, were at a garden party hosted by the King and Queen of England at Buckingham palace. That summer they were late returning for the summer season in Long Island.

The Rogers were to make a number of trips abroad over the next several years. On their European tours they kept company with the cultural elite of the day. During their stays in Italy Millicent met Duke d'Aosta, the son of the King of Italy and, according to her surviving family, the young d'Aosta swept her off her feet and she fell in love with him. The Duke seemed similarly smitten with the young heiress and asked her to marry him, but Italian nationalist and fascist leader Benito Mussolini and her father intervened to nip the romance before it could develop further.[4]

Mussolini had proclaimed that a son of the royal House of Savoy could not marry a foreigner, and Colonel Rogers strongly seconded that opposition. Though Mary was reportedly in favor of the match for Millicent, Rogers resorted to the lever he would repeatedly use to control Millicent and others in the family who crossed him. He threatened that if she persisted in going against his will, he would disown her. At this stage in life, either her affections for the Duke were trivial enough to discount or she simply was unwilling to abandon her life of luxury and the promise of inheritance for love. She complied with her father's wishes.

One also suspects that the eighteen-year-old was fickle enough, and marriage proposals frequent enough, that Millicent was easily able to move on from these engagements. But the offer of marriage to titled Europeans seemed greatly more attractive than the prospect of more typical marriages to young marriageable men back home. For the next few years Millicent, with the encouragement of her mother, seemed determined to play exclusively on the field of romance with European aristocrats. Her next serious conquest was the dashing Serge Obolensky, the exiled White Russian prince, whom she met while he was in Rome visiting his mother. It was a common story in post–WWI Europe. Serge was handsome and came from a colorful and aristocratic background, but his fortune had been lost during the war. His mother, Princess Marie Obolensky, now divorced from his father, lived in a villa in Naples, but the war years, both the German advance on Russia and the Russian Revolution, had cost her all but the jewelry, a famous trove of emeralds from her tiara, sapphires, and rubies, that she had managed to bring with her. She lived comfortably, but the court life she had once known as a Russian aristocrat was over. Serge, first a student at the University of St. Peterburg, had transferred to Oxford, though it was polo and riding to the hounds that most interested the expert young horseman. He returned to Russia to join the Russian cavalry during the war and marry Catherine, the daughter of Czar Alexander II. Resettled in London, Serge had industriously joined first the grain-handling machinery business and then stock brokering. Catherine frequently visited her mother—whose money was running out—in Nice, leaving Serge to lead something of a bachelor's existence.[5]

"It was back at Rome during the holidays when I went to visit Mother that I met Millicent Rogers, an exquisite American girl with the wide, slant eyes of a deer, which I noticed she accentuated with eyebrow pencil. She was visiting Europe with her parents and her friend Lela Emery," Serge wrote in his memoirs, *One Man in His Time*. Everyone knew that Millicent was fabulously rich. She and Obolensky were introduced at a picnic given by the Italian countess, "Tookie" di Zoppola. "Millicent was terribly attractive, one of the most beautiful girls I have ever known. She was an exotic creature, with a curious languid manner. Even her voice, soft and pensive, was that of an Oriental, and she generally dressed the part."

He began taking her out when she visited London some weeks later, and yes, he asked her to marry him! "We got unofficially engaged," he wrote in his biography, but of course, he was already married. It was Millicent's influence, he claimed, that caused him to ask Catherine to begin divorce proceedings. "I was really fascinated by her," he wrote. Catherine, who had a thriving musical career and "a complete life of her own," was complacent about their marriage and began the process toward divorce.

Serge kept up the chase for Millicent. At the end of the London season the Rogers took a castle in Scotland—Cortachy Castle—and Serge was invited to visit. His married status did not seem to disturb the Rogers, who either considered his title more important or did not think him a true contender for Millicent's affections. Lela Emery was with Millicent and her parents. A young Scotsman, Ali McIntosh, was the designated escort for Lela, Serge for Millicent. The weekend was a classic hunting and house party in the Scottish countryside. Cortachy Castle was an ancient and famous castle, cold and draughty. That year it was unseasonably cold and the party of friends found it necessary to bundle up both inside and out. A big shoot was scheduled for the grouse-hunting season, and Serge noted with humor that Ali put on his kilts as soon as he arrived. The freezing cold out on the moors tested even the Scot's mettle against the elements on the heath. Huddled at dinner and around the fire, Millicent decided to tell a story she had learned about the castle. Ali, irritable after so much cold, quickly said he knew the tale, but Millicent ignored him and continued with her story of the drummer of Cortachy who had put a curse on the Airlies who hung him. Ali told its sequel and at least Lela Emery must have been impressed, because, eight years later, she married him.

Serge also thought his chances with Millicent were looking up. "After the stay in Cortachy, things looked pretty bright again for Millicent and me. We saw each other constantly; although I must say she really was something." He seems to refer to her skill at being ambiguous and keeping him hanging on. "She was still talking to me in complete tangents—perhapses, maybes, we'll sees." He was taken aback when she suddenly left the British Isles altogether. Soon, through the grapevine, an extremely efficicent mode of communication among European society, he heard that she was spotted in Switzerland with a gallant young Argentine, Arturo Peralta-Ramos. A true gentleman, Serge's response was merely a cartoonlike, "Blast him!" Serge would prove quite a survivor himself. He went on to marry another American, the daughter of John Jacob Astor, Alice, and preside over a successful hotel business.

Lela Emery kept a diary of her travels. Her daughter, Countess Sheila de Rochambeau, recalls, "It was hysterically funny because they couldn't stay in any one town for more than two weeks because Millicent would get engaged. All men with titles made up to her when they learned who she was. She was also very beautiful." Their traveling party had to keep moving. The girls were amused by so much attention and so many proposals, but underneath there was a sense of concern for Millicent. They, like her family, worried whether she would be loved truly for herself. All the attention, and the young men wanting to be her fiancé, caused a heady whirl that could be disorienting. It was no wonder that Millicent had written to Jimmy Thompson that their engagement was ended. Her world seemed to be getting fuller of men and opportunities for a future much grander and more exciting than marrying her old Southampton sweetheart.

Lela and Millicent were young enough to have things other than men and marriage on the their minds. They were eager for experiences. One evening in Monte Carlo, the Colonel and Mary Rogers went out for the evening without them. The girls set out on their own to the casino, but the doormen turned them away. They were only eighteen years old, too young to be admitted anywhere there was gambling. For young women who were so typically protected and chaperoned, they showed a noteworthy degree of resourcefulness and pluck by ducking into the ladies' lounge, where they proceeded to scratch out the year of birth on their passports and change the date to make them appear to be twenty-one. Like twenty-first-century teenagers, they produced false IDs and presented them at the door. The ploy worked and soon they were inside betting on the first table on the right, which they heard to be the customary spot for good luck.

The adventure seemed to be their secret until they went through customs to return home to New York. The agent noticed that Millicent and Lela's passports had been altered. Colonel Rogers was brought into the matter, and according to Lela, who called him "Pop Rogers," there was all hell to pay.[6]

Millicent, now twenty and spirited, irked her father in other ways. Her spending habits, in what would become a lifelong pattern, exceeded her means. When she had overspent her allowance by $871.88 in the spring of 1922, Rogers took her to serious task. He wrote her a letter after one of her sprees in Europe.

You are now twenty years old and presumably should have arrived at a mental condition in which you could perform the simple mathematical problems of addition and subtraction, and to have known quite distinctly that you had spent more money than you had. I cannot imagine, under the circumstances, a more idiotic thing for anyone to do, having just arrived from Paris and having bought quantities of clothes to immediately rush off and buy a Red Crepe Beaded Gown for $250.00, when you only had $1000 to carry you over until the first of June.

She had run up a bill of $457.50 at Cartiers, "the most expensive place in New York," Rogers huffed, and he then proceeded to lecture: "If any of these items were necessary, by going to a smaller and cheaper jeweler, you could have gotten the same return for less money."

He then tried to rein her in with the same stern tone he might use with his business subordinates rather than with a headstrong daughter. Cajoling was not in his repertoire.

Though signed "affectionately," the message was certainly clear.[7]

CHAPTER SIX

Breaking Away

THE WINTER SOCIAL SEASON ROLLED ALONG WITH ROUTINE festiveness through the holidays at the end of 1923. It was punctuated by a much-anticipated event scheduled for New Year's at the Metropolitan Opera. The popular baritone Antonio Scotti would celebrate his twenty-fifth anniversary at the Metropolitan with a gala performance of *Tosca*. Mary was an avid opera fan and Millicent was a leader of the Monday Night Opera Club, a social venue for Manhattan's young socialites organized around opera appreciation and attendance.

When Scotti took his last bow, flowers were tossed over the footlights and one admiring matron even sent a basket of white doves, which were tied to the handles with ribbons so they wouldn't flutter too far onto the stage. Then the lights went up and the audience adjourned to the Biltmore Hotel for the party to follow in the ballroom. Scotti stood at the entrance to the party extending his hand to arriving guests, and it was noted in the papers that Mrs. H. H. Rogers was one of the first in line. Mary was accompanied by Millicent and the Marchesa del Monte, a young Italian noblewoman and opera aficionada.

"With their black, glossy hair and being of the same height, [they] looked as though related to each other," *Town Topics* noted. Because Millicent entered the national fashion consciousness later as a blonde, it is sometimes difficult to envision her as she was in 1924: a brunette beauty, attendant to her mother, who was mentioned in the same breath and columns as other society doyennes such as Mrs. Otto Kahn, Mrs. Charles Dana Gibson, and the Duchess of Rutland. They were only slightly farther back in Scotti's receiving line.

The Rogers were checked into the Ritz-Carlton Hotel, where they had been staying since they had returned to the city from Southampton at the end of the Long Island social calendar in late fall. So much of their life was in Southampton that their stays in Manhattan were invariably in the apartment they maintained at the Ritz. They had spent Christmas in Tuxedo Park that year, but returned to Manhattan. As was their custom, preparations were being made for their planned trip to Europe on January 12. Mary, the Colonel, and both Millicent and her younger brother, Henry Jr., planned to sail on the French American ocean liner, *Majestic*, the upcoming Saturday. Mary supervised the preparations for their cruise from a suite of rooms at the hotel. With typical vigilance, the daily newspapers had reported the Rogers travels plans and announced their residence at the Ritz. The week before their departure was always a flurry of activity as the hotel staff worked to ready the array of steamer trunks for delivery to the dock.

A definite weariness had by this time set into the young heiress's tone about her romantic life. "Every time I was seen with someone, I was reported engaged," she lamented.[1] She was the darling of *The New York Times* and *Daily News* society columns. She had to do little more than show up at a social event to get her name in the paper. Her mother and father continued to manage and meddle in her marriage-ability prospects, until she huffed to a group of peers gathered one evening at the Ritz that she was going to marry the next man who asked her and be done with the whole marriage business.[2] She had also mentioned to some of her friends and suitors that she had begun to fear that her parents would force her to marry "a person distasteful to her."[3] Her madcap remark about marrying the next man who asked was reportedly overheard—and noted—by Count Ludwig Salm von Hoogstraten, who had already taken serious note of the young Millicent, though he had managed to woo her beneath the Rogers' social radar. He had been living at the Ritz that fall and was often at the same social occasions as Millicent.

The Rogers had spent the prior winter in Europe and upon their return had gone directly from the pier where their ocean liner docked on Manhattan's West Side to Southampton. Once they migrated into the city and moved into the Ritz, they hosted and attended a myriad of parties and social gatherings through late autumn and the Christmas holidays. Count Salm was often there. He had also been out at Tuxedo Park right after Christmas for a fancy dress ball at the local club. A couple of drunks hassled him for his attention-grabbing costume, a fantasy marine uniform he had worn as an extra in the film *Il Principe rosso*, made by a friend in Austria. The Count thought their real grievance was that he danced almost exclusively with Millicent and they sat alone together on the side between dances.[4]

The Count had been in the United States since the previous spring, and had moved into the Ritz-Carlton that winter. He was reputed to be "the greatest of dancers, and he was at it every night. He has immense attraction, and he had no way of getting a woman crazy about him quicker than by dancing with her," gushed an admirer to the papers, who also noted that "He was handsome, distinguished and foreign-looking. His accent added to his charm."[5] His features were distinctive, with a chiseled jaw and long equiline nose. He was slender and dressed elegantly for every occasion. Confident and courtly, he set quite a few feminine American hearts aflutter. He was a bit exotic.

Salm came from an impressive, long line of Austrian nobility and titles that wove themselves through centuries of European history, and he had had the upbringing that went along with it. He was considered to be the senior member of the aristocratic Salm line, and his history is full of hunting parties, manor weekends, Viennese balls, and European chivalry. His younger brother Otto had married socialite Maud Coster of New York City and Tuxedo Park in 1915.

The older Salm had served with a crack Austrian cavalry regiment during the war. He fought his first duel with pistols when he was barely twenty. He had distinguished himself as a tennis champion in high school at the Gymnasium in Baden. As a young cavalry officer he showed up the Germans in Wiesbaden with his dancing, "where the girls had only German officers and trainees as their dancing partners. My wardrobe, mainly from England, was simply wonderful," he wrote later. He spent the winter of 1913 in Paris with an elegant mistress who introduced him, he claimed, to "the wittiest and most important people in Paris." But the war brought that shimmering world to an end.

Salm wrote in his memoir of debts and the limits of his family's support even before the war, but after the Great War, he found, "When my yearly income, which had added up to six thousand dollars before the war, had melted down to forty cents, I made the heroic decision to work." He became an agent, for everything from butter to jewelry. His money was running out when an old school friend, another count, started a film association and offered him the leading role in *Miss Dorothy's Avowal*. The budget was so meager that he did his own makeup. Roles in two other films followed, but in a moment of real prescience, he concluded that the glamour of the movies wasn't what it was cracked up to be. Audiences, he wrote, "Don't know how often you have to get up at six o'clock in the morning for this, and fall into bed deadbeat at twelve o'clock or later." He was tired of Europe and the promises of an American film agent. He cashed in what remained of any investments in the Berlin and Viennese stock markets and went to London, where he did what so many others had done before and would do after him, he looked to America. "With avowal in my heart and a brand new English wardrobe" he boarded the *President Harding* cruise ship for New York.

His memoir, *My Dear Peter: Confessions of a Father*, written in 1928, includes a classic tale of coming to America. Despite his European heritage and sophistication, his story is not unlike that of a young Iowan traveling from the rural heartland to New York City.

For economy he shared a cabin on the ship out of London and met a Montana sheep breeder who convinced him to stay at the Hotel Commodore rather than the glitzy, European-style Ritz, once they docked in New York. Like most new arrivals to New York, Count Salm claimed he'd reached "the end of my strengths" from the "shocks" of life in the city after three weeks. The dizzying heights of the buildings, the slow elevators, the marvels and challenge of the hotel switchboard, broad vowel sounds, and brusqueness of the staff all rattled him. The shoes he left outside the door of his room at night to have polished were uncleaned the next morning. He took taxis until the expense stunned him into using the subway, but the express and local stops were confusing. He ended up on one occasion far afield in Bowling Green. Even his trophy English wardrobe didn't look quite right once he'd entered the bustle of New York. He thought people stared at him. But he landed work at eighty dollars a week for a petroleum company and felt "already Americanized." His observations about Americans, New Yorkers in particular, create the picture of a thoughtful, often humorous, sometimes earnest man in hopes of a better future. "Nicely modest, without underestimating himself, willing to start again as apprentice, is how the European can use the little plus in average education and his European experience as floating assets for usurious interest, when he has reached the standard of the working competency of his American colleagues by diligence. He definitely won't have to starve in America," Salm wrote of himself in his awkwardly translated memoir.

He also remarked publicly that he was hoping to marry a rich woman. Catholic, and divorced from his first wife, he thought he had (this would be disputed later) his government's permission to remarry. He arrived in the United States with five thousand dollars in his pocket, documentation of his divorce in 1912 from his Viennese first wife, and the frank intention to improve his financial plight through marriage. His divorce deposition described him as a Roman Catholic "and legally divorced." He was chasing a woman he'd met in Vienna and Berlin and had intentions of marrying, but he took his time about making their plans formal and seemed to be easily distracted by other women. The previous fall they had agreed to stay friends, but not to marry. By his account, she had decided, they could not afford "as two people, who although loving each other candidly, but only had modest means" to get married.

Though he would tell several news organizations that he had met Millicent the year before, one of his friends in New York, Betty Sherwood, had been with him when he seemed to first set eyes on Millicent Rogers in a Broadway jazz palace in the late fall of 1923. The Roaring Twenties were in full swing and Millicent was one of the smart set who appeared at the hot new clubs in middy sheath dresses. Prohibition was in effect, and lots of flappers, Count Salm noticed, kept flasks belted to their hips. Millicent and her friends often danced until the wee hours of the morning. "The count was quick to ask about her financial status. He frankly told me he was gambling everything on a rich marriage," said Sherwood. Though he frequently escorted Sherwood—a pretty hat shop owner—around town, he made his intentions to her quite clear: "It is too bad you are not worth a million; I would marry you," he told her.[6] He may also have been realizing that the pretty young flapper who caught his eye was the same heiress he had seen pirouetting on the ice in St. Moritz.

Salm was nearly forty years old, twice Millicent's age, and according to social columnists at the time, reported to "look much younger than his 40 years." The introduction of a European nobleman twice their daughter's age was hardly noted by Millicent's parents that winter at the Ritz. In his own memoir, Salm claimed that he got to know Millicent that winter in the Monday Opera Club, where she headed the group called the "Junior Set." He recalled later that "her pretty and interesting face, her magnificent poise and her elegance could not fail to arrest attention." He encountered her at other parties that he attended with his former fiancée and where Millicent was with another escort. "We had only a few dances and our conversation was no more than casual." Then in his telling, "Days went by, and I thought no longer of her, any more than I did of the Queen of Sheba, when one night I rediscovered her in the Palm Garden of the Ritz. She offered me a cigarette and asked me to remain with her until she was called for." It is a rare glimpse of Millicent, seductive, tendering a cigarette, and waiting for a light as she cast her spell over the older European count. "I found her conversation witty and fascinating. My first impressions of her were definite, for my eye did not deceive me and my critical judgement of her, too, was lasting," he wrote.[7]

There is an inscrutability about Millicent at this juncture in her life. Young Millicent, it must be remembered, had been treated like an invalid into her teens. She had lacked social experience and been unduly dependent on her family until her debut, three years earlier, had thrust her onto the New York social scene with a vengeance. There were various, sometimes conflicting, considerations governing her behavior: What was good for her health, what was appropriate for a young lady, and what was correct for someone of her social station— and then in addition, what Harry and Mary would accept.

She was more programmed than matured in her early twenties and despite her attractiveness and travel, she was sometimes withdrawn, even shy. Perhaps the ballyhooed allure of her financial worth had made her doubtful of her own value, creating a strange clash of outward know-how and bravado, and private insecurity. The seeds of creativity that would blossom later may have been sown in this period of coming to grips with the image that her wealth and reputation projected without any real or personal contribution from her. Her true self, her essence, the things a young woman hopes will fuel her lovability and romance, were treated, publicly at least, as almost beside the point. The previous winters in Europe had left no doubt that she had a siren's appeal for men, but she was always very aware that money was a significant part of the attraction. She had learned a little skepticism toward men, their attentions and hasty proposals. She had become a bit more resistant—headstrong even—to the management of her parents. She may have come to think, as another American socialite, Edie Beale of Grey Gardens, counseled her daughter in the film version of her life, "First you get married and then you can do anything you want."

Whatever was in her head, Millicent was quite competent at executing her intentions. As her family and staff at the Ritz went about preparations for the upcoming trip abroad, on Tuesday, January 8, 1924, she stepped out on some business of her own. She went out in the early afternoon and was hardly missed amid the flurry of her family's farewell logistics. She was well but not extravagantly dressed, and wore a string of pearls when she hailed a cab to take her downtown. She was eloping with Count Ludwig Salm von Hoogstraten. The marriage license had been acquired the day before. They had sought the advice of an attorney two days earlier, but he had counseled them to get her parent's permission to marry. Otherwise, he cautioned, Millicent's rich and powerful father was likely to disinherit her. Millicent felt sure her father would oppose the marriage and the attorney's advice only stiffened her determination. She wanted to marry entirely in secret, and she did not intend to tell her parents until they were on the boat to Europe. The prospect of the scene that was likely to follow when her father got the word made the plan seem an act of wild daring on her part, but she hoped to pull off a fait accompli. According to Salm, she urgently wanted to avoid the matchmaking that she believed her parents had in mind for her.

Millicent claimed she had been taken by surprise when she learned quite by chance that their departure for Europe was to be in several days, rather than in two weeks as had been originally planned. Her parents, she believed, had taken note of the growing affection between her and the Count and intended to spirit her away from him. Knowing how closely the press followed her romances, she and Count Salm hoped to avoid detection by fudging their names to the marriage bureau.[8] She signed in as Marie Harriet Rogers, daughter of "Harry Rogers," and gave her age as twenty-one.[9] Count Salm presented himself as Ludwig Albrecht Konstantin Maria Salm, age thirty-seven, and filled in that his occupation was dealing in antiques on Madison Avenue. It was partly true, though he was also trying to set up a small auto parts business in New Jersey at the time. She hoped the deception would keep their names out of the newspapers the next day, at least until their boat left. With a "discreet friend" present and another witness they recruited at City Hall, they were married in the chapel of the Municipal Building in downtown New York by the deputy city clerk, without much fanfare. That would follow.

Millicent's motivation for this marriage can only be guessed at. Perhaps she saw an older European man both as her ticket to freedom from an all-enveloping family, and a continuing source of the strong security she was used to. Simple rebellion was no doubt one ingredient of her decision. Of course, there was the lovely burst of glamour and gossip for the other debutantes to talk about. More profoundly, this was the first expression in her very tumultuous life of her search for glamour, for beauty, and for love, unfettered by convention, and yet relatively free of the flamboyant champagne-in-a-slipper partying lifestyle that typified many of her generation. She was making the grand leap that would firmly separate her from her cosseted childhood and establish her in the adult world (titled Europeans, no less!) that she aspired to join.

After the wedding ceremony, Millicent and her groom, rather than go to the Ritz, dropped into the dining room of the Hotel Vanderbilt to privately congratulate themselves and regroup. Salm invited his attorney, H. B. Goodstein, to join them. He examined the marriage certificate, pronounced it legitimate, and asked about their plans. He begged them to tell Millicent's parents that evening. The couple returned to the Hotel Ritz separately.

Millicent immediately encountered the family doctor in a corridor of the hotel and told him what she had done. A worldly, avuncular man, he laughed out loud. "Well, Millicent, you have had enough choice here and in Europe. You're not a child anymore. If you have taken this step, you probably know whom you've chosen and what you wanted. Good luck!" When he promised to put in a good word with her parents she asked him to come with her to tell them, *now*. Salm waited anxiously in his own room. After some time, the phone rang. How had it gone? he asked. "Very bad, Ludi, Darling," she reported. Her parents had sent her to her room and wanted to know nothing more of him or the wedding. According to the count's record, the newlyweds spent the night apart, in either a show of true cowardice or great deference to her parents in hopes of receiving their blessing later.[10]

At six the next morning there was a knock on his door. When he answered it a gentleman, fully dressed in business clothes, stood outside and asked for his marriage papers. He explained he was the secretary to Colonel Rogers. Count Salm coolly suggested he should go to City Hall and consult the registry. The war had begun.

Colonel Rogers, rather than meet with Salm personally, called his brother Otto, whom he was acquainted with from Tuxedo Park, and asked him to come to the Ritz at three o'clock. Otto called Ludi, saying he expected this meant that Rogers was coming round and they were about to come to an understanding. No sooner had Count Salm hung up the phone with his brother than Millicent phoned, with good news. "The situation is looking better. Daddy has had our papers proofed at City Hall. They're okay. He is providing you and me with an apartment at the Ritz, but wishes not to see you." She sounded giddy and told him to start packing for the trip. She no sooner hung up than there was another knock at his door. This time it was reporters. All the papers had the story.

Millicent stepped out of the hotel for several hours, but when she returned at four o'clock a horde of flashbulb-popping photographers and newsmen was at her heels. Colonel and Mary Rogers had retreated to their suite and refused to talk to anybody. Rogers testily referred the newsmen to his attorney for comment. The Rogers cancelled their scheduled cruise, and the bell captain was dispatched to collect their trunks from the waterfront. Instead of sailing, they left promptly for Southampton, only to find a crowd of what today would be called paparazzi. The Colonel, fuming, instructed the driver to keep going and they turned the car around for Tuxedo Park. There would be no comment. Millicent and her Count remained to face a press uproar that was gaining in sensationalism by the moment.

The *Daily News* reported the elopement, explaining that "Count Ludwig was a member of the Belgian branch of the princely house of Salm-Salm, one of the most ancient lines of nobility in Austria." Soon the story took on hype and spin, referring to "Count Ludwig Salm von Hoogstraten, the so-called Austrian nobleman who plucked a $400,000 plum from the tree of Standard Oil." Forty million was more like it. A full-length picture of Millicent, taken the prior season, with her arms stretched over flower urns like a neoclassical goddess accompanied the story. By the third day it was "Count's Gold Tinted Love . . . He wanted a girl with a million and said so frankly."

The day after the wedding, Ludwig appeared in the hotel lobby, trim and smartly dressed in a gray knickerbocker suit with gray golf stockings. He looked "like a picture from a trade journal catering to the men's wear element" according to *The Washington Post*. Millicent wore a fashionable *trottier*, a stunning couture suit of black, and a small hat. A red scarf added dash to the ensemble. The Count and Millicent had answered a list of questions that had been sent to their suite. Now, he shot back at further questions, "We have no immediate plans beyond avoiding newspapermen." He was suave and genial, a charmer, a cavalryman, a tennis champion, and a ladies' man, and now, the husband of Millicent Rogers. Millicent, in contrast, made no attempt to hide her anger with all the press attention. Posed sitting on a table, she remarked haughtily, "I am criticized because I had the nerve to do what most American girls lack the nerve to do—the unconventional thing."[11]

Then came the bombshell: Had the Count been formally engaged to someone else, Mrs. Grace Sands Montgomery Coffin? The story grew richer as it began to surface in the newspapers. It seemed to overshadow the elopement itself. The newspapermen who got wind of the Coffin engagement worked fast enough to make it to the apartment where Grace Coffin was staying with a friend in hopes of avoiding publicity. Her friend, Gianetta Traini, a singer, was an old friend of Count Salm in Europe. She had also met Millicent in St. Moritz. She created something of a stir as an intermediary between the Count and Mrs. Coffin, when she paid a visit to Millicent and Count Salm several times a few days after the marriage. She was mistaken by the press as a disappointed sweetheart, but she claimed her visits were simply to "pay her respects" to the couple. It's likely she was also helping to smooth the ruffled feathers and ego of her friend, Grace Coffin. *The New York Times* reported that Count Salm had invited Grace Coffin to the Ritz for dinner the night before his wedding, but he had somehow lost the nerve to break the news to her either out of cowardice or courtliness. According to Madame Traini, he phoned her after Grace Coffin had left the Ritz and asked Madame Traini to tell Mrs. Coffin not to be unhappy.[12]

Traini had known Count Salm for five years, since they had met at her home in Berlin. Her late husband had owned a string of newspapers in Germany and was one of Count Salm's best friends, she explained. Comfortable speaking with the press, she invited the reporters into her Fifty-seventh Street apartment and willingly answered their questions. One *New York Times* reporter mentioned her good looks and noted that she greeted them in Chinese costume. Whether this was a costume for a singing role she was rehearsing or merely a chinoiserie robe she chose to wear is unclear, but it contributed to a splendid scene as the blue-eyed blonde held court for the press.

"It is ridiculous to say that the Count is a fortune hunter; that he was running after money. He never ran after anything. He never pursued women; they pursued him," Traini asserted. "I do not think he was ever really in love until he met Mrs. Coffin and, of course, Miss Rogers." That seemed to throw a little gasoline on the fire, but she was quick to add, "I knew for some time that he was going to marry Miss Rogers. So did Mrs. Coffin." But, she claimed, they simply had not known *when*. The count wanted very much to avoid the publicity that would follow the announcement of his engagement. Then she offered up a tidbit for those pursuing the question of when and where Count Salm had actually set his cap for Millicent. Traini said that she had known Millicent in St. Moritz and that *she* had shown a photograph of Millicent in skating costume to the Count and "he was very much impressed by her beauty even before he knew who she was. 'How beautiful she is,'" she remembered as his reaction to the photo. The Count had been seated with Madame Traini and her husband at a party somewhat later in Montmartre when Millicent Rogers made an entrance. The Count exclaimed, "That is the girl in the picture. Who *is she?*"

The Washington Post also ran the interview and interjected in its story, "Berlin cables state that the count met her in Berlin before this date." The paper eagerly followed its German lead and beat a trail to the American born Baroness von Weichs, known in film circles as Fern Andra, the "Mary Pickford of Germany." Reports from Berlin stated that the Baroness had been engaged to Count Salm in Berlin. She dismissed the story as "an exaggeration," and explained they had been "very, very good friends" as she scolded them, somewhat teasingly, with a suggestive smile, "Don't ask too many questions on *that* score." The list of Count Salm's women began to add up, to the delight of the tabloids—and the chagrin of the Rogers.

The newspapers mined the Count's relationship with Grace Coffin for all it was worth. And indeed, it seems Count Salm had once been in love with her, or at least thought of marrying her enough to make his intentions public, if not formal. To add to the circuslike atmosphere, film star Rudolph Valentino arrived at the Ritz and told reporters that before he sailed for Europe in mid-December he had had lunch with Mrs. Coffin, a widow, and Count Salm, who had talked of plans to marry. Among Salm's documents, now in the public record, was a testimonial concerning his Austrian divorce, stating that he was now free to marry Mrs. Grace Sands Coffin. When this particular item was mentioned in one interview, the Count gave an answer that he seemed to think explained everything: "That does not mean anything. That was an idea I had in July."

There were rumors that Mrs. Coffin contemplated legal action—a breach of promise suit—after he had eloped with Millicent, but in her public appearances she was nothing but gracious. "I will not say a word. Not a word for a million dollars," was the somewhat tortured message she sent out to reporters through Madame Traini, though in private she declared dazedly, "It is impossible." *The Washington Post* had reported that she had obtained a passport, given up her apartment, and arranged to store her furniture with her sister in preparation for a wedding and honeymoon with the Count.[13]

Count Salm's brother, Otto, acted as an emissary to Grace Coffin in the days following the elopement. *The Washington Post* found him seated in Madame Traini's apartment with Mrs. Coffin, whom reporters seemed unable to resist noting "had a real physical likeness to Countess Ludwig," as Millicent was now called. Grace Coffin was described in the same account as "a sobbing, hysterical woman." In order to escape the whole debacle, she and Gianetta made plans to sail for Paris the following week. Madame Traini, acting as Coffin's spokeswoman, continued to put the best face on matters for the press, asserting that Grace Coffin and Count Salm "had found they were 'incompatible.'"

The press didn't rest. "Love Finds a Way in Spite of Match Making Mama," was a headline in the *Sunday News*. Even the *Southampton Press* got on board with "Prominent Society Heiress Astonished Friends with Sudden Marriage." One paper produced a French "publicist," Miss Suzanne Boltard, who was staying at the Hotel Chatham and had known Count Salm through the French Embassy in Vienna. She was interviewed about the Count's prior attentions to her. There would be a rehash of Millicent's first engagement and the buzz about her and the Prince of Wales. "New York and Washington Society Heiress Astonishes Relatives by Becoming Bride of Austrian Nobleman," blared *The New York Herald*. "Count Danced Into Marriage" was another. It was front-page news in every New York paper. "H. H. Rogers Heiress Weds at City Hall" was *The New York Times*' more restrained account. By Thursday, three-quarters of the entire front paper of the society bible *Town Topics* was devoted to Millicent. This "unconventional marriage," it pronounced, was a "sensation."

The papers hungrily moved from matters of romance to finance. "Fortune hunter" was what the newspapers—echoing the Rogers family sentiment—called Salm. No reporter could resist mentioning that Millicent was likely to inherit $40 million. Salm's financial prospects were meager. He did meddle in the antique business in New York, but it was his brief career as a movie extra in Europe that stole the limelight. His role among a cast of thousands in *The Queen of Sin* as a Roman legionnaire (some said swordbearer) stole the thunder. He had also played the part of a lover in a German film called *Red Rider*.[14] It was assumed that a Count would have property in his homeland but it turned out that the ancestral estates of the noble Salm-Salm would not pass to him since his grandfather, Prince Constantine, had married a German commoner, and the convoluted land, title, and marriage laws at the time did not allow it. Yes, he was the eldest son, counted as head of the ancestral house of Salm, but he would not hold title to the ancestral estate in Reichenau, Austria. He was on record saying that he was looking for profit when he came to America. The papers soon reported that Colonel Rogers had cut Millicent's inheritance to fifty thousand dollars because of her marriage.

That wasn't all. The story took a further turn toward soap opera. One "other woman" commented: "Everybody is saying that Count Salm picked a prize in Millicent Rogers, but if you ask me she got the world's greatest lover." It was not the kind of public notice the Rogers were accustomed to. When Millicent read the papers she would soon see that she was now referred to as Countess, but the title had come dear. By January 12, four days after the elopement and the date the Rogers had originally scheduled to sail, Millicent was reported "peeved." It's hard to imagine that she would have felt otherwise. When the new Countess was asked for a talk, she responded angrily, "I will not talk to anybody. The papers are full of lies." The Count, on the other hand, remained suave and jaunty. To a female reporter at the Ritz who was blocking his path, he cajoled, moving past her, "You are sweet, but I have nothing to say." He had already shared with the press his hope that the Rogers family would warm shortly to his marriage.

The story trailed off into a collection of often contradictory details and explanations. Salm was quoted as suggesting the Rogers knew of the plan. "I think they wanted her to marry someone else," but he claimed he and Millicent had had "a big talk" with the family "before we did it. We told them Tuesday morning before we went downtown and they knew all about it." Again from Ludi: "From the moment I saw her I loved her. And she says it was the same with her. We met at a party last May here at the Ritz-Carlton." So much for the Jazz Club version of their meeting. He remembered dancing with Millicent. "Since then we have become quite famous you know, for our tango. We have danced it together everywhere," he said proudly. Salm attributed the plan to elope to Millicent, because she feared her parents would force her into a marriage against her wishes.

While the Count and new Countess's romantic pasts were put under a microscope in the papers, they seemed to play out a waiting game with Millicent's parents. The Count, at least publicly, interpreted the couple's continued stay in the Rogers' apartment in the Ritz as some evidence of his in-laws' approval and forgiveness. But Colonel and Mary Rogers did not come to call on the couple. Reporters who approached the parents in Tuxedo Park were turned away. Millicent and the Count had lunch at the hotel with the Austrian Vice-Consul and dined out with the Count's brother and sister-in-law over the next several days. The newlyweds boldly attended the Wednesday Supper Club, making it their last appearance before sailing for Europe. Their entrance caused several of the society matrons to blush, but not "the pale face of the one-time Milly Rogers when she noticed an occasional glance in her direction," observed *Town Topics*. She was not repentant.

A week after the elopement the newlyweds boarded the liner *Veendam* for the Netherlands. Millicent told reporters it was their honeymoon trip, to last, she said, at least six months. No friends or family came to see them off, though Count Ludwig's brother Otto was traveling with them. Attention was paid to Ludwig's attire, "a rather old-looking brown overcoat, gray suit, and a gray fedora hat with black band," according to *The New York Times*. The writer decided he looked dapper. The getaway was almost spoiled when Otto Salm could not find his passport and became quite agitated as federal officials came onto the pier to question him. It was Millicent who kept a cool head and took charge. She told Otto to calm down and be quiet as she explained to officials that the passport belonging to Count Otto was quite in order and had the necessary visas, but had been packed in one of the party's trunks by mistake. "I saw to it. Quit fussing," she told him, echoing the same childish imperative she had once used to the notice of her elders on her brother. She was convincing, a Countess now, and comported herself accordingly. Otto was permitted to board, and the passport was later found in his trunk.

"I don't know what I can say of where we are going or when we are coming back," Millicent demurely told reporters, who felt obliged to report that she looked tired. She did manage to pose with her husband on deck for the photographers until the movie cameramen started to crank the handles of their cameras, and then she burst out, a bit stagily: "I was never so tired of anything as I am of the newspapers. I'm so bored with them—bored beyond words! I do not wish to see another one for the rest of my life." She would not be so lucky.

Then in a burst of girlish enthusiasm that now seems to betray Millicent's youth and inexperience to a touching degree, she shared her vision of what life would be like in her new marriage. After a visit to the Count's ancestral home, she told reporters, she and the Count would go to the South of France where her husband would practice tennis for the upcoming Olympics. "I shall go to Africa while the Count is engaging in Olympic tennis play as a member of the American team, and try to find a new brand of monkey."[15] Then the ship's whistle announced their departure and the *Veendam* cut through the icy floes of New York Harbor and slipped out to sea.

CHAPTER SEVEN

Countess

OUT OF SIGHT AND OFF THE AMERICAN SOCIAL STAGE, Millicent and her count escaped the press attention she found so wearisome. As their train pulled into Paris, only one reporter awaited them. "We felt like in paradise," Salm recorded in his memoirs. He was equally pleased that Millicent's parlor maid, an American black woman, had become ill in New York and was unable to make the journey, so an older Frenchwoman was hired to serve her. He preferred the Frenchwoman's morning greeting, "*Bonjour Madame, bonjour Monsieur, avez-vous bien dormi?*" to the American maid's whistle, gloomy weather reports, and humming of Negro spirituals.

They were immediately swept up into the social whirl and magic of Paris. Salm was breathlessly proud of his beautiful young wife who caused a stir wherever they went. "A beautiful woman gets admired nowhere else as honestly and discreetly as in this city," he wrote. Millicent seemed to bask in the admiration and revel in her new liberation. She bought a lorgnon, had the lense removed, and when she'd had enough of being stared at by a rather dowdy American woman one day, she stared back through the lorgnon and waved with her fingers through the hole.

However, neither Salm nor Millicent were truly ready to adjust to a new standard of living, and like ostriches burying their heads, they continued to live without imposing limits on themselves. Recalls Ludi: "Couturiers, furriers, milliners—one was young and in love. I didn't have the heart to even ask how and when are we going to pay? Forebodings of the future arose in me though, but it seemed to, as if all people had to give Millicent all the jewelry and all the beauty, simply because she was so beautiful, so endearing and so young."

Fashionability mattered so much that the trip Millicent had hoped to take up to St. Moritz to visit a girlfriend was cancelled when the couturiers in Paris delivered her new purchases too late for her to go. Salm huffed that the loss was the clothiers', "who lost a special chance of advertising in St. Moritz, if Millicent appeared in their fashions."

They traveled to Cannes several days later and he looked on proudly when she entered the casino. All conversation stopped as Millicent, wearing an all-white couture gown, descended the staircase to the dining room below. Salm and his brother Otto followed behind and listened to the comments as she passed by. "*Qu'elle est belle! Qu'elle est ravissante!* How lovely! Adorable! *Che preziosa!*" For several months their life seemed charmed, as she enchanted French society and Salm trained for the upcoming Davis Cup and Olympic games on the courts in Cannes. Though he was now forty, he hoped to achieve some of his prewar success next month in the upcoming competition in Vienna. While he brushed up on the court, his mother came to Cannes to meet Millicent and it was a relief that the two got on well.

By March Millicent knew she was pregnant. She went to bed early and the Count began to stay at home with her, despite her urging that he go out to the casino alone. He preferred to stay, reading by her side, and holding her hand until she fell asleep. Sometimes he slipped out to have a cigar on the beach. On the nights he did go out alone, he returned to her early and wrote in his diary, "I was so in love!" Their idyll soon ended when his Viennese attorney came to visit. He explained that Millicent's baptismal certificate was missing from the package that was required to record their marriage in Vienna and they would have to travel to the consul in Nice to authenticate her papers. They detoured to Milan, where Salm trained on the tennis courts with his brother to prepare for a tournament in Lugano. By then Millicent's black parlor maid from New York, paid by the Colonel's attorney in New York, had joined them and she was sent ahead to Lugano with their luggage and their dogs. Always an animal lover, Millicent and Salm had two dogs they took everywhere with them. The Sealyham Terrier named Paddy was their favorite.[1]

Public titters over Millicent's elopement had subsided in New York, but the Rogers family stewed in private. Mary, it was assumed, was less affronted by her daughter's marriage than Harry. She had a sense of romantic glamour, and she had hoped for a title for Millicent at one point, certainly when the Prince of Wales had courted her. She also kept her own counsel on the matter so as not to further aggravate Harry, which was wise, since he was becoming known for his tempers and rages, especially when he was drinking.

But their overall dissatisfaction over Millicent's marriage continued to rankle. They considered Count Salm little more than a fortune hunter, and no sooner had he and Millicent set sail than Harry Rogers had hired an investigator. His first commission was to investigate the validity of the wedding ceremony performed at City Hall. When it was determined that the marriage was indeed legal, Rogers decided to challenge whether Count Salm, a Catholic, was truly divorced from his first Austrian wife. Word came back that Count Salm had petitioned the Pope to have his first marriage adjudicated, so Rogers would need to take a different tack. The investigator, no doubt instructed by Rogers' hard-nosed lawyer, Adrian Larkin, was dispatched to Europe with instructions to "spare neither pains nor money in his efforts to lay bare every detail of the former life of Colonel Rogers' highly heraldic son-in-law." He was to delve into the Count's romantic past, and his commission explicitly stated that if Count Salm had "sown many wild oats the Rogers family would never recognize him, and that in the event of their daughter electing to remain his wife, in view of such revelations, she would very likely be disinherited."[2]

Another indicator of the Rogers' attitude toward the marriage came from Millicent's uncle, William Coe, who was Harry's cousin. William wrote to his son Robert, five years older than Millicent and the closest to her in the larger Rogers' family constellation. They had been playmates on the lawn at their grandfather's home in Fairhaven, and now Robert was enrolled at Oxford. His father wrote him a birthday missive that included notice of five hundred dollars that he had added to his bank account to mark the occasion. Along with the news of their life in Oyster Bay, the state of the camelia plants, and repairs to the greenhouse, he added a paragraph about Millicent halfway through his three-page letter:

> The Millicent affair is a bad one. They sailed on the "Veendam" a couple of weeks ago in a $400 cabin with very little money. Before he [the Count] left he wrote the story of his life and how he won Millicent and sold it to the "American" and it is now appearing daily in that paper. It shows completely what kind of a chap he is. The feeling in close quarters is that the marriage will not last a year. It is too bad. I am sending you the "American" articles that have appeared so far. If Aunt Cara would be interested in them you can turn them over to her.[3]

Indeed, Count Salm had sold his story to the weekly tabloid, perhaps in hopes that the story would move the Rogers' to his side. He was paid $2,500 for the account. Later he would explain that he only wrote it because he and Millicent needed the money, but such public exposure was considered unseemly in the Rogers' social circles and did not help his cause.

The day after William sent his letter to Robert, several letters to him and his wife arrived from Robert, who already knew about

Millicent's elopement and the sensation it had made. In it he mentioned that he hoped to see his cousin and her new husband since they were both on the same side of the Atlantic. William hastily dashed off a one-page missive, cautioning Robert against seeing her.

In your letter to Mother you expressed the hope that you would see Millicent. My advice to you for the present is to keep away.... Uncle Harry and Aunt Mary have not seen her since the day she announced her wedding and have not seen the man since the wedding. I heard a lot about the matter yesterday afternoon and it is indeed a very sorry mess. The "American" articles show just what kind of a man he is.[4]

The letter included little else except a brief weather report and advice to keep up his exercise. It seems intended solely to wave off Robert from seeing Millicent and is the best clue to the unwavering disposition that the Rogers family had developed toward the marriage.

Other reports began to leak back to Southampton about the couple. "New York society was a small, small world back then. It was all WASPs and everyone was married to their own cousin three times over. They always knew what each other was doing. You couldn't help it," says Joyce Mann, the daughter of one of Millicent's Southampton friends. The most damning news was that Millicent and the Count were so short of funds that they had taken up dancing for money in clubs in Paris and throughout southern France. Both were considered superb dancers; Salm was noted in New York for his tango, so it was not surprising that they had fallen back on the one thing they seemed expert enough at to sustain them, dancing. "The Colonel was furious," claims Mann. "They weren't suited for jobs. The Colonel no doubt understood that, and we knew he was trying to starve them out."[5] The newspapers mentioned it delicately. They simply wrote of the couple dancing in clubs, which could have been taken to mean they were spotted dancing during an evening's entertainment. To those who read between the lines, it telegraphed their dire financial straits.

Millicent had been given twenty thousand dollars by her father at the time of the marriage, but with the caveat that it was all she was going to get.[6] In the opinion of friends and relatives the sum was intended to keep the couple living simply. While it was a princely sum by most American standards at the time, it was hardly sufficient to maintain the glamorous new couple at the standard of living Millicent was accustomed to, and by May the money was gone. It would be noted through all of Millicent's life that she knew next to nothing about handling money, and once when told that her account was low she remarked that couldn't be possible because she still had checks in her checkbook.[7]

Tidbits of news about the couple's itinerary made their way into the papers. The *Chicago Tribune* reported from the Riviera that Count Salm had several disastrous evenings playing chemin de fer in the casinos. It was true, said the papers, that he and Millicent had accumulated a trail of unpaid hotel bills and resorted to the dancing to settle some of their accounts. Perhaps it was the news that Colonel Rogers had been waiting to hear. In April Rogers quietly set sail for Europe, ostensibly to enroll Millicent's brother, Henry Huttleston Rogers III, in preparatory school at Oxford in England. Ominously, attorney Adrian Larkin sailed on a different ship for Paris on the same day.

In Milan, Millicent and the Count received a telegram from Larkin, telling them her father would be in Paris for three days after dropping her brother off at school, and that he wanted to see her. She had written him and her mother that she was pregnant. Count Salm, sensitized to the Colonel's rebuffs, felt jittery. He had become suspicious that his wife's parlor maid, paid by the Colonel, was used to inform on the marriage and their movements. He was unsettled that Rogers was traveling with his attorney, but Millicent assured him that Larkin often accompanied her father on his travels and was also his friend. Though she, not he, had been summoned to Paris, he intended to break his training regimen in order to go with her. When he couldn't get a seat on the same train, they decided it would be more prudent for him to stay behind until she called with word that her father was ready to meet him. The Count consoled himself by rationalizing that Rogers had come out of fatherly concern for Millicent's health and also to receive the results of the investigation into the legality of her marriage in Europe, a topic Larkin had also raised. He had specified that getting the Austrian marriage papers in order, by whatever means necessary, was required by Rogers before the Count could return to America with his wife. A visit to Vienna would be required to do so, making it impossible for Salm to accompany Millicent on the voyage home that Rogers now proposed to her. If Salm intended to play tennis in Vienna in several weeks, he would have trouble fitting in an American trip. The Count was suspicious of Rogers' motives, but Millicent insisted her father wanted to take her to New York solely to be examined by their longtime family doctor. She agreed to look for housing for them when she was there and that he should follow her after his tennis competition.

It was cold for May in Paris when Colonel Rogers arrived. He allowed himself and Larkin a week of preparations in the city before he launched his offensive, in the style of the military maneuvers he was so admiring of during his army career. Though his trip abroad had been ostensibly undertaken to settle Millicent's brother at Oxford, her brother had seemingly made it to school on his own or with another escort while the Colonel went about his mission in Paris. Count Salm's father was summoned to Paris from the Austrian family's estate in Mienta to meet with Colonel Rogers. Two days after Millicent arrived in Paris, she called Salm to come. To his chagrin he had to leave the Sealyham Terrier, Paddy, behind, when the conductor wouldn't let the dog travel without its muzzle. Salm knew things weren't going his way in Paris when Millicent met him at the station and didn't even notice that he hadn't brought the dog. She looked nervous and agitated. Her father had reserved two adjoining rooms for him and Millicent in the modest St. James Hotel. Colonel Rogers had established himself in the luxurious Champs Elysees Hotel where for the next three days he would orchestrate meetings with all interested parties in the sumptuous hotel parlor.

In the St. James Hotel, where the couple retired at the end of the day, hotel staff commented on the worried looks on the faces of the couple.[8] They were continually together, dining out, visiting dancing places nightly, and taking long walks in the Parisian spring in the afternoon. They lived as if they were having a last fling, yet their faces gave them away.

The two fathers and Count Salm had meetings together all week at the tonier Champs Elysees Hotel. There was money on the table, and the senior Salm tried to prevail upon his son to give up his wife in order to replenish the family's empty coffers. This rich American industrialist was their best hope at financial survival. It was clear to the Colonel that his daughter could not live in the style to which she was accustomed—and he believed entitled to—on the Salm money and her meager allowance from him. There had been those rumors back home that the couple was "forced to dance in Paris cabarets," clearly considered a come-down from balls at the Ritz and royal palaces. The added notion that they danced for money was too horrendous to remark upon.

Rogers also seized upon the question of the marriage's legality in Austria. He had a report from Vienna in mid-February that prewar marriages consummated under the old Catholic regime (as was Salm's first marriage in 1912) would not be granted a divorce without special dispensation of the Pope. It seemed that a civil divorce alone was not sufficient in Austria at that time, according to a ruling of the high court. The court had raised the question of the legality of the marriage of Count Salm and Millicent.[9] Count Salm had engaged an attorney to make a statement that the marriage had been approved by the Viennese authorities. He presented his new marriage documents for official registration in Austria, but the Catholic church, it was reported, refused to recognize the legality of the Count's divorce under the postwar edict of the Viennese government that granted civil dispositions. The news seemed to play into Colonel Rogers' hand. He repeatedly asserted that his insistence on Millicent's return to America was based in some part on uncertainty about the validity of her marriage in Austria.

The situation became what Rogers had hoped for from the unhappy start of this marriage. Though the deliberations were wrapped in a gossamer decorousness of continental teas and good society manners, there can be no mistaking what Colonel Rogers was trying to do in the elegantly decorated parlors of the Champs Elysees. He was bargaining to buy back his daughter by dickering with her husband and the husband's father. Adrian Larkin sat in on the talks. The subject was the price. The finagling had about as much finesse as George Steinbrenner's buying and selling a baseball player, or tribal sheiks allocating a desert bride.

A young woman of Millicent's intelligence surely saw her father's intervention in her marriage at this point for what it was. We do not know her reasoning, and she very likely wanted to think that her father believed he had her best interests in mind. He wanted to protect her, and what could be worse than not having enough money to live as she had so far? As far as we know, she did not rise to fight the negotiations or resist the terms of the settlement; perhaps she felt powerless to do so. She was also hopelessly dependent on the fount of riches her family provided. Her idyll with Salm in Paris and Cannes had proven the point. She didn't know how to do without. We can only guess if the shine was off the relationship. It is possible that as she dutifully cared for Salm in Paris when he fell ill with lumbago she found life with him, a man twice her age, less satisfactory than she'd hoped. Rescue by her father from the financial problems, and a trip back to his luxurious and well-run households, were not totally unwelcome developments.

Her pregnancy was a trump card she could have played either way. It could have given her reason for returning to the comfort of her American life and expert medical care in the United States, or she could have insisted on staying at the side of her husband. Four months pregnant, lacking a permanent residence, and the prospect of following her husband on his itinerant training schedule in the months ahead, she decided the first option made more sense. She accepted—or capitulated to—the terms of the negotiation. She would return to New York with her father, and once there she would have nothing to worry about for herself or her child. She clearly couldn't go on dancing forever. It was apparent that Salm had no prospects for making a living. When she left Paris she gave him two thousand dollars and a car they had acquired during their sojourn. As she would also write shortly to her mother-in-law, she did not consider her husband capable of earning a living.

Millicent was present at the hotel with Salm midweek, but on Thursday and Friday only the elder Salm and Colonel Rogers met in private. The ransom they arrived at for her return to New York with her father was one hundred thousand dollars. Friday evening Count Salm and Millicent dressed in evening clothes and went to the little bar in the Hotel St. James where they each had a cocktail and then went out to dinner. Before leaving, Millicent asked the hotel maid to pack her trunks for an early morning departure. The floor valet asked Count Salm if he would like his baggage packed also, but the Count replied that he was remaining and asked for a wakeup call for *madame* at 6 and himself at noon. They were back at the hotel at midnight.

Some time during the evening Millicent made time to write a letter to Count Salm's mother, the Countess Adolfini Salm von Hoogstraten, whom she addressed as Mamma Fini. She described a conference with her father that had taken place during the past week. "I think I can manage to arrange everything for all of us: mother, daddy, Ludi, the baby and myself," she wrote. She had taken to calling the expected baby, "Le Cochon." She explained that the Colonel wanted her to return to the United States to protect her health and straighten out legal matters. "... it seems there is a great question in America of the legality of our marriage as there is in Austria." In fact, the legality of her marriage in the U.S. had been proven. It was its uncertainty in Austria that her father had seized upon to challenge its validity. She added naively that her father had promised not to try to influence her to stay in America. "I have practically consented," she wrote. "They are thrilled at my going to have a child, and I am sure if I do what they want now, by the time it comes they will have come around to our side." She wrote of the loneliness her departure would mean, but expressed her opinion that Ludi loved her enough to understand that she was going only to try to get everything she could for him, including every advantage for their child—"and that means money."

Her deprivations, if they can be called that, had made her glinty-eyed. The experience of being financially strapped in Europe had stiffened her resolve to do what was necessary to get access to the money she believed was her due. In her correspondence to Count Salm's mother she explained that she could capitulate to her father in Paris, and once safely back home in the United States begin to make headway toward a reconciliation between her father and her husband. But the "vagabond" life she and Salm had been leading would be cited in formal separation documents filed later. Her last night with her husband in the hotel was choked with emotion. They fell asleep crying, holding hands.[10]

Millicent was up at six and packed and ready by seven when her father arrived by limousine. She wore a traveling suit and brimmed hat with a veil when the porter ushered her to the car. There was the rustle of resignation and determination to their departure. She and the Colonel boarded the boat train for Le Havre for the steamship *France*, which would sail at one o'clock.

Word, perhaps through the hotel staff, had already reached the press, but once on board Colonel Rogers shouldered past all inquirers. No one was to be admitted to their stateroom for the customary bon voyage toast, he instructed. Millicent kept her head down, her tear-filled eyes visible even through her swath of heavy veil. She ignored questions.

A few persistent reporters broke through to Rogers. When asked where the Count was, Rogers replied that he was in Paris to the best of his knowledge. "Anyway he was there yesterday morning," Rogers added, characteristically obtuse. He declined further comment and forbade Millicent to answer questions.

Salm stayed back at the St. James into the afternoon of the day that Millicent and her father left. He ordered his valet at noon to pack. Before checking out he sent a telegram to his brother in Monte Carlo urging him to head to Vienna immediately for the Austrian Davis Cup team tryouts. As Ludwig boarded the Orient Express at one o'clock he was ambushed by reporters. He kept up a good front. Colonel Rogers, he explained, had come to Europe to bring his son, Millicent's brother, to Oxford. Serendipitously he and his daughter had decided she should return home to New York with him. "My wife does not feel like traveling or standing the summer heat over here, so she is going to America with her father and will remain there till I have finished the games and fetch her." He continued, "It is untrue that there is any trouble in the family and untrue that her father came over to take her to America."

The reporters seemed to buy his story. The *New York Times* reporter who cabled the story to New York added that the Count "certainly had not the appearance of a deserted husband. He was erect, bright and smiling and displayed none of the resentment which characterized the interviews he gave reluctantly several months ago," at the time of the wedding. Talking to reporters as he directed the loading of his luggage onto the car that would take him to the station, he could not resist putting an extra helping of spin on the story. He admitted that Colonel Rogers had been distant to him at the beginning of their relationship, but he said that his recent relations with him had been most cordial. He added that his father-in-law now seemed "charmed." He may have mistaken charmed for relieved, now that Rogers had him positioned where he wanted him, at the forfeiting end of a buyout. The sensation of impotence against Colonel Rogers and the power of money gnawed at him. He had noticed that while the negotiations with Rogers had been going on, Larkin, behind the scenes, had summoned the parlor maid, luggage, and even Paddy the dog up from

Lugano in a sleeping car. There hadn't really been much question as to how the proceedings would go. With his two trunks, two suitcases, four overcoats, three tennis racquets, and a battered green felt hat clutched firmly in one hand, Count Salm moved on.

He stuck to his story the following evening when the Orient Express from Paris pulled into Vienna and the Associated Press reporters were there to greet him. "The rumor of an estrangement between myself and the Countess is buncombe," he declared.[II] "I won't say anymore. I am sick and tired of interviews. I have been submitting to them for the past six months, and I gave the Paris press one prior to my departure. I am well, but tired. I have come to Vienna to play in the Davis Cup matches," he declared, before hailing a taxi for the Hotel Bristol where his brother and tennis partner awaited him. He was scheduled to play on the Austrian Davis Cup team against Switzerland on May 16, five days away, and he hoped the Olympic tennis matches would follow. Then, he said, he planned to join his wife at the Rogers' home in America.

The cover story didn't work for long. The account of a financial deal between Count Salm and the Rogers would appear in the next day's *New York Times*, with a blow-by-blow account of the prior week in Paris. "Col. Rogers Bent on Salm Separation" was the front page item of *The New York Times* on May 12. The subhead stated "Countess Sailed in Tears" and "Her State of Health Said to Account for Grief at Parting, Even If Only Temporary." It was Millicent's good fortune to be spared the newspaper accounts that raged during her passage. If she felt bought, she did not say so in any public way. She had, after all, been apprised of the financial realities. A week at sea with Larkin and her father must have seemed an eternity. Quite ironically, Gianetta Traini, the singer who had functioned as Grace Coffin's spokesperson during the postelopement news, was also on board.

It was 8:30 and just barely dark enough for the lights of the city to cast their evening spell over Manhattan as the French ocean liner

France docked at the West Seventeenth Street pier. The harbor that had been choked with ice when she sailed in January now carried the soft scent of spring to its arriving passengers. As Rogers' valet and Millicent's maid went to gather the baggage, Millicent dragged behind. The baggage was grouped alphabetically, but in order to dodge the press that was bound to be waiting, Millicent went to the A section rather than the R. The Colonel joined her there, carrying her sealskin coat over his arm. Reporters noted that he carried himself with "evident satisfaction" over triumphantly bringing his daughter back home, but before he could wholly bask in the success of his mission, a customs inspector spied the coat and needed to make certain that it had been declared. Rogers passed the chore to his valet, and went back to the luggage area himself. In his absence newspapermen swarmed around Millicent, who laughingly declined to answer their questions, repeating, "I have nothing to say." As she was hustled into a chauffeur-driven automobile that would take her and her father to the Ritz, the newsmen noted that she looked girlish. She wore a black satin dress and a close-fitting black hat with a white feather sticking out the top. If her pregnancy showed, the press had better manners, in this case, than to mention it. The sea of reporters gathered around her parted, allowing the car that would whisk her back to a life of entitlement and riches to speed away.[12]

The following morning *The New York Times* trumpeted, "Col. Rogers Is Back With His Daughter—Declares Story That Pair Had to Dance in Cabarets to Earn a Living Is Untrue."

CHAPTER EIGHT

Exit the Count

MILLICENT RETREATED TO HER PARENTS' HOME IN Southampton for the summer and stayed out of the news for the rest of her pregnancy while her parents worked the social scene with cruising and fishing parties given aboard the *Fan-Kwai*, Colonel Rogers' electrically powered yacht. They were often mentioned in the society pages. Rogers was photographed in July in a photo that is both flattering and seems emblematic. He is jauntily turned out in a sport jacket and vest, a summer bowler hat and spectator shoes, a grin on his face and a cigar in his hand. It is a photo that shows the man at his smart, jovial best. He can only be described as self-satisfied.[1]

In July, while she was playing golf at the Shinnecock golf club, Millicent lost a diamond ring Salm had given her. It was a solitaire diamond worth $2,500, a Salm family piece from his mother, that the Count had offered to have reset at the time of their engagement.[2] She asked her father to replace it, but he refused.[3]

There was some anxiety about the impact of the pregnancy and birth on her general physical constitution, hearkening back to the doctor's warning when she had fallen ill with rheumatic fever during her girlhood that childbearing would be risky for her. The pregnancy, however, proved uneventful. Colonel Rogers grumped in private about the Count wasting no time in trying to conceive with her so that his heir would tie him to the Rogers' finances, but the Colonel was confident that the deal he had struck in Paris would end all claim to Millicent and her money. Millicent, her letters revealed, had quite another plan.

From New York she wrote again to her mother-in-law. She was "horribly lonely without Ludi," she said, and then she cheerfully proclaimed that the legal complications her father had spoken of were finished, "and now I can go ahead trying to get some money." She wrote that Ludi "was never made to work. . . . He hates it and he's too nervous. The movies are so cheap and horrible here that I hate the idea of his having to go back to them, especially in America, and that's all he could do to make fast money. And we literally haven't a bob between us. Selling things is all right until there is nothing more to sell." She also worried that if Salm came to the United States and found work in the movies, there would be more scandal.[4]

Pending motherhood had stiffened her resolve and she continued to write more calculatingly about money matters. The fallout from her marriage had clearly given her a fresh perspective on the social world she had once so fully inhabited and embraced. Of her elopement with Ludi, she wrote, "He and I got pretty thoroughly in wrong over here by getting married as we did. Every one was against us, and they still are. All daddy's friends would be rotten to us; all the people who cater to money, all the people who don't care for me and those who don't care for him."

She believed that she had won points with her father for her acquiescence to his will so far. "From refusing to give us one cent they have offered us (I'll admit under bad conditions) $12,000 per year, but that was the first offer and others may come." She seemed to pour her heart out to her mother-in-law, one of the few who championed her marriage. "Ludi and Daddy don't love each other at all. If they met it would be fatal," she wrote, asking her mother-in-law to keep her husband in Europe. "He'd be most unhappy here and if I felt he wasn't having a good time and people were nasty I wouldn't be able to bear it. I love him too much and I want to keep him from being miserable the way he was last winter." In conclusion, she added, "I'd rather have the baby here alone with them where I can finish what we have started even though it's not easy and come away having gained my point, gotten money and calmed things down."

Throughout the summer she did seem to work tirelessly to those ends. By late July she updated her mother-in-law: "I've gotten all the baby's things out of the family," which included a six-thousand-dollar-a-year commitment and pay for a nurse. She called herself "a sick bunny" with the flu but added that she had nothing worth complaining of with the pregnancy. "I am in for only four months more." She dismissed any discomfort and closed "with all sweet thoughts" and instructions to "kiss Ludi for me."

What Millicent and Salm did not understand—yet—was that they were in the hands of a master strategist, attorney Larkin, who was under instructions from Colonel Rogers to do all that he could to make Count Salm's return to his bride in the U.S. next to impossible.

Wary that some conspiracy might be brewing, Salm and Millicent had decided on the eve of her departure from Paris to number their letters so they would know if correspondence between them was missing, but a number of delays and omissions occurred just the same. Part of the Rogers' bargain with the Salms had made clear that Salm was not to talk to the press at any length about the state of his marriage. Yet on the American side, Salm began to discern a well thought-out plan to discredit the marriage and to suggest its denouement was under way.

The first evidence was a story in the American newspapers that said he had declared himself a "free husband" and was romancing the beautiful Hungarian actress, Lya de Putti, famous for her vampish roles on screen. He learned about it when he received a telegram from

Millicent, asking, "What is all this talk about Lya de Putti?" It was not until he saw the article in the Paris editions of the papers that he understood what Millicent's telegram was asking. The story had large individual photos of him and Lya, declaring that he wanted to marry her after his divorce. He was furious, but he kept his promise not to speak to reporters. Larkin and Rogers had warned that any comment or denial would only fuel divorce rumors in New York. He contacted Lya, whom he claimed never to have met. They made an appointment to meet in the lobby of the Hotel Adlon, where a reporter who was courting her explained the story had been a hoax.

The rumors continued. Salm smelled a rat when he was contacted by a German lawyer who claimed that Colonel Rogers had offered to pay Lya fifty thousand dollars if she would let herself be filmed "in flagranti" with him. He was never able to determine whether the story was true or not, but now he was alert to a campaign against him. When he sought legal advice about how to squelch the rumors of divorce, a legal clerk opened a drawer of clippings from mostly American papers and tabloids that continued to suggest a divorce was in the works. A misinformation campaign seemed well under way.[5]

Then there was the question of the legitimacy of his 1912 divorce and his marriage to Millicent. It was a Byzantine tangle that required his full-time attention. In mid-July Salm was granted recognition of the marriage under Austrian law and made reservations to travel to New York. Then he heard from Larkin that there were still doubts in the U.S. about the validity of the proceedings, and he should wait in Europe for an emissary from Larkin's practice, a Mr. Kelly, who was headed for Vienna to try and straighten things out. Millicent, impatient with the time it took to receive or send a transatlantic letter, began telegramming. She had been advised by her father's legal counselors to tell Salm to delay his trip because a refusal to recognize their Austrian marriage papers in New York was likely unless they achieved a "canonical" or Papal decree. "Urge Pope," she instructed Salm, who replied, "Pope is Pope, cannot be urged." Her next telegram read,

"Daddy wants to send good lawyer to Vienna, to urge the Pope." In a moment of levity, Salm replied, "Think lawyer is too expensive, better invite Pope to New York, will be delighted about the journey." Salm understood that a canonical divorce would take years. Kelly arrived, and according to Salm, "must have shaken his head in disbelief and had his own thoughts . . . on the marriage huddle in Austria. It's truly scandalous, that in a so-called state of law one authority disperses dispense, [sic] which are declared invalid by another authority of the same state." Millicent, meanwhile, had gotten her own lawyer, a "Catholic specialist," named Conway, who agreed that Salm's divorce and his subsequent marriage were legitimate.[6]

Now seven months pregnant, she was becoming increasingly anxious, a situation that her father fully exploited. She wrote that she had been rushed into Manhattan in the middle of a heat wave for a conference that was full of accusations about Salm. There were assertions that he had misrepresented his divorce, that he was covering up a relationship with Lya de Putti, and that he had conducted himself poorly toward ball boys in a recent tennis competition, a complaint it was assumed would vex Millicent, who was punctilious about courtesy. The assembled advisors expressed doubt that the child would be legitimate if Salm did not stay in Europe and nail down the accreditation that Larkin insisted upon. They also suggested that she would be made financially independent and granted a sizable income if she would consent to a divorce. She hadn't buckled, she wrote to her husband.

He thought she sounded depressed. She said her parents comforted her with gifts and presumed things would get better for her after the birth of her baby. Then came a letter from Conway, Millicent's attorney. He had been contacted by Larkin, whose advice to Salm was to become a Hungarian citizen in order to avoid any legal dispute of his marriage. "With which stupidness had they turned my poor wife's head?" he asked himself when she passed the information on. But he traveled dutifully to Budapest and went through a series of ludicrous steps to satisfy the lawyers, including allowing himself to be adopted by a Hungarian clerk in order to avoid establishing residency over a lengthy time period. He now understood "that the whole 'Hungarian idea' had only arisen from Larkin's brain, who had stayed true to his principles of keeping us separated from each other." He told Millicent as much and hurriedly traveled back to Vienna to get ready for his trip to the U.S. A telegram from Millicent was waiting. "Daddy is offering us a thousand dollars monthly, if you oblige to not come to America without his permission," it read. Salm fully understood that Larkin and Rogers' goal was to keep him from coming to the U.S., and worse, he realized, "My wife had unknowingly descended to the enemy's camp."

He resolved to go to New York again, but first went to say goodbye to his mother at her manor in Reichenau. She showed him letters from Millicent. Each expressed Millicent's deep love for her son and her sorrow over leaving him in Paris. She asserted that Salm should go to Hungary, establish his citizenship, and marry her again there, perhaps in a church. Salm became more certain that his wife had been brainwashed. She promised, though, she would arrive ten days after the baby's birth with her belongings.

The letters threw him into a quandary. Should he follow his instinct and be with Millicent, or protect the financial legacy of his child? He opened a third letter addressed to him anonymously. "Dear Count Salm! Millicent is well, I have seen her in New York, I have seen her in Cannes, where she was different, happier, better, as she was as a girl. She is fickle, as she was always. In two months she'll betray you. Come, before it is too late, look after her. You can't ever expect any money from the father. Millicent is nothing but a social butterfly like all these girls nowadays," signed, *a friend.*

The content of these letters tortured him over the next few days, but he took comfort in knowing that the marriage was valid and their child would be legitimate. He sourly concluded, "I had been disenfranchised and without rights been portrayed as a bothersome foreigner." He followed Millicent's request. He did not travel to New York.

As Salm must have wondered when he tossed in bed at night over the next few months in Europe, what was his wife's motive? Had she been persuaded that he was a deceiver and fortune hunter? Was she still determined to rejoin him? Did she want out of the marriage, and was conveniently hiding behind Larkin? Or was she simply being shrewd and would beat Larkin and her father at their own game? Was she as much a victim of Larkin's machinations as he? He could not know for certain. One of Millicent's talents and great attractions to men, which she would cultivate in her dealings with them for the next twenty years, was to be inscrutable. She would not reveal her motivations.

Count Salm, on the other hand, comes into better focus during these months of manipulations and machinations. At first there is (perhaps suggested by the sing-songish translation of his memoir) an almost Hardy Boys jauntiness to his willingness to jump through all the hoops the Rogers raised in front of him. Then a cynical tone began to take over his account of the saga that he, a middle-aged man with some experience in life, was living through. He vacillated between a hard-nosed understanding of the way he was being jerked around, and a lovestruck hopefulness that Millicent could deliver a happy outcome.

In late September Millicent gave birth to a healthy eight-pound boy, Peter Alfred Constantin Maria Salm. Both Mary and Harry Rogers were at the Lippincott Sanitarium on Lexington Avenue when the birth was announced with the news that both mother and baby were "doing fine." Millicent had chosen the name Peter and the rest was according to the Salm family tradition. *The New York Times*, which rehashed at length the circumstances of her marriage, reported the birth and then added that not only had Millicent's allowance been cut off at the time of her marriage, but that legal arrangements had been undertaken to withhold her $40 million legacy.[7]

Millicent, so Count Salm was told, would need a small operation to completely recover from her delivery, so the chances of her traveling to unite with him soon after the birth were unlikely. The nature of the needed procedure was undisclosed, suggesting a certain delicacy about all gynecological and "female" matters.

During the interim Salm hunted without success for a job in Vienna and Berlin. He became frustrated that his marriage predicament acted as an impediment. Some companies seemed to find the services of a husband of a very wealthy and well-known American attractive, but they were jittery about the reports that the marriage was foundering. When he auditioned for film parts, the producers expressed reservations that as the husband of a millionairess he would actually need the money and could be depended on to work in the future. His travel funds were getting perilously low, so he took a few assignments in the antique business and anxiously waited for word from Millicent, who wrote to say that she thought it would be better if he didn't come because it would aggravate her father, who might cut off the promised funds. She had also written to his mother again to say that the needed surgery was postponed until March. She asked her mother-in-law to keep Salm in Europe to appease her father and not risk losing the financial ground she'd gained with him.

Mary, meanwhile, had made a trip to Europe, but avoided him. When asked by reporters, on her return, if she had seen the Count, Mary smiled and placed her hand over her eyes, glancing to the right and left, suggesting that she had seen him only at a distance.

Salm managed to save five thousand francs, some of it from hocking the cufflinks and beads on his dress shirts, for a trip to New York and he waited patiently in Paris to hear from Millicent. Finally, as Christmas was fast approaching, he decided to travel to the U.S. if only to spend Christmas Eve and New Year's Eve with Millicent and Peter. He wrote enthusiastically of his plans to Millicent, who telegraphed him back not to come for "vital reasons," that he soon came to understand meant that Larkin intended to prevent him from being admitted through U.S. Customs. He was likely to be interned at Ellis Island and sent back on the same boat, she said, requiring her to fight her way through throngs of reporters with their child to see his father from behind bars. The scandal would be huge and undo the goodwill she had created with her father, she argued. Salm rushed out to the Austrian consulate for advice and was told that despite his visa and passport being in order, a complaint at the Austrian consulate made by the rich and powerful could affect his entry. Millicent sent him a check for $250 for Christmas, half of the present her parents had made to her.

In January, Count Salm came down with the flu and his doctors prescribed a stay in the south of France. He prevailed on the director of the Hotel Carleton, who knew him from his tennis training, to offer him a room at a reduced rate. He consoled himself with the idea that he could be in Paris in a day to welcome Millicent if she arrived in Cherbourg or Le Havre. Within days he was up and out on the courts, readying for the upcoming Davis Cup trials. As he moved around town he sensed that he was often followed by detectives. His old friend, a concierge at the hotel, confirmed his suspicion.

In a spasm of optimism while staying in Cannes he passed a dress shop with an arresting gauzy white dress in the window. Convinced that it would suit Millicent and that she would most likely have sold her good dresses in order to return to him, he bought it impetuously. "How nice it must be to have wealth, to be able to give her everything that the heart desired," he longingly soliloquized as he made the purchase. The storekeeper swathed it in tissue paper and wrapped it for him in a beautiful box.[8]

Millicent, too, had contracted the flu in New York, and her parents had taken her to Mary's house in Palm Beach, Florida, for her recovery. Her needed surgery would be scheduled there, she informed Salm. She wrote to him that the doctors had advised against his coming to see her because she needed complete rest.

Salm believed that the ultimate undoing of his marriage occurred in Palm Beach. "The influence which Palm Beach and the social life, which is common there, had exerted on Millicent, seems to have been poisonous," he wrote. He blamed her weakened physical condition, the advice of lawyers, and the counsel of jaded girlfriends who urged her to opt for money and the posh life she was accustomed to. "Her enfeeble (sic) health and the worry about her child made her forget the love for her husband, who had little to give apart from his love and his name," he concluded. Toward the end of April Millicent wrote asking him for money in order to bring Peter, whom she called her little "bunny," to come and see him. He wired her fifty dollars.

Three days later, she wrote him a Dear John letter that was delivered as he stepped up to play in a round of the Davis Cup. Full of accusations and rationalizations about the future of their child, the letter suggested to Salm that it wasn't written by Millicent. But, he had to conclude reluctantly, it was in her handwriting. "Had she had a momentary mood, a little nervous breakdown, who knows what had been brought forward against me?" he asked. When he returned home a second letter awaited him. It was signed "And that's that, Millicent," which caused him to break down, and to accept that their marriage was ending.[9] Their battles would now be waged through lawyers.

That fall there were signs that Millicent had spread her wings to re-embrace life in New York. An incident that made the pages of *The New Yorker* suggests she was awkwardly scrambling for an identity:

"One thing about a Parisian accent; it is insidious, even in its effect on its possessor," began the October 3, 1925, item, "Accent." It told the story of how a lady entered the well-known dress salon, Hickson's, speaking only French. All salespersons who spoke French were unfortunately out to lunch, but the lady continued in French, and "lapsed into English long enough to remark that she would conduct her business only in that civilized tongue." A messenger was sent to a neighboring restaurant to retrieve a French-speaking salesperson. The lady shopper proceeded to purchase six gowns. "And having concluded her business in a civilized language, The Countess Salm, née Miss Millicent Rogers, left the shop."

As she began to reappear in society, Millicent made her usual splash. The following winter a photo of her, dark hair bobbed, wearing dangling earrings and a knee-length lamé dress that captured the spirit of the early twenties, appeared in the Palm Beach papers. "A good time was had by all and society don't mean maybe when Tony Biddle threw a party at the Club Montmartre at Palm Beach, Florida, the other night. Many celebrities were present, but dominating them with all her beauty and spirits was the Standard Oil heiress Countess Millicent Rogers Salm, whose squabbles with her broke but titled husband have gained notoriety both here and abroad," read one caption.[10] It was hardly surprising that Salm blamed the Palm Beach milieu for corrupting his wife's affections.

If Millicent and Count Salm had believed that the birth of their baby would soften the Rogers' family's resolve against the marriage, they were mistaken. His battles with the Rogers had only begun. He was a supplicant now, and the powerlessness of his position became explicit during the next year as he attempted to visit Peter. Millicent increasingly seemed to be lulled into acquiescence. Her attempts to make peace—which seemed to mean getting her father to support her and Count Salm in their marriage—had failed. Unable and unwilling to make a dramatic stand, which would have meant forfeiting financial support to assert her independence, she let things slide.

It is not clear just when Millicent abandoned her plan to barter with her family for a return to the marriage. But it was obvious that she had. The Washington Post seemed to know that she had booked herself passage on the ocean liner Berengaria in order to travel secretly to Europe with her brother so she could sue the Count for divorce in Paris even as he and his mother traveled to the U.S. to enlist the help of the American courts to gain access to his son. "It has long been rumored among Millicent's friends that she is determined to rid herself permanently of her titled husband," the article of January 11, 1926, asserted, and the reporter claimed that Count Salm was intent on a half million dollars to grant Millicent her freedom. But when word of her preparations to leave began to leak in Palm Beach, she cancelled the reservation. When the ship sailed she was on Breakers' Beach, in Florida, with Tony Biddle III of Philadelphia, who had frequently been her escort that winter.

She was once more wrapped in comfort and security, and life in Palm Beach, a social mecca in winter at the time, offered plenty of diversions. Colonel Rogers had successfully flexed his muscle with money. His peers apparently sympathized with his situation, or at least that was the attitude of those who attended a Virginia Railway board of director's meeting. "Poor Henry," they said, now that he had to deal with a Count in the family. That process, they surmised, must be costly.

Count Salm, all things considered, was amazingly generous to Millicent in his memoir of these difficult years. He believed that she abandoned their marriage and was held hostage to her father's demands in order to provide for their child. Confident that she had known the greatest happiness with him, he commended her "sacrifice." As the very act of her elopement illustrated, she could have a mind of her own. It was true that she had no money without her father's, but it is equally true that her decision, for whatever reasons, to abandon the marriage would make her rich. Money was the club that her parents wielded over her, and she had submitted.

Count Salm was forced to begin a separation suit against Millicent in order to win a visitation agreement to see their son. He and his mother had arrived in New York on December 1, 1925, and established themselves in the Ritz-Carlton, but the Rogers, upon hearing that they were en route to the U.S., left for Palm Beach the day before the Salms' scheduled arrival. By the end of the month, almost fourteen months after Peter's birth, Count Salm had evidently relinquished all hopes of a reconciliation with Millicent. He retained a lawyer to file a separation suit against her, charging abandonment and demanding custody of Peter. In a statement issued through his attorney he said that he was "finally convinced that the affection which his wife had for him has been alienated and that she now joins with her advisers in rendering his efforts to see his child uncomfortable and difficult." Some speculated that he had grounds to sue and collect from Colonel Rogers for alienation of affection of his wife, but he decided to focus on gaining access to Peter, and some control over his upbringing.

Millicent set up winter residence in Palm Beach next door to her mother's house, named "Waikiki." Salm's suit against her asked that she respond to it in Manhattan, bringing their son within the jurisdiction of the Manhattan courts. It had taken three attempts by the Palm Beach sheriff's department before Sheriff Baker managed to serve her the papers. Onlookers assumed it was exactly the sequence of events that Colonel Rogers had hoped for. The Count would have to take formal steps for ending the marriage before he could see his son.

Millicent had followed her legal counsel and consented, at least on paper, to let Ludi see Peter between two and five o'clock, four days a week. But she dodged his request that Peter be baptized a Catholic by stating that he had already been baptized the prior December in Palm Beach. There would be no formal christening as Salm and Countess Fini had hoped.

Salm assumed the Rogers were trying to both frustrate him and deplete the resources he would have available to pay for lawyers. The trip to Palm Beach and the standard of living there threatened to strain his means, forcing him to rely on the generosity of his friend, William P. Ahnelt, owner and publisher of *The Pictorial Review*, who was both a friend and tennis enthusiast. Ahnelt and his wife had entertained Salm and Millicent in their comfortable fifty-two-acre country estate, Ahnelt Hall in Deal, New Jersey, shortly after their elopement. Besides his suite at the Poinciana Hotel, Ahnelt offered Salm that most valuable of gifts for someone in his circumstances, a private telephone line for conferences with his attorney in New York.

Colonel Rogers was determined to orchestrate all the details of the Count's visit with his new son. It would be formal and carefully monitored. Millicent was staying in "La Chosa," the luxurious Pillsbury house on Banyan Road, adjacent to "Waikiki," with the baby and his nursemaid. Several private detectives were on duty to safeguard the baby, as the Rogers were concerned he would be kidnapped.[11] Millicent, her father decreed, was not to see her husband. She stayed out of sight.

After their lengthy trip from Europe to New York, Count Salm and his sixty-five-year-old mother, dubbed the "Dowager Countess" by the press, traveled to Florida and arrived on the Seaboard Air Line at West Palm Beach station early in the morning. The Count remarked that the surrounding countryside was "flat like a plate." He was not dressed when the train pulled into the station. The reporters, expectant, were already there, yawning and drinking coffee. Fifteen minutes later Count Salm emerged from his sleeping car dashingly turned out in a tweed suit and jauntily carrying a cap in one hand and tennis rackets in the other.[12]

Two private detectives from the Palm Beach Detective Agency, compliments of Colonel Rogers, met him and the Countess Fini on the platform and whisked them into a taxicab that would take them to their hotel. Entering the Poinciana Hotel, Salm sparred briefly with reporters, then, rather than waiting for the elevator, abruptly bounded up the stairs to his fourth-floor room.

It was after noon when he came downstairs, dressed in a gray business suit. His mother had preceded him and gone for a walk.

At the sight of the reporters who awaited him, he tried to escape on the hotel's piazza, but he was soon surrounded. Irritable at first, he became more cordial. He explained that it had been arranged that he would see his son at the Poinciana at three o'clock. The baby would remain with him for two hours and then he planned to play tennis with his friend William Ahnelt.

The afternoon unfolded with great drama. At one minute to three a big red Rolls-Royce pulled up to the portico of the Poinciana. A private detective sat up front next to the chauffeur and two detectives flanked the nursemaid and baby in the backseat. The detectives scrambled out so that one stood on either side of the nursemaid as she climbed out of the car, clasping the baby close to her chest to shield him from photographers. The entourage marched into the hotel lobby and asked for the Count's room number. While the reception clerk shuffled through the registration, the nurse sat Peter on the counter. He laughed and clapped his hands, oblivious to the circus that surrounded him. He had blond curls and dark eyes and had been dressed in a pink jumper with white socks and sandals. Millicent often dressed Peter in pink, a practice that Peter would cheerfully chide her for as a young man when he heard it from friends.[13]

One of the detectives spoke to Salm on the house phone to say that they were coming up to the room. Detective Griffin alone accompanied the nursemaid and baby upstairs where the Count and dowager Countess awaited them at the doorway. The Countess handed Peter a white rattle with an unusually large feathery rooster on its top which delighted him. Then the happy moment took a downturn.

Count Salm, clothes-conscious as always, disdainfully took in the escort, identified as Detective Griffin, who was wearing tight tennis trousers, a very tight blue coat, and straw hat. He had plunked himself down on the Countess's bed. Salm tried to dismiss the detective, saying that he would call for him in the lobby when it was time for Peter and the nursemaid to leave, but Detective Griffin held his ground. He told Count Salm that he had instructions that the baby was not to remain in the hotel all afternoon, and that they would all take a walk on the beach. The Count took exception. He said that as a father he had some say in the matter, and that the baby would stay with him in the hotel if he said so. The exchange became heated. Excited, Salm lapsed into a pronounced German accent and spoke in German asides to his mother. In a deep voice, he read aloud the court order stating that he was entitled to a two-hour visit with his son. The conflict in the air caused the baby to drop his rattle and begin to cry. The Countess, her nerves unstrung by the long and tiresome journey, sought to pacify Peter with a teddy bear that had a squeaker in it. When he cried only louder, the Countess burst into tears.

"Shall we meet you outside?" the detective asked curtly. Count Salm stiffened. "No, I want to see my son in my room."

"That's impossible," snapped the detective. "I'm under orders and I'm going to obey them." They continued to wrangle. The baby cried louder, the Countess sobbed harder. Finally the Count exclaimed angrily, "Well, I don't want to see my son at all today, then, if I can't see him alone." The nursemaid grabbed young Peter and started for the door, which the detective had already opened. In the hallway the Count stormed, "I want to have my son with me alone. I didn't come down here to see the mother. I don't give a damn about her." They followed along to the elevator and he kissed the baby good-bye as tears streamed down both their cheeks. "Da, Da," he muttered to Peter before the elevator arrived. "Don't you want to give him a dolly or two?" he asked his mother. "Not now," she said.[14]

After the elevator doors closed behind the detective and nursemaid, the Count and his mother returned to their rooms. While the Countess had a cry, her son sat down to comfort her. Then he phoned his lawyer, who arrived in minutes, and the two men left together for several hours. When Count Salm returned the reporters were at his heels. He announced through the closed door that he would "see no one, and that is final."

His outrage was greater the next morning, when some of the conversation between him and his mother appeared in the local paper, convincing him and his lawyer that the hotel room had been bugged. He was more infuriated when the newspapers decided to interpret his decision to play tennis with his host, who pressed him for a game before dark, as neglect of his son. The length of his visit with Peter was compared unfavorably to the time he spent on the court.

The following afternoon, probably as a result of his lawyer's intervention, went better and Count Salm, his mother, baby Peter and the nursemaid spent several hours at the beach without a detective on duty, but the awkwardness of the carefully programmed visit was apparent. While Peter played in the sand in a red swimsuit, Count Salm, the nursemaid, and his mother visited nearby. Titled Europeans, for whom nannies and nursemaids were commonplace, were hardly people accustomed to sitting in the sand for long periods with toddlers. The artificiality of the situation seemed to wear on all concerned.

Count Salm, nursing a considerable grudge, left to take his mother sightseeing in Washington, D.C. Then it was back to Europe, where in late May he was reported hissing unsportsmanlike remarks to his tennis opponent in Berlin. As his detractors had pointed out to Millicent, he always did have a temper on the court. The Colonel had won. His relentless campaign against Salm had ground down the man. The burden of his battle with Rogers wrought changes in Salm's once sunny temperament on and off the tennis court. The differences were as much about the triumph of one man's will over another as they were about money.

There is little doubt that Count Salm was a fortune hunter—and that he loved Millicent. The two truths need not be mutually exclusive. His struggle against Colonel Rogers and his growing comprehension of the overwhelming, implacable power of his opponent, only give poignancy to his story. The Count was a continental gentleman with the belief that he would prevail through patience and courtliness, and he was unprepared for the low tactics of a mean, money-centered man who, beneath the trappings of his social achievement, military distinction, moneyed fame, and fortune was a rough-edged bully intent on getting his way at all costs, no matter how crude. Though Salm may not have begun as such, he becomes a sympathetic figure, a victim of Rogers' and Larkin's manipulations.

By the following December, Millicent and the Count's relationship was strictly formal and adversarial. They would for the next five months play their parts dispassionately. While he sought a judicial separation, a full divorce not existing under Austrian law, citing her desertion in a New York court, she filed a separate action in Paris for an absolute divorce on grounds of nonsupport. The Rogers continued to erect obstacles for Salm. Larkin successfully countered his suit for a separation from Millicent which would allow him to establish terms of visitation with Peter. The Count was required to emigrate to the United States in order to become a permanent resident so he could press his suit there. It was six months before he could acquire the appropriate emigration passport. When he arrived at U.S. Customs he was detained. All of his luggage, including every shoe and cigarette case, was opened. It became clear that the authorities were looking for something in particular.

He began to panic when letters to him from Millicent that he was carrying in order to present them as evidence in court were confiscated. The letters, opened and perused, were returned, but an officer asked where he was hiding his diamonds. When the Count said he didn't have any diamonds, he was ordered to undress for a strip search. His lawyer, Goodstein, arrived just in time to put an end to the nonsense. He was told that Customs had been tipped that he would be trying to smuggle in his mother's diamonds to pay his court costs. The offense would have required that he be deported as a criminal. With a pat on the back from an apologetic Customs inspector, he was allowed into New York, where the letters he carried, carefully arranged and numbered, would prove worth more to his cause than any gemstones.[15]

When Salm introduced Millicent's love letters as evidence to the court in his New York suit, they were quickly leaked to the newspapers. On December 9, *The Washington Post* ran the letters Millicent had written to Countess Adolfini on the eve of her departure from Paris with her father when he negotiated her return in 1924. The Colonel's lawyers seemed determined to humiliate the Count in the New York hearings by highlighting the ways that Millicent's money had paid for their honeymoon and supported him during the previous year. He was quizzed about the series of newspaper articles entitled "How I Wooed and Won Millicent Rogers" that he sold to a tabloid newspaper for $2,500. He claimed that he did not write the articles, but authorized the use of his signature as author, with Millicent's approval. He had simply needed the money, he explained. The proceedings were ugly. Several times the Count lost his composure and shouted at Rogers' attorney. Much was made of the fact that he did not pay for Millicent's wedding ring and had trouble remembering the exact date of their marriage.[16] By March both sides had had enough, and the action shifted to Paris, where Millicent had filed her divorce suit.

The Count adjourned his suit there when it was announced that a financial settlement of between $350,000 and $500,000 had been reached. The settlement came as additional love letters from Millicent to the Count were being read in court as evidence for Count Salm's plea.[17] The Paris court made the complaints of both sides public when it announced its verdict. The letters seemed to disprove that Millicent had been unhappy and forced to live a "vagabond" life with the Count as well as her suit's assertion that the Count neglected her and obliged her to appeal to her family for support. Both sides did their fair share of mudslinging. She alleged, but did not offer proof, that he had been intimate with other women. She claimed to be deeply wounded by one letter to her: "I wish to tell you that it is useless for you henceforth to correspond with me. The attitude you and your family adopt toward me is such that I ask myself how I lived so long with you. All is finished now and I desire never to see you again." The Count complained that she tried to make him "an utter nonentity . . ."[18]

Millicent's lawyer had vigorously opposed the reading and publication of the letters. The financial agreement, seemingly struck overnight, brought an immediate end to the proceedings. In mid-April, both Count Salm and Millicent appeared in Paris for the final divorce decree. Millicent received custody of Peter, whom she had left in the United States with her mother. It was agreed that the Count would have liberal access to him and a voice in arranging his education, specifying two years of education in Europe. Behind the scenes, Colonel Rogers had made the settlement contingent upon the Count's agreement that he could not see his son alone or unsupervised.

Yet no bitterness was apparent between Millicent and Count Salm when they met in court. The Associated Press reported, "In fact, she smiled sweetly at him when the decree was announced." Rather chivalrously, Count Salm spoke to friends and the press the day after the decree. "I believe she still loves me. I am sure she is the only woman I ever did or can love. Money never entered my mind as far as she was concerned," he stated.[19] Then he turned on his heels to return to the Hotel Carleton in Cannes, where he was living. If his remarks were intended to weaken Millicent's resolve to be finished with the marriage, they had no impact. It was over. Millicent's gaze had fallen elsewhere. She would soon marry again.

CHAPTER NINE

Enter the Argentine

UNLIKE MANY YOUNG WOMEN WHO HAD MADE HASTY ILL-advised marriages and trailed home later with a baby, Millicent, unchastened, rebounded in society without missing a beat. She was the hit of Ziegfeld's Palm Beach Night show in 1926 as she exited the club in a shimmering knee-length dress at three in the morning. It was the first photo taken of "the Countess" since she had returned from Europe, and it was picked up in society pages up and down the East Coast. Her appearance presaged what *Time* magazine would say of her twenty-five years later when a "Milestones" item remarked "Millicent made an unhappy career of marrying in haste, repenting in opulent leisure." As news of her separation suit became public, she was once again considered an heiress to watch and would-be suitors were alerted to her likely marriageability. The papers buzzed about who Countess Salm would captivate next even as her divorce dragged into 1927. Though she had actually lived only five months with Count Salm, the marriage took three years to legally unravel.

✳　✳　✳

Millicent plunged into her second marriage barely six months after the finish of the first. A twenty-five-year-old woman in 1927, she must have felt some urgency to get on with life beyond her parents' world, and marriage was still the best way for a young woman to accomplish that—even though her first attempt had been foiled by her father. Two months after the divorce from Salm, her name began to appear in newspapers and magazines as Mrs. Millicent Rogers, and often "formerly Countess Millicent Salm" was tagged on. A transformation had occurred since she was the fluttery ingénue and young bride on the deck of the *Veendam*, talking about an unspecified duration for her honeymoon and finding a new breed of monkey in Africa.

In the fall of 1925, a year after Peter's birth, Millicent was required to go to court in New York to defend herself in a nagging suit from Emil Kammerer, a Viennese attorney whom Count Salm had engaged to get the Austrian approval for her marriage. At this time, even before her divorce was final and her independence was official, she had a new air of gravitas. The young woman who appeared in court was a composed socialite. She was the only woman in the courtroom crowded with twenty-five men. She casually perched her elbows on the arms of the chair, and one court reporter remarked, "Her self-assurance was complete." She telegraphed her boredom with this whole business of now settling with a lawyer for a marriage that was about to be undone anyway. Yes, she answered, she had given Kammerer a power of attorney, but she had not understood what it was for. Yes, she had paid money to him that he claimed was a retainer. "Yes," she added, "and I have paid other bills for my husband, too."[1] The issue of this legal bill would not go away, though in the end she paid only a third of it. The remainder, her lawyers successfully maintained, was the responsibility of her soon-to-be ex-husband.

Backed by her family's money, her social status, and her father's newfound approval, Millicent began to emerge as a more mature and confident personality both publicly and privately. The following spring she purchased a 180-acre farm four miles north of Bennington, Vermont, in South Shaftsbury.[2] It was a property that was also attractive to her mother, who had begun to chafe in her own life and marriage and would later go to live there. The acquisition of property and the advantages of wealth had taken on a new luster for Millicent after her "vagabond" life throughout Europe during her brief marriage. To her ever-watchful public, it seemed that she had bought into (or been bought by) the life she had returned to. With energy and vitality, she assumed her new role as Mrs. Millicent Rogers, glamorous new divorcée.

Arturo Peralta-Ramos had made an appearance in Millicent's life six years earlier in Paris. The tall and handsome South American playboy captured her interest during her trip to Europe in 1921 when she was traveling with her parents. Peralta-Ramos's family dated back to the early Spanish settlers. Their distinguished ancestor, Colonel Patricio Ramos, had come to the new world with José de San Martín, the national hero of Argentina, to overthrow Spanish rule, and his descendants, through trading and various mercantile ventures, became major landowners over the next century. Ramos had married a widowed woman named Peralta, and their descendants became the prosperous Peralta-Ramos clan that by the twentieth century owned the newspaper La Razón of Buenos Aires.[3] By South American standards they were aristocrats, but their wealth did not approach the great fortunes that the American tycoons, like the Rogers family, had amassed in a generation. Their prosperity was sufficient so that despite the fact that Peralta-Ramos lacked the cachet of a European title, he was not dubbed a fortune hunter. Whatever Arturo Peralta-Ramos lacked in money and title, he made up for with fiery swagger.[4] In his early twenties he had been a playboy in Buenos Aires until he went for a joyride in his father's new Bugatti sports car and crashed it into a tree during his father's absence. He and his brothers had been strictly forbidden to drive the treasured car. Terrified of the wrath that was likely to follow from his father and with the financial assistance of his mother, he took off for Europe. A cadre of five Argentine cohorts— glamour boys, according to the family—went with him. In Paris he and his friends introduced and demonstrated the newest South American rage and export—the tango. They formed dance teams and entered competitions. Their suave manners, dapper clothes, and a Latin wild streak captivated the young society women they met in clubs and restaurants in Paris, Millicent among them. No stranger to the dance floor herself, Millicent easily mastered the steps, and she and Peralta-Ramos were noticed when they paired up on the dance floor.

"They were a bunch of Spanish greaseballs," chuckles Arturo Peralta-Ramos II, reconstructing his father's entry to his mother's life. He made enough of an impression on the twenty-one-year-old Millicent at the time of their meeting that she had abruptly left Cortachy Castle that season and was shortly afterward spotted with him in Switzerland, to the expressed disappointment of Serge Obolensky. Peralta-Ramos reentered her life the year before her divorce, when she returned to Paris.

Millicent's mother provided the bridge between the Rogers' New York life and Europe. A Francophile herself, she kept extending the length of her visits to France and by 1925 had set up a house in Paris. Married life had become increasingly difficult for Mary and the Colonel, whose irascibility was not limited to bullying their daughter. After twenty-five years it was mostly an alliance of family and money matters. When in Southampton, Mary stayed in the Italianate "Beach House." Harry more often occupied the adjacent property, 1,200 acres and "The Port of Missing Men" on the bluff overlooking the 530-acre Scallop Pond. He conceived of it as a grand estate, a backdrop for his role as a gentleman sportsman of the Gilded Age, and spared no expense. Eleanor Brown, the designer he commissioned from McMillen, Inc., remarked at the time that, "Colonel Rogers wouldn't come into New York to look at furniture.... Everything had to be trucked out to him—a considerable distance in those days. "But the effort was worth it," as "... most of it stayed." The colonial cottage of the old sea captain, Jackomiah Scott—located on the property—was remade as a hunting lodge with beamed ceilings and roaring fireplaces. An underground tunnel with a hidden door led from the bedroom wing to a multipurpose room on the waterfront that, viewed from the pond, resembled a sculpted ship's stern. John Russell Pope, the creator of the National Gallery of Art and the Jefferson Memorial in Washington, D.C., was commissioned to make it suitable to entertain the Colonel's wealthy American and European friends who came to hunt with the Colonel in his "beat drives" for pheasants and wild turkeys on the property, a pastime he had developed a taste for while staying in the English countryside.[5] The final H-shaped colonial revival building included a spectacular natatorium, connected to another tunnel bordering the bedroom.

Mary and Harry occupied their separate households, which minimized their quarrels, but they appeared amicably together for family and social events. Meanwhile, Mary shifted her attention increasingly toward Europe. The society matron who had clucked over her debutante daughter's balls and marriage prospects seemed to have relaxed into her own life. In Paris she cultivated friends and studied painting. She also kept a country home in Senlis, where she often hosted avantgarde figures from Paris. A photo of her wearing a French beret and puffing on a cigarette in Senlis in 1925 seems the archetypical record of her European lifestyle and liberty. She and Millicent began to spend more and more time together after her daughter's marriage and estrangement from Salm, and they both developed a taste for the somewhat dissolute high life of France. Her home became a salon for the fashion designer Madam Elsa Schiaparelli and the aspiring designer Van Day Truex.

The tensions caused by the elopement behind her, Millicent gravitated to her mother and the expansiveness of her French life in Paris and Senlis.[6] As their descendants point out, Mary was an organizer, Millicent was a liver. It was Mary who could be counted on to arrange for the nanny and nurses for Peter, the dinner parties, the housekeeping staff. The hum of her households and organized social life offered stability and structure for Millicent. One assumes they shared some disenchantment with their respective marriages, so the vivid and creative personalities that befriended them in late-twenties Paris decorated an alternative life that they could live on their own terms, free of New York's pestering media and the temper of the domineering Colonel Rogers.

It was Mary and the Colonel who traveled from New York to Paris with the two-and-a-half-year-old Peter to unite him with Millicent after her divorce. Millicent burst into tears when they walked down the gangplank off the *Olympic* in Cherbourg, France. It was a moment of such uncustomary emotion and confusion that when Millicent boarded the train for Cherbourg Station to see where Peter and his nurse would be seated she left her son still standing on the platform with her father as the train pulled out of the station. Colonel Rogers mustered his old commanding presence to remedy the situation. He had railway officials wire ahead to stop the train at the next station, where he raced by automobile with his grandson to catch it.

Peter stayed in Paris with Mary while Millicent returned to New York in July of 1927 with her father, who wished to spend the rest of the summer in Southampton. Word of her courtship in Paris with Arturo Peralta-Ramos had begun to leak to the papers. A "rumored engagement" was reported.[7] One French newspaper reported that Millicent was married again. Reporters ambushed Colonel Rogers when he got off the *Olympic* in New York Harbor.

"Is it likely your daughter will marry again?" one asked. "I sincerely hope so," was his rejoinder. "I can say that when she does contemplate marrying again the engagement will be fully announced. That is so, isn't it, Millicent?" he said, directing the throng of reporters to her. Millicent merely nodded and smiled at his side.[8] She had clearly come home with a plan. Two weeks later she sailed again for Paris.

She moved fast in New York to prepare a place for herself that would be ready when she returned to New York to set up residence in October. She would no longer be living with her parents on East Sixty-fourth Street. Ten days later she leased a ten-room apartment at 1035 Fifth Avenue, between Eighty-fourth and Eighty-fifth Streets, facing Central Park, for $9,500 a year.[9] The following week she sailed on the White Star liner *Majestic*. She arrived at the pier fashionably dressed in a sheer pearl-gray costume with a large picture hat. She typically traveled with thirty-five pieces of luggage and two maids in attendance. One carried Millicent's jewelry case and the other handled her dog, described in the papers as "a valuable Pekingese."[10] When the boat arrived in Cherbourg the following week, Arturo Peralta-Ramos was there to meet her. He had been waiting two days for her at the Hotel Casino.[11]

Millicent had told friends that she believed the chances for happiness for an American girl were greater if she married a man of her own nationality, but she was not able to follow her own advice.[12] There was beginning to be a pattern to the men in her life. They were smooth operators, handsome, cosmopolitan sorts, men's men who rode horses and hunted and enjoyed the pastimes of the gentry. They also dressed expensively and stood out on the dance floor. Their inability to earn a real living or make a success by American standards was another common denominator. The foreign quality invariably attracted her. Peralta-Ramos had never been to the United States. But like Count Salm, he was debonair, with good looks and continental polish. It would be remarked, as the list grew longer, that she collected them as she did jewelry and dogs. They were arrestingly handsome, and perhaps their good looks and sex appeal obscured some of their long-term shortcomings.

Peralta-Ramos, twenty-five, was six foot four with dark hair and an olive complexion. He typically sported a soft gray fedora hat. He enjoyed good food and fine living, and in their pursuit he and Millicent, free now of the supervision of her family, set out on a highly romantic fling in France. The young Argentine liked to drive around the countryside to sample the wine and food in fine restaurants. He boasted that he could tell the provenance of a wine by sniffing the cork. The newly divorced Millicent was full of life and avidly appreciative of his broad sensuous style. Arturo knew how to treat a woman, and Millicent was charmed with his savoir faire. They were a late-twenties "Two for the Road" setting out on two- and three-day drives together (no chauffeur!) visiting forests and the château country. Sometimes they would have several courses of a meal at one restaurant or château and travel on to another where they had called ahead to hear what the dessert was.[13] Millicent still lived with the nagging awareness that her weak heart could shorten her life, and this young Argentinian's hedonistic ability to live richly and savor the moment was a great attraction. It was a relief after having lived each day for the last several years under pressures and reproaches from her parents, while the happiness she had sought with Salm dissipated, and the hapless Count was neutralized by her father.

Rumors of their pending engagement swirled around Paris until Arturo told friends in Paris that they planned to be married in October and put an end to the speculation. The following day he left Paris for London where he intended to have his wedding clothes made.[14] The Rogers' formally announced the engagement from Southampton the following week. No date was set, but it was expected to be in late October. The New York Times article retold the story of her first marriage and characterized Peralta-Ramos as a "wealthy Argentinian." The story also mentioned that Mary Rogers had recently purchased a magnificent palazzo on the Grand Canal in Venice.

When Millicent and her new fiancé sailed into New York Harbor aboard the Olympic, it was Peralta-Ramos's first glimpse of the city.[15] Peter, now almost three, was with them, tended by his nurse and Millicent's maid. This time her answers to the reporters' queries about her intentions to marry were clear and easy. "Oh absolutely, yes," she beamed. "We are engaged to be married," said Peralta-Ramos, adding, "I do not know when this marriage will take place, or where. This is my first visit to the United States, and I do not know even where I shall stop until I have met my friends at the pier." They made a striking couple, he in a dark blue suit with brown shoes and his soft gray fedora. Millicent had on a black taffeta dress, a fawn-colored coat, and a matching hat. The Colonel, who had been detained in Southampton, did not come to meet them but he had reserved rooms at the Plaza Hotel (then known as the Savoy-Plaza). Mary, who stayed behind in Paris, was expected to return in September to help plan the wedding. However, this wedding did not go as planned, either.

Friends and the public had been casually told that the wedding would take place in October, but by early November, there was still no announcement. On November 5, Millicent and Arturo registered at the St. Regis Hotel in New York, where they told reporters from their third-floor suite that they would be marrying soon, but no date was given. The newspapers perked up when it was reported that she had ordered several thousand dollars worth of clothes from the designer Jeanne Lanvin for her trousseau. The following day they left in the Rogers' limousine for Southampton. The public was tipped off to an upcoming date when reservations were made in the name of Mr. and Mrs. A. P. Ramos on the Grace liner *Santa Elisa* for Valparaiso, for November 11, but the grave illness of Millicent's maternal grandfather, George Hillard Benjamin, pressured them to have the wedding as soon as possible. The Rogers had intended to host a wedding with their social register friends and family, but these uncertainties held their plans in flux and forced them to keep the wedding mostly a family affair.[16]

Behind the scenes there was much anxiety for yet another reason. Peralta-Ramos was Catholic, so the couple planned a ceremony in the Roman Catholic Church of the Sacred Hearts of Jesus and Mary in Southampton. Millicent was not Catholic and would not convert, but she agreed that any children they might have would be brought up in the faith. The source of the anxiety was that the couple was waiting for a dispensation from the Pope allowing Millicent to be married by the Catholic Church after her divorce from Count Salm. Millicent was claiming that her first marriage to Salm was invalid because Salm's first wife, to whom he had been married in the Church and divorced, was still living. Millicent's marriage to Count Salm in a civil ceremony was not recognized, and so subsequently could be overlooked. It was wincingly ironic that the marriage she had worked so hard to prove legitimate, asking Count Salm to "urge Pope," she now needed to disprove and disavow.

Day after day the dispensation did not arrive and the wedding was repeatedly postponed, even as her grandfather hung onto life by a thread. The couple stayed poised for a quick marriage.

As soon as the decree came through on November 8, they asked to have the ceremony performed in the church's rectory at five o'clock. Her cousin Robert Coe was best man and her friend Katherine Mackay was the matron of honor. Her brother Henry and her parents were also in attendance. Just as the quiet ceremony was finished, news and cameramen rushed up, but Millicent and her groom dashed laughing from the parish house. The bride, vivid and vivacious, carried a huge bouquet of chrysanthemums as she and Arturo climbed into the Rogers' car that would take them back to the Beach House. The front of the house was banked with flowers when they arrived.

Colonel Rogers received as much attention as the groom. Typically stern and uncommunicative with reporters, he beamed through their questions. The papers got wind of the fact that he had set up a trust fund of half a million dollars for the newlyweds and extracted from Peralta-Ramos his signature on papers waiving all future claims on the Rogers wealth. In addition, he had written them a check for $500,000, as a wedding gift. The couple was expected to make their home in New York after their trip to South America, and Rogers had introduced Peralta-Ramos to J. P. Benkard & Co., a brokerage house that dealt with Standard Oil securities, where he would become associated when he returned from his honeymoon. He obviously thought that Millicent had gotten it right this time, with a suitably aggressive, wordly man's man. It was a major life change for Arturo, too. He was no stranger to luxury and wealth, but marrying Millicent had opened the doors to an ease and way of life that must have exceeded his boldest expectations. He had hit the jackpot.

Mary and the Colonel left the Beach House shortly after the ceremony to travel back into New York City to be at Mary's father's bedside on Park Avenue. Millicent and Arturo then sent word to the newspapers that they had nothing to say to them. Colonel Rogers went so far as to turn off the phones for the rest of the evening.

There was an odd story distributed by the Associated Press the next day, reporting that a sudden attack of illness would prevent Millicent from sailing to South America, and noting rumors that she had suffered "a nervous breakdown." Millicent may well have been exhausted by the excitement and anxiety surrounding the wedding, and her fragile health was always a consideration, but the story seemed to have no factual basis. It may have been media hyperbole, or was perhaps the result of her own attempt at subterfuge. On November 10, she and Peralta-Ramos slipped quietly out a side door of the Plaza through the hotel's florist shop. He wore a dark blue suit and Millicent, chic as always, was dressed in a black suede coat with lynx fur and a black felt hat. They hailed a battered old taxicab and sank deep into the backseat. At the Grace Line pier in Brooklyn where the *Santa Elisa* would sail at noon, they were met by Millicent's brother Henry and Robert Coe, who escorted them to the gangplank, where an ocean liner official and a policeman were necessary to escort them up to the deck through photographers and newsmen. Millicent put her pocketbook over her face. Ramos used her felt hat to cover his, but once on deck he decided to take a moment to answer questions. He explained they were taking a roundabout route to Argentina in hopes of having a long and quiet honeymoon.[17] Three-year-old Peter was left behind with his nanny and grandparents.

A week later when the *Santa Elisa* docked at Cristobal, Panama, Peralta-Ramos and Millicent saw a revue and went dancing. Reporters sought out the couple when they dined at a café, but Ramos deftly deflected their attention, telling one and all, "We are perfectly happy and contented, but wish to be left alone."[18] Wherever they went, they were hard to miss. When the couple boarded the train between Buenos Aires and Córdoba, where the Peralta-Ramos family had an *estancia*, or ranch, an extra car was needed for Millicent's array of steamer trunks.

CHAPTER TEN

After the Honeymoon

ILLICENT AND ARTURO RETURNED FROM ARGEN-tina five months later, in March. They arrived on the Munson liner *Western World* in their usual style, with nine trunks (having evidently picked one up along the way), six lovebirds, a macaw, and a Trinidad wildcat. Fellow passengers reported that Millicent had spent much of the voyage in her cabin while Arturo was betting on the miniature horse races in the smoking room. She was pregnant again.[1]

Time magazine noted their return "after a brief honeymoon" and continued to describe Arturo as "a warmly handsome and appetizing youth." It reported that "he will shortly settle down to toil as a member of J. P. Benkard & Co., Manhattan brokers." *Vogue* ran a demure photo of Millicent, now Mrs. Arturo Peralta-Ramos, wearing pearls and looking soulful after "an extended trip to South America." Then Millicent suddenly became seriously ill in June. A case of double pneumonia required bedrest, so she retired to the Port of Missing Men in Southampton. *The New York Times* warned: "Mrs. Ramos's Illness Nearing Its Crisis." Mary was summoned from Paris, but when she arrived four days later on the cruise liner *Leviathan*, Millicent's condition had improved. Such scares—and recoveries—were to be common features all of Millicent's life.

The following November Millicent gave birth to a second eight-pound son, Arturo Peralta-Ramos II. Recovered and resettled in New York, she turned her attention to decorating her Fifth Avenue apartment and traveled frequently between her mother's homes, now in Paris, Venice, and Southampton. Mindful of her health, she occupied herself with quieter domestic concerns, including needlepoint, knitting, and the compilation of family recipes that would grow over the years into ten thick volumes of scrapbooks. The recipes, rich and for large gatherings, are a culinary history of their time, with such items as potted pheasant and cold calf's head vinaigrette. Always whimsical, Millicent could not resist tagging many of them with personally relevant titles, such as "Steak Millicent Ramos," "Lobster Huddleston," and "Oyster Soup Port of Missing Men." She included "Soup Countess" and "Frankfurters Southampton." Many of the recipes were old favorites from the cooks of her childhood and the picnic favorites that had been served on her father's yachts, such as "Cold Eggs Kanawha." Others offered a rare glimpse into an earthier side of the glamorous young heiress, such as her whaling great grandfather, Captain Peleg Winslow Gifford's "Quarter Deck Fish Chowder," heavy on the port and cream. Compulsively thorough, she would gather several hundred recipes and fill volumes before she was finished. She cooked few of the selections herself, but handed the recipes over to her cook.[2]

The needlepoint rugs she designed and made caught the attention of interior decorators and caused admirers like Cecil Beaton to later remark that if she had not had money she might have become "a serious artist in one field instead of a dilettante who dissipated in a delightful way her talents by illustrating books for her children, making acres of needlework carpets . . ." While she took pleasure in these pursuits during one of the rare lulls in her drama-filled life, the public spotlight moved from her to her parents.

The following year, 1929, Mary and Harry Rogers divorced. The family's fame had shifted, as the newspapers, in referring to Colonel Henry H. Rogers, now added, "widely known as the father of Millicent Rogers." Just as Mary and the Colonel's divorce was making headlines, Count Salm, obviously for financial profit, began publishing his memoir of his marriage to Millicent in daily installments in the Berlin publication, *Nachtausgabe*. *My Battle for My Son* was a legacy for his son Peter in which he set out to explain and justify, as he put it, "just why papa cannot come along home and play with you." It included, in the words of *The New York Times*, a "pathetic admonition to little Peter, adjuring him to beware of gossiping and mendacious tongues which in later years might seek to poison his mind against his father. 'If anybody ever trickles poison into your ears, then whack him over the head with this, my legacy,'" he instructed his son. He also claimed in his "cynical yet debonair and occasionally swashbuckling manner," according to the *Times*, that he did not understand the real reason for the break from Millicent. He claimed that "a subtle campaign of slander, espionage, systematic propaganda, threats, and representations of a dire future in store for the wife and child because of his inability to support them," had been waged against him. "Lawyers looking for fat fees and persons who did not understand your mother separated us. A husband and wife who loved one another were torn apart—that is why your daddy cannot come to your home. You do not know him and he does not know you as a father should know his son and that is why your momma and daddy do not have a common home. It was wrecked for all of us," Salm wrote. Millicent and her parents regarded the memoir with disinterest or disgust. Its plaint fell on deaf ears. The Rogers were embroiled in their own domestic disputes.

Mary and Harry's deepening differences could no longer be bridged with money and multiple households. Mary, who had established a residence on the Avenue Montaigne, just off the Champs Elysees, petitioned for divorce in the French courts. She charged Colonel Rogers with desertion. Harry had also set up a residence in Paris two years earlier, fueling conjecture that a divorce would be coming. With Mary already there a French divorce, it was presumed, would be less costly and receive less publicity than in New York. Mary had spent most of the previous winter in New York, but she did not stay at the Rogers' home. Adrian Larkin, the same trusty counsel who had accompanied the Colonel to Paris to negotiate Millicent's separation from Count Salm, was now assigned to handle Mary's charge.[3] In a strange updating of roles, Mary was spotted having tea with Count Salm at the Paris Ritz. The incident gave the Parisian press a chuckle and rearoused suspicions that she had always approved of the Count more than the Colonel had. Harry gave Mary three million dollars in a settlement when a divorce was granted them in Holland, amid rumors that another woman was responsible for the breakup.[4]

In 1929 the Colonel married Marguerite von Braun Savell Miles, the recently widowed wife of Basil Miles, an American economist and diplomat in Washington. There had been a brief scandal around Miles's death. The Department of Justice began investigating hints that he died of poisoning, but an inquiry didn't result in charges. His Budapest-born widow had previously been married to Peabody Savell, a U.S. engineer in Paris. Rogers' former secretary Edward Kern then made headlines lodging a conspiracy suit against Rogers after bad blood developed between Kern and Marguerite, who, Kern said, had falsely claimed to be the illegitimate child of the Emperor Franz Josef. Marguerite attracted controversy and drama, but such petty concerns hardly dampened the Colonel's high style. He installed a big swimming pool with Pompeian-style statuary and winter heating in The Port of Missing Men, and commissioned a yacht to be made in Germany with Zeppelin engines to carry him from Southampton to his New York offices. The pool, it was reported, was the largest private swimming pool in the country.

It was understood among Mary Rogers' intimates that she had fallen in love with the French painter Bernard Boutet de Monvel. Boutet de Monvel, a highly regarded society painter, was one of the more dashing figures in the elegant upper classes of New York and Paris. "The artist's mistress was Rogers' piquantly beautiful mother,

Mary Benjamin Rogers, a gifted painter herself," according to recent accounts of their relationship in the online *Aesthete's Lament*, which captions one of the loveliest portraits ever done of Millicent, painted by Boutet de Monvel. But Boutet de Monvel and Mary were people of an older era, who shared a respect for discretion and the dictums of wealthy society. Boutet de Monvel came from strictly conservative French stock, his father was also a celebrated painter, and it was understood that he and Mary would never marry. According to her grandson Arturo, Mary expected more from Boutet de Monvel. "But she didn't understand that they would always be outside of that society. They would have been outcasts."

Mary, considered something of an austere Edwardian by her descendants, certainly in contrast to free-living Millicent, was a good match for conservative European society. Many of the artists she met in Paris "ran contrary to her conservative nature," wrote Adam Lewis in his biography of Van Day Truex, the young designer who would be credited with shaping much of twentieth-century taste and style.[5] Truex would also figure prominently in Mary Rogers' life. With Boutet de Monvel as her companion, she had Millicent, her grandson Peter, Truex, and her painting, and those things "were all that she needed." She entertained American friends who came to visit, and "like them she was amused by some of the goings-on in the city, but they held to their conservative values and customs," Lewis wrote. Mary was known to scold Millicent for her more adventuresome and willful romantic nature, admonishing her to have greater concern for what the public thought—and to make her marriages work. Meanwhile, Mary was the "cozy" center of her family, especially for her grandsons.

The Colonel was less docile. His marriage to Marguerite Miles lasted only two years, and it cost him yet another three million dollars to bring it to an end through the always expert negotiations of Adrian Larkin. At the time there were rumors that the Colonel and Mary would reconcile, but in 1933 Rogers married Pauline van der Voort Dresser. Millicent, though clearly more closely allied to her mother, managed to maintain a solid relationship with her father and tiptoed around his subsequent marriages in ways intended to not offend or alienate him. She understood by this time the financial consequences of crossing her father.

Disinheritance was the big stick, the threat he always wielded over his family and both his children did their best to court the Colonel's favor. When his engagement to Pauline Dresser was announced, Millicent and Arturo hosted a dinner party in their honor at Southampton in an ironic reversal of family roles. Several days later she and Arturo sailed back to Europe. Her father and Pauline drove into New York City to see them off on the *Bremen* when it set sail at midnight. Millicent and Arturo would return for the marriage ceremony, it was duly noted by the newspapers, in October. Her brother Henry was his father's best man. The Rogers-Dresser marriage turned out to be the occasion for a transforming event, as it played out, in Rogers family history.

There is notably little mention of Millicent's brother, Henry, in the family history. Henry Rogers played an ignominious role within his family. Rather than assume the reputation of the "good child" while Millicent made her headlines with her elopement and angered their father, Harry seemed to slip into oblivion. At Oxford he had taken an interest in filmmaking, but his first mention in the press was for making a pornographic film. The twenty-five thousand dollar loan his father gave him to start the Standard Motion Picture Corporation was not paid back. Even among his relatives he is remembered, according to Michael Coe, the archaeologist and author of his memoir of the Coe branch of the Rogers family, as "a rotter."[6] *The New York Times* wrongly explained the division was because Henry had allied with his mother at the time of her divorce from the Colonel. But the family knew better.

He had always drank to excess, but he outdid himself—and changed family history—one night soon after the Colonel and Pauline were married. It was at a dinner to honor them when he shouted out at his father, "For God's sake, can you stop hanging a marriage license on every woman you screw?"[7] Some tabloid papers claimed that the rift between father and son was because Henry III had struck his mother, in a quarrel when his parents divorced.

The Colonel never forgave young Henry for the insult, and invoked disinheritance as punishment. Wills were his weapons. "They despised each other," Christina Lucia Peralta-Ramos, Millicent's granddaughter, said, explaining the family's sense of the father and son's poisoned relationship. Colonel Rogers was determined to disinherit his son at all costs, and that would have disastrous consequences for the family and future heirs. Even if the Colonel had to suffer huge federal income tax costs, and pay the penalties required to break the trusts that had been created by his father, so be it. Henry would be punished with his father's favorite tool, the withholding of money.

Mary could not side with her son, even when he was trashing her ex-husband's new wife. Her own social and family sensibilities were offended by his conduct and she told him that his embarrassing behavior would have to stop. She distanced herself from him. She went so far as to create a surrogate son for herself in the talented Van Day Truex. "From the moment Mary Rogers met Truex, she unabashedly loved him as a surrogate son. H. H. Rogers III, her natural son, had always been a sad disappointment to her, beset as he was by a serious drinking problem and a life of scandal that had virtually alienated him from both his parents," wrote Adam Lewis.[8] The well-dressed, handsome, and enormously gifted Van Truex captivated both Mary and Millicent and the two began to support him as though he were a member of the family. Truex contributed his decorating expertise to their myriad properties and the women made sure he wanted for nothing. They also introduced him to rising stars in the fashion world, like Elsa Schiaparelli, who were part of that avant-garde of Paris that would go on to fame in the world of design.

Arturo and Millicent lived mostly in Europe during these years. They cruised between New York and France and Italy with nannies and maids to tend to the boys. A second son, Paul, was born in 1931. Millicent invariably traveled with her dogs, an ever expanding pack of dachshunds. They were her pets as well as her accessories, and the family lore is rich with stories of her going so far as to have life jackets made for them to wear during her transatlantic cruises. Her photo albums are full of photos of her much-loved pets. When they were sick she tucked them under the covers and snapped shots of them with their ears bandaged up, bottles at their paws, or wearing a string of pearls. She seemed to dote on them more than her sons.

Millicent devoted most of her time during these years to the role of wealthy wedded socialite, but a creative streak surfaced. It went beyond her earlier children's books and handiwork. Her new palettes were houses and clothes. She began to make an impression in the world of fashion with her fearless insistence on combining the new influences she saw in Europe, even the European countryside, with the classic styles and haute couture she sported in New York and Paris. And she was aggressive about her looks and her taste. In 1930 she appeared on the cover of the August edition of *Life* magazine in a swimsuit.

Millicent had made her entry to the adult world through men, marriage, and the notoriety of great wealth, but she seemed increasingly to hunger for a more creative outlet. She became a perfectionist in pursuit of beauty in all things. One summer when she and Mary rented a house together on the water in Gloucester, Massachusetts, they had new plantings put in to suit their tastes. "They always left things better than when they arrived," says her son Arturo. They also took their own linens on these vacations, and sorting out their sheets and cases, getting them all back properly to their respective owners, was a frequent topic in the correspondence between Mary and Millicent after such trips. True women in the H. H. Rogers money-oriented tradition, they would bicker over liquor bills and other petty expenses. Two strong-willed women in the same house always posed challenges, although they were both committed to achieving a kind of domestic elegance and grace. But beyond housekeeping, no matter how gracious, Millicent began to need a creative outlet. She began to apply her exacting standards to fashion. She was restless and looking for something to do, something that would use her finest assets: taste, beauty, and money.

CHAPTER ELEVEN

Making a Mark in Fashion

THERE HAVE ALWAYS BEEN WOMEN WITH MONEY, BUT NOT all of them had Millicent Rogers' eye for style and the taste to go along with it. In addition, at five foot seven she had a long, lean body to rival that of any model, so she could very powerfully project her own fashion sense. Attractive society women, as a browse through *Harper's Bazaar, Vogue,* or *Town & Country* in the thirties and forties will quickly illustrate, frequently modeled top designer clothes for magazines. It was a time before ready-to-wear fashions could popularize styles in a season, and high fashion, haute couture, depended almost wholly on leading fashion designers. Millicent's money, looks, and sense of style were a potent combination. Her self-awareness at seventeen when she wore a little black dress, Chinese headdress, and lacquered nails to a debutante party suggests she always knew that she had this power. Moreover, she was fond of bending the rules, always a welcome trait in trendsetters.

In her world, clothes played a special role. Proper dress in New York society was de rigueur, and her mother had set a high standard. Like Millicent, what Mary Rogers wore was often reported in the society columns that covered the balls, dances, and society doings in the 1920s. At seventeen Millicent was photographed by the leading fashion magazines wearing the restrained and tasteful fashions considered appropriate for her age and occasion. Those clothes were classics without a lot of dash. The photos were more about her passage into life or marriage than the fashions she wore, though one suspects they were chosen with meticulous care. As her photo history shows, she had a penchant for stagey costumes that ranged from Greek empresses with flowing tresses to flamenco dancers with spit curls. It was not until the 1930s that Millicent began to escalate her role in fashion and develop a distinctive personal style.

When she made her high-handed entrance at Hickson's demanding to speak French, she showed her willingness to throw her weight around, whether or not it was becoming. It was a perquisite of money. Fashion was both a creative pastime and a shield of sorts. Her standards were exacting, but original. As Annette Tapert and Diana Edkins explained in their book *The Power of Style*, "... the driving force behind her inimitable style wasn't a hunger for recognition but a passion for life's aesthetic pleasures." In the authors' opinion, shared widely by Millicent's descendants, her quest for the aesthetically satisfying was inspired by her nearly fatal childhood illness. She had both a sense for fine things and a particular, distinctive joie de vivre. She didn't feel she could postpone or wait for gratification because she didn't know what tomorrow would bring.

It is too easy some fifty years later to ascribe Millicent's interests and passions as reactions to the threat that rheumatic fever posed to her life, but there does seem to be some truth to the theory. Her family had, as Tapert put it, "nourished her artistic and literary sensibilities" during her illness. And yes, with their travels and lavishly designed homes "they were considered style setters and cultural adventurers," creating a family path that she followed. But for whatever reasons of her own, she added dash and flair to almost everything she touched. Taste is invariably hard to define or explain. It just is. Hers was inarguably her greatest personal asset next to money.

Perhaps because taste doesn't automatically come with wealth, it was the asset that Millicent readily cultivated to her advantage and great distinction. With money she could indulge her taste and put it on display, and she was determined to do so.

Her particular style began to be noticed when she returned from Europe after living in Austria, where she had taken note of Tyrolean fashions—the dirndls, aprons, and hats of the local townspeople. She was exacting enough to go into Innsbruck and sketch the nineteenth-century costumes that she saw in the museums, then ask the St. Anton village tailor to replicate them per her instructions— and modifications—when she got home. She commissioned local seamstresses to fashion jackets, dresses, peasant-style blouses, quilted skirts, and hats that she mixed with the high fashions of Paris designers like Elsa Schiaparelli and Mainbocher. This was a time in fashion when style-setters like Wallis Simpson, who bought luxury items, including nightgowns, expected two or three fittings before the items fit them appropriately.

Millicent's Tyrolean variations were widely noted when she returned to the United States in 1938 and the fashion editors who had merely taken note of her when she appeared in their debutante and society notices now snapped to attention. She incorporated a peasant style into high fashion and became a sensation. "Byzantinely beautiful, independent in taste, she has a real sixth sense for clothes," *Vogue* purred over her in the January 1939 issue, adding that she was "as *soignée* on skis as she is in her town clothes."

She was pioneering a freedom of style, to amend rather than follow the dictates of fashion, that would be hers through life. It was somewhat audacious for a woman to create rather than follow fashion commands in this period, when designers and fashion editors largely told women how and what to wear. Being well-dressed amounted mostly to following the rules. Largely through Millicent's example and fashion evolution, the freedom to personalize style would become the hallmark of a deeper and more lasting American approach to fashion, especially later, during her tenure in the American Southwest. It was her knack for integrating into high fashion certain unrefined elements, whether Tyrolean peasant touches or Navajo Indian pieces, that set her apart. She not only had the magic touch to put together disparate pieces, but she had the bold spirit to do it in the first place. She pulled it off.

Millicent had a cult of admiring followers. Members of the Southampton Beach Club, which Millicent frequented almost every summer when she returned to Southampton from Europe, counted on her to introduce them to something new. "She was absolutely beautiful and she always had some new interest and the endless energy to bring it off. We used to say that she needed only three hours of sleep a night. Everyone looked up to her style and copied whatever she did. One summer she had on dirndls. Everybody had to have a dirndl and most of them didn't look as good as she did in them," remembers Joyce Mann. Mann, her friends, and Mann's mother's friends, who were closer to Millicent's age, were all Millicent's admirers. Millicent was considered organized in the way she went about her social life and wardrobe. There was no haphazardness about her, suggesting that she approached clothes and style in much the same way some women would a profession, which is what fashion very nearly became for her. It was her ability not only to create her own look, but to shape the vision of her designers, that left her lasting mark on the larger fashion community. It is sometimes forgotten that in Millicent's time, the thirties and forties, stylish adult women were the trendsetters who wielded influence on the fashion world, much as celebrities do today. "Nor was it a period when young women had any standing in the smart world," wrote *Vogue*'s legendary Paris editor Bettina Ballard in *In My Fashion*, her memoir of her career and life in fashion. "A woman was not considered important in Paris until she was well in her thirties and had her children behind her so she could concentrate on a fashionable life." This description fit Millicent perfectly. Ballard included Millicent in her chapter "The Women Who Make Fashion." "Several American women of that period occasioned a certain fashion stir in Paris. Millicent Rogers (by then Mrs. Ronald

Balcom) lived very little in Paris but bought all of her clothes there. She probably brought as much beauty and dignity to the Schiaparelli era as any of Schiap's loyal followers." Ballard emphasized "the extent of the personal taste that she used in choosing her clothes. They still look today the epitome of fashion," she wrote in 1960. She believed that Millicent's photographs in *Harper's Bazaar* and *Vogue* made her an object of fashion curiosity in Paris in the 1930s. "Had she attached any importance to being a fashion leader, she could have led them all. Hers was a true natural elegance."

There is something more about Millicent's ascendance as a fashion icon that reaches beyond the simple explanation of an unwell adolescent who turned to art and style as an outlet. Her style sense and her meticulous execution of it began to put her into focus by the time she appeared in Paris and New York in the early thirties as Mrs. Arturo Peralta-Ramos. While quietly willful as a young woman, she had basically let her family, money, and society direct her life thus far. But when it came to style and fashion, she was her own boss. In her life's story this was the juncture where money and creativity—and disciplined will—fused to empower her. Perhaps the greatest gift to her life during this time was her exposure to fashion genius at work.

Millicent was not afraid to experiment. Her relationship with the Italian-born couturier Elsa Schiaparelli, whom she befriended at her mother's homes in Paris and Senlis, France, is one example. Schiaparelli was a surrealist and her design sense was shaped in part by Salvador Dalí and Jean Cocteau, with whom she worked in Paris. She would also become the most influential designer in Paris in the thirties, "known for her intoxicating, impeccably executed mixes of femininity, frivolity and wit," wrote Lorna Koski in *W*.[1] Schiaparelli, like Millicent, was inventive, and liked to match previously incongruous elements in her designs. She used gabardine, previously kept in the province of tailored clothes, for evening coats. She is credited with introducing padded shoulders, unique synthetic fabrics, wooden jewelry, rustic woolens, and "shocking pink" to the fashion world of the

1930s. In 1934 *Time* magazine put her on its cover for her contribution to modern fashion. She and Millicent seemed destined for mutual admiration, as the same pairing of unlikely elements interested both women.

Schiaparelli integrated sophisticated and complex artistic concepts into her clothes, which appealed to Millicent. A suit, the "insect Dress and Jacket" that Schiaparelli designed for Millicent, revealed the importance of the designer-client relationship during couture's "Golden Age."[2] Schiaparelli's plastic buttons and painted metallic insects seemed way ahead of their time in 1938. Schiaparelli admitted that Millicent exerted a profound influence on her work. She reflected on Millicent, "If she had not been so terribly rich, she might, with her vast talent and unlimited generosity, have become a great artist." Millicent had no need to subject herself to the rigors of professional creative education and success, yet she was determined to discipline herself and learn to meet her own standards of excellence. She did not compete with the professionals she partnered and patroned, but she inspired many of them to reach for and to help her to realize her own fashion visions.

Her tact and gentleness with the mighty creative egos of the fashion world were considered part of her appeal. When Schiaparelli fitted her with a dress, Millicent would study her reflection in it, and admire it with the designer. Then she would add, "Sciappi [her pet name for her], it's the buttons. It would be much more beautiful with different buttons!" And so it went, her patient and tactful amendments helping to improve a design and ultimately get what suited her. She disarmed the designer first, then treated her addition to their design as a brilliant discovery that they shared. The designers, almost artistic egos all, did not resent or resist her suggestions. Partly, one assumes, because they immediately sensed she was right.

The current fashion designer Arnold Scaasi was a teenager working for the legendary designer Charles James when Millicent would come into James's ateliers for fittings. Her pending arrival would always create a stir among the staff. His job at the time was merely holding the pins while James made his adjustments to her dresses, but he recalls, "Everyone was awed that Millicent was so very beautiful."[3]

During the titled Golden Age of Couturier, Millicent's taste was eclectic, another reason that she was dubbed an originator of "hippie chic." The term, of course, could only have been applied in retrospect well after her death in 1953, because "hippie" entered the popular lexicon in the sixties. Still, she did not limit herself to one designer or style. She wore Hermès (a leather cape, no less), Grès' classical Grecian-styled gowns, Mainbocher, and Schiaparelli interchangeably. Jeanne Lanvin and Valentina styles were also in her collection. She sampled them all, as they applied to her interests and imagination. It comes as no surprise that in November 1935, when *Harper's Bazaar* ran a feature called "One Woman's Winter Wardrobe," which was the magazine's prescription for how fashionable women should dress that season, the accompanying photo is of Millicent, "Madame Arturo Ramos," leaving her mother's house in Paris in a navy wool coat lined with feather monkey by Schiaparelli. Millicent added a monkey muff on her arm. While the article asserted that the stylish woman that winter would always wear a beret, Millicent wore a Tyrolean hat of her choosing and led her own dachshund alongside. She looked smashing, on her own terms, and had added her own twist to *Harper's* vision.

Diana Vreeland, the unrivaled doyenne of fashion from the late thirties when she became fashion editor of *Harper's Bazaar* through 1971 when she stepped down as editor in chief of *Vogue*, was a friend of Millicent's who championed her fashion sense long after Millicent's death. She wrote of Millicent when she curated the Metropolitan Museum's exhibition "American Women of Style" in 1975: "She was dressed by the leading couturiers, but always, with complete assurance, she went way beyond the fashions of the time to create her own special style. She used couture to make her clothes exactly as she wanted them."

Vreeland, known for her own extraordinary style, took some cues from Millicent. They were friends, products of a similar upbringing, and crossed paths on numerous occasions in Europe and New York. After a trip to Austria in 1936, Vreeland made note in her journal of a coat—a jacket really—that Millicent had been wearing during her visit. It was a ski coat that she had modeled after an Italian truck driver's, down to the same orange lining. She had added a red fox collar. The effect, fresh and eye-catching, was a classic example of Millicent's confidence, and her ability to reach out to an unrefined element, and incorporate it into her own look.[4] Through the admiration of the fashion world's players, she earned attention and promoted the style.

The same thing would happen when Vreeland was fashion editor of *Harper's Bazaar* in the late forties and Millicent arrived in New York wearing a chest full of turquoise and silver beads and a Navajo concho belt. The next thing she knew, she was being photographed by the fashion photographer Louise Dahl-Wolfe and the classic American Southwestern look, so seminal to Ralph Lauren and designers to follow, had been launched. Millicent's style was her own, but its lasting impact was made through her friends, advocates, and admirers in the fashion world. Her manner, mellowed from the headstrong miss who insisted on speaking only French that day in Hickson's, also accounted for the spread of her influence. It had become apparent that fashion, for Millicent, was part play.

Vreeland had admiringly witnessed, and made note in her memoirs, of an exhibitionist streak in the young Millicent at a debutante ball at the Ritz some years earlier in New York. Millicent began the evening wearing a black silk dress with a bustle and train by the popular French designer of the day, Patou. On the pretext of having sat on some ice cream, she excused herself and returned wearing a robe of looped taffeta. Later she claimed that she had spilled coffee, and went off to change her clothes again, reappearing in another enchanting fashion. The fashion world grooved on the legend of these episodes, and it was Edna Woolman Chase, editor of *Vogue* between 1914–1952, who retold it in her autobiography, *Always in Vogue*.

In the late thirties Millicent made a sensation by adding Tyrolean accessories to the tailored classic styles of major designers, and then she returned from Europe with a moleskin cape, muff, and hat, dyed bright red. The fashion world leapt to attention. She and her fashions merited three pages in *Vogue*, two for her city suits and furs and another for her skiwear. Millicent, hatless and wearing sunglasses, dressed in her knife-creased ski pants (Springerhosen), her square-toed ski boots, and an "easy well-tailored blue jacket, her neat pale blue sweater—all an object-lesson in ski simplicity. A simplicity that American ski-runs might better see more of," preached *Vogue*.

Millicent's assertion of her distinctly original style was not limited to her wardrobe. She was just as exacting when she bought a car, the luxury Delage Aerosport Coupe she had seen on display at the Paris Salon in 1937. She specified that the silver-gray exterior should be repainted a darker shade of gray to go with the deep red calfskin upholstery, and to the astonishment of the French carmaker in the Letourner and Marchand workroom, she pulled out a tube of lipstick, and drew the changes she wanted on the fender and center rear fin.[5]

Millicent's most important relationship in the world of fashion was made in 1930 when she went to London with a group of friends to see a talked-about young designer named Charles James. Though born in England, James would become known as the most truly American designer. In a field largely dominated by French, Italians, and Russians, James uncannily understood where American style was going after World War II and proceeded to capture its essence. Millicent's name became paired with his at the height of his fame when she functioned as both his patron and muse. In the quickly changing world of twenty-first century fashion, it is hard to imagine the influence that a few key and highly respected fashion designers wielded in their time. Nearly unknown to all but fashion industry experts and aficionados today, Charles James was considered a giant, a fashion innovator on the tip of every fashionable woman's tongue in the forties and fifties. His sculpted ball gowns in lavish fabrics and inventive colors were his signature styles, though his coats and capes trimmed with fur and embroidery also left their mark. His designs have been variously called abstract, architectural, and sculptural. He considered himself an artist, and history has largely remembered him that way, for his sculpted bodices and voluminous skirts, the intricate drapings that were his trademarks. Among designers, he is often acknowledged to have been "the best," so it should come as no surprise that he would be linked to Millicent, who sought out excellence. Christian Dior credited him with creating the "New Look," as modern women stepped out of prewar fashion and gazed ahead. Millicent was equally credited with pioneering the modern "look," a style she crafted by being her own stylist. In the world of fashion, the two seemed to complement and to feed off of one another.

It has also been noted that James was one of the oddest and most difficult personalities in the legends of fashion history. He seemed "the very model of Hollywood stereotypical fashion designer: compulsive, effeminate, occasionally hysterical, frequently hectoring, always demanding . . . kissed by the furies," wrote Jay Cocks in a review of the Metropolitan Museum of Art's show "La Belle Epoque" in 1983 that featured James's designs. Yet he and Millicent got along, and in her matchless manner, soothing, demanding, and yet flattering, she managed him.

James's and Millicent's relationship was considered one of the most famous and fruitful designer-client collaborations in American fashion history.[6] By his account it began in 1943 when he designed a nightgown, a "deshabille" of white and rose organdy trimmed with lace and biscuit-colored ribbons," for her when she was hospitalized with a bout of her recurring heart ailments.[7] Instinctively he understood style and finery as a tonic for his client. He created more than forty-five original designs for Millicent, and her financial patronage was essential to his business success in the late 1940s. Her contribution to his larger success went beyond the clothes she actually commissioned from him. He involved her in an arrangement with museums to commemorate his clothes, thus cleverly becoming the architect of his own glorification. Through a clever scheme devised by James,

Millicent underwrote the cost of the clothes that became enshrined in museums. She would pay double the price for the initial dress and donate it for a tax deduction. He would then give her a replacement dress at no cost.[8] He described (perhaps spun) the arrangement: "... it was agreed that I did have the right to give her a wardrobe. [It] did reflect brilliantly on me and made clear the value of HER inspiration, by which finally a large hunk of the dress industry benefited." Thus, he simultaneously made Millicent his premier American client and engineered the donation of his work to major American museums that would further establish his reputation as a major American designer. Millicent accumulated a studied collection of his creations for her wardrobe, to be placed in the Brooklyn Museum with the patterns, muslins, completed dresses, and documentation of their structural evolution.

In correspondence to Millicent, James wrote of bill A. and bill B. "In this, I have entirely forgotten or struck out of mind all the dealings which went to make up the total of 6,000 in bill A. I have simply arranged a gift to the Museum for the sum of 6,000, which is entirely payable out of your untaxed income and should NOT cost you more than 1,000, and therefore saves you between four and five grand."[9] As Bettina Ballard explained it, "The clothes that he finished for his rich customers never really belonged to them in the mind of Charlie. They were his masterpieces, his creations, his architectural triumphs—whatever he chose to call them—and women were simply a means of displaying them to the world."

Still, he was attentive to his clients' desires and understood flattery. In his correspondence to Millicent, he listed the dresses he was creating for her, and paused to lament, "I haven't got the cream violet satin." Juxtaposing hardheaded business and creative matters, he figured she would probably want to keep the big red and brown dress he had designed for her, but would be willing to give up a grey satin and ribbon dress. "You see," he wrote, " we have been working quite seriously on this project and the Museum are [sic] delighted to have it, for they feel you are perhaps one of the most representative figures of today and best able to stand for the development of taste." He was a handful, and his clients, including Millicent, kept coming back for more. They were seduced by the way they looked in his clothes, almost always regal, streamlined, beautiful, and totally original. James's designs for Millicent continued to be marveled at by present-day admirers when many were displayed to the public for the first time in the 2010 exhibit, "High Style: Masterworks from the Brooklyn Museum Costume Collection at the Metropolitan Museum of Art." Nearly a quarter of the fashions on display in the landmark show once belonged to Millicent.

When James died in 1978, his widow Nancy James explained, "Millicent Rogers inspired him more than anyone. He felt that she could help him to resolve a design when he wasn't certain how to finish it."[10] James was direct in his own admiration of Millicent and wrote to her in one letter, "... when you came into my house everyone at once knew what they were to do, and how to do it. And that special quality of bringing out people's work at its best was what gave you a special rating." He quickly, however, segued: "NOW about business. Your present bill is in front of me." His statement was for $4,825.[11]

Millicent typically overspent the money that she had and as late as 1949 she owed James money. She had a platinum, diamond, and sapphire ring (one sapphire, 84.81 carats; four baguette diamonds, 1.25 carats; and fifty-six round diamonds, 2.21 carats) assigned to him to cover her bill. Yet the strain of paying her bill did not dampen her desire for his clothes. In 1950 she corresponded with him about an order. "The cinnamon coat arrived and—it has no pockets! The collar also is not just right for me but I'll take this up when I get back to New York."[12]

Their relationship developed into a friendship beyond typical designer/client roles, though it was certainly forged with Millicent's purchasing power. Like James, she was a tireless perfectionist intent on exact tailoring, and together they wrestled with the sublime and stupefying challenge of fashion design and creation. Though James was considered by many to be a tortured artist, a sort of odd genius, he was capable of a lasting and warm personal relationship with Millicent. During one of her serious bouts with illness, he wrote to her on airline stationery while aboard a United flight: "Dearest dearest Millicent, All laughs aside I'm more than worried about you. I'm so damned inhibited that I can't make plausible my feelings toward you and somehow I always feel just round the corner instead of where I want to be. Already in life you've given more happiness than you have perhaps received and there is a credit balance due you. Physically in <u>looks and shape</u> you are at a peak. Last year you were raddled and now you seem to have lost ten years . . ." In another letter, typed on his 699 Madison Avenue letterhead, he wrote admiringly, "I have missed you very much, and your very sweet sense of reason and poetry all mingled up in an Emily Dickinson, Mark Twain, Socratic manner." Conversely, she could take him quite to task for any skittishness in their professional relationship, especially when he pressed for money. "Dear Charles, In answer to your various letters, I do think yours suddenly is a queer way of acting. A while back when you needed money in Europe I sent it to you in exchange for a suit the whole of which I finally got a year later." She then berates him for long delays in delivering her orders and billing in excess of their agreed price. "What is all this business of saying I promised you $10,000 on delivery. . . . If you are going to double your clients accounts, you are not going to have clients long. I can tell you, you are being very unwise."

They continued to bicker over money. Even the diamond ring that Millicent provided to settle their account in 1949 caused a prickly correspondence when James pawned it to pay expenses. He wrote to Millicent's secretary Mathilde Seif, "In fact this morning we arranged that I would give you the pawn ticket for the ring and that when the estate was cleared you would take the ring out of pawn and return it to Mrs. Rogers, and pay the difference to me directly in my absence to the tax authorities." Obviously miffed at the pace of payment and capitalizing on the ring, he ended with a threat to sell it outright "for three thousand two hundred dollars tomorrow and apply the payment to Mrs. Rogers bill."

Somehow he and Millicent managed to weather these altercations over money. They seemed to be merely passing squabbles over filthy lucre among creative creatures. The following year, Millicent wrote that she had sent the brown and red dress and gray evening dresses that he had designed for her back to him for his museum show purposes. "I'll do it this time for you, my love—but you don't know how I loathe other people wearing my clothes and the way I feel about them afterward." Again, there is a discourse on money. "I have received your bill of September 19th and—whether you want it or not—herewith my check #A3650 in the amount of $1000.00 on your account. As I told you over the telephone, I cannot make payment to any third party. This, you will have to take care of. But what about that $500.00 that Mrs. Seif cabled you in Paris last December? My accountant, Mr. Taylor, has asked about this. Expect to be back some time around the first of November and will of course, see you then. Love, Millicent."

In letters that James wrote to Maximilian Furs on Fifty-seventh Street in New York, he ordered six thousand dollars worth of "royal pastel" skins to be selected by Millicent for making into a cape and a coat that she had commissioned him to design. So confident was she that James could improve on others' designs and tailor-make anything more to her taste that she had him design her furs, dressing gowns, blouses (she had forty-eight of them), even the so-called squaw skirts that she adopted in the Southwest. He and she spoke the same language about clothes and life. "You know as well as I do how terribly life seems to shorten itself, and all of a sudden one just isn't in the same age bracket at all. And Lord knows we don't have a second chance that we clearly know about. I don't think I ever realized acutely till I was forty how LIFE IS WHAT WE MAKE IT EVERY DAY. I always figured I hadn't really begun to do things, or that they could all be done over again," wrote James to Millicent, in a letter that sounded hauntingly like Millicent herself. Always aware of the fragility of life and its shortness, Millicent would share sentiments much like James's in correspondence to family and lovers. Both she and James shared, for whatever reasons in their respective pasts, a mindfulness of the shortness of life. That and the love of beauty and creation in haute couture seemed to bind them.[13]

CHAPTER TWELVE

A Stylish Life

MILLICENT MOVED BETWEEN NEW YORK, PARIS, Venice, and Austria in the late twenties and early thirties in a life devoted mostly to decorating her homes, dressing well, and entertaining in style. She was glamorous and restless, motherhood was not her top priority, and her three young sons, like many children of the well-to-do at the time, were raised chiefly by their nanny, the stolid Dade, a devoted and stabilizing presence in the family. Matronly and starchy, Dade was a regular in the family photos of the thirties and forties. In the nursery and the years beyond, she allowed the children to be sometimes seen, and very seldom heard. The boys were trained to answer when spoken to with the simplest and shortest response. While strictly enforcing their mother's rules for the household, Dade was attentive to the boys and provided a constancy in their young lives that was otherwise lacking. "As children we saw very little of our parents," concedes Arturo, the middle son. "We were accidental aspects of her life."

Their grandmother filled the void by organizing her grandsons' schooling in Swiss boarding schools and making summer arrangements for them at her homes in France, Italy, and Southampton. Her demeanor was more austere than Millicent's, and she had no trouble taking charge of their care and making decisions that concerned them. She was more likely to help with their homework and listen to their concerns than their self-absorbed mother. But she was no pushover. Paul, the youngest, was packed off to boarding school at the age of six, and the three brothers began to rely mostly on each other for support in their mother's 1930s approximation of modern jet-set life. There was not much room in that life for children and their specific concerns.[1]

Millicent was better at whimsy than management, and during her spells with illness she reverted to her sketchpads, much as she had done as a sick youngster. But now she made up stories for the boys and illustrated them with imaginative drawings. They were wonderfully inventive. One in particular that has been preserved was a variation on Hans Christian Andersen's "The Mermaid and the Prince," about a sea creature who must take to the land to marry her prince and the homesickness that follows. In the twelve remaining drawings done in colored pencil, the heroine "married the Prince but she had no friends and her sisters don't know her." Her description of the mermaid's sense of alienation smacks of her own experience after her elopement. "In the summer her feet hurt and she dreams of home. . . . She gets homesick and grieves in secret." Perhaps most reminiscent of her own life, the mermaid's prince meets the Sea King, a tyrant one might assume was modeled on Colonel Rogers. The theme seems pulled directly from her own life. Her sons vividly remembered her stories and her drawings into adulthood, perhaps because they provided some of the few occasions when her attention was wholly focused on using her talents to amuse and to please them.

Millicent's sons' relationships to her would unfold in different ways during their early years in Europe and after. She bewitched them, both by her presence and her absence, in much the same way she had other men in her life. They revered her, wanted more of her love and attention than they got, and they were always willing to seek her out, somewhat beseechingly, even as they grew older and spent longer periods of time apart from her. "There was great love when we were with her," says Arturo, but he emphasizes that he and his brothers actually spent little time with their parents. As children he and his brothers lived in fear during the long stretches, usually weeks at a time, that Millicent suffered some sort of paralysis, stroke, or weakness due to her heart and spent time in bed. Tiptoeing around her, uncertain about her survival and their subsequent future, the boys worried about her frail constitution.[2] It was Paul, the youngest, who suffered the most anxiety and hung onto his mother's apron strings. Arturo steered a more independent course as the middle son, and was buffeted between the needs of his younger and older brother.

Three years younger than his half brother, Peter, Arturo was often included in Peter's visits with his father, Count Salm who, after his divorce from Millicent, was only permitted to visit with his own son in the company of another person, and Arturo would do. He was often called upon to fill this role, and during the years after Millicent's divorce from Peralta-Ramos Arturo saw more of Salm than his own father. He also played the role of protector to his younger brother. Paul was slight and easily picked on by other boys at boarding school, where he was enrolled at age six, so Arturo, older and scrappy, defended him. Once he sent his younger brother money for books when the fee had been neglected by their mother. On one or more occasion, the Peralta-Ramos boys were left at school over a holiday after their classmates had left. Paul responded typically by being hurt; Arturo was angry.

"She was a terrible mother!" asserts Arturo. He says it bemusedly, as though he had made peace with Millicent's foibles long ago. He and Paul would also develop different adult relationships with their mother during the intervening years. He was combative with his mother during her lifetime. As an adult, Paul wrote an unpublished novel about a young man who loved his mother but did not receive her love in return. Peter's trajectory would be very different, in part because of a bequest from his grandfather, Millicent's father. As usual, with the family, the controlling element was money and inheritance.

In the fall of 1934 Millicent's father, Colonel Rogers, came down with pneumonia while staying at his suite at the Hotel Pierre in New York City. Despite three surgeries, he could not be cured of the infections that continued to plague him through the winter, even when his surgeons prescribed repeated blood transfusions. In May, Millicent and Arturo rushed back from Europe to be near him, and by July they were keeping a vigil at his bedside along with Rogers' third wife, Pauline Dresser. On July 25, at age fifty-six, Colonel Rogers died at the Southampton Hospital following a fourth surgery. The day after his death, his obituaries were filled with tales of his military distinctions, his inheritance, and his extravagances, including his famous collection of old ship models, his Pompeian-style swimming pool, his Long Island shooting preserve, and his state-of-the-art express yacht.

After a funeral at the St. Andrew's Dune Church in Southampton, his body was taken by train to Fairhaven, Massachusetts, where he was buried with military honors.[3] His old friend and loyal attorney, Adrian Larkin, now gray and hard of hearing, was a pallbearer. He had seen his companion and employer through many family dramas, and it is possible that only he knew of the bombshell that would soon explode over the Rogers family.

The first week after the Colonel's death news broke that he had divided his estate into thirds, one for his widow, Pauline, one for Millicent, and one for Millicent's son, eleven-year-old Peter Salm.[4] The Colonel had stayed true to this threat to disinherit his son Henry for outlandish rudeness to himself and Pauline, and in 1934 he had drawn up a new will substituting the young Peter Salm for his son, Henry. Peter also became the chief beneficiary among the heirs because his grandfather left to him, in addition to his one-third share, the Southampton estate, with The Port of Missing Men and the Beach House on it. There were a few stipulations regarding its occasional use by his widow, but it was to belong to Peter. The will's passage to probate was the trumpet call for the legal battles to begin.[5]

It was the beginning of a tumultuous year for Millicent, who beneath the quiet exterior of a life of repose in New York and Europe was once again at a crossroads and poised to re-create her life. While she and her husband made appearances and stood up together throughout her father's illness and demise, their marriage was unraveling. As early as 1932 there had been rumors of divorce. They were denied by Arturo in the Paris newspapers. It is unclear if there was an exact cause for the Peralta-Ramos/Rogers breakup, but his descendants offer several hypotheses. Arturo was headstrong, as his exit from Argentina after crashing his father's favorite car, demonstrated. He was athletic and charismatic, but not intellectually stimulating, something that Millicent had begun to want in a partner. He was also a Latin male with a hot temper, and in some family members' criteria, subjected Millicent to a double standard. His son Arturo heard whispers about a relationship between his mother and the handsome Austrian ski champion and instructor Rudolph Matt, who was often in company with the family. Matt was in family photos taken in the Austrian mountains and ski resorts starting in 1932, the year that there were first reports of a divorce. What her son Arturo did hear was that Millicent had broken "the rules" between her and her husband. His father had a maxim, he said: one infidelity was allowed, two strikes and you were out. There were quarrels and outspoken differences, common knowledge in the family. The contentious atmosphere of Millicent's own upbringing seemed to have left its mark, and she did not shy from confrontation.

By October following the Colonel's death, Millicent had filed and received a separation agreement settling the couple's property rights and fixing the custody of their sons with her. One New York Times account said, "Ramos planned a possible career in moving pictures." He had resigned from Benkard & Co in 1928, reportedly dissatisfied with the securities business and had accepted a job as a purchasing agent in New York for his grandfather's elevator company in Buenos Aires. Shortly after Colonel Rogers' death a story ran in the *American Weekly,* a paper that typically sensationalized the dramas in the lives of the rich and famous, saying that the final blow to the Peralta-Ramos marriage was Colonel Rogers' will, in which Arturo's stepson, Peter Salm, was a major beneficiary while his own sons' inheritance was nominal in comparison.

Perhaps more noteworthy and barely commented upon, the $150 million fortune that Colonel Rogers inherited from his father was now estimated at 20-some million, and more than 16 million of that was expected to go to Federal, State, and British governments in taxes and lawyers' fees. One of the great fortunes in American history had been dissipated, and the most immediate cause was the obscene outburst that Henry had hurled at his father and stepmother at dinner several years before. In order to disinherit young Henry, the Colonel had to break the family trust, which laid it open to crushing taxes. As a result, Millicent was no longer megarich, she was merely quite wealthy. Given her lifestyle, that meant she would feel the pinch of financial reality on occasion, for the rest of her life.

Millicent's divorce from Peralta-Ramos may have been timed to follow her father's death and her establishment of a firm grip on the inheritance. Colonel Rogers had liked Ramos. He had liked especially that Ramos helped his daughter manage her money, which the Colonel had always taken her to task for doing badly. Free now to move toward divorce without risking her father's ire, Millicent filed for separation ninety days after her fathers death.

In February, as her friends had intimated to reporters in December when her divorce from Peralta-Ramos was final, Millicent married Ronald Balcom, a fiercely handsome New York stockbroker nine years her junior. He had been a successful broker, and seemed to come with his own portfolio, though his image in the press was as a "young man known to café social circles." They had first met in Southampton where he frequented parties her father and stepmother had hosted at The Port. They had secretly gone about acquiring the necessary papers to enable them as foreigners to be married in Vienna, in February after her December divorce from Peralta-Ramos. The civil ceremony this time was in Vienna's *Rathaus*, the lovely spired Gothic city hall that overlooks the picturesque Rathaus Park.[6]

One society columnist in Tuxedo Park claimed that he had gotten a call from Mary Rogers asking him to confirm the news that Millicent had married again. "Ronnie!" she exclaimed, caught unprepared. Balcom was a *bon vivant* himself, always on the social scenes in New York, Paris, and Palm Beach where he made society page news before and after his marriage to Millicent for escorting a myriad of glamorous East Coast and Hollywood women, including the actresses Claudette Colbert and Norma Shearer, and Lady Ashley.

A definite pattern to Millicent's choice in men had emerged. She always fell for the best-looking, most debonair, and most sexually exciting suitors. What is surprising is that after two failed marriages, her criteria for marital happiness didn't evolve to take the shortcomings or pitfalls of the previous marriages much into account. This time she married a fellow American, which she had declared essential to marital happiness after her second marriage to a foreigner failed, but Ronnie Balcom's nationality was not considered his chief attraction.

Ronnie Balcom was a direct and open American sort of man; less temperamental and complicated than her first two husbands. He wasn't jaded, and she assumed that he would make a good father for her boys. Yet in other ways he fit the same mold as her first two husbands. He was first and foremost known for his extremely good looks. Her contemporaries found him a "Greek God of a man," a fabulous dancer who wore expensive clothes, one who was widely admired for being a fine athlete. He played tennis and golf, was a champion bobsledder, and an exceptionally fine skier who would fit easily into the life she envisioned sharing in Austria. While he and Millicent would have no children to tell the tale of their romance to subsequent generations, a few friends believed they understood the attraction. The daughter of a close friend of Millicent's during the 1940s discreetly explained that "Ronnie's" appeal to Millicent, as she had gotten it from her mother, was his skill as a lover. Of course, Millicent's son Arturo puts it more bluntly: "He had a penis the size of a horse." A Palm Beach matron more politely explains, "It was the way he was constructed ... He couldn't wear Bermuda shorts without falling out."[7]

In addition to his other assets, Balcom cut an elegant profile with his taut muscular physique in ski sweaters and springerhosen ski pants on the ski slopes. He was the perfect male accessory to the life that Millicent now envisioned for herself in Austria where she had built a house in Tyrol and intended they would spend most of their time. She liked living in the mountains and believed that the fresh air and the pine forests had a positive effect on her health and constitution.[8] She walked the nearby mountain trails and skied, in moderation. In the town of St. Anton she built "Shulla" house with its sweeping view of the Nasserein area below, and the long arched driveway up to it was lined with pine trees that her eldest son, Peter, helped to plant. As her New York apartment had been noted for its Chippendale furniture, fine china, and a bedroom of gray and yellow with Queen Anne furnishings, her St. Anton chalet was lauded in fashion and style magazines for its mix of fine Biedermeier furniture, bright carpets, and lovely Austrian porcelain stoves; again, a mix of fine European style with a dash of folksy peasant charm. From its chalet-style balconies and elegant yet cozy interiors she began to export her latest mix of fashion ingenuity, eagerly reported in *Harper's Bazaar* and *Vogue*. Her "soignée school of dressing" was hailed from New York. She looked incredibly chic, hatless with sunglasses, invariably wearing tailored sportsclothes in the photos that made their way back to the U.S. In lieu of fussy hats, she wore scarves, hoods, and visors, and posed on sundecks and porches for lunch with friends with the ski slopes and chalets in the background. The red moleskin cape and mink hoods that she wore captivated her American fashion audience with their dramatic flourish.

Millicent's new life abroad was interrupted by the lawsuits concerning her father's will. The summer following her father's death the new Mrs. Ronald Balcom was back in the U.S. challenging the will. Her stepmother, Pauline, would have rather had an outright bequest for her third of the estate than the income that she would share with the others from the trust that the Colonel had established. Pauline had also—unwittingly, she claimed—signed a waiver that would cut her income from any inherited trust to half if she remarried.[9] A year after Harry's death she was in court in an attempt to prove Rogers was incompetent when he had executed the will. She claimed that she had expressed her notion that Henry was "incompetent" to her daughter-in-law, Millicent, at the time.

Adrian Larkin, now one of the executors of the estate, held his ground. To Pauline's assertion that she had been inadequately informed about the new will, Larkin said that he had visited her in January 1934. "I had with me the new will and a copy of the old will," said Larkin. "I put them both down and compared the different items. . . . I explained to her that Henry's trust would reduce the interest amount in her share. I did not read to her the long part of the remarriage clause but I told her that it was the same as in the old will. Then she up and said a little impatiently but very pleasantly, 'Harry has explained all of this to me. Where do I sign?' Then she signed the waiver."[10] In court Pauline testified that she was recovering from injuries suffered in an automobile accident at the time and had not wholly understood what she was signing. Personal letters read in court in which she had written about her feelings of exclusion from Rogers and his life mesmerized the press and painted a somewhat sorry picture of Rogers in his last few years. In one letter dated January 1934 she asked him to cut down on his drinking and continued to explain "a feeling of Babylonian exile. . . . And there are great endurance tests for you and for me in the tomorrows of our relationship, so, if I am to be a part of it, able to help, I must be made to feel so not that your distrust in womanhood has made you draw in your shell."[11] Millicent, her new husband, and Henry III sat in the courtroom listening. Henry would have liked nothing better than to have seen his father's latest will discredited, as then he might have been restored to his position in the old will—before his disinheritance—as recipient of the one-third share that would now go to Peter. Quite a mix of emotions must have run through Millicent's mind as she listened to the testimony in the courtroom.

At one point Pauline discussed a phone call that Millicent, still married to Arturo at the time, had received from her brother Henry in Europe, while Millicent and Arturo were staying with her father and stepmother in Southampton.[12] Henry had called to discuss breaking the will, which he knew disenfranchised him, at the time. Everyone had been worried about the will. Had Pauline won her contest of the will, based on her claim of the Colonel's "incompetence," it might have opened the door to Henry III to be heir again. Millicent kept mum during the proceedings. Pauline, who, the will stipulated, had to live in the Southampton property within six months of her husband's death or forfeit it to Peter, appealed for funds to maintain the two-thousand-acre property. Pauline's challenge had cost the estate $40,000 in counsel fees, and she lost her suit. The will was upheld.

It was an odd twist of fate that Peter Salm, product of the very marriage that the Colonel had fought hardest to unravel, became his biggest heir. The Colonel did leave Millicent's two sons by her second marriage, Arturo and Paul, $50,000 each. Whether he believed they would be included as their mothers' heirs or he was signaling that Peter was his choice, in lieu of his own son, to carry on a family dynasty, is uncertain. But he had clearly warmed to the little boy that had been so often in his and Mary's charge in Southampton and Palm Beach. To Peter he also left "my Great-Great-Grandfather Gifford's grandfather clock and pistol which he carried in the Revolution and his four-poster bed." Despite Pauline's assertions, he sounded frightfully competent to the end. The quarrels weren't over. The reading of the Colonel's will, and to some degree Pauline's argument with it, had loosed the family demons.

Now Millicent made her moves. She served her stepmother Pauline with a demand to return estate jewelry valued at several hundred thousand dollars, given to her by the Colonel as a wedding present. He had bought for his third wife an emerald and diamond bracelet valued at $85,000 and a $42,000 emerald ring and a $95,000 diamond and platinum ring from Madame Marie el Khouri of 561 Fifth Avenue. The Colonel had remarked to a broker that the jewels were "a getting-well present" to his wife while she convalesced after the automobile accident she had suffered, but Rogers also told his secretary to enter the purchases on his books as investments. In addition, he gave her $49,500 in cash. Millicent challenged both the jewelry and the cash.[13] She claimed the money was a loan and should be repaid to the estate. Needless to say, she had broken off friendly relations with Pauline after the will was offered for probate. Next she went after the Southampton property, The Port of Missing Men. The Colonel had stipulated that if Pauline did not occupy The Port for longer than six months, it would go to Peter. Pauline claimed that she had been unable to occupy the house because Colonel Rogers had made no provision to maintain it. The five thousand dollars she had won by court order for that purpose, she claimed, was insufficient. Millicent, with a raptor's speed and intent, contended that Pauline failed to file an intention to occupy the estate and had as a result forfeited her life rights to the property. In fact, Pauline had filed her intention, but at the very end, the 179th day of the 180-day period. Millicent declared that this last-minute act was insufficient. She lost that claim.

In the "Caviar and Cordials" society column of the *Journal*, columnist Reggie reported, "Never a dull moment in the H. H. Rogers will contest ... understand that the latest move by the estate will be a REFUSAL to pay any bills contracted By Mrs. H. H. Rogers while she was married to her husband. . . . This will tie up practically everyone concerned in the lawsuits ... it's this week's best bet that the main beneficiaries of the estate will be the LAWYERS ... as has been the case in SO MANY large estate settlements."[14]

CHAPTER THIRTEEN

Wills as Weapons

THE ROGERS BEGAN TO ASSUME A NEW ROLE IN THE PUBLIC consciousness during the mid-1930s. Scandals, large and small, plagued them. A year before the Colonel's death there was a shooting in the wee hours of the morning at the The Port of Missing Men that wounded the butler and sent women in evening gowns and men in white tie scurrying for cover. According to the papers, it was a brawl between "the upper crust and the 'below stairs' people." The missteps, intrigues, and indiscretions of the powerful rich were quickly masked by decorum and money.

The same year Millicent's brother, Henry, made headlines when the musical comedy star, Evelyn Hoey, the toast of Broadway that year, turned up dead in his Indian Run farmhouse near West Chester, Pennsylvania. He had experienced great difficulty making a life in the shadow of his successful, hard, and hard-living father. To escape his playboy image, he told some friends, he was going to start at the bottom and work his way up, and he got a job as an electrical engineer with a transmission company in Cleveland, Ohio. Henry seemed to be on a stable course when he married Virginia Lincoln, a pretty society girl, whose father was a prominent physician in Cleveland.[1]

But Henry soon tired of the electrical work and quit to produce motion picture shorts from New York. There were whispers that he was involved in pornography. His drinking, public outbursts, and out-of-bounds behavior had already alienated him from his father after the Colonel's wedding to Pauline Dresser. Then during a weekend in 1935 when his wife went home to visit family in Cleveland, Henry III went off to a farm he owned in Pennsylvania. Evelyn Hoey was one of his weekend guests. After a boisterous drinking party Evelyn was found shot to death and Henry and two male companions were investigated by the police.

One friend, William J. Kelly, was charged and granted bail under suspicion of murder. Both men were exonerated when the authorities ruled that Evelyn had committed suicide, but the case took its toll on Henry's already troubled reputation both within and outside the family. A report from the investigation alleged that when he and Evelyn arrived at Indian Farm he had taken a photo of another girl out of his luggage and provocatively placed it on the dresser in his bedroom. A quarrel and heavy drinking ensued, and the young actress dashed upstairs in the farmhouse to shoot herself in a spasm of jealous passion. Henry collapsed over the incident and sought seclusion in a sanitarium, but he pulled himself together in time to challenge his father's will.[2]

Perhaps ill-advisedly, young Rogers decided to take on his widowed stepmother. He claimed Pauline had exerted "undue influence" on his father when they were honeymooners and he appealed to have his father's estate redistributed to himself, Pauline, and Millicent. His contest would have cost Peter Salm one third of the proceeds from his grandfather's estate. Millicent filed an answer to his appeal in which she stated that to her knowledge, her stepmother exercised no undue influence on her father. She had clearly decided to protect her son's interests over her brother's. It was also apparent that her own interests were aligned more closely with her son. As Peter's guardian, Millicent had the liberty of dipping into his earnings from his trust fund or drawing down the principal on his behalf outright. She would also have the use of The Port of Missing Men, valued in the newspaper at the time at $15 million.

Then, in one of the stranger twists during the many courtroom dramas that unfolded surrounding the Colonel's will, his second and ex-wife, the former Marguerite Miles, "Daisy," as she now called herself, showed up in court to support young Henry. She made a dramatic appearance, wearing a dark wide-brimmed hat and fur-collared coat, to testify on behalf of her former stepson's plea for exemption from paying twenty-five thousand dollars that his father's estate claimed from him.[3]

During the same year, 1937, the Colonel's widow Pauline remarried another New York socialite, Walter Hoving, president of the Lord & Taylor department store, who would eventually head Tiffany and Co.[4] As Millicent had, Pauline took refuge in the next marriage, that convention by which society women advanced or at least found a safe harbor from unflattering publicity and financial uncertainty, much like the heroines in novels of the period. Her marriage to Hoving put an end to the battle over The Port of Missing Men, which reverted to Peter and his guardian, Millicent.

A challenge to Millicent came promptly after her father's death, from another quarter. Count Salm reappeared, asking the New York Supreme Court to appoint a guardian for the estate of his son Peter.[5] His petition conceded that Millicent had lived up to the divorce decree regarding Peter's upbringing, religion, and visitation requirements, but it asked that a guardian be appointed for the boy's property. The petition was made during one of Peter's visits to his father in Austria and seemed a hasty gambit by Salm to lay claim to some of the Rogers' money, this time the five million dollars that his son's guardian would have control over.

Salm pulled no punches in the application to remove Millicent as guardian. He described his ex-wife as "inexperienced and helpless" in financial matters. "She has been since the day of her appointment and probably will continue to be an absentee guardian. She very recently arrived in this country from Austria and I am informed that she expects to return to that country or elsewhere abroad soon." Millicent and her attorney came back swinging, claiming that Salm's challenge was little more than an attempt to gain control over Peter's inherited property. Their response that the Count's right of visitation "does not absolve Count Salm from the obligation of supporting the boy, she said, but she and her late father found it necessary to assume the obligation," seemed to settle the matter.[6]

Millicent and the Manhattan attorney who had been appointed co-guardian for Peter asked the courts for cash payment of the one-third share of the trust fund willed to him by his grandfather. Under the Colonel's will, Peter could not touch the principal until he came of age, making the integrity and ability of the overseer to manage the money for the next ten years an important consideration The fund earned income of approximately $175,000 annually for the young heir.[7]

Furthermore, Colonel Rogers, by specifying that all inheritance taxes and expenses should be paid out of the capital of his estate, seriously strapped his heirs. Estimates of the main estate varied wildly, but *The New York Times* in a detailed account said that the total estate was $17,100,000, and that the Colonel's will specified that all taxes had to be paid before the proceeds went to his heirs. Those taxes were more than $13 million.[8] A separate trust of about $9 million left by H. H. Rogers softened the blow, but it, too, was subject to taxes. Millicent was left with one third of the proceeds from these two sources, which was about $3 million. Liquid assets were becoming scarce. The tax bill threatened to exhaust the estate to the point that there would not be enough money to create the new trusts that were intended to produce income for the heirs.

These courtroom scenes and appeals pitted almost all family members against each other in often Byzantine ways. There seemed no end to the permutations and perambulations of taxes and money, inheritance and divorce. A whole new Millicent, quite different from the languid and diffident beauty so often photographed at other stages in her well-publicized life, angrily pointed a finger to wave aside courtroom photographers who snapped her as she left the court in Riverhead, Long Island, where she sought to win custodial rights to the estate left by her father for her son. There would be no reprieve from the financial and legal agendas.

Money, so enabling and wonderful on one hand, now had shown its ugly face, casting doubt on nearly all the relationships Millicent had known. It had been almost comic when so many unknown European noblemen had proposed to her in pursuit of her millions fifteen years earlier. It had been sobering when her father had managed to buy off her first husband and his family, and to some degree her own young romantic self. The reasons for Peralta-Ramos's disaffection also came into question when her inheritance diminished. She had attacked the stepmother whose wedding dinner she had once so graciously given, and her own brother was now her enemy in court. If she ever had, she could no longer pretend that her relationships to others could be separated from money. It was an end of innocence. She would always now look at people, family, friends, and lovers, through a different scrim of understanding and wonder who her true friends were. Her money unquestionably controlled the dynamic of her marriage. When Ronnie spotted a luxury Delage sport coupe in 1937 in Paris, he appealed to Millicent to buy it. She said no. But the following year she went ahead and bought it, after having it modified to her style specifications. She held the purse strings.

It is no wonder that Millicent embraced living in Europe. With Mary's homes in Paris and Venice and her own in St. Anton, she could leave some of the scalding effects of the invasive publicity behind and retreat, richer or poorer, to a more controllable and perfect world in the snow-covered mountains of St. Anton.

CHAPTER FOURTEEN

Expat Idyll

MILLICENT'S YEARS IN AUSTRIA IN THE VALLEY OF the Arlberg mountains, as recorded in the photo albums that she carefully kept, have a particular glow about them. In many of the candid snapshots she is smiling, in marked contrast to the stern, somber-faced poses she struck for the fashion magazine photographers. In Austria, her three sons were often photographed by her side. Posed on one of the several balconies at Shulla House, they looked like an abbreviated version of the von Trapp family. Millicent typically dressed the part and sported white peasant blouses under dirndl dresses. She was often photographed flanked by Ronnie Balcom and Rudi Matt. Both men are tanned and square-jawed and the threesome looked more like movie stars than common citizens. It's no surprise that Millicent caught the eye of the expatriate crowd and became a style icon. Most afternoons she had tea at the Post Hotel in the village. In her stylish clothes and dark glasses, she attracted the attention of tourists and fashion professionals alike. Her charisma was noted back in New York.

Millicent may have sought peace in distance from her family's legal squabbles and the probing press in the United States, but she was not isolated from the American scene. Her friend Diana Vreeland visited her in Austria, and upon her return to New York featured Millicent in the pages of *Harper's Bazaar*. Mrs. Ronald Balcom was, according to the article, ". . . Perfected, but ever changing. Creative in her approach to life. Many women have acquired taste; she has it by instinct . . . Byzantinely beautiful, independent in taste, she has a real sixth sense for clothes." Beneath the photos of the interior of her Austrian house, the Schonbrunn serving set of dishes, her Biedermeier beds and furnishings, a Viennese harpsichord and green porcelain stove, the article rhapsodized on her life. Purred the reporter: "She follows the snows with the seasons and spends almost seven months of the year on skis. She has not one little dachshund, but eight. . . ." *Vogue* chimed in: "In a winter of pretty froufrou, she passes up the houps and bouffants for her own soignée school of dressing. Schiaparelli suits are her uniform."[1] *Vogue* had already described her as "incredibly soignée." *Soignée* was the working word. The magazines clearly considered her quite sublime.

Even in Paris, unquestionably the center of the fashion world at the time, Millicent made an impression. "Paris stood up and took notice when Millicent Rogers arrived. They thought she was the first real American woman with any style," said Horst, the iconic fashion photographer who photographed Millicent in many designer gowns. The "very visible Americans in the Paris fashion world that the public emulated included Millicent Rogers (then Mrs. Ronald Balcom) . . ." wrote Eleanor Dwight in her biography of Vreeland. *Vogue's* Paris editor Bettina Ballard explained the influence that a stylish rich society woman could exert on style trends: "Women of fashion were . . . dictators in the sense of a luxurious and capricious way of life." The social standing of these women depended "on their power to make others emulate the way they dressed or entertained or talked and on their ability to make fashionable the people and the places they preferred." Wallis Simpson, the commoner for whom the King of England (had he been the source of the teenage Millicent's "English kisses?") gave up his crown, was so inspired by Millicent's mix of Tyrolean and designer clothes that she commissioned Schiaparelli and Mainbocher to make Tyrolean outfits for her honeymoon.[2] A shop specializing in Austrian clothing soon opened in Paris. Babs Simpson, editor of *Vogue* after Millicent's heyday, was very much aware of her impact. "I greatly admired her because she was a great beauty photographed by everyone, and I thought her creativity was wonderful. People who had money dressed well because they bought their clothes in Paris. It was taken for granted that they dressed beautifully, like running a house well was taken for granted, but Millicent was admired for her creativity. Today we forget that people lived very conventional lives then. They didn't expect to do things differently, but *she* did."[3]

In a world parallel to the fashion centers and arbiters, domestic life took on a kind of normality for Millicent and her family at Shulla House. Millicent's three sons liked Ronald Balcom, their new stepfather.[4] In some ways he was like the father they had never fully had, and was widely considered a wonderful man, warm and athletic, who looked after them when they were home to visit. Younger than both their mother and respective fathers, he was less self-absorbed and more accessible. On the scene when the boys were home from boarding schools in Austria and Switzerland, Ronnie often took them skiing and biking, and for several years they operated like a genuine family. Arturo had started out cool to his stepfather, but more of his resentment was directed at his mother, who infuriated him when she changed her name from Peralta-Ramos to Balcom. Eventually he was won over by Ronnie's open manner and good spiritedness. He was remembered in his paternal role as "a nice guy" even when Arturo itemized his shortcomings as his mother's husband.

Balcom and Millicent led a somewhat charmed life, or so it seemed from the outside. Though Millicent's legal battles dragged on with lawyers in New York, she and her third husband spent most of their time quietly in the Arlbergs. They lunched on the sunny decks of Gstaad, overlooking the snow and peaks that surrounded them, and for contrast they skipped over to Paris where Mary Rogers kept a house or dropped down to stay in her palazzo on the canals in Venice where they were likely to see Valentina, George Schlee, Noël Coward, Barbara Hutton, Iris Mountbatten, and Harry Bull, the editor of *Town & Country* magazine. The smart set in prewar Europe frequented the Grand Hotel or rented apartments in Venice for the season. Lanfranco Rasponi, a society writer and performing arts reviewer, was there and wrote about it in his biography, *The International Nomads*, forty years later. He recalled "Millicent Rogers, one of the most bewitching creatures ever to grace society . . ."

Her sons would warmly remember the summers they spent with Mary in Venice where a staff of eight tended to them and their grandmother's houseguests. Millicent always took a governess along for the boys, but there were a number of people among the adults they looked forward to seeing. Van Day Truex was there and the boys considered him to be a relative. They preferred his company to their governess's.

Truex had risen by this time to be director of the Parson's School of Design in Paris and was also a great favorite of the style doyenne Lady Mendl (formerly, Elsie de Wolfe). Millicent's immediate life during these years seemed charmed, and spilled over with interesting people and experiences. The struggle for survival that the Great Depression was causing for most Americans at home was remote from the luxurious living in Shulla House, Venice, and Paris.

Yet Millicent was aware of shortages in the lives of those surrounding her. She extended herself in her small alpine community, which aside from the skiers and rich tourists eked out a bare livelihood. The kitchen of Shulla House became something of a soup kitchen for needy villagers. At Christmas she loved playing the part of lady bountiful, inviting village children and their families to her house to enjoy the festive decorations, food, and beautifully wrapped presents that she handed out freely. She became known locally for her kindhearted generosity to anyone in need.[5] But this respite of happiness would soon be sabotaged by things unpredictable and beyond the remedy of money: War and illness.

The expatriate Americans lived the high life until they could no longer ignore what was happening in Europe. In 1933 Hitler had become Führer. Then in 1935 he denounced the Versailles Treaty which limited Germany's remilitarization after the first world war. In 1937 German air forces and Spanish rebels destroyed Guernica, Spain. The Nuremberg Laws forbade intermarriage between Aryans and Jews. For anyone keeping track, the signs were ominous. Yet almost everyone hung on to the European idyll.

Millicent's sense of home in Austria, a carefully controlled little universe created to suit her down to almost every detail in her house set amid so much natural beauty, was palpable. In a letter to her friend William Jones Allen, who was in the European division of the State Department in Washington in 1937, she wrote of traveling back to Nasserein from Paris on Christmas Eve. Glowingly, she recounted her homecoming. The boys had been fetched back from school and were there to meet her at Shulla House "round and smiling." She described how the servants and houseguests were clutching two dachshunds under each arm when she arrived at the door. "The snow is powder and the weather's cold, clear, and clean. My darling, the mountains are beautiful, if not more beautiful than ever, more beautiful I think for one realizes that we will not have them long with the world going on as it is."

She was beginning to feel uneasy: "Bill, Bill, will nobody realize anything, will no one see what is going on in Germany, the undercover Nazi world, the spying . . ." She told the story of her journey back to Austria. "The officials were as usual polite at the border and looked into everything with their usual Austrian charm," she wrote, but she quickly took note when they "asked me whether I had enjoyed the Venetian summer (How do you suppose they knew?)" They asked whether she was staying as usual in St. Johann and she replied, a bit defiantly, that naturally she was staying "all winter and probably next summer, too."[6] Their queries included a question about the arrival of a routine houseguest, whom she explained was staying in Washington working on the "Europe situation." There were murmurings about the Nazi threat.

In a provocative ending, she wrote, "Darling, I wish you were here with me. But I shall write you all I see and hear and it will be the next best thing." Whether her sentiment was romantic, or she was subtly volunteering to be an informant, her suggestions were intriguing.[7]

Millicent seemed to be a step ahead of her mother and other wealthy Americans in Europe, who did not want to think about war. Adam Lewis in his biography of Van Day Truex noted that Mary Rogers and Lady Mendl, as late as Easter in 1939, believed "if only no one would talk about the war, it would not happen." Many Americans shared the illusion. In a like manner, the citizens of Venice not only shut their minds to the thought of war, but also closed the shutters of their windows to avoid the sight of Joseph Goebbels when he visited their city. "They tried not to see the Nazi flags fluttering from every gondola and bridge during his procession down the Grand Canal."[8]

Millicent stayed as long as she could in Europe, but at the end of 1937 she sensed that political unrest would bring her stay in Austria to an end. She insisted that her mother and Van Day Truex come for Christmas at Shulla House with her, Ronnie, and the three boys. She consulted with Truex about which of her Biedermeier furnishings she should ship back to the United States. He advised her to send everything back to the U.S. and work out details with a decorator when she got there.[9] They celebrated Christmas with Millicent's typical lavishness, inviting the villagers in for food and gaily wrapped presents. Mary declared that she would not tolerate any talk of war. Lady Mendl, who lived at the Villa Trianon outside Paris, announced that she had no intention of ever leaving.

In 1938 the political situation worsened when German forces annexed Czechoslovakia, but the expat aristocrats wanted to believe Neville Chamberlain when he declared, "I believe it is peace for our time. . . ." Soon all the expats would have to revise their convictions.

Millicent, a more astute student of history and politics, knew better. When the brown shirts marched into the center of St. Anton and a Nazi took the podium, she snapped a photo of them for posterity and began to plan her exit. She paid none of the bills sent to her the next year in Austria and assumed responsibility for the bills owed by her neighbors. A large debt accumulated over the course of the next year. When Hitler actually marched into Vienna, as she had expected, a Nazi official purchased her house and then informed Millicent that the money could not be taken out of the country. She applied the money received for the house to the bills that she had cleverly assumed, and her own debts, and the accounts were almost even.[10] The German annexation of Austria the prior spring had stiffened her resolve. Suddenly the turmoil of Europe was all around.

By some accounts, Millicent stayed longer in war-threatened Europe than was prudent. Her affection for Austria and a certain reluctance, some say stubbornness, to bow to political authority seemed to determine her actions. When the Nazi flag was hoisted near her house in St. Anton she erected a taller flagpole on her property with the American flag. On several occasions she stood down the Gestapo officer sent to order her to take it down. She claimed that since she owned the property it was American soil where her house sat. She also delayed her departure in order to help set in motion rescue routes and escapes for Jewish friends and acquaintances whose plight had come to her attention. She arranged to pay off the Swiss border patrol who were under German directives to turn back Austrian Jews who fled into Switzerland across the Alps. Her old friends in the Ciano family in Italy, whose young scion had once proposed to her, helped her carry out her plan. She also tapped her good friend, Margaret Mallory, whose family owned Mallory Shipping Lines in Italy, to acquire space on the company's tankers for her stowaways.[11]

Then failing health converged with political causes to set the pace of her own departure. She had suffered a small heart attack in Paris in 1938, causing her to fall back on her mother's help and requiring that she limit her exertions and convalesce when she returned to

Austria several weeks later. The episode was another incentive for her to prepare to return to the United States, but she was also increasingly concerned for the welfare of her son Peter.

Peter had been born in the United States, but his Austrian parentage and the fact that her divorce from Salm had specified that he would be educated in Europe had become a matter of concern. She was not certain that a belligerent Germany would honor his American citizenship, so as soon as Germany moved into Austria she quietly transferred Peter to school in Switzerland, where Arturo and Paul were already enrolled. She may have had other things to fear. Arturo says she was involved in hiding the son of Austrian chancellor Kurt von Schuschnigg when the Germans moved into Austria and deposed Schuschnigg during the *Anschluss* in the spring of 1938.[12]

The previous month another challenge had come from France. Count Salm, apparently broke, had legally appealed to his son for an allowance of $20,000 a year and an extra $10,000 annually to cover the expenses of Peter's visits to him. Peter's estate was valued at $3,250,000. Salm claimed in an affidavit, "I am 53 years of age and have recently and suddenly as the result of political upheaval in Austria, sustained severe, financial reverses, which have deprived me not only of my capital resources but, as well, of the means of earning an income." He had moved to France because of the war and stated that his seventy-five-year-old mother and he wanted to see Peter much more frequently. Ever since his divorce from Millicent, he had been allowed a week with Peter every month and a month during the summer. To the Count's appeal for money the Supreme Court Justice in New York supported Millicent in ruling, "Scraped of all camouflage this is an attempt by the father to be 'declared in' on his son's estate." His request was denied.[13] This latest appeal seemed dangerously acquisitive to Millicent who, having sent Peter to Switzerland, stepped up plans for her own departure from Austria.

Even nature seemed to conspire to unsettle her life at this time. Back in Southampton the Great Hurricane of 1938 had seriously damaged The Beach House that her parents had created to such acclaim in 1919. The record storm that savaged the New England coastline had left the once glorious estate uninhabitable and any return to Southampton would be to The Port of Missing Men that now belonged to Peter, and her as his guardian. Yet she did not want to make her new American home at The Port of Missing Men. She harbored negative feelings about her domineering father's life there, and after years of use and the hurricane, even though it was set farther inland than The Beach House, it needed work.[14] She would continue to spend time at "The Port," as family and friends referred to it, but it was not to be her true home ever again. She and her mother had rented a house in Gloucester, Massachusetts, the previous summer, while the fate of "The Port" was still in doubt because of the dispute with her stepmother Pauline. As was their wont, they quickly took charge in Gloucester and hired a landscaper to replant the gardens with the flowers they preferred. As usual, they left the property better than they had found it, and to their own liking. They also provided their own hemstitched sheets, so accustomed were they to their own brand of domestic luxuries.

Millicent had kept an apartment in New York during her years in Europe, but the threat of war had shifted her focus. Like many fashionable New Yorkers during the war, she cast her gaze on the capital. Washington, D.C., now the focus of world power with a sense of purpose and swagger, was the next happening place to be.

She and Ronnie made several trips to Washington during the next year. While staying at the Shoreham Hotel, they were entertained by her cousin Robert Coe, who worked for the State Department. It did not escape *The Washington Post* that Millicent had been spotted looking for a house to buy.

Millicent hoped to hang onto some of the gracious country living she had become so attached to in Austria, and a bit like Marie Antoinette's overprecious visions for the Trianon, she had a vision of a country life in which she could live off the land during wartime. A Tidewater estate 170 miles from Washington caught her fancy. She envisioned making it into a working farm with cows, pigs, and chickens on the property so she would not be dependent on wartime rationing. Even after the *Anschluss*, when war did not openly break out, Millicent returned to Austria, but it was not until Paris fell to the Germans in June of 1940 that she joined the exodus of rich American expats who headed home and uprooted her family.

Pandemonium had hit the booking offices and ocean liner companies. Millicent was unable to get reservations for her sons, herself, her husband, and the staff that would travel home with them. So she sent Peter, Arturo, and Paul with their nurse on a Cunard White Line ship from Paris, while she and Ronnie traveled to Lisbon to catch a boat from there. Millicent's pack of dachshunds, which had grown to sixteen, were sent with Dade and the boys. Each of her sons was given a teddy bear to carry with a stern warning never to let it out of his sight. Peter, sixteen at the time, and Arturo, thirteen, carried them grudgingly. When their ship docked at New York Harbor, a family retainer was on the dock waiting for them. The attending staffer immediately took the teddy bears from the boys and stashed them safely in the car before turning his attention to greeting the weary young travelers, recalls Arturo. Millicent, it seems, had sewn a fortune's worth of jewelry into the bellies of the bears, keeping them safe from customs officers and wartime authorities.[15]

CHAPTER FIFTEEN

To the Manor

MILLICENT ALIGHTED ON AMERICAN SHORES WITH A new creative vision for her life. Claremont Manor, a seventeenth-century Tidewater estate on the south shore of the James River in Surry, Virginia, in the shadow of Richmond, became her new stage. Fashionable New Yorkers and Washingtonians had adopted the region for its proximity to Washington, D.C., and its relative economy compared to Long Island and Newport. Claremont Manor was considered one of the loveliest private properties in the country, a house where every U.S. president since the Civil War was said to have been a guest in what *The Washington Post* called the "oldest large house in America." The land, received in a Virginia Colony land grant in 1621, adjoined the old tobacco plantation belt. Its colonial garden and lawns extended for twelve acres and the entire three-hundred-acre property ran for a mile and a half along the waterfront. Daffodils and magnolias bloomed by the acre in spring. The house, dating from 1750, was originally copied from Claremont Mansion in England, home of the Duke of Kent, father of Queen Victoria. Grand, gracious, and exquisitely beautiful, and poised on a terraced lawn a hundred feet above the river, it exerted a strong attraction on Millicent. She and Ronnie had originally shopped for a house in Washington, but at the last moment Millicent was captivated by the historic estate.

Almost from the moment she saw it she had a vision of what her life could be there. She engaged the highly regarded architect William Lawrence Bottomley, famous for his restoration and design work in Colonial Williamsburg and other classic residential architecture, to upgrade the building. He had designed modern additions to Claremont Manor for its previous owners in the 1920s. Bottomley's genius was his ability to install a contemporary floor plan within a classical shell that reflected the architectural traditions and preferences of the region. He was the perfect choice for Millicent's undertaking to make Claremont Manor a grand property that could house her European furniture and art collections and be the seat of an American lifestyle to rival her gracious household in Austria. The slave quarters on the property became guesthouses, and the little office, a relic of plantation days from which the overseer tended to business, she converted into a music library. She added a greenhouse, tennis courts, and a pool. Possibly she was reaching for even more in Claremont, since she no longer had a true claim to The Port of Missing Men as she had before her father's death, and Claremont, with its gardens and classic architecture, promised to be an American setting for the kind of life she had known in her youth.

Bottomley removed the Greek Revival porch and replaced it with a stone landing and steps. A paneled chimney breast was designed for the north side of the porch chimney where Millicent installed one of her beloved porcelain stoves from Austria in a curved alcove. A spiral cherry staircase was added to dramatically fill a whole wall between the chimney and the west wall of the south wing. A modern feature, an elevator, was added to the basement dining room and cleverly concealed inside an armoire on the north wall. The biggest triumph was a sunken paved area outside the dining room, accessed by French doors.[1] Millicent envisioned gracious dining and entertaining in her pale blue dining room accented with cerise, while outside, the grounds fulfilled their bucolic role in her scenario by producing fresh vegetables and eggs.

She seemed to have an ulterior motive as well. Her marriage to Ronnie was unraveling under the pressure of relocation and the return to American life. In Claremont she saw the makings of a new beginning and something of a retreat.

She meticulously redecorated the house. "Everywhere the collector's hand is in evidence, deliberate, distinguished, sure," wrote a reviewer, adding, "the house reflects the worldliness, the eclectic taste of its much-travelled present owner." From Paris she had brought her beloved Watteau, Fragonard, and Boucher drawings, *gros-point* rugs, crystal lustres, and girandoles. She hung French modern paintings in clusters, a somewhat new decorating conceit. Van Day Truex came to help her augment and locate her much-admired Biedermeier furniture, and a striped sitting room with beaded needlepoint cushions arranged on a pullman-brown velvet sofa was admired and photographed by decorators and design publications. The needlepoint rugs and a footstool were her own handiwork. Much as she had mixed dress designers and her own tastes to arrive at a unique reduction, so she consulted with Truex and their mutual designer friend Billy Baldwin. "I consider it a desecration in Virginia to change even one single architectural detail," she told Baldwin. Perfectionist that she was, she delegated to him, "Inside, you can do whatever you want because that is entirely up to you; you're going to see it, and you're responsible." She ended up with a palatial home that embodied the essence of her style.[2]

Millicent brought several aspirations to Claremont Manor that were not shaped by the architecture. With her marriage to Ronnie ending, Claremont would be the first household that she would create and live in as an unmarried woman. It would be a harbor for herself and her sons during the war years. She purchased tractors and trucks in order to begin the farming and livestock operations she envisioned to sustain them. More predictably, she envisioned the house as a spectacular stage on which to entertain wartime Washington. She would import many of the same guests that she had known and entertained in Southampton and Europe. Politicians, spies, designers, actors, writers, and socialites of all stripes would dine and party at Claremont.

A worrisome new theme—her health—was also beginning to be prominent in her life. As the frequency of her bouts with illness were increasing, the house and its peaceful grounds would also provide a place for her to convalesce.

Her neighbors and the townspeople of Surry often saw her walking the road along the river, peacefully strolling the groves and gardens, usually by herself, and always well dressed. In warm weather she invited her neighbors' children to swim in her pool. The larger-than-life socialite, who seemed to the press never to step off the social merry-go-round, had in fact, as was sometimes evident in Austria, a real fondness for outdoor beauty and quiet domestic pleasures. Her letters to her mother during the first few years at Claremont are full of animated descriptions of her garden, the spring plantings and willow tree buds. Honeyman, her lawn man, cut her honeysuckle by mistake, "when I wasn't looking," she wrote. "I'm having a fit. He will have to replace it with Jasmine."[3]

Living in the quietly gorgeous countryside gave her a chance to evaluate her life. It was not always easy to reconcile the high-flying society woman and the other, earthier soul. In one particularly soulful dispatch telling of her fondness and focus on the grounds and plantings, she wrote to her mother as if with an inaudible sigh, "I might have had another life." Whether less money, a better defined direction, the right marriage partner, or a single focus on design would have made the difference, she didn't say. What is noteworthy at this juncture is that she was reflecting on her purpose, the life that she had lived so far, and the future. She never gave up on the future.

Her independence predictably found a new expression in fashion. At Claremont Manor Millicent strove to once again re-create her wardrobe to match her surroundings. She reached out to the designer Mainbocher, who created ornate upholstered dresses for her. Rather than dirndls, she commissioned big full skirts and voluminous-sleeved blouses with ruffled and tassled collars to suit her newly elegant but pastoral surroundings. They hearkened back to the era of her Biedermeier furniture. Ever an original, she might have been offended if one had compared her to the heroine of the book that was sweeping the country, Gone with the Wind, but her big skirts and pinafore bodices definitely suggested a couturiered Scarlett O'Hara look. Her bucolic indulgences, a bit precious, were more in the manner of Marie Antoinette. She may have taken a hint from her mother's friend, Lady Mendl, the fashion doyenne she had observed in Paris, who attracted fashionable France with her lunches and parties at the Villa Trianon before the war. But Millicent needed no model. She had her own knack for gracious style and luxurious living.

Despite Millicent's energetic attempts to change and to re-create her life, the dissonant state of her health began to interfere more and more with her activities. Her weak heart faltered under stress, and sabotaged her efforts to move forward decisively. What seems truly admirable is the way she managed to roll with the episodes, as though they were merely inconveniences that with patience and proper accommodation would soon pass. She learned to live with them.

She invariably turned her bedridden stretches into productive periods for self-improvement or inquisition. As a young girl she had learned languages and drawing. Later in life she designed jewelry. During one hospitalization she took the opportunity to deepen her understanding of music. In a Virginia hospital she quickly perceived that her floormates were a deaf man and a woman whose only passion was listening to the Amos 'n Andy Show on the radio, so she had her maid bring in the "Marconiphone" and spent several days immersed in the records Mary, a true music lover, had sent. Up to that point she had not been a fan of Bach, but in writing to her mother, she declared she was now a convert. Her only complaint was of visitors who told her not to turn down the music but then talked over it, "So one could not hear the music or what they were saying." She seemed never self-pitying.

"Believe me, there is an art to illness as to any great state of being," she wrote to her mother when Mary was suffering from a kidney infection. "One has to find the compensation, and then learn to accustom oneself to a new and different set of circumstances and reactions (mental and physical). For the always healthy person who finds himself ill, he must take stock of himself and make peace with things that he usually passes by, with no time to consider."[4]

In 1941 Millicent suffered a small stroke and found it necessary to check in as a patient at the Medical College of Virginia in Richmond. In a letter to her mother she wrote, "Dr. Higgins is pleased with me. I'll have to take it a little easier." She recalled a previous episode with her heart. "Not everything seemed to come together the last time. War, business, holidays, and houseparties. We hope it won't be like that this time." She had hopes of making a quick recovery but wrote several weeks later, still in the hospital, "I don't know when they will let me out of here and I don't really care. It seems as though all the tiredness which has been accumulating like old furniture in an attic is just beginning to ooze out of every pore. And I lie on my bed doing nothing, watching the river. I don't know how I ever could have gotten so tired... I didn't want to stay and then I felt better. Now that I have begun to relax it doesn't seem as though I've sat down in the past ten years. And I don't want to read or see anyone or discuss anything. I suppose pretty soon I'll begin to come to again."

Her illness illuminated the widening fissures in her marriage: "... it's tight nerves when Ronnie comes and then utter flatness... I do wish Ronnie would relax and stop fussing—anyone would think he carried the weights of the governments on his shoulders. If it isn't Rosie [one of her dogs] peeing it's the awful expense of having a house in Washington and me in the hospital. He won't go quietly down and live in the house. Instead of coming up here and fussing about things hasn't entered his head and if I told him he'd be offended or something for Washington isn't as gay as New York (the elegance and chic?!x!!) are lacking. I wish he'd take a little trip. I think it would do us both good." In the same letter she made clear that her marital distemper was deeper than these minor frustrations. "I wonder how long it will last. Not long if it wasn't for the children . . . I guess it's my fault for I should have known better than to do it in the first place and I have to pay for it now. And get along the best I can. There isn't any explaining such things is there?" She told a story to illustrate Ronnie's lack of sensitivity: She had had a sore foot over the summer that she had asked him not to touch. "This last month I have one foot out of the bed. He takes it and squeezes . . . I've asked him not to touch it, as it gives me shivers up my spine. But like a naughty little boy he can't resist. . . . It's his way of being affectionate, but it does something to me. Yesterday he squeezed it and put a pencil between the toes and I burst into tears."[5] In other correspondence and remarks to family members she mocked him for calling her Mary Mil. *Yes, Mary Mil this and yes, Mary Mil that.* His solicitousness worked against him. She criticized him now for having few opinions of his own. Despite his overall congeniality, she had come to consider him simply not smart enough for her.

Family and friends could see that Balcom bored her. Handsome and well-dressed, he looked the part for a man—or accessory—in her life, but he was not, she complained, interested in the arts, theater, or paintings. He cared mostly for sports and athletics. "He just wasn't intellectual or edgy enough for her," explained her son Arturo. He uncharitably added, in hindsight, that Balcom was a "wimp," and a "yes man." Others described Balcom as the kind of man who could talk about his golf game through a whole dinner party. Paul, Millicent's youngest son, philosophized some years after about the breakup of Millicent and her last husband: "They couldn't get along." Asked of her breakup with his father: "They couldn't get along." Of her first marriage to Count Salm, he answered wryly, ". . . they couldn't get along."[6] Millicent, it was noted by others, "was no easy wife."[7] She lived with an unflagging sense of drama and intensity. She was used to getting her way. She had learned how to bicker and quarrel at the feet of her quarrelsome parents and continued the tradition. Her poor health, requiring a partner's patience and solicitude, created a great sense of urgency around her when she was well, and she was always prone to romantic extravagance. She never broke. Arturo, her last living son, cannot remember ever seeing her break down and cry.

After the New Year rang in 1941, Ronnie easily returned to his life in café society. He retreated to skiing in Sun Valley, Idaho, and six weeks later filed for divorce in Boise. The charge was cruelty, common grounds for getting a divorce when there was no other legally acceptable reason. Within weeks he was pictured side by side on the sunny ski slopes with his old chum the actress Claudette Colbert. He hardly seemed to miss a beat in rejoining the world he had frequented before their marriage. He would be photographed on the dance floor with Norma Shearer and appear in a *Life* magazine feature on Palm Beach highlighting a community centered around fine "homes, swimming pools, and private clubs." The model of gentlemanly discretion, he never talked much about the years he was married to Millicent. Even his next wife in 1946, Lucille Parsons Vanderbilt, says he hardly mentioned Millicent. She claims to have no idea of why he'd fallen in love with or married Millicent. She offered the age difference between Millicent and Balcom and Millicent's heart trouble as reasons for strain in their marriage. He jumped into a lasting marriage with another rich woman in marrying Vanderbilt, and the new twosome made a reputation for excellence at golf, tennis, and skiing. Even as a widow, Lucille pauses to recall her husband's "beautiful body." The public encounters between Ronnie, Lucille, and Millicent after his remarriage were a credit to good manners and social station. Everyone, according to Lucille, was "just lovely" to one another.[8]

After the divorce Millicent reverted to her maiden name and became Millicent Huttleston Rogers, often referred to in the press as Mrs. Huttleston Rogers. Her mother sometimes addressed her in their correspondence by her middle name, Abigail. They were fond of name play and Millicent sometimes signed her letters Mary Millicent, or Abigail, but Ronnie's use of Mary Mil and Milly had ruined those nicknames for her. In one postscript to her mother she noted, "I like the Abigail—But I do so *Hate* Milly." She would never be a Milly.

With her sons she had fun mocking how she had always been referred to in the papers as the Standard Oil Heiress. One Christmas her gifts were tagged "for the SOH."

Millicent's relationship with her mother had also evolved considerably. By the time of her return to the U.S. she was grudgingly close with Mary, who had been disapproving of her marriages and divorces yet was always willing to step in and help put the pieces of her daughter's life back together. Millicent did not need much emotional shoring up, but Mary helped her to organize her life. Mary had originally been quite ambitious for her daughter. It was important to her to have the good opinion of society. At heart a conservative, she did not like scandal. Consistent with her opinionated nature, Mary couldn't keep secret what she thought, and could be piercingly critical. She was an imperious scold, often lecturing Millicent on the importance of marriage and how to treat a husband.[9] Millicent, to the contrary, was generally not judgmental. When her mother told her that a friend had cheekily criticized how she had raised Millicent and her brother, and the lives they had led, Millicent jumped in generously to absolve and reassure her mother. "I think you make a mistake accusing yourself of failures that no one can remedy," she wrote. "Life is a series of cause and affects [sic]." Her letters to her mother and her sons were increasingly philosophical on matters as diverse as love and war.

Millicent's strongest, least compromising opinions were reserved for matters of style. In relationships, she tried to soothe rather than exacerbate differences. It was a skill she had developed as a survival tactic against her confrontational father. She intervened with flattery and a cool head when there was a difference of opinion with her designers or a harsh word between her critical mother and her sons. Now she seemed to complement her mother. Each compensated for what the other lacked. Mary was the saving grace for Millicent's sons, who counted on her for the summer vacations and niceties that their beautiful but often distracted mother would overlook.

Mary, too, had changed since her days as an aspiring society leader with grand gestures and parties as Mrs. Henry Huttleston

Rogers of Southampton in the 1920s. She was no longer the woman who marched into automobile showrooms and made high-handed demands. Her years and her associates in prewar Paris may have mellowed some of her more conservative notions. New York's high society had twirled its last waltz in prewar Europe. There was still, in the late thirties, an echo of Wilbur de Lyon Nichols's prescriptions for social aspirants at the turn of the century. Mary's friend Lady Mendl had remarked from her perch as hostess and style-setter in Paris, "Money, rather than family, is the watchword which now opens the gates. If one wishes to be in society one must have money and spend it—let society feed on it, drink it, and gamble with it. Then one can be anything, go anywhere, and do almost anything one wants. For the truth is that today society is bored with itself."[10] That may have been true. Society from Washington to Boston, with Philadelphia and New York in between, was still a short roster of three or four hundred families who had known each other for several generations and as one Southampton matron put it, "married their cousins." The coming war, thrusting European aristocrats and artists into American society, would bring about irrevocable change.

The bombing of Pearl Harbor in December of 1941 galvanized the country. Mary, who had been reluctant to contemplate war before, mobilized with Millicent for the war effort. They were determined to do everything they could to help. "Mary was charged with a spirit of patriotism. At the Christmas party she hosted, no one talked of anything but the war effort," wrote Van Day Truex, who, like all the rest of café society in Europe in the late thirties, had come home.

As Millicent's heart problems increased, so did her urgency for living. While she had immersed herself in the creation of a new life in Virginia, her comings and goings between Claremont Manor, Washington, and New York continued at a sometimes frantic pace during the war years. In photos she appeared a bit wan, her hair longer and straighter, more naturally styled. She was thinner and her brows, as she had begun to shape them in Europe, were dramatically plucked and pencilled in above their natural line. She seemed to be always on the move, and dressed the part of the busy professional woman in tailored suits and dresses when she appeared in town.

Her principal reason for spending so much time in New York was the Medical and Surgical Relief Committee (MSRC), which was no less an ongoing and helpful concern because it involved a number of socially prominent New Yorkers, and members of the medical community there. She rented an apartment on East Sixty-eighth Street in New York in order to create and oversee her newest pursuit and wartime effort. The committee was founded by her and a group of New York doctors in 1940 and she ran it as executive chairman. She was working in collaboration with well-known physicians and surgeons in New York, and it is of course easy to understand that she was valued for her ability to raise funds. What might have been less expected was that she rolled up her sleeves and involved herself in the daily grind.

The committee's first mission was to collect medical and surgical supplies for British field hospitals. But with America's entry into the war it began to collect and distribute serums, vitamins, surgery sets, medical aid kits, and drugs to war zone hospitals and ships of all the Allied nations. Millicent took on the job with a vengeance. The organization was her brainchild, and working with New York doctors and her own seed money, she managed to expand the MSRC nationwide until it operated in forty-four states. The MSRC volunteers chiefly combed the country for supplies, even writing the widows of doctors asking for instruments that were no longer in use and leftover drugs. It also clandestinely provided medical supplies to the French, Dutch, and Belgian underground operations, for which Millicent, according to Arturo, was offered the Legion of Honor ribbon from France in 1948. It is his understanding that the MSRC fronted underground operations in five European countries and was part of a larger "spiderweb" of spy and rescue activities. He vividly remembers the time in New York when she barred him from her apartment because she was hosting a secret meeting of the MSRC. She would not explain herself to him later.[II] The allegations are not that she was active in espionage but that she was a facilitator and a public front for some of the activities that were carried out by others.

When Millicent wasn't in New York she could be reached on a direct wire to her house in Virginia. She and the group's medical director, Dr. Joseph Peter Hoguet, made all the decisions of the operation. At its height the MSRC boasted six hundred volunteer workers. After the attack on Pearl Harbor volunteers flocked to be of service and a sense of mission motivated the American public to pitch in for the war effort.

Millicent worked long hours in the gray warehouse headquarters on Lexington Avenue in New York, her office piled high with boxes and metal trunks of supplies. In a precursor of the jewelry-designing fever that would overtake her creative interests shortly, she designed and patented an MSRC medical emblem for sale to raise money for the organization. The serious publicity surrounding her efforts began to add another layer of veneer to her image. *Vogue* and *Harper's Bazaar* covered her wartime efforts and this time she appeared a hardworking professional woman, inventorying prostheses in the MSRC warehouse and making business calls from her office. She posed for the newspapers in stylish but businesslike suits at her desk on the phone, her big bracelets pooled at her wrist. "Medical Supplies for the Allies," trumpeted one headline. "Today her big-knuckled sensitive hands are working for the Medical and Surgical Relief Committee," *Vogue* captioned one of her photos.

Millicent was captured at one point at the end of the day in her New York apartment posed with her feet tucked up underneath her on her red velvet sofa in a high-ceilinged living room decorated with a gold-bordered mirror beneath walls in various hues of green. She could never quite escape the halo of luxury and glamour. In a *Vogue* article entitled "In Defense of Working Wives" the author, Alfred L. Hall-Quest, prophesied a new kind of life in America "of a time when it is essential for every woman to be *of* the world. . . ." The piece prescribed

a new personality for women and its poster girl was, oddly enough—
Millicent. It is almost humorous by today's standards that a thrice-
divorced heiress, society woman, and fashion style-setter who didn't
truly work until she was nearly forty—or need to make a living—
would be celebrated as a model for married working women, but such
were the fantasies of women's magazines and the juxtapositions created
during the war years. She was photographed checking her clipboard,
inventorying the warehouse, and answering calls, rather than in the languid pleasure-puss poses of the past. Millicent surely worked hard.
She raised over a million dollars in donations for MSRC.

Her success was derived from her talent for organization and her
willingness to lean on people whom she knew she could count on for
support or money. Van Day Truex came to work with her and in return she went on the board of the Parsons School of Design, which
by then he was presiding over. She donated generously to Parsons and
when she heard that Truex and some of the faculty were going unpaid
as a result of the Depression economy and wartime cutbacks, she
stepped in with her checkbook to make sure that they received their
salaries.[12] She seemed to enjoy her influence, and the ability to make
a positive impact, albeit with money.

In an act of pure chutzpah, she wrote to President Franklin
Roosevelt, opening with an explanation that she was "the daughter of
your second cousin, Harry Rogers and a granddaughter of Mr. H. H.
Rogers of Fairhaven. There is no reason for you to remember me,
though you came to a dance for me at the Montgomery Club in 1919
from which your wife went home early leaving the home key in your
pocket. . . ." She sought his backing and to have a person assigned to
help the MSRC, "someone with the same ideas of unprejudiced far-
sightedness and sensible ideals who like yourself and Mr. Churchill
isn't afraid to see things as they are and doesn't cater to large organizations." She flattered him: ". . . It is a little unfair to want to ask you
to be on our board since you are President of this nation," she added,
having asked for his help in other ways. In closing she managed to
invoke the most blatant "we-are-the-same-kind of people" bond,

pointing back to their English and Dutch-based aristocracy: "the fact that our families have for 300 years sailed on the same ships, sat at the same church and town meetings, and understood each other's motives. With sincere regards, your kinswoman, Millicent Abigail Rogers."[13] In hindsight she was wonderfully persuasive and willful, and from a twenty-first century perspective, a bit comic. If there was a response, it is lost to history.

Millicent's sons did not make the transition to the United States as easily as their mother. Cosseted by European boarding schools and wealth, they were plainly out of sync and touch with mainstream American culture. Arturo claims that as their ship docked in New York he saw a black man for the first time and asked his governess, "Why doesn't that man wash?" Peter, the elder and a more conscientious student, was enrolled at the Groton School, where by coincidence he became friends with Diana Vreeland's son Tim. What Tim remembers was Peter's glamourous mother. The other young men had mothers who were stylish but matronly. They looked—well—like mothers. But when Peter set a fashionably posed photo of Millicent in which she looked like a movie star in his cubicle, his classmates asked rather breathlessly, "*Who* is that?" When his svelte mother arrived in her chauffeur-driven car to visit at school, invariably draped in furs, fine fashions, and jewelry, she caused a stir, fuelling what by his brother's accounts was an already strangely Oedipal relationship between mother and son.

"Peter was intimidated by her. And awed. He never got over it," says his brother Arturo. Peter was the serious son who seemed to always feel a sense of duty to his lineage on both sides of the ocean. He was a good student, a focused young man who felt a responsibility to live up to his inheritance and husband the property he had been left. He also straddled American and European cultures and society, never quite fitting in as a native son in either place. He looked up to his mother and sought out her guidance, which she readily offered in letters to him as he matured.

Arturo and Paul had a more difficult time fitting into American schools. The transition from Le Rosey in Switzerland to the Malcom Gordon School in Garrison-on-Hudson, New York, did not go smoothly. After the fall semester the director, Malcolm Gordon wrote to Millicent: "In making up my list of boys for next year, I feel quite strongly that it would be best for all concerned if your boys did not return next Fall. I have come to this conclusion after careful study of both boys. In the first place they do not readily fit into our school life, and secondly their attitude is such that I fear we can do little to improve them scholastically or otherwise. We have given much of our time and attention to both boys, because of their lack of any foundation, but except under compulsion and constant pressure they do not work. Neither shows any ambition. Doubtless you are aware of their rather coarse language and profanity." The brothers had been required to share a room to prevent the "petty disorder" that occurred otherwise, he wrote. Gordon boasted that they were happy and in improved health: "Paul has gained pounds and is now strong," but he reiterated, they were not welcome to continue at the school.

Within a week of receiving the letter, Millicent, obviously stung, shot back with a defensive, haughty, and not very persuasive retort. "I fear I agree that the school does not fit them. . . . As I have always brought them up to show independence and to think for themselves I feel that they would do better in a school where they will have more scope, and be under the supervision of men. . . . I feel that common sense, honesty, and independence of thought and character are vital as foundations now so much to the child as to the man he will become, but possibly we do not share this opinion in common and there again I consider that the desire to work and co-operate depends largely on the inspiration of the masters, rather than on the children, since few normal, healthy little boys of their ages are fired with great ambition or desire for work. Nevertheless I can see that from your point of view a studious, quiet child is preferable as he presents to the teacher a much more simple problem than the opposite kind." She added that on the matter of profanity, "on the contrary, I have most certainly not been aware of any such digressions from good taste on the part of either of my children." She finished the two-page typewritten letter: "I believe I have now covered all the things you mention, so let me thank you again for having written. With best regards to Mrs. Gordon, Sincerely yours." Telling him off with the thinnest veneer of politeness over an unconvincing and waspish response, one can almost see her holding her head arrogantly high as she set down her pen.[14]

One-upmanship aside, in her private correspondence, she had to admit, "Brother [the nickname for Arturo] is doing his usual work. He's just never going to be a concentrated student and he will have to learn life through living it."[15]

Practicing what she preached, she transformed herself during the war years from a rich playgirl to a woman in charge of her life. With a new sense of purpose provided by the war and the MSRC she became well-organized in matters beyond style and fashion. Being impeccably well-dressed and stylish no doubt required more time and organization than the average onlooker might suppose, but now Millicent expanded the sphere within her control. She managed to run the MSRC, maintain a presence in Washington social circles, and oversee the Claremont property.

An empowering transformation began. Those who had worked with Millicent, like the fashion designer Charles James, were aware of her assets. "She had a great quality of being able to bring order to the thoughts of others and to give them the sort of advice she herself needed to receive," James explained. It is sadly ironic that as she began to tap and engage her managerial gifts, poor health continued to undermine her stamina. Her letters to her mother are sprinkled with references to the "brown drops" the doctor has prescribed, of her waning energy, fevers, and prolonged recoveries from bouts with flu and colds. These skirmishes, reminders of mortality, only quickened the pace with which she raced against the clock, determined to live as fully as possible in whatever time remained. Now thirty-eight and thrice divorced, she was no longer the pawn of men, money, or her parents but fully mistress of her own life, American-style, for the first time.

CHAPTER SIXTEEN

Wartime and Washington

EALTHY SOCIAL CLIMBERS FROM ALL SECTIONS OF the country are planning to take houses in Washington for the winter 'season,'" reported the *Times-Herald* in 1941. One woman interviewed for the article said a bit breathlessly that she was coming to town "just to be in the swim for I couldn't bear to be so far away from all that excitement." The socially stratified capital had always been able to expand and contract to adjust to Congress and the diplomatic set. Now it had to accommodate the war effort and the wartime players who came in hopes of winning political or social influence.

"Every time you turned around, you brushed shoulders with an envoy, or a military or naval attaché; or a Washington social celebrity or a member of Congress," wrote the society columnist Hope Ridings Miller for *The Washington Post*'s "Capital Whirl" column.[1] Washington, D.C., had become *the* place to be almost overnight.

For Millicent, Washington life, the war, her return to the United States, and life at Claremont Manor would mark her fullest flowering. Never before had she been so busy or engaged in public life, so demonstrably a woman on her own or so free to choose her own loves and make her own rules. The same flair and artistry that she had applied over the years to her houses and wardrobe could now be wielded onto a larger canvas. At thirty-eight she may have felt the clock ticking more than ever, both as the years threatened to diminish the physical beauty that she had relied heavily on to distinguish herself and as her weak heart kept her mindful that she was vulnerable and her days were numbered. In response, she lived as fully as possible, traveling up and down the East Coast between New York and Washington, entertaining, dressing extravagantly, taking lovers, and working for the war effort.

Mary Rogers bought a stately residence on Wyoming Avenue at Twenty-fourth Street in a Washington neighborhood populated with ambassadors and politicians, and for the next three years she would become known in D.C. political circles for the well-attended parties she gave in the twelve-room house with an often noted and widely admired terrace hidden behind exterior walls. She hosted events for the USO (United Service Organizations) and other relief groups which Millicent attended as a guest or cohostess. At one such event Millicent met James Forrestal, the Undersecretary of the Navy, through her kinship with her cousin Robert Coe, who worked in the State Department. She and Forrestal may have orbited each other in fashion and society circles before the war. His wife, Jo Ogden, a former Ziegfeld dancer, had been a writer at *Vogue*. The Forrestals had a house on New York's elegant Beekman Place, and they vacationed on Jupiter Island north of Palm Beach.

But Forrestal was a star in his own right, an intense, driven man who rose on his own in the financial world on Wall Street and led a freewheeling life in the Fitzgeraldian circles of New York before he became one of the premier players on the Washington power scene. He and Jo had a notoriously "open" marriage from the outset. By the time he came to Washington and distinguished himself for his toughness and the ability to get things done, Jo had a major problem with alcohol and periods of mental illness. Ironically, it was she who enlisted

Mainbocher, Millicent's favorite dress designer at the time, to design the WAVE uniform. Due to her psychological infirmity, Jo was excluded from affairs with other Cabinet members' wives. She was known to be a loose cannon, and an impediment to her husband in most social occasions.[2] It came as no surprise that he was attracted to Millicent. "Jim liked affairs," remembers Marion "Oatsie" Charles, then Mrs. Thomas Leiter, a friend of the Forrestals in Washington.[3]

As Undersecretary of the Navy, Forrestal had distinguished himself by building a fleet of American ships that superseded the British fleet as the world's largest seapower. Cocky and handsome in a Jimmy Cagney sort of way, with his pugilistic nose and big ears, he attracted Millicent. This was an American man of more substance than the previous men in her life, including her ex-husbands. She wrote her cousin Bob Coe, when he had been dispatched to the American Embassy in London, "I like, I love, I am enthrawled [sic] with the sweet and thoughtful way you speak of my friend Mr. Forestall [sic]."[4] Coe might have been slightly jealous. He had always been a fan of his glamourous first cousin and was assumed by his brother and other family members to have nursed a lifelong crush on her.[5]

Whether the attraction between Millicent and Forrestal first sparked when she began taking injured navy pilots to convalesce at Claremont Manor, or whether she conceived of the idea because of Forrestal, is unclear. The navy shipped supplies for the MSRC so they may have first made contact through their official roles for the two organizations. But their relationship developed over Millicent's recovery program for the injured pilots. She reasoned that the patients, most of them "shell-shocked," would recover more quickly in a comfortable and gracious home environment with people and animals and everyday life taking place around them, than in the sterile Naval Hospital in Washington. It was a philosophy Forrestal sympathized with and that, ironically, he had subscribed to for his wife. When Jo returned home after a mental breakdown, he concluded it was better for her to lead a "normal life" than continue to undergo treatment for clinical schizophrenia. Forrestal supported Millicent's offer to open her house to four patients from the Naval Hospital for several weeks at a time. He had trained as a navy pilot in Canada and helped her to design the program.

The romance that developed between them was one of the most delicate and discreetly handled of her affairs during the war years. He was a frequent visitor at Claremont Manor, ostensibly checking up on his injured soldiers, but his influence and role went beyond mere war business. He advised Millicent about finding an appropriate school for Arturo after the boy had been asked not to return to the previous one. Forrestal thought a military academy would do Arturo good, and with his guidance and influence, Arturo was enrolled at Staunton Military Academy in Staunton, Virginia.[6] Though he did not last through graduation, Arturo was as impressed with his mother's friend as were most people who met James Forrestal. The Undersecretary's presence and comportment commanded respect, especially from a floundering young man.

Arturo remembers his visits to Claremont Manor and how the Undersecretary's relationship with his mother seemed, to his young man's sensibilities, to be one of "great respect." Forrestal on occasion spent the night when he came, and it was evident to Arturo and the staff at Claremont Manor that the Secretary and his mother had developed an intimate relationship, though they tiptoed delicately around it in public. "Nobody could be more charming when he wanted to be than James Forrestal," says Oatsie Charles, who, in addition to being a friend of both Forrestals, was close to Babe Paley and Bootsie Hearst. They were all members of a high-flying social set in wartime Washington.

As the war years passed, Forrestal's aggressive, burning ways made him a legend in Washington. Seapower was driving the Japanese from the Pacific. He was, even though a civilian, a hero. He was appointed Secretary of the Navy, and then, after the war's end, was named the country's first Secretary of Defense as the three services were merged. Whatever else his charms, he could hardly have been a relaxing companion for Millicent.

That wasn't a problem for Millicent, who seemed at this juncture in her life to like men with dynamism, energy, and sex appeal. Unfettered by marriage, Millicent was making something of a reputation for herself as being "frisky." The war had brought a devil-may-care aspect to the sexual mores of a usually starchy Washington, which had its share of sexual adventuresses. Like Clare Boothe Luce, Martha Gellhorn, and other high-profile women, Millicent joined in the conversation about the world and war with the men. She was not a pretty toy. She fearlessly jumped in to assert her thoughts on political topics and expected her opinions to matter. There was nothing subordinate about her and she wasn't tolerant of frivolous women who acted as if they were. "She couldn't put up with them. They had to have a brain. She liked men who were bright and she wanted women to match them. She thought women underestimated themselves," remembers Arturo. Her friends Babe Paley, Bootsie Hearst, and Margaret Mallory were equally assertive, though it is undeniable that their confidence was in some part due to wealth. They were all empowered by money.

Her Washington experience caused Millicent to consider and pontificate on some of the social and political issues she saw around her. Confidence was Millicent's prescription for American womanhood. She found her female countrymen wanting on the whole. She seemed wholly unfettered by her own lack of formal education, which wit and worldliness had compensated for, in all areas except perhaps spelling and punctuation: "I am not damning their average intelligence but in what country save ours could their [sic] exist The Daughters of the American Revolution.... Their cash lies in what they imagine themselves to be not in what they are..." she wrote to her eldest son Peter.[7] Her keen observations of Washington were on display in the lengthy letters she wrote on lined paper with datelines from Claremont Manor or Wyoming Avenue.

During her convalescences and quiet hours she now shared the opinions that had previously been jotted down in the margins of the books in her library. She was as sharp and alive as ever. To her cousin Bob, she asked, "What about Mr. Adams' 'Degeneration of the

Democratic People?' He strikes home in this city. I have come to the horrid conclusions that the greatest tragedy this country has ever suffered was the potato famine in Ireland which gave us a variety of citizens problematic in Washington. Known as the Irish Catholic Minority and after that we work down to the gentlemen from the gettos (sic) of central Europe and then come—and they are not the least bit calm—the oh so calm and serious and qualified Radcliffe graduates. Those ladies who have theories such as racial equality, give speeches to colored groups and then yell for a lynching when caught short. Next come the gentlemen with flies open continuously . . . who call one 'my Dear Child' while they rob the till. Oh, it's great, great, great to watch them all eating their way through the War—and talking. The only thing one can say is that if it's what the people want they are certainly getting it." She observed and chronicled the scene with gusto, and in the end seemed to place herself somewhere between the women of the DAR and those Radcliffe students. Despite her love of learning and knowledge of the world, she did not seem to identify with, nor put much store on, higher education for women, and despite her references to the Irish and Jews she seemed no more or less bigoted than most Americans of the time.

She segued into talk about her experience with the MSRC, which legitimatized her as a Washington insider. "We have been doing some work with the British and they are, on the whole splendid to work with in comparison with our people. The poor French are impossible. The Norwegians are by far the best and most efficient. With us it is that no one wants to take any responcibility [sic], so that if you are doing something useful you are showing up inefficiency right down the line. . . . Frankly I can't help thinking how useful it will be for the country if a few intelligent men remain alive for the future build up of the U.S.A. for what it's become now is frightening."[8]

Millicent's romantic interests overlapped during the war years. She wrote her mother, "Don't forget I expect you for Xmas in Claremont," and told her that she had already invited Van Truex, "in case you want companionship for the trip down." She also mentions that Ian Fleming might be coming. "If Fleming turns up from England I presume he can stay with us. Hadn't planned on a mass of people, it is too much trouble with so few servants and everyone asking 'Where and when and how? Where is the whiskey?' "[9]

Commander Ian Fleming was on assignment with British naval intelligence in Washington and, not unlike Millicent, had seized the war as an occasion to re-create himself. He had been a London stockbroker until the previous spring when he was appointed a lieutenant in the Royal Naval Volunteer Reserve. His facility for languages and an Eton education made him agent material, and he had a talent for espionage. Along with other elaborate spy plots, he would be credited with masterminding a ploy to use a corpse, dressed up as a British admiral and carrying false plans, for an invasion that would divert the Germans from the real target. He usually carried a small commando knife and a trick fountain pen that ejected a cloud of tear gas, a bit like the gadgetry he would create for agent 007 in his future novels.[10] Tall and strikingly handsome at thirty-two, six years Millicent's junior, he came under her spell, and vice versa. Both were quite taken with what the other had to offer. Fleming had an air of melancholy about him and, like Millicent, was proficient in several languages.

He wore his uniform well, and his long nose, slightly humped from being broken on a football field at Eton, seemed to add to his attractiveness. He and Millicent shared creative imaginations and flights of stylish fancy. He admired a gunmetal cigarette case she carried and made it the model for the one 007 would carry in his James Bond novels. He talked a great deal about sex. His compatriate Mary Pakenham (the future Lady Longford) remarked, "No one I have ever known had sex so much on the brain as Ian." His London flat was full of books about flagellation. Arturo claims that Fleming remarked that Millicent was the most sexually insatiable woman he had ever experienced, which seems a case of the pot calling the kettle black.

Fleming seemed to have felt outclassed, as many men did, by

Millicent's opulent lifestyle. Her impressive collection of Fabergé eggs was second only to Britain's Queen Mary's and was noted in his biography, along with her "zany" temperament and extravagance in clothes. He wrote to Ann, the wife of Viscount Rothermere (Esmond Harmsworth, the proprietor of the *Daily Mail*), whom Fleming would later marry, that he was staying with a spectacularly rich and flamboyant mistress, though he confessed that he loved her. He tended to be confessional about his relationship with Millicent, and insouciant about his affairs in general. "... I had to take to the four roses [whiskey] and write to you, so far as women are concerned I am sorry to say I have been corralled and that it all couldn't be wronger or more confused."[11]

Millicent followed Fleming to Jamaica in 1946 where he had built a plain concrete house with shuttered doors and windows and named it *Goldeneye*. Like Noël Coward and other British intelligence employees, Fleming became acquainted with Jamaica when he attended a British-American naval intelligence conference there during the war. He resolved that after the war he would "just live in Jamaica and lap it up and swim in the sea and write books." On Montego Bay he and Millicent carried on their affair. It soon became a gossip column item in the Washington newspapers.

Fleming's idyllic routine was a morning swim followed by pawpaws and Blue Mountain coffee for breakfast, then more swimming and snorkeling for lobsters. At war's end and after spending much of the previous winter there with Fleming, Millicent bought her own house, "Wharf House," also on Montego Bay. She rhapsodized about the waters, the rugged scenic beauty, the picturesque golf course and racetrack, and prophesied it would become a new hot spot. "It looks as though Millicent had started a movement," wrote another gossip columnist. Noël Coward, Cecil Beaton and a handful of Hollywood celebrities had already discovered Jamaica's unspoiled beaches and wild landscape. The casual lifestyle and easy social scene, a loosely arranged series of dinners and parties at guests' resort houses, were a main attraction for her.

Fleming, on the other hand, was always moody and a bit reclusive. It was said he liked the company of his dogs more than most people, and he disliked parties, preferring dinner and a game of bridge. He was also hard at work on his novel *Casino Royale*. The differences between them seemed to become evident naturally. Socially minded Millicent threw some of the most elaborate theme and costume parties during the winter social season. She re-created an African village on the beach with shields, spears, and smashed skulls for one cannibal theme party that her friend playwright Noël Coward could not attend. He sent his regrets to her in a note asking, "Who are we eating?" much to Millicent's delight. When Oatsie Charles dropped down to Jamaica to visit, she scolded Fleming for the way he treated Millicent. She thought him generally disagreeable and often dismissive to the always composed and gracious Millicent. "He was very abrasive, yet he could be so charming. Even when I told him off he said, 'You're quite right. Shall we have a drink on it?'" says Oatsie.

Fleming figured favorably in Millicent's life in Washington, at Claremont, and in New York. As her guest and lover he exhibited a kind and caring facet of his complex personality, which Millicent described appreciatively to her mother. After Christmas 1945 she felt a cold coming on, but decided to attend a New Year's Eve party in Washington just the same. "I expect that didn't improve matters much but it was quite fun." She and Fleming traveled to New York two days later. Upon arrival they found Millicent's temperature had spiked to 103 degrees. She was promptly diagnosed with bronchial pneumonia and went to bed with a night nurse on duty for the next ten days. Ian, she wrote her mother, was "sweet, helpful, and concerned." While still recovering, she longed to be well enough to travel to Jamaica soon. "I am trying to get myself down there," she wrote, asking if she could stay with Mary in New York when she returned to the U.S. "Ian wants to see something of the country so we thought we would motor up." They had clearly become an item. "Ian relaxed as he got some rest and was more himself after a week here and went off feeling well again. He's really very sweet. The more I see him the more I like him. It is a curious shyness that makes him brusque on the outside and when that wears off comes a nice sensitive inside and his good commonsense brain to back it with," she explained.[12]

Fleming was rather adept at two-timing his women, and Millicent was no exception. He sounded a bit tortured in his missives to Ann, writing, "It's not what you might imagine any kind of affair to be like but just something out of juan in America (half-baked shorthand) when everything starts wrong and goes on wrong and getting wronger and god knows what she thinks its all about and it really isn't all one persons fault but just that both sets of rules are wrong—baseball and rounders, which is really what happens between English and American people, but I find it very galling and uninteresting and very difficult to straighten out and altogether unsatisfactory."[13] This rumination may have had to do with a flurry of newspaper stories suggesting that they were soon to be engaged. "The tall, slim, and glamorous Standard Oil heiress has said yes (or at least maybe) to Capt. Ian Fleming," the society reporter Charles crowed in one of the many columns that kept track of her affairs.[14] The rumors proved untrue, but there seemed to be no question of her deep affection for Fleming. After their relationship came to an amicable end when she took off for Hollywood at the end of that year she continued to keep a marble bust of him in the Claremont Manor.

Millicent may have been just as well out of it. Fleming would go on and marry Ann, and their sadomasochistic sex life would be whispered about in the UK and Jamaica. There were newspaper stories about the piles of sodden wet towels they used to cool their fiery bouts of lovemaking, and the welts suffered by Ann, who later wrote, "I loved cooking for you and sleeping beside you and being whipped by you . . . I don't think I have ever loved like this before." While Millicent would confide some of her sexual hijinks to friends and lovers later in her life, and her son Arturo maintains that she liked experimentation, sadomasochism was never mentioned.

Millicent was no stranger to juggling men's affections. The same espionage world that Fleming moved about in also brought the young Roald Dahl to Washington and into her orbit. Dahl, known to posterity as the creator of favorite children's stories, also made a reputation as a lady killer. The man who wrote *The Gremlins, The BFG, James and the Giant Peach*, and *The Witches* came to Washington as an R.A.F. hero, grounded after being seriously hurt when his plane crashed in the Libyan desert. Head injuries exempted him from active duty, but as a young, well-educated war hero, he was perfect to be assistant air attaché, the liason between the British and U.S. Army Air Force. He was stationed in an embassy post to spy on England's ally, and neatly fit the description of gentleman spy. He even came to the attention of Eleanor Roosevelt, who was reading *The Gremlins* to her grandchildren, and brought him into contact with FDR, and into the President's confidence on many war issues. Some claimed he was a go-between for Roosevelt and Churchill. With his extraordinary good looks and suave manners, he moved deftly through social Washington, shamelessly charming almost every woman who met him. "With the playgrounds of Europe closed to tourists, moneyed society was forced to stay home, and Washington was brimming with wealthy dowagers and their bored, unmarried daughters," Jennet Conant wrote, describing the scene in *The Irregulars: Roald Dahl and the British Spy Ring in Wartime Washington*.

Six foot six with wavy brown hair parted on the side, a finely chiseled profile, debonair in a suit or uniform, and with piercing blue eyes—a legacy of his Norwegian ancestry—Dahl knocked 'em dead in Washington. If there was ever any question about the attraction of Millicent's other loves, even her ex-husbands, there was little doubt about Dahl's. They were naturals, except for the thirteen-year age difference. He was twenty-eight, she was forty-one. What he lacked in years he made up for in confidence. He was long-legged and cocky, fond of pranks and teasing, and, like Millicent, had made a reputation for himself as a frightening mimic. They both seemed to have the same outlook, sharpened by near-death experiences, and the habit of positioning themselves, at least in their own minds, just enough outside the culture they moved in to stand back and poke fun at it. He spoke several languages, including Norwegian, and was becoming a writer. He also had a taste for fine art.

"He was ageless. There was just something about him. Oooh, he was smooth," says Odette Terrel des Chênes, who was asked by Millicent, a bosom friend of her mother's, to dine one evening with Dahl, to keep him occupied while Millicent and her mother went elsewhere. "He was a real charmer," Odette says, still remembering their meal in a Japanese restaurant.[15]

Their age difference seemed not to matter since each projected the same animal magnetism for the opposite sex. Dahl had smooth manners, British wit, good looks, and writer's success, which filled the category she called "having a brain." He, like she, was a free spirit now; his reputation with women was becoming known in D.C. His looks were compared to Henry Fonda and Gary Cooper, and he was continually courted by rich women, whom he entertained with stories of his escapades in Hollywood, where *The Gremlins* was being adapted by Disney for a movie that never got made.[16] "He's a killer with women," the actress Patricia Neal would declare years later after she became his wife and then ex-wife. He was broody, self-centered, and could be unkind, yet those aspects of his personality seemed to add some sort of *noir* attractiveness to his sex appeal.

Dahl's job in D.C consisted mostly of keeping an ear open for whatever he might hear of Britain's enemies, and to that end he was a regular at hunt breakfasts, luncheons, teas, dances, balls, and parties. "Girls just fell at Roald's feet," explained Antoinette Marsh, the daughter of his friend and benefactor Charles Marsh. "I think he slept with everybody on the East and West Coasts that had more than fifty thousand dollars a year." Millicent certainly fit that category, but she had something that Dahl admired even more. They no doubt had a common interest in espionage topics since she was abetting the French underground, and her admiration for Norwegian efficiency through her work for the MSRC would have been a conversation starter as well.

But her special attraction for Dahl was clearly her taste and opulent lifestyle, especially her collection of fine art. When he accompanied his countryman William Stephenson—author of *A Man Called Intrepid*—who was running the British spy operation and becoming a legend himself, to Claremont Manor, Dahl was as smitten with Millicent's home and artwork as he was with the dazzling hostess.

During this period Dahl was also carrying on with the new congresswoman from Connecticut, Clare Boothe Luce, and another woman described by Antoinette Marsh as Eisenhower's girlfriend.[17] But Millicent's lifestyle sustained a powerful attraction for him. In the devil-may-care atmosphere of displaced servicemen and war workers, Roald and Millicent seemed to develop a mutually satisfying arrangement. When he visited Claremont, Millicent assigned her Norwegian maid, Olga, to attend to his room and comfort. Her paintings seem to have been a powerful aphrodisiac between them—or at least for him. "She had something that he found truly irresistible—a great art collection," claims Dahl's British biographer, Donald Sturrock.[18] Dahl gushed about Millicent's paintings in letters to his mother back in England, and his awe was unmistakable, if as glinty-eyed as an auctioneer's:

I took first weekend for a long time at Easter. Went to the most marvelous and lovely house. Owner is Millicent Rogers, a sort of Standard Oil millionairess, and it was all very fine. It was an old colonial house in South Virginia, and from the back verandahs, long smooth lawns sloped down to the James River, which went on rolling along between gardens of cherry blossom and daffodils. Millicent had ten dachshunds, and a great dane and she had a lot of other things. In the small library (which was huge) there were

a) Degas pastel 5' × 3. Very beautiful
b) another Degas pastel, a little smaller
c) A Gauguin 5' × 2'
d) A head of Renoir by Degas

e) Two Renoirs
f) Two Corots
g) One Monet
h) One Manet

In the next room there were twelve Boucher and some Fragonard. All very beautiful and carefully bought by M. I had an enormous bed with gold hanging all around it, and a Norwegian maid to wait on me. As I say, everything was very fine.[19]

Sturrock called Millicent "Dahl's most significant conquest of 1944," but Millicent may have considered him *her* conquest, keeping the balance of power between them more interesting—and static. She kept him on the hook by opening her various homes to him, and showering him with expensive gifts. When he stayed in her apartment on East Sixty-eighth Street she presented him with a gold door key made by Tiffany.[20] He had difficulty mastering the burglar alarm and on his first visit two "of the most enormous armed thugs you ever saw" burst through the door just as he was making himself at home by pouring a whiskey. Yet again it was the art that impressed him, two van Goghs, Gauguin's self-portrait, and a Cézanne he estimated to be worth seventy thousand dollars.

Millicent played to Dahl's interest in art and channeled her seduction through their mutual appreciation of paintings. Dahl's assistant, William Roxburgh, acted as go-between when Millicent alerted him by telegram to auctions of interest. "Long before this reaches you will have received a telegram from Millicent Rogers, who arrived at the Embassy today full of excitement because she has discovered that in some future auction there are to be several pictures which she thinks would please you. . . . I am a little anxious about how much it is all going to cost and have tried to point out tactfully to her that it might be inadvisable to involve you in a sum much greater than the $600 which you left with me." Roxburgh also shuddered that a Norwegian picture Millicent was keeping an eye on for Dahl would cost between

$1,200 and $1,300, "according to Millicent's latest intelligence!!!" Ten days later he is near despair, corresponding to Dahl at Whitehall, "I sent another meaningless telegram to you the other day from Millicent about pictures. Apparently the two that you had in mind were both rather expensive and she let them go. She has gone to some other sale today and may pick up something for you if she sees anything which she is convinced would meet with your approval." Two days later, she telegraphed Dahl at the Dorchester Hotel in London. "Pictures sold prohibitive prices bought only small Delacroix water color 150. Going New York Sunday three weeks, Love."[21]

Millicent generously lent Dahl the house she and Mary shared in Washington the following summer, where he continued to catalogue the artwork and enjoy her hospitality:

> While my house is being painted I have been lent Millicent Rogers house. She is away on Long Island somewhere for the summer. My sitting room there has in it
>
> | | |
> |---|---|
> | one | Degas 5 feet high |
> | one | Degas a little smaller |
> | one | Gauguin 5 feet high of Tahiti |
> | one | Gauguin still life |
> | Two | Boudins |
> | one | Monet |
> | one | Manet (seascape) |
> | one | Vuillard (much finer than mine) |
> | one | Pissaro |
> | one | Degas (portrait of Renoir) |
>
> So its pretty pleasant sitting there even if one isn't doing anything. There's also a Steinway piano on which I PLAY "The Well Tempered Clavichord" over and over again. In my bedroom there's the finest and largest Renoir of Red Roses that you've ever seen, also, a Pissaro, a Sisley and a Burne-Jones; not to mention a couple of air

conditioners. The normal rent of the house is 600$ a month [figure a bit unclear], if anyone wants to pay it!

But home will soon be ready and I'll go back[22]

Though partners in a passion for style and good living, Dahl and Millicent had quiet different social tastes. When Dahl went to New York to see doctors about his perpetually hurting back, a casualty of his plane crash, Millicent invited him to Southampton. Dahl thought his fellow guests at The Port of Missing Men in Southampton were dull. He described them as such to his mother, but he was impressed by their celebrity.

Went to New York last week to see doctors then popped out to Long Island for a day staying at Millicent Rogers house. Fantastic business. There also were Cecil Beaton, Schiaparelli (I call her Shocking) and many other equally strange and artistic types. Women with ruby necklaces and sapphire necklaces, and god knows what else sauntered in and out and down below amidst miles of corridors, there were swimming baths, Turkish baths, colonic lavages, heat treatment rooms and everything else which was calculated to make the prematurely ageing playboys and playwomen age a little less quickly. I didn't like it much.[23]

The next month Millicent threw a gala birthday party for him. *"Didn't tell anyone that it was my birthday, but must have let it out long time ago because the irrepressible Millicent Rogers gave large party with champagne etc including Ambassadors and Undersecretaries of State. I was bored and didn't enjoy it much except for the champagne,"* Dahl wrote.

He seemed to like being on the receiving end of Millicent's generosity while ridiculing it at the same time. Millicent extended her generosity to Dahl and sustained his interest in an almost Pygmalion fashion. It is difficult to tell when and how their relationship moved into more than friendship. An elaborate bracelet she gave him, perhaps one of her own designs, he later gave away to an English girl he was dating.[24] She gave him a gold cigarette case with a pornographic engraving and a lighter, and at one point in their relationship regaled him with stories of her other sexual adventures.[25] She had once had sex with a lover while her husband was asleep in the same room, she recounted. He did not share that one with his mother. Dahl repeated the tale to a friend back in London, making the point that Millicent was wild and fun.[26] Whether she confessed in a spirit of bravado to titillate Dahl or as one weary sexual traveler sharing tales of the road with another can only be conjectured, but they were unquestionably well-suited by experience and in more ways than one made good bedfellows. Dahl was apparently irked when Fleming, another of Stephenson's men in Washington, began his well-publicized affair with Millicent, but he didn't dare ruffle the golden goose's feathers. Millicent was not one to be told what to do in those days. In one letter to her mother she wrote of him in a way that suggests that he sometimes strained her hospitality, or had a slightly inflated notion of his importance to her. "The bell rang and in came Roald with great apology that he couldn't stay long. Though I did not ask him to stay at all. He ranged around looking rather white and looking for booby traps, which were not there. I think what rather upset him was to find that we were not away."[27]

Dahl's British biographer has no evidence that his friendship with Millicent was sustained after he returned to England in 1946, the same year of her rumored engagement to Fleming. But true to character, Dahl resorted to the cruel ridicule that he was known for. He named Millicent "Curvature," apparently a reference to a scoliosis of the spine after her strokes and a partial paralysis of her right arm.[28] She compensated with conscious good posture and even foundation garments designed to hold her upright, but someone who knew her intimately would have noticed. Dahl being Dahl, he couldn't resist referring to her by the unflattering nickname.

Much as she skittered between New York, Southampton, Washington, and Claremont, Millicent flitted between Forrestal, Fleming, and Dahl. Her contemporaries seemed to marvel rather than to judge or criticize. "You could not imagine more interesting men than those," said Oatsie Charles, who admiringly remembered them all in wartime Washington. Millicent seemed more adept at choosing lovers than husbands.

As exciting and fascinating as they were, their lives were not all play, and after the war, all three men's accomplishments were hard-won. Fleming and Dahl would go on to literary fame. Forrestal, the most visible and powerful of the three at the time, went on to accept President Truman's appointment to be the nation's first Secretary of Defense. He was tired and worn down by political sniping and competition. Paranoia overtook him; he was constantly bedeviled by imagined Communist or Zionist plots to kill him. In March 1949, he resigned. Shortly thereafter, he was confined in the Naval Hospital in Bethesda for reactive depression, with a twenty-four-hour guard looking after him. Yet early on the morning of May 22, he managed to hurl himself from a window and fell thirteen stories to his death.

His affair with Millicent had almost certainly been over for some time. Her full and "frisky" years in Washington, a fling of multiple lovers in her own life's trajectory, were over. The surrender of Japan in 1945 turned almost everyone's sights to the more mundane matters of life back home, and Millicent was no exception. She would yet again need to regroup, take stock of her diminishing health and finances, and the prospects for her future.

CHAPTER SEVENTEEN

A Changed World

EN AND THE DEMANDS OF HER WAR EFFORT KEPT Millicent on the move. She was ubiquitous and often hard to track during the war years, but as her correspondence with her mother and sons illustrates, her thoughts about life and the state of the world were firmly anchored. Money and the responsibility of managing it for herself and others began to be an issue, unforeseen before the full effect of the estate taxes on her father's estate became a factor in her life and on her livelihood.

In 1944 she was obliged to address the unfinished business of Southampton and her guardianship of The Port of Missing Men for Peter. He would not turn twenty-one until the following year. Peter had joined the U.S. Army in Surry, and Pauline Dresser, her father's widow, had relinquished her much-challenged claim to the eighteen-hundred-acre property both by her remarriage and her failure to occupy the house continuously, as was specified in Colonel Rogers' will. The house was now Peter's and in dire need of maintenance. The Beach House, the gorgeous palazzo-type residence Millicent's mother and father had designed and appointed in the 1920s, had been washed out in the frightful Great Hurricane of 1938 that devastated much of the Long Island coastline, but The Port was far enough inland to remain largely intact. Millicent, in close contact with her mother, set out to make the house livable for the family again.

She and Mary deliberated over what they seemed to do best as mother and daughter, decorate and furnish fine houses. Though they were known to bicker over liquor bills and they sparred notoriously over the intrinsic value of modern art, which Mary disdained and Millicent admired, mother and daughter invariably rose to the occasion when the project was creating gracious households for fine living. Now, contrary to the public impression of their wealth, they worried about money. Mary's Tuxedo and Palm Beach houses required upkeep and Millicent was renting and refurbishing her apartment in New York in addition to Claremont. They had agreed to rent in Gloucester the following summer though Mary wished only to be there in August, causing Millicent to shoulder most of the rental fee herself.

Much of their correspondence during this time was about accounting, which one assumes Millicent was addressing without the assistance of a husband for the first time—and from within the U.S. rather than as an expat. She paid a note on her Virginia property, rent in Manhattan, and was learning the ins and outs of estimated income taxes. "It is somewhat difficult but not as difficult as imagined," she wrote her mother. Peralta-Ramos had managed their finances when they were married. The story of his opening a drawer that bulged with her unpaid bills was legendary in the family. Balcom, a competent businessman before he married Millicent, had also helped her manage her money.

Now, she needed to take charge of her own finances. The consequences of the debacle over her father's inheritance continued to plague her. In 1943 the U.S. Supreme Court found in favor of the federal government, which sought an additional estate tax of $7.5 million against her father's twenty-three-million-dollar estate.[1] Three and a half million dollars that had gone to Millicent and her stepmother were at issue in the estate's gross calculations. The shortage of money was finally making itself felt in her life, after she had coasted through the late thirties and first years of the war. She instructed Mary on estimated income tax, and worried that she would lose twenty-five thousand dollars in income herself as a result of her tax status. She lamented the costs of "storage, trucking, moving, labor." It all, she concluded, "cost a great deal."

Their practice over the years had been to move furniture, bedding, and dishes between their various locations, but Millicent was tired of the expense and the practice. "I don't feel *capable* or *inclined* to move!" she wrote. In an assertion that would have caused her deceased father to chuckle from his grave, she wrote to Mary, "It seemed to me you have wasted so much money! (the trips, insurance, time) . . ." Then she came to her point, "I don't want to take on Southampton with you because I am quite certain I shall not be there this summer and the boys will probably be in summer camp and I don't want anymore expense than I can help until I pay the government the large sum on the Virginian notes—so you can see that I can't be as cooperative as you would like. I think that if I take the house [Gloucester] off your hands I will be doing about all I can and possibly more." With a note of newfound pragmatism, she added, "You understand I don't wish to be disagreeable but facts are facts and one might as well face them." By the spring of 1944 the first tug of financial awareness added to her domestic concerns. She added in her letter to Mary, "Arturo is much bigger and quieter, and Paulie has got very figitty [sic] indeed. They both want to go back to Claremont." She agreed to take them the following week, in part because she needed to see her doctors. "I have to have three more x-ray treatments as the trouble has started up again. Other than that I feel fine."[2]

With Peter in the army, the responsibility of maintaining, and to some degree restoring, The Port fell to Millicent. Both time and disuse had taken its toll on the $1.75 million property. She wrote to her mother in Washington after she'd been out to Southampton to see it: "The Port was interesting . . . One felt a lot. The passages are definitely unpleasant. I don't like Southampton," she volunteered. Her appearance there and the local rumor that The Port had been haunted when it was unoccupied brought curiosity seekers out to see. It also caused the local papers to rehash the whole inheritance story. "Finally it got so bad that I stopped giving away drinks—one or two was one thing but when it got to strangers in tens and twelves I simply was rude. As for the talk, well of course it brought the usual articles in the Journal and at which point I was <u>extremely</u> rude to one or two people who stuck their noses out. It doesn't matter. They aren't very important because they are blind and everything seems allright to them no matter how wrong it is." Of gossip and speculation she theorized, "... they start the avalanche going blithely down hill, carving the mountain away.... There it is—then it's gone too far for anybody to stop." Her appearance at The Port to sort furnishings and assess what work was necessary fuelled public speculation and was an irritant to Millicent. The publicity was unwanted. When a friend came around wanting to photograph family heirlooms, pictures, and diaries, she lost patience again. "I think it would be a good idea if this family could be left alone for a little while—a year or so might help—at least it would be that much to the good!"[3] Despite her war efforts and failing health, Millicent kept up her high profile in the fashion world. In 1939 upon her return to Washington, *Vogue* had named her one of the year's best dressed. She was no newcomer to such distinctions and at one point even seemed to eschew them, as was politic to do during the war. She was repeatedly named to the formidable Eleanor Lambert's Best-Dressed List. No matter what illness or challenge befell her, style was the thing of her own invention that she could lay claim to.

In New York she wanted a car and driver, but gas rationing made it impossible and politically incorrect. She talked a Checker cab driver named Irving into working for her full-time. She decorated the interior with tiger-skin upholstery and put Irving and the car to use like a private limousine. Irving was treated almost like a member of her family. She dispatched him with her maid on shopping errands and eventually tutored him on how to dress so he could do her bidding even unaccompanied by the maid, matching a shirt or cardigan in the color she had requested. She sent him to collect her friends for her soirees, especially in Southampton. Diana Vreeland remembered Irving fondly in her own autobiography, especially for the night when he was assigned to bring her and the actor Clark Gable out to Southampton for a party. It was a far cry from the coach-built, hand-tailored Delage Aerosport Coupe that Millicent had bought in Paris in 1938. But times had changed.

Millicent's attitude stiffened in her correspondence during the late war years. In letters to her mother and to her sons, she filled lined legal and letter pad pages front and back with her thoughts on public attitudes, the war, her country, love, and, a bit obtusely, her own emotional dynamic.[4] She had time to ruminate at Claremont and wrote of going to New York "just to go to the ballet and hear an opera or a concert or two—It has been quite lonely down here—aside from animals and negroes leaving and a few such things. It doesn't really matter where one is—it can always be nice if one has occupation and work to do."

Yet she struggled when poor health slowed her pace. "I haven't written because the tests made me feel rather punk. Nothing was found except a spastic colon which we knew already. Dozens of tests were made. Some quite disagreeable. Now Dr. Higgins is feeding me vitamins. . . . He has taken me off the brown drops and I am not doing so badly, though I'm slightly nervous about my insides. Some of the pain has subsided and the heart feels o.k.—also I'm getting massage. Dr. Higgins says any heart would be punk with such an inside and it's not such a bad heart—and he'll have me skating yet. I need rebuilding. I say hurrah, hurrah. But I'm pretty bored." She filled her days by overseeing the "planting and replanting every inch of the garden and fought in imagination with all radio broadcasters and commentators."

The girl who had written in the margins of her books in private dialogues with the author was still at it in letters to her sons and mother during the time she spent in bed in the early 1940s. She filled many of her long hours at Claremont with writing. She looked forward to visitors. After her colleague in the MSRC Dr. Hoguet came to see her, she wrote Mary: "I like educated people with whom I can talk and be understood." Rambling, even at times sounding feverish, she always expressed what was on her mind. Smart, willful, opinionated, and definitely not nuanced, her writing projected both restless energy and a blunt moral sense. It exuded the certainties that develop when one is unused to being contradicted. International matters interested her greatly, and she wrote Mary in a stream of consciousness outpouring on the role of the United States and the condition of the Germans:

They will always find an excuse and some people will always believe them because they had Bach and Beethoven and Mozart and Brahms and because they look beautiful when they are young and laugh and have fine teeth and blue eyes. Someday someone will get tired believing how beautiful they are and how well they sing and how they wear roses in their hair and that they are brave and haughty and then they will kill them all, men, women, and children. I can't say it makes much difference who does it, provided it's done. It seems to me that they have shown us how. I can't see either that it matters much whether the Americans are the ones or not. I've never thought that we had to *prove* ourselves. It's always seemed to me that we "were." If other people do not know how we are that much the worse for them. It's always seemed to me so strong in us that it was not worth arguing about and not worth defending . . .

If we have our ideal we will live up to it. If we have faith we will stand by it. No talk proves anything, only acting and if actions are fine they need not be explained—and what we, in ourselves feel that we have done right and according to our pride and belief ourselves to know we must do things—then that too is right for us and we could not have done better. . . . We are too willing and apt to justify ourselves before others as a nation and as individuals. Sometimes we want gratitude. It seems to me that Dumas was right when he said "those who complain of ingratitude are imbeciles, for one must be an imbecile to expect it from any human being." That is likely why the WORD dole succeeds so well. A man gets something for nothing. He gets something he doesn't have to work for in exchange for his vote. He doesn't need gratitude. It's a negative exchange and it undermines the moral fiber of a people. If we expect gratitude in the liberated countries from those we have helped we will be hated. We will be the most hated people in Europe (as we are in North Africa.) I don't like this business of saying "We did this. This is for you." It's dangerous to America—both morally and economically. The world today with aircraft is too small, the games too crude. . . .

I have always wondered in reading history the way people were willing to be burned alive, tortured and staked out when they could pretend to change their opinions. I know why now. People who have life easy have no strong core. They never had to have it. The French, the British, the Norwegians, the Russians, the whole of Europe has been down to the bone—to rock bottom, and when you reach rock bottom you know certain fundamental things—and you are ready to die for them. It isn't business or money or pictures or home. It is the chain upon which civilization is built and you must be ready to give up everything . . .

We haven't had it hard. We haven't suffered or starved or fought on our land and no matter how hard we want to understand we are going to have a hell of a time doing it. The men who have been in battle will—the others won't. What's more, they can't. If one is healthy how can one understand the sick? Sympathize yes, help yes, care yes. But not understanding, and that we will have to face somehow because the world is sick, and the world is facing it and will take it 50 or 75 years to come and it's going to be a tremendously hard job and it's going to take a certain amount of humility and at the moment we have very little—"For frantic boast and foolish word, thy mercy on thy people lord," [she quoted Kipling's *Recessional* and continued] and Rilke—"only those who with the dead

Henry Huttleston Rogers, Millicent's paternal grandfather, was the proud patriarch who created the family's great fortune. In 1906 he posed with his eight grandchildren in front of the grand estate he built in his hometown of Fairhaven, Massachusetts. Millicent, four, to her grandfather's left, held his hand. *(From the Collection of the Millicent Library)*

Millicent's girlhood was divided between her parents' Fifty-seventh Street town house in New York City and a second home in Tuxedo Park, New York. Pictured here in New York at age seven she strikes a solemn pose in her sumptuous surroundings. The following year she would contract rheumatic fever. *(The Peralta-Ramos Family archives)*

The summer following her social debut, 1920, Millicent became engaged to Jimmy Thompson, a young man from her social circle in Southampton and Manhattan. Thompson went to the dock to see her off on a grand tour of Europe with her parents the next winter. Their engagement did not survive the trip. (*©Bettmann/Corbis*)

In 1924 Millicent rocked society with a burst of headstrong glamour when she eloped with Count Ludwig Salm von Hoogstraeten, a relatively impoverished Austrian nobleman. She was 21, he was 39. They sailed for Europe without receiving her parents' blessing. (*©Bettmann/Corbis*)

Millicent's father, Henry Huttleston Rogers, controlled his daughter as best he could with wills and money. He was intent on ending her marriage to Count Salm and bargained with her husband's Austrian family to bring her back to the United States five months after the wedding. Father and daughter are pictured here strolling the grounds at Belmont Park on race day. (*The Peralta-Ramos Family archives*)

A brunette most of her life, Millicent sported a flapper's short haircut when she stepped out as a soon-to-be young divorcée in 1926. She married again the following year. *(The Peralta-Ramos Family archives)*

Arturo Peralta-Ramos, a dashing Argentine aristocrat, became Millicent's second husband in 1927. She invariably traveled with her beloved dachshunds, often numbering eight or more, when she moved between New York and Paris. *(©Bettmann/Corbis)*

In the 1930s Millicent made her mark on the fashion world in Paris and New York. Her flair for adding Tyrolean accessories to the tailored classic styles of major designers became a sensation. In 1939 *Vogue* featured her wearing the moleskin cape, muff, and hat, dyed bright red, that had won her admirers in Paris. *(©Condé Nast Archive/Corbis)*

Ronald Balcom, nine years younger than Millicent and a man of American café society, became her third husband in 1935. Through most of their six-year marriage they lived in Austria, where Millicent had built a house outside St. Anton. Balcom was an attentive stepfather for her three sons and an expert skier. (*The Peralta-Ramos Family archives*)

Millicent's sons Peter Salm (left) and Paul and Arturo Peralta-Ramos flanked Millicent on the balcony of Shulla House in St. Anton when they were home from Swiss and Austrian boarding schools. During their years together in Austria before the outbreak of World War II, this was the closest they came to being a conventional family. (*The Peralta-Ramos Family archives*)

Millicent divorced Ronnie Balcom in 1941 and picked up her life in wartime Washington, D.C. She purchased the legendary property Claremont Manor in rural Virginia and joined in the war effort. Unattached for the first time in her adult life she consorted with an array of dynamic and interesting men. Roald Dahl, 28, was working as a spy for British intelligence when he became her lover and frequent houseguest. He wrote letters to his mother in England about her impressive wealth and art collection. (©Bettmann/Corbis)

Millicent's relationship to Ian Fleming, who was on assignment with British naval intelligence in D.C., introduced her to Jamaica, a haunt of Fleming's, toward the end of the war. Millicent eventually bought her own house in Jamaica amid reports, false, that she and Fleming would marry. (©Sidney Beadell/The Times/ nisyndication)

James Forrestal was Undersecretary of the U.S. Navy and one of the most powerful men in D.C. when he met Millicent. Forrestal was married but came into Millicent's life when she opened her home in Claremont to convalescing navy pilots. Their romance has been described discreetly as one of "great respect." (Courtesy of the National Park Service, Abbie Rowe, courtesy of Harry S. Truman Library)

Though she appeared more often as a poster girl for her wartime efforts, Millicent was still a reigning fashion icon, photographed here in her New York apartment for *Vogue* in February 1947. (*©Condé Nast Archive/Corbis*)

Gilbert Adrian, couturier for Hollywood's leading ladies, designed clothes for Millicent in the 1940s. She modeled his black taffeta gown for *Vogue* in 1947. (*©Condé Nast Archive/Corbis*)

After the war Millicent's friends
Rocky and Gary Cooper from
Southampton introduced her to
Clark Gable. Here they posed at
the Coopers' home with, from left,
Lucien Ballard, Merle Oberon's
cinematographer husband; Rocky
Cooper, the actress Merle Oberon,
Millicent and Clark. In the front
row, film star Van Johnson kneels
next to the Coopers' daughter,
Maria. It is assumed Gary Cooper
snapped the photo. (The Estate of
Gary Cooper)

Benito Suazo, left, was Millicent's
chauffeur in Taos. Their relationship was
a cause for conflict between her and her
friend Dorothy Brett after they traveled
together cross-country to Jamaica in
1950. Benito posed along the route with
Trinidad Archuleta, another Taos Indian
who worked for Dorothy Brett. (Courtesy
of Santiago Suazo, Taos Pueblo)

In Taos, New Mexico, Millicent
quickly adopted the squaw
skirt and dress of the local
Indians. She dyed fabric over
the stove in the kitchen of a
house that Mabel and Tony
Lujan provided her while she
awaited renovations to her new
house. (Archives of the Millicent Rogers
Museum, Taos, New Mexico)

Millicent struck an iconic pose for *Harper's Bazaar* in 1947 in this winged dress of black silk velvet which has, puzzlingly, been attributed to both designers Adrian and James. *(©Bettmann/Corbis)*

have eaten of the poppy may recall the faintest tones without forgetting." It's all pretty true—We are too great to be loved . . .

In an endearing touch, she closes the six-page letter with a whimsical personal account of a visit by a friend who "has a German white mushroom as a beau—the worst thing I ever saw—she brought him around. Surely there must be a limit somewhere. But no. Well, so long. Lots of love, Mil."[5]

Millicent's work for the MSRC kept her more mindful of the war than many women, and it was the endless topic at social events in New York and Washington. She was horrified to hear that her friend, the designer Elsa Schiaparelli, was being accused in some quarters of being a Nazi sympathizer. "Did you see the anonymous article against Scap. Calling her a Nazi—really people are awful. No names mentioned but so obvious, and all because she took vitamins to France and criticized the 7th Avenue hat business—and if she wasn't right and American hats aren't ridiculous, what is!" she wrote her mother. "It was only the pot calling the kettle black. Freedom of speech, but God help you if you do—"

The harder reality of war touched her as a mother, with Peter now a sergeant in the army. His German, French, and English facility made him a natural for intelligence. When he was sent to the field she had a special belt made for his uniform which she padded with five thousand dollars to buy his freedom if he was captured. Most things in her experience could be bought.

From Mary's house in Washington she wrote a long letter in answer to one she had received from Peter. He had, it seemed, been spurned by a young woman, Lucille. Her approach to matters of the heart was no less certain than her opinions on patriotism and national character, and on this subject, she was certainly more experienced. "So Lucille has given you the axe. That's too bad. She'll answer you. Very few people have so little curiosity that they will return a letter unopened, and if they are so lukewarm and dull don't bother with them." She tells him how to see if a returned letter had been steamed open first. (Perhaps a skill learned during her marriage to Salm when her parents intercepted her mail!) She tells him:

Peter darling, remember this, usually girls and women, they will do anything against all their better judgment (if they have it and most do not) if they are made jealous. I have seen women married 20 years who carry on in outrageous ways who obviously care nothing about their husbands, turn into furies if they think they are losing something. Even someone or something they care nothing about. Women are acquisitive by nature. American women are the most possessive of all women—it is their Achilles heel. Everytime. Unfailingly. Very few people in life know what they want and often they only discover it when they imagine they are losing it. A man need only put another woman under the nose of his best beloved to have her eating [out] of his hand. Never fall so much in love that you forget this.... However, her jealousy doesn't necessarily mean that she loves you—remember that also ...

I rather think that a man can have a woman to do what he wants. Only he must be exceedingly careful that in doing so, he does not destroy those qualities and faults that are precious to him. It takes much sensitivity and self-knowledge for this and some humility toward one's own shortcomings. You write that you are "no God's gift to women?" I'm glad you are not. Such men can unhesitatingly be put down and wholly unsatisfactory. They are almost always the "no-goods" of the world who live on their charm to women and their ability to play on weakness.... I think they lose more than they gain ... and they seldom have peace of mind or lasting satisfaction.... I think that you are doing well enough so far. They say that one knows the right person when that person comes along. I doubt that for the simple reason that one's character changes as one learns how to live. Some marriages work out. Most do not. Those that do is [sic] largely because both sides are willing to give to understand. Not for a couple of years but as a life long habit. . . .

It is better by far that the man always keep the upper hand. It is from thousands of years of habit more satisfactory that the woman come second. If she is wise she will find her way as the intuitive member of the two. . . . Great beauty is less essential in the long run than friendship, trust, and understanding. Looks are pleasant, but mean nothing, like fine furniture or pictures or objects that are owned . . .

I ask you to find quality—integrity, a clear brain that has sufficient slyness to be still when stillness is required and that sensibility that does not forever have to have small matters explained that are unexplainable, rather than extreme beauty. This because you will appreciate it as you develop and grow older, more than you will the attractive shell which will coarsen and deteriorate with time—a stupid middle-aged woman is about the saddest sign that the 20th century can produce. The world is full of them and this country has the most. For in this country less is asked of women than in any other, than perhaps our South American neighbors who at least pay attention to the efficient running of their homes and the welfare of their men and children. I'm not damning American womanhood, But I am damning their average intelligence. For in what country save ours could their exist The Daughters of the American Revolution, Shriners, Elks . . .

One wonders what the DAR had done to earn her enmity. She was, after all, the one who had invoked values identical to the DAR's creed when she wrote President Roosevelt on behalf of the MSRC and eagerly mentioned their shared English and Dutch heritage as a touchstone.

Her advice to Peter was based on her own experience. It comes as no surprise that he would eventually marry a European.

In sharp contrast to the grand-sounding advice she handed down, her musings on her own life and relationships were starker. She wrote to Mary:

No one was ever close to me. Nor will they ever be. My nature resents intrusion and fears intimacy. People think they are indispensable to me of whom I hardly think. They imagine friendship which to me is for the most part acquaintance. People go out of my life because they were never in it[.] I want knowledge and happiness. Nothing is good enough forever. No job well enough done. Most people want peace. I don't know what it means. I can't remember when I didn't have to fight to keep my integrity and to hold because (for good or bad) against someone elses will.[6]

She was also having issues with her son Arturo who, though often moody and quiet, had begun wanting to know more about her romantic and marital history.

Dear Mummy Da, [she wrote Mary]
I've been meaning to write for weeks. The reason now is that Brother [her nickname for Arturo] has conceived a sudden passion for writing me long letters about himself and all his thoughts and asking questions and he is much worse than any lover, and it frightens me that his first love should be for me, his mother. It worries me so much that I have to answer carefully, to stay him off. I think it could do him so much damage otherwise. Why it came suddenly I can't imagine but it did and it's a greater problem than the rest. Still, he will have to manage it. I think maybe that if it keeps up I'll have to take him to a doctor for answering. Until [then] I'll try myself. . . . He looks so big and is so uncertain about life. You might write (as though you did not know). Tell him something about our family. He seems to think that in his life he will be on his own entirely, and it frightens him. I've told him but I think he could do with a little more. He trusts me not to tell the things he says, so I don't dare. He's all mixed up. I imagine that the

two bloods don't help. Kipling perhaps was right when he wrote "Let the wheat be all of one sheaf, the grape of all of one vine, ere our children's teeth are sat on edge by bitter bread and wine."[7]

It is interesting that she quotes from Kipling's poem "The Stranger," which has been largely suppressed by publishers over the years because its subject is a warning against racial mixing. Though she had the essence correct, Kipling wrote of corn, not wheat.

She set much store on the various nationalities of her sons' fathers and their mixed heritage. "Paulie [as she called Paul] somehow has more of us, and Peter is all right, the Austrian makes him old and wise, if sometimes a little too gemutlich[8] for his own good—our Darling Peter, he will get along. He is in Belgium now and likes it."

A sad note sounded in 1944 when the family received news that Count Salm had reportedly committed suicide by jumping from his fifth-floor apartment in the Hotel Ritz in Budapest, Hungary. The Count had been arrested and questioned by the Gestapo for three days for alleged anti-Nazi activities and was then released. He told the bartender at the Ritz that he would be rearrested, downed a glass of wine, and leapt from his apartment window, though speculation that he had been pushed clouded the account, especially in the family. The notice of his death in the U.S. invariably included the account of his elopement with "Millicent Rogers, heiress to a $26,000,000 Standard Oil fortune." Peter was enrolled at Princeton when he heard the news. He believed his father had been murdered for withholding information—or leapt to keep his secrets.[9] The latter seemed less likely since his father was Catholic. Count Salm's body was not located, adding to his son's distress. That factor was considered one of Peter's motives when he suspended his education to join the army's military intelligence. His parentage had a way of bringing tragedy and pathos to his place in the family.

What with men, motherhood, war, the MSRC, and fragile health, Millicent had her hands full. Yet, as always, the public saw only her composed exterior. The papers wrote admiringly of her outward style. In appearance she always managed to suggest that she didn't have a care in the world. "Millicent, who never looked better in her eventful life (or happier) recently bought a house in Jamaica," declared *The Washington Post* in the "Society" column at the war's end. "The chic heiress spent all her winters at Claremont Manor . . ." the columnist continued, and wrongly guessed she would soon be living in Jamaica. In the same column it was mentioned that her ex-husband, Ronald Balcom would soon marry again, this time to Lucille Vanderbilt, recently divorced from her husband George. His romantic involvements with Norma Shearer and Lady Ashley had been reported during the previous year.

Millicent reestablished herself in New York society at the end of the war—much as she had done at Claremont Manor—on her own terms. She frequently entertained at The Port, but the cast of friends and guests at her dinners and parties had changed. Her good friend Elizabeth de Bruniere, a former countess who was part of the diaspora of French and Russian émigrés who came to New York after the war, was a frequent guest. Bruniere, who had run the Elizabeth Arden salon in Buenos Aires before becoming the business manager of the Arden salon in New York, was her contempory in style and spirit. "There was no sewing or knitting or cooking," laughs Bruniere's daughter, Odette, "They wanted challenge and to be entertained. They were intelligent and funny and thrived on the new world of artists, writers, and gathering of interesting people. They were bachelor ladies, women of the world by then and very smooth."

Odette's memory of Millicent when she accompanied her mother on their weekends at The Port was of "a most extraordinary person. There was a peace and lightness about her" that Odette likened to Grace Kelly. "She projected a sense that 'I'm just here and I am just myself.'" Millicent's conversation was serious, of books and of music and pleasure in the present moment. There was no "one-upmanship," the staple of prewar society. "They never, ever talked about money. Never," recalls Odette. Their references to men were considered "grown-up talk" and kept out of Odette's earshot, but she knew there was a link between Millicent and Roald Dahl, even when Millicent and her mother arranged for Odette to go out to dinner with him.

When Millicent, who had become a blonde during the war and like the auburn-haired Elizabeth de Bruniere wore her hair in a chignon with waves, entered a room, "You had to stop what you were doing. She was like an apparition," says Odette. The women went out most evenings and while they were thought by some to be aloof and snobbish, their social interest was merely selective. It was as though Millicent had moved on from the old society roster that she now considered boring, and was finally free to choose her own friends and company. Once again, she was reinventing herself in her new milieu.

Millicent continued to run an orderly household in which the staff did its work properly and stayed mostly out of sight, but she shed some of the old formality and social conventions of Southampton life before the war. Her dinners were increasingly casual, and she "hung out" with her houseguests. They dressed informally and most evenings began with little vodka martinis.

Odette, though perhaps impressionable at seventeen, has fixed memories of staying in Millicent's house. She thought her stylish hostess approachable and "surprisingly conversational with a 17-year-old. No one else did that then. She had lots of charm and was totally serene and she just didn't look like anyone else." Odette, a Parsons student on the lookout for style and design, was most taken with Millicent's individualistic style. She was wowed that Millicent came down to breakfast one morning wearing a white men's shirt with the sleeves rolled up, and "something we'd never seen before—a denim skirt. The chic of it all was perfect. Who had ever heard of a denim skirt?!" Once again, Millicent was inventively setting the standard for a new look in casual dressing. Fashionable women like her and Bruniere always "dressed" for their days and evenings; they would not have been seen in robes or dressing gowns even on a casual summer weekend, according to Odette. Dumpiness simply wasn't in their fashion repertoire. But Millicent was moving toward a more relaxed and casual look that she would expand and popularize, causing some to call her visionary, for the next decade.

While she had always attracted attention with her designer clothes and attention to fashion, with the mixing and matching of refined with unrefined elements in Austria, she began to cut a different, clean-lined "American" fashion image in the forties. She sported the newest type of shoes for summer, espadrilles. Button earrings, no bracelets, and no necklaces were considered proper jewelry for a lady during the daytime. Millicent was partial to gold and wore her large signature pearls at night. She was also partial to big jewelry. It was whispered that she wore so many rings and bracelets to anchor her hands, which now trembled after her many small strokes and heart attacks. She did finger exercises to strengthen them. As in so many areas, Millicent freely skipped ahead of the trends with her white shirts and rough fabrics, tweaking high fashion with casual elements. Yet her hallmark became her impeccability, and that merely embellished and modernized her legendary appeal. Odette Terrel des Chênes vividly remembered her mystique, almost seventy years later: "She looked so fabulous but you knew there was more depth to her. You wanted to go in there and find out about it." It was a trait that had fascinated more than a few men and women, and would continue to attract.

There were other signs of a sea change—a new freedom and ease with herself, playfulness even—in Millicent's life. Colonel Rogers had named the guest rooms at The Port, some humorously. There was "The Room of the Dog" with its collection of Bennington Pottery canine figures on the mantel. "The Room of the Haunt," with dark beams and dormered windows overlooking Scallop Pond. The Attic Room and the more colorfully named "Room of the Ruined Roman Virgins," which was usually assigned to male guests, while The Room of Canton with its Oriental antiques, rugs, and ivory carving was for women. But seventeen-year-old Odette was assigned The Room of the Ruined Roman Virgins, which she, her mother, and Millicent had a laugh about. When Odette, a tidy sleeper by nature, woke in the middle of the night with the sheets all off the bed, she thought of the supernatural and ran to her mother's room. She and Millicent were convinced that the room was haunted and the next day Millicent called a priest for an exorcism and followed his advice that she close the house until it was complete.

Whether it was the spirit of fun or spiritual yearning, Millicent and Elizabeth also attended séances and on one occasion in New York went to see a famous medium who claimed to read minds and speak with the dead. They were attracted by the showmanship and the paranormal promise that the boundary between reality and spirit could be penetrated. Odette reasoned that the tight bond between Millicent and her mother during those years, beyond the fact that they were sophisticated women of the world—those "bachelor ladies"—was that "They were both displaced persons. One because of the past [her mother] and one because she didn't like the rules of the game. Millicent was a free spirit and could afford it. She could do what she wanted to when she wanted to, and I envied her." That was the effect she had on fashion editors and society women alike. They envied her freedom and flair.

Odette was on the terrace at The Port with Millicent and her mother on the day that a package arrived for Millicent. Inside was a gold toothpick that Millicent brought out to show at lunchtime. "It was the most outrageous, craziest item and we all laughed about it." The moment, the conviviality, the absurdity and luxury of a gold toothpick stayed in her memory, emblematic somehow of Millicent's rarified life.

Millicent invariably charmed the younger generation with her composure, her openness, and her willingness, atypical at the time, to treat young people like adults rather than children. She invited Michael Coe, grandson of the Colonel's sister Mai, to visit The Port of Missing Men when he was in his teens for a three-day visit in hopes that her younger sons would help to entertain him. He was piqued by the prospect of visiting his glamorous older cousin and her sons. "Millicent was like a legend in the family. First, nobody ever got divorced like her. We felt like we were country cousins," Coe says.[10] It was Peter, his elder by several years, who made the effort to make him feel comfortable with his mother's grand style of entertaining and wide array of guests. Peter had been a babe in arms whom Millicent had brought to visit Coe's grandfather at Planting Fields on Oyster Bay, the year he was born.

Coe was intrigued with his "great looking" older cousin whose reputation for being gorgeous, smart, having a sense of humor, and radiating charm while at the same time being down to earth had always preceded her in the family. "She knew everybody, and at The Port there were designers and painters and people from the Southampton Yacht Club. She was interested in painting and collected Cézannes," he recalled sixty years later. He was smitten to find her "so highly intelligent and so informed." It was understood in the larger Rogers' family constellation that the Colonel's will had cut Millicent out of a large part of her inheritance and handicapped her financially. Coe also knew about her ne'r-do-well brother and understood that Millicent's mother, Mary, was "a fine person and a family favorite" despite her divorce from the Colonel. He noted the Japanese butler, who commented cavalierly to him in a heavy accent: "All they do is dwink." Valentina, the fashion designer, focusing on resort wear that season, was also there with her husband George Schlee. Coe could not help but notice that Millicent's Great Dane, an enormous dog by his standards, was not housebroken when it made a big pile in the living room. Most noteworthy was how calmly Millicent handled the event. "It didn't seem to bother her one bit and the maids took care of the mess." It was a heady affair for the callow fifteen-year-old, who concluded that Millicent was "not just a fashion model"—and could be all the things he'd heard about her at once.

Lanfranco Rasponi, a writer on society and performing arts, wrote of Millicent in his book *The International Nomads* that she was "one of the most bewitching creatures ever to grace society...." He also noted a trait that had become her hallmark by the end of World War II: She was always late. "Had she not been a Standard Oil heiress, she would have been condoned anyhow, for she was that rare person who lighted a room upon entering it. Although she adored going to the theater, she never saw the first act of any show." He wrote that on one particular evening he escorted her to *The King and I*, and afterward they were to have supper with the star, Yul Brynner. Millicent, he wrote in his account of the conversation, "quite seriously she said to him 'I have a marvelous idea for you. The number of people, like myself, who cannot avoid being late is such a large one that twice a month you should advertise the inversion of the two acts. All of us would return to see the initial act and then you could eliminate performing the second, for during the first half, the theater would be empty.'" It was an audacious suggestion, what would later be called thinking "out of the box." There is no record of what Yul Brynner thought, but one assumes that with her gracious delivery he was either charmed or amused, but hardly offended.

Tardiness, Rasponi noted, had become part of "smart" behavior in the forties, but for Millicent it had always been a tendency and was becoming increasingly so. It was assumed that as a young woman she had preferred arriving late in order to make an entrance, but concern over her appearance as she grew older seemed to compound her reasons for lateness. Now age and sickness had taken their toll on her looks and she required extra time to make the appearance she wanted. She worked to compensate for the new weariness that sometimes slipped into her face. She insisted on looking perfect. The flawless grooming that she had made her trademark took time, and she was not to be hurried—nor would she go out—until she looked exactly the way she wanted. She studied her face and makeup and often called in a hairdresser, who slowed rather than speeded up the process of readying to go out. Her son Peter recalled a certain madcap heiress *joie de vivre* during these years. One evening when Millicent came home tired and "tight," she undressed for bed and took off her jewelry and tossed it in the air. It was several years later that a housekeeper found her employer's missing diamond necklace caught in the chandelier overhead.[11] Much of Millicent's past and present converged during wartime. Even her old flame Serge Obolensky was now in

New York, married to Alice Astor. He squired numerous society women to the opera and parties. Peralta-Ramos was now in the U.S. and made the society columns for merrymaking at a party at the Westchester Bath Club. A food fight developed, and Peralta-Ramos challenged the host to make a pyramid out of tables and chairs. When he did, Peralta-Ramos turned a seltzer water siphon on him and the evening escalated when one of the female guests put a berry pie in Ramos's face. The debacle was picked up by *The Washington Post*. In an incredible bit of snobbish whitewash, Westbrook Pegler wrote in his column, "Fair Enough," "It hardly needs to be said that the Westchester Bath Club is regarded as a very desirable adjunct to the social life of our county and of Greenwich, Conn...the guests, though rich and hearty are never vulgar but unfailingly refined, never ill-mannered or noisy.... There is an elegant way and there is a low and vulgar way to squirt a siphon or throw a blackberry pie or smear pie over the evening clothes of a company of merrymakers." Pegler concluded that the "high quality of the fun-loving mischief-makers" was what made the difference in the acceptability of their pranks. There is not a sign that his tongue was in his cheek.

At war's end Millicent's life was adrift in a three-point social swirl between Southampton, Montego Bay, and Claremont Manor. Her friends Rocky and Gary Cooper, Noël Coward, Claudette Colbert, and a list of Hollywood celebrities and movie stars were regulars at Wharf House in Jamaica and Claremont Manor, when they weren't in Southampton, but their locus was Hollywood, the new capital of America's imagination. Once the purposeful war years were over, Hollywood began to eclipse New York and Washington as the epitome of glamour. The movie business was entering its golden age. Sophisticated screen images and luxurious fashions began to reshape postwar America's popular ideals.

Millicent had befriended and commissioned dresses from Hollywood's new leading couturier, Gilbert Adrian. He was the man responsible for dressing a new crop of glamorous movie stars on and off set, including Greta Garbo, Jean Harlow, Joan Crawford, and his wife, the Oscar-winning actress Janet Gaynor. Adrian was known for his magically glamorous evening gowns, in a quintessential American style. He designed Greta Garbo's clothes in *Mata Hari*, and gave Joan Crawford the broad shoulder pads that spawned a whole new trend in postwar fashion. But his greatest claims to fame were the evening gowns he designed for stars, like the cast of women in George Cukor's *The Women*. He seemed to have a knack for perceiving the personality of his clients and putting some wit into his designs for them. He took Millicent's look of fragility and heightened it with extremely feminine dresses that draped and floated at night, in contrast to the simple tailored lines she wore during the day. With his elegant yet sexy and mature styles, he spearheaded the rich new American look toward haute couture that swept through financially and emotionally crippled Europe after the war. Millicent, who had been widely admired in European fashion circles before the war, helped carry the message that American design was leading the way. She looked the fair femme fatale, fluffed and feathered like an apparition from *Swan Lake*, when she modeled his layered net black ball gown, the décolletage adorned with black feathers, in *Harper's Bazaar*.

Adrian and Gaynor were naturals for Millicent. Their origins were humbler than hers, but they were a stylish, creative, and modern version of the demimonde life that Millicent and Mary had cultivated so expansively in Senlis and Venice. They were the logical hosts to help her establish herself in the new culture of celebrity-driven Hollywood. Rocky Cooper, the stepdaughter of the Wall Street scion Paul Shields from Southampton who was married to Gary Cooper, also joined in the chorus recruiting Millicent to Hollywood. She volunteered that Tyrone and Annabella Power's house across the street from the Adrians was available.

Several factors converged to make Hollywood Millicent's next destination, but there was really only one catalyst. She was smitten by the last major love of her life, the movie star Clark Gable. The Port had always been frequented by Hollywood stars, many of whom had family connections to Southampton or with success enjoyed the wealthy fun there. Millicent's friends Rocky and Gary Cooper hosted their friend Gable when he came out to Southampton during his vacation in New York. They introduced him to Millicent. It was in Southampton's social swim, a location in which she starred, that she met Gable, the most handsome and glamourous actor of his day. They quickly become an item and regulars at social gatherings that included other Hollywood stars. One summer afternoon they were casually photographed together on the porch of the Cooper's house with Van Johnson, Merle Oberon, her husband, and Rocky Cooper. It is assumed Gary Cooper snapped the photo. The sand dunes and beach grass lay visible behind.[12] Her eyes averted from the late afternoon sun, Millicent stood next to Gable, her weak arm cradled next to her waist in a pose that was becoming distinctive.

Gable, six foot one and dark and handsome, was a true movie star and a hunk, an American man who had leapt into the female consciousness as a fantasy heartthrob, never more so than after he seized Scarlett O'Hara on the velvet staircase when he starred as Rhett Butler in *Gone with the Wind* in 1939. Millicent referred to him as Captain Butler in private to her friends and family. The prospect of falling in love seemed to quicken her postwar pulse and revitalize her energies. Like her other loves, he was a beautiful object: dapper, but more a Hemingway type of man's man than her past roster of smooth Europeans and Englishmen. He was enough of a cad to fit the pattern she had already established—and he had a well-paying job. He and Millicent, from the start, were a pair worthy of Hollywood central casting. She, the composed, impeccably stylish heiress and he, the dark, debonair leading man of Hollywood. "Millicent was a slender, exotic beauty with enormous style, and Clark liked her very much," wrote his biographer and former personal secretary Jean Garceau, who was more restrained in her characterization of the relationship than Millicent's associates. Diana Vreeland put it more emotionally, as women friends often do. "Millicent liked beautiful men, and she was just *mad* about Clark Gable. Mad!"[13] Not only was Millicent a-twitter over Gable, but she didn't hesitate to refashion her life and image to seduce him. On one occasion her attorney, Jerome Sinsheimer, came to her New York apartment to attend to her legal matters. His appointment with her ran into the hour that Gable was expected to arrive. When Gable arrived downstairs and was announced by the buzzer, Millicent went into an uncustomary flutter and told Sinsheimer that he would have to leave immediately down the back stairs. Apparently, the scene she envisioned for his arrival did not include his finding her bent over papers with her attorney.[14]

From the outside it seemed as if Millicent had perhaps met her match. She seemed to put down her guard with Clark, and for the first time in her life he was *her* conquest, instead of vice versa. Instead of coolly being courted, she joined in the chase, asking her driver, Irving, to drive him to Southampton, summoning him to her home and parties. It wasn't like the secretive walkups to her marriages, or the cool conniving with her men in Washington. Compared to those courtships, she threw herself at Gable. The caretaker of Claremont Manor, Jack Arnold, remembers spying Clark Gable and Millicent swimming nude in the estate's elegant pool.[15] Gable himself was shopping for property to buy in fashionable Surry, Virginia. "They were having a big love affair," declared Vreeland. As the "season" in Southampton came to a close, Millicent decided to pack up and boldly follow Gable back to Los Angeles. She had set her sights on the man, still staying, as she had done numerous times before in her fast-moving life, at the forefront of American glamour as it migrated to the new postwar capital of image and dreams, Hollywood.

CHAPTER EIGHTEEN

Bangles and Baubles

ILLICENT FLOWERED IN MANY DIRECTIONS DURING the war. By its end, she had established herself as an independent woman and head of household at Claremont, and she had also defined herself as a woman who worked as the director of a charitable cause—with undertones of intrigue and underground activity in support of the French and perhaps other resistance organizations—in the war effort. Whatever satisfaction her new roles and competence provided her, she did not seem to work for outward recognition, but avoided it, just as she showed disinterest in awards and citations in the fashion world. The French government offered her the Legion of Honor for her work as Executive Director of the MSRC, but she declined. Her efforts, she explained later to her sons, needed no other acknowledgment. She also stated publicly that fashion distinctions were of little interest to her. Though she was again named to the New York Dress Institute's ten best-dressed list, when asked what designer she patronized, she responded, "I'm like everybody else. When I need a dress, I just buy one and then wear it until it's no longer wearable." Her answer, disingenuous as it was, seemed tailored to match the earnest public mood of the time against frivolity and excess. "The whole thing is rather silly," she stated with uncharacteristic candor for a woman whose broadest reputation rested on being fashionably dressed.[1] She also added that she did not like fussy clothes and was partial to simple lines. She had never been hostage to a single designer. Yet style and design still greatly interested her, and she put her energy into a new expression of it.

What is truly remarkable is the way that Millicent ranged from bedridden passivity to social ubiquitousness during these years. She flitted between New York, Southampton, Washington, Jamaica, and Claremont Manor, in spite of her foundering health. Her illness and the long spells of seeming inactivity took their toll on her physical stamina, but they didn't touch her spirit. If anything, they incubated her newest creative enterprise—jewelry making.

Millicent had always loved jewelry. She had notably run into trouble with her father for that fascination, back in 1922, when she went overboard at Cartier. As in all matters of style, she had expensive taste and was inexorably attracted to the best. There were both contemporary and antique pieces that she had acquired from Cartier, Boucheron, Chaumet, Verdura, and Schlumberger. She bought the jewels, surreal liquid-looking brooches, that Salvadore Dalí designed for Verdura.[2] She typically mixed the old and the new as it suited her. Her height and the increasing angularity of her features as she aged made her favor big pieces.

Though jewelry etiquette for women in the 1940s rigidly prescribed minimalism, even down to when and what kind of watch to wear by day and evening, Millicent had her own sense of what was appropriate. "She had a flair for the dramatic and she wasn't afraid to wear big jewelry. Millicent could carry off a big piece and she knew how to wear it," explains Edward Landrigan, chief executive and successor to Verdura. She wore Verdura's big starburst brooches. She flouted all fashion prescriptions when she wore the designer Valentina's big brooch, a spectacular Russian Order of Saint Catherine set with huge diamonds on her white blouses, "as casually as someone else might have worn a gold circle pin."[3]

As her taste evolved, the only way she could get the kind of jewelry she wanted was to design and make it herself. So she did with jewelry as she had done with coats and dresses; she tweaked exisiting designs and custom details to suit herself. There was yet another reason for her focus on jewelry in the 1940s. It was camouflage for the tremors and paralysis caused by her strokes and weak heart. Making jewelry was far more personal than designing a dress with a couturier. Using her fingers to first mold the wax and then wield the small tools for refining a piece was therapeutic for her hands. Both the product and the process suited her. Her friend Maria Martins, a noted Brazilian sculptress, encouraged her. Millicent had been sketching jewelry designs on tracing paper and yellow legal pads, the same paper she used for her five- and six-page letters to friends and family, since her heart attacks in France and Austria in the 1930s. She sent her early designs to Tiffany, to the master French jewelrymaker and designer Jean Schlumberger, who had begun his career creating buttons for Elsa Schiaparelli.

While it is unclear who first sat down with Millicent, hand to hand, to teach her the craft of jewelry making, the various influences on her work and design are understood. She had been a prodigious collector and admirer of fine jewelry in New York and Europe. In Paris she sent one of her first designs to René Boivin, whose wife Jeanne Poiret had a stable of women designers, a feature Millicent may have found attractive during her early efforts. Poiret was the sister of the famous Parisian couturier Paul Poiret, whose clothing designs Millicent was acquainted with, and they traveled in the same well-connected top fashion circles.

Jeanne Poiret Boivin, a designer herself, deviated from the popular Art Deco styles in Paris of the time to create large pieces with exotic themes, and reintroduced "barbaric" bracelets. She created chunky, often mechanical pieces with Abyssinian swirls in yellow gold as well as floral designs and depictions of animals and sea creatures, even mermaids and unicorns. They fit the descriptive "sculptural" that was applied to Millicent's later work and inspired her to experiment.

Until the 1940s Millicent had turned her designs over to master goldsmith Joseph Fried and the famed jewelry designer George W. Headley for production. A longtime patron of À la Vieille Russie, eminent jewelers in New York who specialized in the work of Fabergé, she sought advice from the owners, friends by now, who advised and guided her pursuit of the craft. Through her social contacts with leading designers and artists, she always started at the top. She and Verdura, a member of the Italian royal family who had designed Coco Chanel's famous cuffs and favorite jewelry, were birds of a feather who had probably crossed paths back when Millicent the post-deb was being courted by the heir to the Italian throne, and again in Venice and Paris, well before Verdura opened his New York studio in 1939. Through jewelry design they soon developed a creative bond, a pared-down version of her relationship to Charles James. Martins suggested that Millicent cultivate the sculptural aspects of jewelry that intrigued her and encouraged her to learn the mechanics of the craft and even to set up her own bench. It was something of a bold foray into her newly chosen creative realm. Even master jewelry designers of the time most typically did not "fabricate" or manufacture their own creations. Fried taught her the fundamentals of metallurgy so she could create and cast her own gold and silver designs.[4]

As she had with fabrics, hats, dresses, cars, and home interiors, Millicent now put her creative stamp on jewelry: She developed concepts quickly and reworked them meticulously. Headley, a leader in the field, remarked that she was not easy to please because she "knew exactly what she wanted. She had a fabulous eye for color and texture and a daring knack for juxtaposition. There's a sense of enjoyment in all her work. She had a way of transforming the mundane into something interesting, refined, and above all personal," he told *Connoisseur* magazine in 1984. She paired whatever elements, precious and semiprecious, that suited her fancy. Her son Paul remarked that as her proficiency increased, so did her arbitrariness. Everything she did was directed by her own tastes and preferences. She thought nothing of mixing red glass with rubies, if she liked the impression they made. The small and precious provided a creative outlet, totally within her control. Her designs were appreciated for their flair and individuality, and according to Penny Proddow and Marion Fasel, coauthors of *Hollywood Jewels*, were considered "ultrachic" both then and now.[5]

Making jewelry was more than a hobby. Once again, as with dress clothes, she seemed to divine the direction design was headed. It was hardly by accident that Paul Flato, considered the American jeweler extraordinaire, asked Millicent to lend her imagination to his "whimsies," the stylish pieces that were different from the serious jewelry fashioned from diamonds and platinum.[6] Flato's "whimsies" were lighthearted, often humorous pieces to wear in the daytime. The market for them continues to this day, as evidenced by advertisements (most notably in *The New Yorker*) by major jewelers in New York City featuring bejeweled animals, insect, and bird designs. Millicent's study and appreciation of Jeanne Boivin's Parisian creatures had primed her imagination for such design.

With Verdura, who had apprenticed with Flato from 1935 to 1939, Millicent sometimes sat in the back studio of Flato's Fifty-seventh Street shop in Manhattan, designing. Verdura was paid for his contributions while Millicent was not, but some reciprocity was arrived at between them. It seemed to be enough for Millicent to know that her work was of a caliber to suit the masters. Their tutelage and access to fabrication techniques compensated her for her designs. Millicent's most noted design was her puffy heart, an outsized asymmetrical heart with stones that she wore with dress fashions in *Vogue*. One facsimile of it was purchased by Joan Crawford. That this heart, full and hardy in contrast to her own weak and failing organ, would become the design for which she was best known, was a bittersweet irony. Her stars, asymmetrical, sensual and fleshy, were nearly anthropomorphic. They were as modern as the stars that New York jeweler Kenneth Jay Lane, an admirer of Millicent's, would later create for Jacqueline Kennedy Onassis.

A revolution in jewelry design was on: It was a shift from the classical European designs and standards to American modernity, and Millicent happily joined in. After the war European jewelers hewed to classic styles, while American jewelry found its own idiom, lightened by kitsch and playfulness. Flato, considered the greatest of all the Americans, offered a pair of gold nuts-and-bolts cuff links, cited as an example of the American tradition of "elevating the humble."[7] By 1948 *Harper's Bazaar* had noted that "Millicent Rogers has turned craftsman. Her tools, in a small gray felt bag, accompany her on her travels. The jewelry has the archaic feeling so apparent in contemporary art; often the precious metal is used with the freedom of a primitive artisan carving in wood."

She liked designs derived from nature and featured dragons, horses, stars, and flowers. Her work was bold rather than delicate, and as usual, she sparked a craze among fashionable women. "Jewelry embarked upon a whole new trend when she picked up a leaf, stuck a pin through it, and gave it to Boivin to copy in gold and diamonds," Cecil Beaton recalled. She liked the weight and feel of heavy metals, eighteen- and twenty-four-carat yellow and green gold. Millicent's enthusiasm was contagious. She taught Rocky Cooper and her mother Veronica Shields in Southampton how to go about the design process and soon they, too, began carrying their felt bags and bits of gold, as less exalted women did knitting, wherever they went.

Millicent's heavy jewelry also served as a foundation garment. Her son Arturo emphasizes the way that the heavy gold necklaces and bracelets were designed to hide her paralysis. Their weight kept her head and hands in place, he says, and her heaviest necklaces were often anchored to her bra strap to keep her upright, as would a brace. Yet her closest observers were able to detect an increasing problem. Fulco Verdura, gentler than Roald Dahl had been, noted "the funny way she walked." She repeatedly, in the forties, struck the same pose for snapshots: arms crossed, with her left arm cradling the weaker right one.

She occupied herself with jewelry making during her bedridden stretches, and if she wasn't designing on paper, she shaped small wax molds from red or black dental wax for casting. She had always set up her boudoir to double as a studio and sitting room, a place to receive visitors as well as to study and to sketch, but now when she was convalescing she often slipped a piece of wax into her visitor's hands and told them to make something with it. When they left she might recover it, and have it cast into a bauble or piece of jewelry to present to the creator as a surprise gift later. With gold at thirty-five dollars an ounce in the 1940s, it was an imaginative and generous gesture. Cecil Beaton added jewelry making to the list of skills, like needlework and carpet making, that "used up the energies that might otherwise have been channeled to serious artistic accomplishments." Her friend and designer Elsa Schiaparelli joined the chorus. "Her jewels were of rare beauty and strange design. . . . If she had not been so terribly rich, she might, with her vast talent and unlimited generosity, have become a great artist."[8] The distinction between copying and inspiration is a flimsy one because jewelry design cannot be copyrighted, but Millicent seemed definitely to inspire others with her creations, much as she had done with dresses. It seems clear to Judith Price, director of the National Jewelry Institute, that "she paid her way in" to the field, but that she inspired others, nonetheless.

Such designs were in the vanguard of what would become immensely popular in the forties and fifties, when Millicent was at her most prolific. The evolution in her designs showed up as accessories to her own wardrobe and gifts that she tendered to her friends. She made a large gold necklace of gold beads with large flat pendant plates for her acquaintance Dame Edith Sitwell. Though they had met only once, Sitwell called Millicent "one of my greatest friends." Sitwell took "Figures of Growth," as it was entitled, to the British Museum as a spoof. The museum curators studied it for four days believing at first that it was a pre-Columbian piece from the tomb of an Inca. They marveled at how the gold had been stiffened in ways that did not exist in pre-Columbian times before they were told of its provenance. It clanked when Sitwell wore it.[9] As Millicent's technical skill increased, so did the complexity of her designs, often molded in wax first, then cast or forged in twenty-two or twenty-four carat gold, malleable enough for the bashed and battered look she preferred.

Millicent's pouch of jeweler's tools became her newest omnipresent accessory. On her trips to California, which were becoming increasingly frequent, she typically settled into her train compartment with her gray felt bag of tools and molding wax, distracted from the duration of the journey by the pleasure of making jewelry.

CHAPTER NINETEEN

A Leading Man

THE ROMANCE BETWEEN A BEAUTIFUL BLOND HEIRESS WHO kept seeking lasting marital happiness and America's leading man could have been scripted in Hollywood. It seemed to observers, and perhaps even to Millicent, that the classic happy ending was taking shape. Millicent set her sights on Gable as she had no other man, allowing herself to pursue him with flair and aggression. She took Rocky Cooper's advice and rented Tyrone Power's bungalow across the road from Janet and Gilbert Adrian in the northeast end of the San Fernando Valley. The Coopers promoted the romance with Gable after they had introduced them in Southampton in 1946. They'd been friends with Gable for many years. Gable's third and most recent wife, the actress Carole Lombard, had dated Gary Cooper in her teens when the two were both under contract to Paramount. Gable and Cooper had once been rivals, leading men who almost always were considered for the same roles. In fact, producer David O. Selznick had once wanted Cooper to play Rhett Butler in *Gone with the Wind* before Gable was offered the part. Successful survivors of the system and members of the close-knit Hollywood community of the forties, they'd become good friends who regularly skied together in Sun Valley where they sometimes played with their pals Bing Crosby and Ernest Hemingway.

With seven of her beloved dachshunds and twenty-some trunks of clothes, Millicent moved west and prepared to take Hollywood (or at least its leading man) by storm. She traveled on the train with the Coopers, who were enthusiastic about her move. When they crossed the desert Millicent looked out the window and remarked to Cooper, who was quickly becoming America's favorite onscreen cowboy, "It's been so long since I've seen this part of the country. Where are the long-horned cattle that used to roam these parts?" Cooper answered, "I've lassoed them all in my pictures."[1]

As Millicent traveled to the coast, the public was already speculating about her next marriage. "Millicent H. Rogers Rumored Planning to Wed Clark Gable," announced Cholly Knickerbocker in his syndicated gossip and society column on July 25, 1946. He offered lots of details. She had been expected, he confided, to fly to England to marry Ian Fleming, but instead she ordered a new twenty-thousand-dollar wardrobe to take to LA, and abruptly cancelled plans to visit Prides Crossing, a smart summer resort near Boston. Friends had been told, he said, that she was making a ten-day trip to Los Angeles, but she was taking some of her finest paintings from her New York apartment, which hinted at a longer stay. Gable had returned to Los Angeles a week earlier, noted Cholly, and phoned Millicent continuously.

On the road, Millicent seemed the archetypical Easterner, commenting on the Western landscape and the livestock, but at the end of the trip she found a Hollywood that made her feel right at home. Lady Elsie Mendl, who had entertained her and her mother Mary so lavishly in Paris, was living with her husband in Benedict Canyon. Even the Duke and Duchess of Windsor were in town on an extended visit, though there is no evidence that Lady Mendl, their hostess, entertained Millicent and her old beau, the former Prince of Wales, and the Duchess together.

Millicent was charmed and energized by the Adrians' California way of life, a gracious yet laid-back lifestyle enhanced by Gilbert Adrian's flair, which was on display in his house as well as his studio. The ten-acre Adrian property included a spacious country house akin to those rambling Connecticut country estates where Adrian had grown up. He and Gaynor partied and hosted luminaries from the Hollywood design world and MGM stable of actors and playwrights. The dirt roads lined with citrus groves lent the valley the feeling of open country, though it was populated with the homes of movie moguls and their stars. The social life was wildly glamorous when the movie kingpins and stars socialized.

Across the road from the Powers' house where Millicent stayed, the Adrians were a vital resource for everything from setting up housekeeping to buying a monkey, which was a matter of the first order for Millicent once she had moved in. Adrian had a pet monkey, a blond gibbon about three feet tall, that fascinated Millicent. The monkey house with an awning cover that he'd designed for it, striped and tassled like something out of the French circus, was admired by his fellow stylists, designers, and guests. Millicent hoped to find a smaller ape that she could teach to ride on her shoulder. Adrian directed her to a dealer in exotic pets in Thousand Oaks, an hour away,[2] but her friend, the British actor Reginald Gardiner, presented her with a small black and white gibbon at a champagne lunch in her honor. He made a toast saying he hoped it would give her "as much pleasure, love, and joy as Clark gives you." Millicent was delighted and named the monkey Topaz. He became her newest accessory.[3]

Predictably, she had no trouble making it into the Hollywood smart set; she knew a good many of them, the Fondas (relatives on the Benjamin side of the family), Powers, and Coopers from Southampton, and the stream of celebrities like Cecil Beaton and Noël Coward, her pals from Montego Bay, who were now in Hollywood. Within months of her arrival she was noted in *Modern Screen* for being at movie mogul Jack Warner's parties, and she and Clark Gable were an item in Louella Parsons' and Hedda Hopper's gossip columns for the *Los Angeles Examiner* and the *Los Angeles Times*.

According to Lyn Tornabene, one of Gable's biographers, "Hollywood in the immediate postwar years was the most glamorous spot on earth . . . for a moment in the history of hedonism, there was no place like it." He explained that in the years after the war "money wasn't the universal problem. Drabness was, tackiness was, deprivation was. Hollywood seemed to suffer none of it. There were parties every hour of the day and night, nightclubs like Ciro's and the Mocambo to dance in." Chasen's and Romanoff's were the dining spots, and after the dearth of men during the war, there were now lots of men around, some of them, on-screen and off, considered heroes.

Gable had flown combat missions for the Army Air Corps and came across as a man's man. He drove a sporty gray Packard convertible around town and his publicity agent had tailored him in the image of a sportsman, a man comfortable with horses, guns, and fishing. He was to all appearances from the same mold as Millicent's three ex-husbands, though he was in fact a poor boy from Appalachia who had dropped out of high school at sixteen to pursue acting. His father had labored in the same oil fields that her grandfather had made his millions exploiting. But his stardom and life experiences had seasoned him, and his greatest attraction for women was what Joan Crawford, one of his former loves, called his "animal magic." Most women's knees buckled when he was around. "He was the most masculine man that I have ever met in my life," Crawford cooed. The newspaper reviewers invariably called him "all man," which was what American audiences liked their leading men to be.

Janet Gaynor added some levity to the admiration. She had known Gable for years. She and he often rode home together from the MGM studio at the end of the day. She considered him a good sort and a regular guy, despite his outrageous attraction for women. He also had a reputation as a heavy drinker. Before his marriage to Carole Lombard he had been known for being tough and inconsiderate.

He didn't remember birthdays and anniversaries and lacked chivalry off-screen, but he had mellowed since her death and the war. He was becoming more gentlemanly, on and off the movie set.[4] He just seemed to like women, even if he took most of them for granted, which made them both more comfortable and attracted by him.

He and the lithe and stately Millicent, exquisitely dressed, made a striking couple, and it must have been a glorious high for Millicent to appear at Hollywood's toniest social occasions on the arm of America's leading man. She was the pale regal dame alongside the dark knight. This time, however, the bar was remarkably high and the competition was stiff. Hedda Hopper wrote of Clark Gable in the *Los Angeles Times*, "Women flocked around him like moths around a candle—duchesses, show girls, movie stars, socialites—name them, he could have had them." "Women, women, women, women," wrote biographer Tornabene, summarizing the situation when Millicent entered the fray.

Perhaps the competition piqued her, for the following year, 1947, she settled in further by moving from the Powers' house in the San Fernando Valley to Rudoph Valentino's august Italianate villa at the head of Benedict Canyon on eight acres overlooking Beverly Hills. The scenic hillside property up a winding road with sweeping views was lined with stately cypress tress and Italian gardens, stables, and a circular drive. It suited Millicent's yen for fine houses and established her apart from Gable in his eight-room white brick home in Encino, but she soon tired of the dark broody house away from nature and the social life of the Valley. Clark showed her a property in the rolling hillside northeast of his house that she intended to purchase, and she eagerly began plans to build. It seemed a statement that she was a presence to reckon with, and that she had come to stay.

But all the while, her energies were diminishing and the trajectory of her life was faltering. She spent many of her days quietly in the grand surroundings of Falcon's Lair, the name Valentino had given the property before his death. There she sat with her tools crafting jewelry throughout the day. She spent more and more hours in her boudoir creating the looks that would dazzle the multitudes at her entrances throughout Hollywood at night. "Millicent was likely to show up anywhere, and wearing a parachute if that was her mood," remarked Gable's assistant, Garceau, who despite the gifts and expensive lunches bestowed on her by Millicent, never befriended her, and seemed to enjoy dissecting her to others.[5]

Millicent did little to dispel the mystique that her money created. When she took Garceau to lunch at Romanoff's in Hollywood, she pulled out the gold toothpick that had so amused her and her guests when it arrived at Southampton. Garceau watched her pick her teeth. She was making a reputation for herself as rather eccentric and "willful." She was hard to miss when she appeared in public with her pet monkey on her shoulder or draped around her neck the way other women wore fur boas. She was certainly not bashful about her pursuit of a conquest, and sent some of her twenty-four-carat jewelry creations to Garceau, in hopes of gaining her favor in her campaign for the heart of her boss. Garceau was unmoved.

Millicent presented Clark with a buckle, cuff links, shirt studs, and a ring, all of her own design in eighteen- to twenty-four-carat gold, for Christmas. She gave Garceau a green-gold ring called Green Leaf, engraved inside with her name and date, but Garceau would not be won over as one of Millicent's confidantes or champions. Garceau summarized their luncheon: "We did a little polite fencing over the chicken *en gélee* as she tried to find out what Clark thought of her. I was at my blandest and most obtuse."[6] She was loyal only to her boss—and possibly the prospect of her continuing livelihood, which included living and working out of Gable's house in Encino.

Millicent pressed her suit with fearless flair and style. She knew Gable had enjoyed serial affairs and romances with Joan Crawford, Paulette Goddard, Loretta Young, and Grace Kelly. Yet the field of competition didn't seem to daunt her. She had confidence in her panache and the star value of money. According to Tornabene, "Clark's girls," as the author referred to Gable's stable of consorts and love interests, "snapped to attention" when Millicent came on the scene.

They'd all heard about her money, and Louella Parsons flagrantly called her Miss Moneybags. She also wrote in one of her columns that Millicent spent up to a million dollars a year on clothes. A million dollars was a high estimate considering that Millicent's finances had been trimmed by her inheritance, but couturier dresses cost as much as a median family's annual income, according to Jan Reeder, executive curator of the Brooklyn Museum, where over two hundred of Millicent's dresses were housed after her death.

By any standards she was a clotheshorse, and spent excessive amounts of money on her wardrobe. At the time she understood very well the worn maxim that clothes make the woman. They certainly helped to make her and her reputation for wearing whatever struck her fancy, and helped her compete with the entrances of Hollywood's leading screen beauties. As had always been the case, Millicent was noticed, and Hollywood was a new stage on which not only to compete for the affection of American's leading man but to exhibit her creative style in clothes. When she appeared draped in sapphires at a producer's party or in a champagne shantung dress at a charity benefit, she was definitely noticed.

She spent money lavishly. During the transition between the Powers' house and Falcon's Lair, Millicent checked into one of the bungalows at the Beverly Hills Hotel. The décor wasn't to her liking so she went into the well-known upscale designer Tony Duquette's shop on the hotel grounds and asked him to completely redecorate her unit. Duquette knew her by reputation and that she was a friend of Gilbert Adrian's. Millicent agreed to purchase the items that went into his temporary installation. When she checked out she took most of the changes and furnishings with her, but after several months Duquette began to worry that his bills to her were still unpaid. He was used to being paid promptly by his wealthy customers. Finally, he approached Adrian about what to do. "You sap, don't you know she only pays her bills once a year?" guffawed Adrian. Duquette waited anxiously, but sure enough, his payment came in full at the end of the year, when Millicent's business manager paid her bills.[7]

Millicent's relationship to Gable kept the gossip columnists a-titter and a bit confused. Millicent, it was reported, "lived quietly." Gable, with no explanation, missed Sonja Henie's blowout party at the Crillon Café, and Louella Parsons speculated that he was reducing the pace of his social life to be with "his current heart." Yet on occasion they did appear at large soirees. One evening at Jack and Ann Warner's nine-acre estate just down the road from Millicent in Benedict Canyon, Elsa Maxwell gave a party. "Such fun we haven't had in a long time," gushed Louella Parsons. It was a theme party of sorts. Men were invited to costume twelve glamourous women. Irene Dunne, Claudette Colbert, Lana Turner, and Millicent Rogers were among them. "Millicent Rogers was a good sport and let herself be turned out as a frump," reported Parsons, who noted that she attended the party with Gable, "And I must say he was devoted to her." She also developed a reputation for her spirited wit after she responded to an esteemed windbag at one Hollywoood party who noticed her attention waiver and boldly asked, "Am I boring you, Millicent?" "Not yet," she replied.

What Millicent may not have grasped about partnering Hollywood's leading man was that almost everything social in Hollywood was business. The columnists, the stars, the producers fed on the tidbits of any given day about scripts, roles, divorces, and marriages as they related to the movie business. Millicent was mentioned, but she wasn't news the way Deborah Kerr, a prospective leading lady in Gable's next film, would be. The publicity machine was driven by flacks for the studios who were interested in pairing their leading men with gorgeous movie stars, also on the publicity make. Millicent was not such an asset. In Gable's case, Hedda Hopper and Louella Parsons loved him like their own and protected his image. They passed notes back and forth, calling each other babe and darling, thanking each other for scoops and evading scandals. It was one big club.

Clark Gable was a hit with Millicent's sons. They looked up to his manliness. Paul, a teenager in the mid-forties, fondly remembered traveling by train with Gable and his mother. The blue and green paisley dressing gown, one of Clark's many, that he gave to Paul when he complained of the cold in his compartment was a keepsake for many years.[8] In spite of his distinction as a man's man, Gable also set fashion. Clark was named one of the World's Ten-Best-Dressed Men, though he claimed he only owned six suits. When he took off his shirt in the Frank Capra movie *It Happened One Night*, and was seen bare-chested rather than wearing an undershirt, the sale of men's under-shirts reportedly plummeted. He, like Millicent, wielded enough influence to set trends. Though Gable was not the aristocrat or true sportsman that Millicent's husbands had been, he often played the roles of such men, and that was often as good as the real thing in Hollywood's house of mirrors.

Though that "animal magic" seems to have been the stuff that truly fuelled their relationship beneath the surface, Gable and Milli-cent had several surprising things in common. Gable shared an affec-tion for the Tidewater region of Virginia and at one point had tried to buy the Four Mile Tree plantation downriver from Claremont Manor. They had the same birthday, February 1. Both had hastily married older partners while in their twenties. The same year that Millicent eloped with Ludi Salm, Gable had married his acting coach who was fifteen years his senior, and his second marriage was to a woman seventeen years older. His third wife, the movie star Carole Lombard, had died in an airplane crash returning from a war bond drive. He was clearly the marrying kind, as was Millicent. Clark also demonstrated a strain of meticulousness that only someone of Milli-cent's perfectionism in matters of home and design could admire. He lived in the same house in Encino that he had occupied with Lom-bard. After the war he put in a pool that took workmen three months to install. The dirt, excavation, and overall contracting delays infuri-ated him. He didn't like the mess and he explained to friends that he'd had enough of sleeping in dirty beds and hearing loud workmen's conversations when he was in the oil fields as a kid. Millicent, a model of quiet composure and a master at managing remodeling and deco-rating projects, must have seemed an antidote to the chaos.

If there was a flaw to his sex appeal it was his bad breath. Even Vivien Leigh had mentioned it when they filmed *Gone with the Wind* together. During his early career he had suffered from gum disease. The recurring infections were so bad—causing delays in filming during movies—that he finally had most of his teeth pulled and replaced. Halitosis was one consequence, one that Millicent later mentioned to her friends and sons.

If Millicent suspected that the quiet ticking of her heart was now measuring out a slowing and a decline in her powers, it was also true that Gable had seen his greatest days as an actor. Ever since he had appeared unshaven in a love scene with a braless Jean Harlow in *Red Dust* and played the gangster who slapped the actress Norma Shearer on film, he had been the matinee idol to reckon with. His role as Rhett Butler established him nearly in a class of his own as America's male sex symbol, yet when he took up with Millicent, his actual acting career was considered in decline, according to his biographers. His new pictures, like *The Hucksters*, would fail to have the box office or critical success of his prewar movies though he continued to be hailed the "King of Hollywood" by adoring columnists, and he seemed enduringly cast as America's leading male heartthrob.

War, financial restraints, the reconstititution of The Port, Ian Fleming's tortured fickleness, and her hospital episodes during the war were all a continent away the year Millicent was in Hollywood. She let little interfere with the creation of her newly elegant profile, and at last she seemed in control of her image, even in the papers. A rowdy night of drinking by her brother at Ciro's that got his name in the news for being boisterous and out of control was the only exception. His former legal battles and tribulations had clearly not daunted his drinking or his style. News that Arturo had been in a car accident in Virginia came as another reminder of family ties beyond California. She left Los Angeles on the 20th Century Limited to be by his bedside for several weeks in May of 1947. While she was gone, her relationship with Gable was being undermined.

By their mutual friends and admiring public, Millicent was considered madly in love with Gable. But according to the whisperings of her rivals and gossip columnists, her determination was hurting her cause. At least once, she had brazenly booked herself a table at a restaurant where he dined with another woman, to rein him in as he courted someone else. She was stalking him, watching him. Their relationship began to grow frayed.

Their denouement came when she discovered him—for the second time—with the starlet Virginia Grey. Grey had been a regular date whom he had seen intermittently before and after the war. A cosmopolitan herself, Millicent had overlooked his first dalliance with Grey. She discounted the relationship as "the bee looking for pollen," her euphemism for sex without love. But eventually Clark took his infidelity too far.

Clark called ahead to say he was working late on location and couldn't be at the intimate dinner party Clifton Webb had invited him and Millicent to one evening with the Adrians. Millicent went alone and the Adrians drove her home at the end of the evening. She'd had more than a few glasses of champagne herself. Clark had given her a key to his house in Encino and she decided to use it. She packed up a bottle of champagne, his favorite Iranian golden caviar, and called a limousine to drive her. The house was dark but for a small light in the living room. Something told her to ask the driver to wait. Once inside she heard sounds from the bedroom and froze. In that instant so much slipped away from her; but she managed to put the caviar and champagne in the fridge and left a note next to the baguette, explaining it was "ready for you and your new lover's breakfast." She added, "I never wish to see or hear from you again." She left Gable's housekey on the table, and then rode the numbing drive in the dark back to her house. Once there she sat down and wrote him a letter. She composed a small fiction, preferable to saying that she sat in his darkened kitchen and listened to the sound of his lovemaking.

"I followed you last night as you took your young friend home," she wrote. "I am glad you kissed and that I saw you do it, because now I know that you have someone close to you and that you will have enough warmth beside you. Above all things on this earth, I want happiness for you."

In one of the typically Millicentian bold, abrupt moves that had punctuated her life, she then sent a copy of the letter to Hedda Hopper. Hopper promptly published it, in its entirety, in her column in the *Los Angeles Times*.

My Darling Clark, I want to thank you, my dear, for taking care of me last year, for the happiness and pleasure of the days and hours spent with you; for the kind, sweet things you have said to me and done for me in so many ways, none of which I shall forget.

You are a perfectionist, as I am; therefore I hope you will not altogether forget me that some part and moments of me will remain in you and come back to you now and then, bringing pleasure with them and a feeling of warmth. For myself, you will always be a measure by which I shall judge what a true man should be. As I never found such a one before you, so I believe I shall never find such a man again. Suffice that I have known him and that he lives.

You gave me happiness when I was with you, a happiness because of you that I only thought might exist, but which until then I never felt. Be certain that I shall remember it. The love I have for you is like a rock. It was great last year. Now it is a foundation upon which a life is being built.

I followed you last night as you took your young friend home. I am glad you kissed and that I saw you do it, because now I know that you have someone close to you and that you will have enough warmth beside you. Above all things on this earth, I want happiness for you.

I am sorry that I failed you. I hope that I have made you laugh a little now and then; that even my long skinniness has at times given you pleasure; that when you held me, I gave you all that a man can want. That was my desire, that I should be always as you wished me to be. Love is like birth; an agony of bringing forth. Had you wished it, my pleasure would have been to give you my life to shape and mold to yours, not as a common gift of words but as a choice to follow you. As I shall do now, alone.

You told me once that you would never hurt me. That has been true, even last night. I have failed because of my inadequacy of complete faith, engendered by my own desires, by my own self-ishness, my own inability to be patient and wait like a lady. I have always found life so short, so terrifyingly uncertain.

God bless you, most darling Darling. Be gentle with yourself. Allow yourself happiness. There is no paying life in advance for what it will do to you. It asks of one's unarmored heart, and one must give it. There is no other way. When you find happiness, take it. Don't question too much.

Goodbye, my Clark. I love you as I always shall.[9]

Her heart may have been broken, but she had not lost her poise nor her composure. She had maintained the control and art in writing the letter that enabled her to make the man who had spurned her uncomfortable in public. It was one thing to receive such a letter, and quite another to find it in the morning newspaper. She was no dummy, nor innocent. She surely knew he was dating starlets; all of Hollywood knew, and she had even openly positioned herself to scrutinize the competition. Perhaps a premonition, and the shedding of inhibitions after a few drinks, may have emboldened her need to discover the truth for herself that night. Perhaps she had been composing, even polishing this letter in her mind while she spent days and weeks working on her jewelry designs in a shady room at Falcon's Lair.

Whatever the facts and the reasoning, it was a gutsy thing to do. The letter no doubt staved off the humiliation of her failed and widely known suit of Gable, countering the snickering that his infidelities would no doubt cause—if they had not already. Millicent by now and through most of her life had a sense of her own dignity and self-worth. Her bearing had been regal from the beginning, and it should be remembered that as a young woman she was subjected repeatedly to scrutiny, scandalous allegations, court appearances, and hounding by the paparazzi. She was practiced at walking with calm assurance through a firestorm.

It was the first time that she had been rejected. She was unaccustomed to the sensation of loss and anger that accompanies the experience. Yet she'd always had pluck and aplomb, given the circumstances. There was no resemblance in Hollywood to the tearful veiled twenty-two-year-old who had been hauled home from Paris at the side of her domineering father. She had obviously learned along the way that there was merit in taking the offense in such matters.

Was she truly in love with Clark Gable, or was he just the next best gorgeous man for her collection, a conquest so widely admired, a trophy that every woman wanted? By her own confession, she loved him, and her calculated suit for him suggests that she sincerely cared. But coming from a woman as much of the world as she, her letter also suggests that a nearly pathetic self-degradation had crept into her affections. Could she really be so generous to a man she loved and wanted who had spurned her? Did she hope to learn how far she would go in pursuit of him? The end of this affair must have suggested to her, even someone of her overriding confidence and chutzpah, that this was her last grand love affair—or chance at a lasting partnership, marriage even. Had she landed Gable, she would have created the classic happy film ending, finally marrying the King of Hollywood and playing the role of his queen, composing together a beautifully handsome couple. Gable had clearly been charmed by her magnitude, style, experiences, and class. She was more like the grand characters his leading ladies portrayed than who they were in real life. Millicent's heirs acknowledged the seriousness of her loss, yet they were reluctant to see her as much less than the victor in any situation. The seriousness of the breakup is glanced over quickly, with slight bemusement, as seasoned parents might discuss the first of many heartbreaks for an ingénue daughter. Her son Arturo maintains that after the breakup he spoke with Gable, who wanted to reconcile with Millicent, but Arturo, nineteen at the time, advised him that it was not possible. There is scant record of his relationship with Millicent in the three leading biographies of Gable, suggesting that she played a lesser role in his life than he did in hers—or that their relationship was less newsworthy than his liaisons with other movie stars. Whatever the emotional truth, Millicent left Hollywood quietly after the letter. She did not linger to play the martyred lover, or languishing Camille, hoping for his return. Her tenure in Hollywood was more of a selected short than a full feature, and the promise of a shimmering new life quickly faded. The high times were over.

According to Arturo, her pet monkey had taken to drinking with his owner and died of alcohol. An African gray parrot had fallen in the toilet and drowned. In her "Chatter in Hollywood" column, Louella Parsons wrote: "Millicent Rogers, bag and baggage, has gone East. She'll stop in New York, put her two sons in school, and then go on to her home in Jamaica." She continued that Millicent had not cared for living in Valentino's old house, which may have fed the fan rumor that the house had always been haunted by Rudolph Valentino's ghost. "She suddenly decided that with a home in Jamaica and one in Virginia which she did like, she'd pull up stakes. She's sending to Jamaica thousands of dollars' worth of reed furniture she bought here. As for her romance with Clark Gable, well, just between you and me, that never was very hot. They were friends and that's all." Gable also played down the breakup. "We're friends," he said to Hopper, and shrugged. It was a line any Hollywood actor could deliver in his sleep. Ironically, it was not a frisky young starlet he was next associated with romantically, but another East Coast socialite, a former old flame, Dolly O'Brien. Yet it was Nancy Hawks, top of the best-dressed list with Millicent the previous year, and former wife of the movie producer Howard Hawks, who clung to Gable on the gangplank long enough to delay the departure of the *Queen Mary* the following summer when he left for Europe. The Hollywood whirl would go on without Millicent.

CHAPTER TWENTY

After the Affair

ADRIAN AND GAYNOR WATCHED MILLICENT REEL OVER the breakup with Gable. In spite of her high-minded letter, she took it hard. After all, it was the first time she had chased a man. She had been enthralled enough to step down from her pedestal to stalk him, and that spectacle was public, thanks to the Hollywood gossip machine. Through the summer of 1947 she sank further and further into depression until the Adrians thought a change of scene would do her good. Arturo, recovered by now from his car accident, and a friend had made their way west to stay in his uncle Henry's house in Hollywood, but Millicent had only made time to see him a couple of times.

In late summer the Adrians proposed a trip to New Mexico. Gilbert Adrian had gotten a taste of its unruly charm during his visit in the thirties. He discussed it with his wife and they agreed. A trip to Taos might be just the thing to take Millicent's mind off Gable.

When Adrian visited in the 1930s he had sought out Mabel Dodge, a famous heiress and debutante from Buffalo, New York, who had made a reputation for herself in Taos. She had once been a socialite in Europe and Greenwich Village before she moved to New Mexico with her third husband. Wherever she went, she cultivated a salon, modeled after her acquaintance Gertrude Stein's famous circle in Paris. In Taos she divorced Maurice Sterne and married a Taos Pueblo Indian, Tony Luhan. Her story was notorious on the East Coast, but she seemed undeterred by what others thought. Adrian, free-spirited and artistic, had heard about her when he lived in Connecticut and he had wanted to meet her. Once he began working in Hollywood he made a trip to Taos on a lark when he had a break between pictures. The journey by car from Los Angeles was a daunting undertaking before interstate highways, but he was curious about the stories he'd heard of people living in little cabins in Taos and falling madly in love with the landscape.

When he arrived and looked up Mabel Dodge Luhan, known for opening her home to distinguished and interesting people she'd known in New York and Europe, she took him in and showed him around. An art colony for painters from Chicago, the East Coast, and Europe had taken root in Taos in the twenties, and Mabel was a magnet for notables from other places when they visited the small western enclave. She and her friend Frieda Lawrence, the widow of the writer D. H. Lawrence, who had come to Taos at Mabel's invitation, showed Adrian around. Like most visitors, Adrian fell in love with New Mexico and quickly bought a five-acre piece of land with a falling-in adobe house fifty miles south of Taos in Pojoaque, closer to Santa Fe, the state capital. The "cabins" he'd heard about were in fact the adobe brick houses made from local soil that were endemic to northern New Mexico. The light, as advertised, was perfect, and the altitude of northern New Mexico provided an escape from the high temperatures of the San Fernando Valley in summer.

Millicent needed coaxing. She didn't want to go to New Mexico. She came up with one reason after another to decline: the duration of the trip, the heat, her own malaise. While her son Arturo was dismissive of the depth of her distress over the breakup with Gable, her younger son, Paul, more consistently in her company, registered the depth of her hurt. "She was very depressed," he recounted. But finally, she agreed to go.

Mabel Luhan, who kept in touch with Adrian, had contacted him to let him know that a prime property was about to be put up for sale in Taos. She thought he should come and take a look at it. He booked seats for himself and Gaynor, Millicent, and her maid and cook Ethel, on the Santa Fe Railroad from Los Angeles to Lamy, New Mexico. By car they made their way to their friend's, the sculptor Allan Clark, and his scenic ranch near Santa Fe.

The Adrians' gamble paid off. Millicent was energized immediately by the old Spanish town's architecture and sights at possibly the most beautiful time of year along the Sangre de Cristo mountain range. The cottonwoods lining the creeks and valleys turn yellow and gold in the fall and late summer, and afternoon thundershowers deepen the hue of the red soil and the purple tinge of the sage, creating an effect that can only be called enchanted. Millicent, they knew, would respond to such beauty.

Another implacable instinct twitched in Millicent to brighten her spirits and renew her energies: collecting. New Mexico, and Santa Fe in particular, were full of things to discover in markets and trading posts that sold Native American jewelry, rugs, belts, silver, and Spanish colonial artifacts. The Adrians took her to The Thunderbird Shop on the plaza in Santa Fe across the street from the landmark hotel, La Fonda. It was both a quality silvercraft store and a gathering place for clients and visitors. Tea, coffee, and liquor were served around two tables that lent the store the atmosphere of a salon. They introduced her to one of the owners, Miranda Masocco, called "Mirandi," who served tea and showed Millicent the "pawn" jewelry that intrigued her. They were finely crafted Indian pieces that were pawned when their creators brought them to trading posts and agents to sell. Some were the finest samples of native craftsmanship, and Mirandi could get the best. She also designed jewelry.

Mirandi immediately recognized Millicent from the magazines when she entered the Thunderbird wearing an elegantly tailored suit and makeup that looked professionally applied. A friendship sparked between them almost instantly. Mirandi had her own sense of humor and style. Millicent praised the dyed gravel Mirandi used as a background to display some of the store's designs even though some of her other clients and townspeople thought the storefront was too far out. "But Millicent came in and raved about it. She liked it," recalled Mirandi. Their shared appreciation for the unusual bridged their thirty-year age difference. Mirandi was perceptive enough not to ask Millicent too many questions about her past. The prescient twenty-year-old quickly surmised that "Millicent just wanted to get lost. If I had lived the kind of life she had, I thought I'd be sick of it, too."[1] Millicent and the Adrians invited Mirandi to come with them on their trip to Taos.

Taos, intended only as a diversion, was a gamble. All Millicent had done in life to this point had mirrored the time and trends in which she was living. Born into great wealth, she lived the high society life provided by the new class of robber barons. In the twenties she mocked convention and partied with hip flasks like the flappers, and her elopement with European nobility was also something that was done by daring wealthy young women at the time. She lived in Europe when being an expatriate was the thing to do, and like the others, she returned in wartime. When she arrived in Virginia, money and notables were making their way there or had already arrived. She joined the war effort when that was the popular thing to do, and discovered the joys of Jamaica with an in crowd. Her migration to Hollywood mirrored an American trend, at least as the country moved to California in its imagination and cultural interests. Her life so far had mirrored American trends, even when she added her own innovations, as she did in fashion. She always rode on the crest of real and perceived glamour. The one exception to this trajectory was Taos.

Taos was on nobody's list. It had only been discovered by a rare few. Its heyday had been in the 1920s, after artists Ernest Blumenschein and Bert Phillips had stopped there when the wheel on their wagon broke, and decided to stay. In their wake, a community of established artists had settled in, ostensibly for the fine light and primitive subject matter. As willing transplants they established a social culture free of many of the distinctions and restrictions of East Coast society. They created a world of their own, layered over the agrarian and colorful, often mysterious Indian and Hispanic cultures. On their heels had come a few pioneering Eastern socialites and writers, equally enchanted with the place and determined to live off the grid of their former lives. Taos had its kooks and crazies. But for others a brief visit to the town, initially a curiosity with its one-story adobe houses and dusty roads at the foot of the rugged northern New Mexico mountains, often turned into a longer stay, and consequently the culture was reshaped by an influx of ideas and wide-ranging personalities, most of them taking zealous delight in their new surroundings.

Mabel Luhan's marriage to a Pueblo Indian gave her a unique position in the community. She settled into a long ten-room house on the edge of town with a view of the Indians' Sacred Mountain to the north and the town of Taos to the west. Her hospitality to nearly anyone of note from the East, including Georgia O'Keeffe, Carl Jung, and Thornton Wilder, was widely known. She recruited artists and writers like Lawrence and Frieda with an iron will. Almost anyone who was anybody that passed through Taos had been invited—summoned—to her. Her hospitality, it was soon learned by the recipients, was not without cost, which was usually unchallenged homage to her and her whims. Yet even when she was controlling, she was hard not to like, this woman of Eastern privilege who seemed honestly to trill over the working hum of her big adobe house with crackling fireplaces, dovecote and cat, rutted road and old fenceposts. The transformation that overtook many newcomers to Taos, a change of sensibility toward the admiration of simple and rustic things, had claimed her.[2] Others, like Frieda Lawrence, who had returned to Taos after the writer's death in France, and Dorothy Brett, an English aristocrat, writer, and painter who had first arrived with the Lawrences in 1924, stayed as well.

There were undeniable drawbacks to Taos. It was remote and backward in many respects, a town of unpaved roads where children rode horses to the central plaza after school. In late winter and spring many residents had to abandon both cars and horses to the mud and walk home at night. Doctors were in limited supply. The poorest patients paid their bills with chickens and heads of lettuce. Dr. Ashley Pond could boast that he had the first television, a black and white, but in order to get reception he had to drive around town with it in his car. It was the basic simplicity of the community that seduced its worldly and sometimes wealthy transplants.

It was no mean feat to get to Taos in the thirties and forties. No train went farther than Santa Fe, and the twisting road sixty miles up through a steep-sided mountain gorge could only be traveled by horse or—carefully—by car. The journey was taxing and often impossible in winter. The seven-thousand-foot altitude made many visitors short of breath. Mabel frequently stopped halfway on the journey to rest overnight along the Rio Grande in the town of Embudo, hardly more than a stagecoach stop and a few farms. Few travelers chose to emulate Kit Carson, a Taos resident in the mid 1800s who had managed to dash the sixty miles to Santa Fe on horseback, in just a day. The appeal of Taos largely traveled by word of mouth to visitors who heard reports of something arresting about the place, be it a fertile salon culture, the stunning view of the mountains, the atmosphere of the Old West around Taos plaza where Indians sat huddled against the chill air in Pendleton blankets, the mystery of the Pueblo, or just that it was a good place to hole up and hide for a while.

Mabel championed the simple life. In her memoir, *Winter in Taos*, she wrote of Taos's appeal to outsiders. "I saw it from their viewpoint, my patchwork of a house and my rickety stables and corral that was picturesque enough to be a suitable background for the Holy Family, with its horses and sheep and pigs dawdling against the pale, weathered wood; but with my family here, it suddenly appeared rundown, inefficient and, in contrast with their own spick and span farm at Youngstown, it was, I realized, quite reprehensible."

From Mabel Luhan in the thirties to John Nichols, author of *The Milagro Beanfield War* in the 1970s, the dusty evocative charm of Taos caused creative and restless souls to pause over a shift in the wind or the sound of pigeons in the morning. The sagebrush, piñon, and chamisa cast a spell on psyches usually cluttered with weightier matters.

Taos quickly separated out the hardiest souls, and many from their trust funds. The secret of its lasting allure may be best explained with Millicent Rogers as a classic example. She shared the secret with Luhan, Lawrence, Dorothy Brett, and other devoted émigrés to Taos, whose ranks she was about to join. It wasn't just the sheer beauty. It was that she was *ready* for Taos.

CHAPTER TWENTY-ONE

Changing the Scene

The morning that the Adrians planned to drive to Taos was a replay of their departure from Los Angeles. Millicent was reluctant to go. She was happy enough poking around Santa Fe, but Gaynor told her the scenery would be magnificent and that the trip would take only an hour. Adrian hired a limo to soften the effects of the bumpy road. He'd booked rooms at a guesthouse on the edge of town with space for the Adrians, Millicent, her cook Ethel, and her new friend Mirandi.

Travelers approaching Taos from the south twist their way up the Rio Grande gorge, then climb steeply out of it and emerge over a low ridge. Abruptly, a dramatic view opens up. A broad flat valley spreads before them, cut as with a knife by the dark Rio Grande canyon. Twenty miles ahead, across the flat mesa, rises Taos Mountain, and at its feet lie the Taos Pueblo and the town. In the far distance the Sangre de Cristo Mountains continue to rise, stretching north to Colorado. It is a heart-stopping view, and for Millicent it was fuelled by surprise. Stepping out of the car, she surveyed the scene from the side of the road. "Why has no one ever told me about this?" she gasped.[1]

The party stopped for lunch at the Sagebrush Inn just south of town. Millicent immediately remarked on the blankets and rugs decorating the walls and floors and began comparing them to French, Flemish, and Spanish tapestries. Her enthusiasm waned on the short drive into town as they passed by the cheap motels, a small dusty post office, garages, and cafés, but by the time they reached the town plaza Millicent had spied the Indians, some wrapped in blankets. There were cowboys in tight jeans with kerchiefs round their necks and Spanish women with their hair swept up and secured with fine combs, all part of the fiesta atmosphere of San Geronimo Day, a celebration going on in town and out at the Taos Pueblo, the mud and adobe community inhabited continuously by the native Indian population for over six hundred years several miles outside town.[2] It was late September and the Pueblo Indians (as they prefer to be called, rather than "Native Americans") were celebrating the Feast of San Geronimo, an annual day of celebration with pole-climbing competitions, a footrace between different sides of the Pueblo, and a market for the native wares and jewelry made by the local and neighboring tribes.

When she and the Adrians drove out to the Pueblo, Millicent was intrigued. Something moved in her when she stood on Indian land and watched the people. She had always striven for calm and serenity in her manner and presentation, and here before her were a whole people and place that practiced those virtues, seemingly within their nature. The Indians just *were*. They didn't gab and make small talk. They also wore and traded silver jewelry that attracted and intrigued her. There was an element of the treasure hunt wherever she went.

Quite by coincidence, or so the story goes, her son Arturo, who on his way east had come with friends on an outing, approached her across the main yard, the plaza, of the pueblo. Thinking her still in Los Angeles, he says he was astonished to discover that the woman, noticeable for her carriage and deliberate movements, much like his mother, *was* his mother, in this place.

The next day they went up the hill to Mabel Luhan's rambling adobe house. Taos, as seen from Mabel's patio, beneath a canopy of gold and orange-leafed cottonwoods, was as resplendent on a late September afternoon as at any time of year. Luhan was expecting them for dinner. The conversation was filled with Millicent's questions about the Indians. She was fascinated with the Indian preoccupation with creation, life, and death, which came up repeatedly in the discussion.

Mabel's house's "simple" appeal charmed Millicent. In the next few days, the company, the climate, and the scenery converged to make a lasting impression on her. The autumn days were warm enough for picnics, yet the cool nights required shawls and serapes. There was a different pulse to life in Taos that began to revive Millicent's flagging spirits.

Later in the day Mabel took them out to see the property for sale that she had mentioned to Adrian.

Mabel's friend Judge Kiker had bought the eighty-acre property west of town to fish on. He and his family lived in Santa Fe and came up to Taos in summer. When they took possession of the land, they had discovered an abandoned *morada* (old country church, common to Hispanic Taos and northern New Mexico) that the sheepherders on the property used for worship. The house, a term applied loosely to the dilapidated structure there, was a historic adobe building with the original vigas (exposed log ceiling beams to support the thick mud roofs), and it lacked a foundation. There was no plumbing, so the family carried water from a local spring in the meadow below up to the outhouse and main house.[3] But what the property lacked in accommodations, it more than compensated for with views. Perched on the side of a mesa, it looked over the meadows along the small *rio* running to the Rio Grande through farm and grazing land. The prize vista loomed beyond. Majestic Taos Mountain rose at the base of the Sangre de Cristo range to the northwest where the Indian pueblo and its unadulterated lands nestled at its feet. By noon in summer and fall the view across the meadow and fields spread out in emerald green and gold. Late in the day the shadows undulated between purple, blue, and gray. It changed, but always seemed the same in that way of Western skies. The natural splendor of Taos, and the Kiker property in particular, cast their spell over Millicent.

The quest for beauty of one kind or another had always driven Millicent. She loved beautiful men, beautiful clothes, arresting jewelry, and beautiful houses. She had known the opulence of Southampton, Paris, Manhattan, and the splendor of the Arlbergs in Austria, the seaside ambiance of Jamaica, and the colonial charm of Virginia. New Mexico offered her another, different kind of beauty: raw and earthy and on a grand scale. She was, as she had always been, alert to discovering new beauty, and her response to it was the same. She tried to buy it.

When the property was mentioned again during the visit, Millicent asked the Adrians if they were planning to purchase it. The Adrians explained that they had a large second property in Palm Springs, closer to their work in Hollywood, and that they were reluctant to invest in another. "If you're not going to buy it, I am," Millicent told them, quickly casting the die that would shift and re-create her life again. Before they left town, she had called for her driver to bring her station wagon from Virginia.

Millicent was now forty-five. It was a time in the country when postwar America was obsessed with newness and economic growth. New cars, new houses, new washing machines, and new values. In her life so far Millicent had experienced more than most women dreamed of. There had been great wealth and status, luxury, glamour, playboys, European titles, and aristocrats at her feet. Her boys had become young men. It was an age when many women thought not much lay ahead in life, but that wasn't—nor had it ever been—Millicent's approach. She invariably saw possibility. Perhaps unknowingly, she needed a new stage to play on. As her spirits revived, her vision expanded.

She had never settled for the ordinary. After three marriages and three sons she was positioned to create a new life, if only she knew what or where it would be. Hollywood had been hardly more than an exploration, a largely unsuccessful dalliance for a woman who was footloose and independent for perhaps the first time in her life. Europe and New York were behind her. She needed a fresh outlet for her creativity and her lust for beautiful and precious things. The natural beauty of Taos drew her. She may have had a slight foreboding that the final grand chapter of her illustrious and colorful life was about to begin and that she would find the adventure she desperately needed in New Mexico. She moved swiftly. She had never been one to waste precious time.

Luhan seemed as taken by surprise at Millicent's decision as were the Adrians. Perhaps she heard the first warning shrill of the competition that would develop between them. Millicent had money to rival Mabel's and she was also beautiful, something Mabel was not. Mabel had been a pretty younger woman, but she was now close to seventy, portly, and matronly. She still sported her twenties-style bob and bangs, though she was, overall, noticeably sagging. Mabel's taste in clothes, flowing Isadora Duncan–type dresses, was dowdy; and she clung to the proper silk and lace fashions of the Northeast, out of place in New Mexico. Millicent, on the other hand, always adapted. She stepped into Martha Reed's dress shop next to the Taos Inn and bought a few of the long, squaw-style skirts she admired. She enjoyed wearing shirts and skirts made of cotton. Like the woman in a denim skirt and espadrilles on the porch in Southampton, she had an unerring eye for chic, even in this dusty outpost.

Yet the contrasts between her and Mabel ran deeper than style. The two women had a good deal in common, had they been willing to focus on their similarities. Mabel had positioned herself quite consciously as a "New Woman" as society, especially female society, emerged from Victorian mores and restrictions. One of her biographers, Lois Palken Rudnick, described her as "sexually emancipated, self-determining, and in control of her own destiny," all things that could be equally applied to Millicent. Yet Millicent didn't seem interested in positioning herself or being considered a symbol to society, and Mabel quite consciously did. Luhan's letters and memoirs show a woman who saw almost everything she did in political or sociological terms, even her marriage to Tony Luhan. She was an intellectual and utopianist, who believed that the Indian would constitute a "bridge between nations," and she saw Taos as the birthplace for a "new American Civilization."[4] Ironically, Mabel was an undeniable snob, interested only in people distinguished by background or accomplishments who lent themselves to her circle and soirees. Millicent, on the other hand, was noticeably casual about people. She liked interesting individuals from any social stratum. She was confident and well-established enough in the worlds she had emerged from that she did not need Mabel's acceptance or blessing to thrive in Taos, an indifference that caught Mabel off guard.

Mabel was often full of bluster and attitude. When another wealthy new arrival, the unassuming Helene Wurlitzer, came to town, funded by the musical instrument manufacturing company of the same name, Mabel arrived at their door and announced herself as the social arbiter of Taos. "By dint of what?" was Helene Wurlitzer's calm response. She was kept busy with her own affairs as a patroness of the arts and proceeded to go about town ignoring Mabel. Millicent was subtler, but she was not going to be hostage to anyone, including Mabel Dodge Luhan, at this point in her life. Mabel would unquestionably be a valuable acquaintance and resource, and God knows, Millicent had had a lifetime of practice at managing controlling egos. But Mabel did have something that greatly interested Millicent, a relationship with the Indians.

The true friend that Millicent found in the midst of Taos's egos was Dorothy Brett, one of Taos's favorite and most colorful figures. A titled English aristocrat by birth, Brett had studied at the Slade school in England to be a painter. She was part of London's Bloomsbury set, hobnobbing with Bertrand Russell and Aldous Huxley before coming to New Mexico with the Lawrences. Partially deaf, she sported an ear trumpet and spoke in crisp, precise diction. A brimmed sombrero hat was part of her New Mexican uniform. As she aged, her shock of white hair and enormous bosoms loose and low under her smocks and shirts gave her a distinctive appearance. Almost twenty years older than Millicent, she was one of the town's true characters, part of the threesome that included her, Mabel, and Frieda Lawrence by the time Millicent arrived in town. The trio bickered endlessly with each other and often ganged up two-to-one over imagined slights and differences, yet they persevered like the town's three witches. Brett, despite her lofty social origins, was down on her luck financially, even though her work, focused largely now on the Indians, was ranked alongside the works of Taos's finest artists. But it sold slowly, and without other sources of income she relied shamelessly on the financial kindness of friends to get by. Millicent's arrival to Taos brought new hope to Brett and an alternative to the social dynamic between the three doyennes.

Millicent bought a painting off the wall of Brett's studio for three hundred dollars shortly after she arrived in town, without Brett realizing she was the same woman who had been wearing white shorts and lunching with the Adrians at the El Patio restaurant on the plaza when Brett had met up with Gilbert Adrian to go fishing. When Millicent bought several others the next year, Brett acted as if she had met her savior. She understood Millicent was "The Standard Oil heiress," and with childlike enthusiasm she boasted to her brother Oliver back in England, "Millicent Rogers will look after me." Mabel and Frieda took a dim view of her enthusiasm.

Money may have been the opening salvo of their relationship, but Brett and Millicent seemed to forge a genuine friendship. They both came from high society. They loved art and the Indians. While Brett no doubt envied the comfort of Millicent's life and its financial certainty, Millicent must have found Brett's dedication to her art highly admirable. Even if she understood that its seeds were self-interest, Millicent accepted Brett's friendship. Brett was often her companion in the Indian markets, and she liked to accompany her on her explorations and shopping trips to Indian country. Brett's established contacts with the Indians at the Pueblo helped pave the way for Millicent in return.

Millicent promptly purchased the Kiker property with Mabel and Tony Luhan's blessing. Accustomed to nothing but luxury in her life so far, she had signed on to wrestle with the five small rooms, including a kitchen and dining room lined up along a single wall, and to make them habitable for herself. She named the property "Turtlewalk" for the turtle-shaped cluster of small rooms. Among Indians, the turtle is the sign of the female.

The house was beginning to fall down and the dirt sifted through the ceiling in places. As was true with most adobe houses, large amounts of dirt (in this case, twenty-two truckloads) had been loaded onto the roof as part of the New Mexican technique of insulating against scorching summer heat and scathing mountain cold. But the ramshackle house and property had been passed on to its illustrious new owner just as it was.

Millicent went about the business of moving to Taos with quiet determination and resolve. She was practiced at taking charge of houses and shaping them to her whim and design, though she may not have been prepared for the independent work habits of *Taosenos* and the Indians. She checked into La Fonda, the venerable hotel off Taos Plaza that was run by the Greek Saki Karavas. Saki, characteristically at home in a lounging jacket and smoking a cigar, charmed Millicent and especially her son Paul with his storytelling and generosity, yet soon Millicent began to look for accommodations that would better suit her and run later into the season.[5] Paul, who seems to have considered travels with his mother a fine adventure and an opportunity to catch up on her attention, noted that "Taos was most likely the wrong area for heart problems," but Millicent disregarded his advice.

When the Adrians returned to Los Angeles, Millicent asked Mabel and Tony to help her prevail on Dick and Kay Dicus, who ran the Dicus Guest Ranch where she had stayed with the Adrians, to stay open through the winter. Mabel laid out the situation, somewhat inflating its grandiosity: "I have a friend, a Standard Oil Heiress and she'd like to come with her three sons, a chauffeur, and their governess to stay." In fact, only two sons would be with Millicent initially, and they were bound soon for school back East. There was no governess. Mabel didn't mention that Millicent had two dachshunds with her.

The Dicus Guest Ranch was a good choice for Millicent. Dick and Kay Dicus hailed from Baltimore, Maryland, and bought the property, an intact hacienda with an enclosed central plaza, before the war. They agreed to extend their season on her account. The arrangement was a hit for both sides from the beginning.

Dick Dicus was a handsome six footer with sharp blue eyes and a mustache whom Millicent liked immediately. He had joined army intelligence during the war, and he was also a sculptor, painter, and architect who designed Spanish Colonial furniture in a woodworking shop he kept in town. A raconteur by nature, he often stayed up late into the evening playing chess with Millicent in the music room of the ranch while Kay Dicus and their daughter, Susan, went to bed. Sometimes Millicent beat Dicus at chess, which Susan believed attested to her skill, since her father would never let anybody beat him out of deference or courtesy. He didn't treat Millicent with special courtesies, which she appreciated. Soon she asked him to design the renovations to the house she had just bought. She also asked him to take her to the neighboring Indian reservations to see the ceremonies she'd heard about. When they came back he told his wife and daughter that she'd bought a lot of things, mostly jewelry, from the Indians. He had carefully watched her interact with them and remarked when he got home, "She didn't bleed them like other Anglos." He explained that Millicent had genuinely seemed to care about and respect the Indians.[6]

Millicent asked Tony Luhan to provide Indian labor for the work on her house. It was typical, and invariably noted by the local population, that outside Anglos who came to Taos seemed to overlook the native Hispanic population, whose numbers were far greater than the Indians, and who had populated the community since the late 1500s when the Spanish came to the region. But the fascination, especially for Mabel, Millicent, and Dorothy Brett, was for Indians.

Taos was a gentler, less stratified society than Millicent had known in other places. Her stay at the Dicus Guest Ranch introduced her to the town's easy ways. A cook prepared meals for the proprietors and their guests, and served everyone together in the dining room. It wasn't unusual for fourteen people, most of them local friends of the Dicuses, to sit down at the table for the cook's specialty of chicken cacciatore while classical music played on the Victrola. Frank Waters—author of *The Man Who Killed the Deer* and other books—Mabel Luhan, Dorothy Brett, Frieda Lawrence, and Thornton Wilder, in town at the time, and a painter, John Young Hunter, were friends of the Dicuses who came to dine on a regular basis.

"They were all bohemian souls," remembers Susan Dicus. Her mother was used to the little tensions that always ran between Mabel, Frieda, and Dorothy, and she deftly navigated around them. Tony Luhan, a fan of Kay Dicus's soup, always seemed to know the day she was making it and came to hang around the kitchen. At mealtimes, Tony, like many of his kinsman, was famous for often not uttering a word. Cocktails flowed freely. Guests played the piano. Tony often excused himself to play his drum, and some evenings, when spirits ran high, Susan Dicus saw her mother with a rose in her teeth.

Millicent established herself in the three front rooms of the Dicus house, looking west toward the Rio Grande Valley, and she was soon treated like a member of the family. The young Susan Dicus was enchanted with the beautiful and elegant lady who had set up residence with them. Sometimes Millicent silently entered the room where Susan was practicing the piano and sat down next to her on the piano bench as she played Schumann and Bach. Millicent smelled wonderful to her, an amalgam of powders and French perfume. Millicent, always comfortable with children, invited her into her room to play dress up with her jewelry, real pearls, emeralds, and rubies that she kept in a trunk under the bed.

Kay Dicus was furious when she realized that Millicent, who had arrived with two of her dachshunds, was bringing stray puppies and dogs back from the Indian reservations and keeping them in one of her rented rooms. Millicent responded to Dicus with the same serenity Michael Coe had witnessed when her Great Dane pooped on the living room floor in Southampton. She was just a little apologetic. A flicker of admiration rose in the young Susan's heart as she realized, "Millicent did just as she wanted." In this case, however, she got rid of the strays.

The girl began to notice something more than the fun and novelty about Millicent and asked her parents, "Why is she so sad?" They explained to her that Millicent wasn't always well. She took her breakfast in her room and started her day slowly. She spent hours by herself reading.

Inevitably Millicent began to make an impression on the townspeople. She didn't look like other middle-aged women in town who wore shirtdresses and jeans, and if they'd been long in Taos were a bit weathered by the dry air and harsh sun. Millicent, to them, looked like a movie star herself, perhaps like Grace Kelly. She was a glamourous apparition in beautifully tailored expensive suits or dresses when she arrived and she carried herself deliberately, a bit regally. Once she adopted the squaw skirt, it became part of her signature look. She seldom appeared wearing anything else. "She lighted up a party because she looked so special," explained Martha Reed, in whose dress shop next to the Taos Inn Millicent had first tried on the skirts. They frequented some of the same parties in town and Martha, a fashion observer herself, noted that Millicent's taste was very sedate, never girlish or flippant. When she came in to shop she didn't try on clothes in front of customers or salespeople. She moved about quietly and privately. Reed also realized that the basic skirts Millicent bought in her store were being copied and refined by Millicent's designers back East.

A typical squaw, fiesta, or broomstick skirt, as they are called, made by Martha Reed's Indian seamstress, sometimes contained fourteen yards of fabric, pleated by hand when wet.[7] Millicent commissioned Charles James and Schiaparelli to make them to her specifications out of fine fabrics and with couturier workmanship. Millicent also began wearing the short-waisted jackets worn by the Indian women on the Pueblo, trimmed with silver Navajo buttons and butterflies, copied in French velvet rather than the shiny napped fabric (also used to upholster the cushioned seats of the Santa Fe Railroad cars) that the Indians preferred.[8]

The Taos that Millicent discovered had not been as stressed as the rest of the country by the war. Dish soap was the only thing that people had stood in line for on the plaza during wartime rationing in Taos, and with hunters and ranchers galore, there was always meat to eat and the bounty of an agrarian community. There was a gentle Western inclusiveness to the townspeople, common enough in places that still contained an echo of frontier mentality. People looked for commonality and forged friendships without a stamp of social or certified achievement by outside standards.

There was also a like-minded society in Taos and Santa Fe of Eastern defectors who'd come West. While there was an underlying layer of Eastern contacts and values, invariably those who stayed became hybrids of Western free-thinking and Eastern wealth. In reviewing Flannery Burke's 2008 book about this era, *From Greenwich Village to Taos*, the *Wall Street Journal* reviewer Alexander Theroux dubbed the newcomers "oddballs" and "crackpots," but they were, more accurately, a self-selected group of people who balked at settling into prescribed rules and roles back wherever home was, and northern New Mexico seemed to offer them an interesting alternative. Millicent, like them, was not looking for a society to fit into or a club to join. She rubbed shoulders in Taos with Claude Anderson, a prosperous Montana cattle rancher with family money from the Kodak camera company, back East.[9] He wore tweed jackets and a cravat at his throat and gave parties where liveried waiters in white jackets served cocktails on trays. Such formality, impressive if uncustomary to the locals, may have made Millicent feel at home, but the charm of Taos lay elsewhere for her.

The work on Turtlewalk progressed, but the house wasn't yet livable, so Millicent moved from the Dicus hacienda into the "Tony House," a property owned by Tony Luhan at the edge of the reservation, yet still in town and a stone's throw from the house that Mabel lived in. The Luhans owned a small constellation of houses and studios that came to be known informally as "Mabeltown." The house she shared with Tony would become known as *Los Gallos* (Spanish for the ceramic roosters that lined the roof of the portal) or the "Mabel House" to locals. Tony mustered a crew for Millicent made up mostly of a group of his nephews from the Pueblo. The arrangement delighted Millicent, who spent long hours working on renovations at the house. Now that her cook, Ethel, from Virginia, had joined her, she routinely fed dinner, usually roast beef, to the men at the end of the day. She also served liquor, a taboo with the Indians, who called it "bad water," and which Dick Dicus had warned her against.

Tony Luhan routinely stopped by to check on the workers and stayed through dinner, while Mabel was home seething with anger over his lateness. Tony, it was whispered locally, was having an affair with someone in the neighboring community at this time, and Mabel was at something of a low point when the glamorous Millicent, twenty-three years her junior and still carrying a little Hollywood stardust, came to town.[10] Tony's practice of stopping off at Millicent's to see the boys from the Pueblo and to eat and drink with them caused the most significant tiff between the two women. Mabel, overwrought, inflated the situation. She cited it to her lawyer, Judge Kiker, as cause to pursue a divorce from Tony.

When Millicent got wind of the story she called Frank Waters and asked him to pay her a visit. As he wrote in his memoirs, he "found her a beautiful, sensitive, and sensible woman." She told him she had called because she understood he was close to Tony and Mabel. "She thinks I'm trying to steal Tony away from her. How preposterous! What do I want with an aging Indian when there are so many young and attractive men of every kind? He isn't invited here; he just comes, and I have nothing to do with him. Nor can I control the boys eating and drinking; I have my dinner served in my own room."[11] It was the right response at the time, although her feelings for Tony would develop in intensity and complexity.

She didn't want to hurt Mabel and asked Frank's advice. He agreed to play mediator, but Mabel was on her high horse. "I can't stand this any longer," Mabel stormed. "I'm going to get rid of him—this old man so infatuated with Millicent that he comes home drunk late every night! He's never here. Let Millicent have him for whatever he's worth to her. Judge Kiker will get me a divorce." Waters prevailed upon her, but he believed that Mabel's interest in Indian life and religion diminished from that time on. His sympathy seems largely to have been with Mabel, whom he had known for more than twenty years. Then, too, Millicent, with her money, glamour, and dash was not always a natural fit with the strong creative personalities, often tough-minded and strident, that populated the Taos bohemian scene.

Some of them, especially the European émigrés like Russian Alexandra Fechin and the Greek Saki Karavas and his mother, Noula, cottoned to Millicent, but she made her mark mostly with the Indians and as a patroness of the arts. She lived quietly once she settled in, and her health precluded her participation in some of the hi-jinx that more unconventional Taoseños were known for. Millicent's efforts focused on creating her environment and fashioning her look. Dorothy Brett helped her on occasion with both. One of Millicent's enterprises was the subject of perhaps the most famous and endearing photograph of her—taken by Arturo—when she was staying at the Tony House. Wearing a fiesta skirt and a velvet squaw jacket, she climbed up on a kitchen chair in order to dip velvet into a pot of dye on the stove. She was wearing rubber gloves and high-top squaw moccasins. A bare lightbulb dangled overhead. It is a rarely glimpsed Millicent, clearly at play.

Brett contributed her artistic vision as work progressed on Turtlewalk. Fortified with a few drinks, she started painting the decorative patterns on the vigas in Millicent's living room that would became one of the house's hallmarks. She would arrive in the afternoon and then she and Millicent would sit on Millicent's bedroom floor to mix paints of every shade in empty tin cans until Millicent approved a color. Brett's Indian chauffeur and all-around handyman, helper, and friend, Trinidad Archuleta, helped her paint from a ladder and carry the paint pots and brushes from room to room as they tried to match shades and tones, with Millicent enjoying the process and the company.

Always a self-styled character, Brett set tongues wagging when she was denied a table at Frenchy's, the popular restaurant that served European fare and attracted a clientele from as far away as Denver. It was a favorite of the Anglo community and prosperous visitors. Frenchy, in fact, the Austrian Theodore Hutton, ran his restaurant with a high hand and enforced a dress code. Women were required to wear dresses for evening. Dorothy Brett, who refused to wear anything but slacks and Western wear, even when she went out at night, was denied a table when she arrived for dinner "inappropriately dressed." She went home, and when she returned was seated wearing a fur coat—with not a stitch on underneath. The story traveled fast in a community that appreciated spirited irreverence.

Millicent, too, would run afoul of Frenchy, who met customers at the door of his restaurant often in a dirty chef's jacket and high toque, imperiously checking out the clientele more like a bouncer at a New York club than a gracious restaurant host. According to her son Arturo she handled him with uncustomary brusqueness when she thought he had gotten uppity with her. "Don't give me any of your shit. You were my first husband's bootblack in Europe," she lashed out at him, momentarily becoming once more Colonel Rogers' daughter. It is one of the few remaining references to Millicent speaking harshly—or profanely—though Arturo claims she could unleash a string of foul language, usually in private, when she was provoked.

Millicent more often won admirers with her regal manner—and her pocketbook. Earl Stroh, a respected painter in Taos, had met Millicent in New York. When they were reacquainted in Taos, Stroh, an avowed perfectionist, was further impressed. Her art collection of Renoir, van Gogh, and Rubens put his eye out at her dinner parties, and there was mutual respect between them, one perfectionist for another. Stroh remarked that she was not truly educated about art, but that her "eye" was impeccable. Their admiration was mutual and Millicent bought several of Stroh's paintings just as the struggling young painter was about to leave on a trip to Bolivia and was almost too financially strapped to go. He never forgot the favor.

When Millicent invited her friend Mirandi in Santa Fe to come visit her and to stay in her house in Taos, Mirandi was equally amazed at the number of Renoirs hanging on the walls and to find one in the very guest room assigned to her. Her sense of Millicent's past expanded gradually. Millicent allowed that her memories of Austria were not fond, but that she had loved Paris. "She was a very private person, and she never sat and bragged about anything or anyone. I could be so comfortable with her and we talked about everything—except her," recalled Mirandi.

Eventually, there was an exception. Millicent recounted the story of her elopement with Count Salm and talked of the deprivation she had suffered at the hands of her father. She told Mirandi that her father had cut off her money and that she and her husband suffered as a result. "'We needed money, and we were so cold in Paris, I cannot tell you,'" she told Mirandi, gesticulating with an elegant flip of her hand. It seemed a strange confidence, intended perhaps to illustrate that she had known some discomfort in her life, or perhaps she was simply trying to bridge the gulf of experience that invariably existed between her and others. Mostly their talk focused on the shop and their shared interest in design. Millicent typically entered the Thunderbird silver shop in Santa Fe and asked her friend, "What new have you got to show me?" Sometimes she burst in excitedly, "I can't wait to show you what I bought." Collecting was their bond.

Mirandi had a regular table that sat ten persons at the popular La Fonda in Santa Fe where she often lunched and entertained clients and friends. She told the hotel's manager that anytime Millicent

Rogers was in the hotel she and her friends could sit at "Mirandi's table," and Millicent seemed charmed by this simple gesture of friendship and acceptance.

Millicent made a reputation for herself in Santa Fe on Canyon Road, the unpaved quality venue for art and commerce where she nearly bought out the Spanish Colonial and native furniture carried by Eleanor Bedell, a Santa Fe furniture merchant and character of her own distinction. Bedell is remembered today as a woman who wore Saint Laurent suits and packed a 22-caliber pistol on her hip. Millicent appreciated these colorful figures—and they worked to supply her with what she wanted: the secret to winning her favor.

From as far as Santa Fe, Mirandi had heard about the tensions between Mabel and Millicent in Taos. Mirandi was also a friend of Frieda Lawrence, and word traveled. Mirandi was hardly surprised: Everyone knew that Mabel ruled the roost before Millicent came. The differences between the two became increasingly evident to Mirandi. Even Cholly Knickerocker in his New York society and gossip column, "Getting Around," reported to his mostly Eastern readers: "All is not well, one hears, between the two leading ladies of Taos, N. Mex., society. That little sleepy town is quite awake now that Millicent Rogers has pitched her tent there and Taos' first lady, Mabel Dodge Luhan resents her intrusion. Both ladies just love the Indians. And just in case you don't know, Mabel is married to one, Tony, who wears long pigtails!"

The slender young Mirandi would find herself somewhat awkwardly cast in a caper of Mabel's. She had worked temporarily as a model in New York at Bergdorf Goodman's when she traveled east to get her citizenship papers. Mabel knew she was working at Bergdorf's when she and Tony made a trip to New York. In an act of condescending manipulation that baffles modern sensibilities, Mabel sent her husband Tony, dressed in his Indian blanket, moccasins, conchos, and pigtail, into Bergdorf's with instructions to ask for the floor where Mirandi was modeling. As was his manner, he stood in the back of the elevator, somber and silent, on his way to the floor with the fashion show. The Eastside matrons who were arriving with their friends and daughters nearly jumped out of their skins when they encountered Tony—dark, motionless, and dressed as he was—at the back of the lift. "Millicent died laughing at the story," Mirandi recounted. Millicent, in stitches, would ask her again and again to "tell us about when Tony came to see you at Bergdorf's."[12] While she enjoyed the tale, one can hardly imagine Millicent, who held the Indians in such high regard, pulling such a stunt at Tony's expense.

Millicent's comportment became her distinguishing trait, though it is understood now that her erect posture and disciplined carriage were practiced to avoid detection of her paralysis and the onset of small tremors that would sometimes overtake her. It all added up to an elegant impression, sometimes likened to an otherworldliness of calm and serenity.

Mirandi had also introduced Millicent to the poet, writer, and scholar Witter Bynner, a longtime resident of Santa Fe whose provenance was Brookline, Massachusetts. He'd been educated at Harvard and was friendly with D. H. and Frieda Lawrence, Ansel Adams, Willa Cather, and Igor Stravinsky, among others who came through New Mexico. Though known to be a homosexual, Bynner considered himself an arbiter of most things, including female beauty, and according to Mirandi, "He thought Millicent was probably the most beautiful woman he'd ever seen. He found her to be mysterious and sexy and totally seductive."

Predictably, Millicent had her detractors. The labels "heiress" and "millionaire" distanced her from many in Taos, and her visage, glamourous and impeccable, caused some to assume she would be a snob. "She was a stuck-up lady," concluded Dalton Montgomery, when Millicent gave a building contract to the Indians that his family business had bid for. His father worked for Mabel and carried home stories that Mabel was jealous of Millicent, her good looks and her money.[13] Millicent also, like many of the accomplished and prosperous Easterners who adopted Taos, overlooked the Spanish population in her enthusiasm for the Indians. Most locals regarded rich Easterners, at least at first, with some suspicion, though people who worked for her, like Rafael "Ralph" Vigil, who lived across the river from her property and became her trusted foreman for Turtlewalk, were almost immediately won over by her generosity and kindnesses. She built the house Vigil and his family would live in, and included him in the parties she threw at her house on the mesa. He also came to realize that her graceful manner was consistent and genuine, not something reserved to impress certain people. Ralph told his son Norbert that he could tell when Millicent had come down to the barn to pet the horses or was in the vicinity of the garage where he was working because her perfume reached him seconds before she swooshed around a corner in her long skirt.[14]

One young high country cowboy on his way to Hollywood where he would become an actor and producer of westerns was staying in Taos and acquainted with Mabel Luhan. Max Evans had heard a lot about the interesting new Rogers woman who had been involved with Clark Gable and was making a splash in Taos. The typical small-town gossip, some of it wrong, was going around about Millicent. Frank Waters, for instance, inexplicably ascribed her wealth to a series of rich husbands instead of her family fortune. Some people said she'd been involved with Cary Grant.

Max was curious. He was a regular at the bar of the Sagebrush Inn, a popular meeting place in Taos known for its notable art collection on the walls. One evening when Millicent was there, he asked the bartender, Clay Crawford, for an introduction. Dressed beautifully in a bright blue squaw skirt, a red blouse, and wearing lots of turquoise, she made a lasting impression on Max. They sat and visited for two hours talking mostly about art, from the Impressionists to the Indian jewelry that she so admired. He was impressed by all she already knew about the Taos art masters and her opinions on the New York art critics whom she described as elitist, because they gave Taos artists short shrift.

But the impression that lingered from that evening of conversation was "She was really a lady, full of respect and kindness. Her conversation about music and art was uplifting. Not only was she beautiful but she treated a little dumb-ass cowboy as if I was her equal."[15] Many who encountered Millicent just briefly or only once remember the intense and total focus she turned on them. She was always seductive. She focused on the moment and the people in her sight, and she never hurried. Yet Millicent could be discriminating. On several occasions Mirandi watched her correct someone for a remark she considered dumb or incorrect. "If you were sitting at a party and someone said something stupid she'd set them straight." said Mirandi. Millicent politely but firmly jumped in with a line like "I think you were a bit wrong there...."

Millicent could be quite assertive with her own family members, as her relationship with her mother evidenced. When Mary visited there was the usual clash of personal styles. She had challenged her grandsons, uneasy in adolescence as they juggled their Austrian and South American heritages, European educations, and American lives, that they were not truly American. She often took over at family dinners, asking all present to account for themselves, shining the conversational spotlight on the boys' latest educational or behavioral failure. When Paul flunked out of his Eastern preparatory school, Choate, she called him a "failure." Millicent was irritated and vented in a letter to Paul's teacher and tutor, John Joseph, her confidant in such matters. "Mother did such damage this summer by calling him a failure. God these well-meaning women, anyway . . . the personal unfulfilled dreams that must be put upon the young as nightmares in disguise of upbringing and character building . . . 'you will only find happiness in duty and in living as other people do, in giving your children the advantages we gave you and your brother.' BALLS!" Millicent worried that Paul's "pride will be hurt if another school rejects him. I hate to try again."[16]

As her waspish, if disingenuous, letter to their old schoolmaster Malcolm Gordon suggested some years earlier, Millicent tended to let her sons go their own ways. She was grateful to Joseph. "You taught him [Paul] a lot about himself, you taught me a lot about him and for that I can never thank you enough. He has never had any man near him of even a medium amount of sensitivity so that you with all your great good humor and understanding gave him a strong foundation of inner strength so I wonder if I can bridge this crisis in his life now. . . . I think he feels he has not got something in him which is the American pattern. Mother again; she told him he was not really American being half Argentine." She broached the subject directly with her mother, but by letter, once Mary had returned home, berating her for "scolding Paulie the way you did when he came back from Hartford."

Millicent extended herself freely to children. Florence Bramante and her cousin Donna Montgomery, Dalton's daughter, were young girls when their mothers took them along to have tea with Millicent at Turtlewalk. They remembered her beautiful, fine-boned face and how full of life she seemed. Her voice, to little girls, seemed "flutey" and she lit up a room with her quick hand gestures and erect posture. She was perky, and she served finger sandwiches and lots of "goodies" to them, including lemonade. Her arresting looks and elegant manner were a notable contrast to the rougher-hewn mavericks and artists in town. In a place like Taos, she also managed to move well beneath the radar of many of the citizens.[17]

Turtlewalk, expanding to eight rooms from five, came along slowly. Spanish labor was required to make and lay the adobe bricks and like most local houses, the floor plan was arrived at more by directive than architectural plans. Millicent seemed unworried and endlessly patient, but Dorothy Brett recalls a process that tried the tolerance of everyone else involved with it. "Slowly through the summer the walls rose. Millicent with her inexperience, with no plans drawn, would find that what she had in mind did not always work out right. Walls would go up, walls would come down, windows would be put in, taken out and put in somewhere else, there was so much shifting and changing that we, the spectators began to wonder whether a whole house would ever materialize. The patience of the builders, the friends working for her was strained to breaking point, but somehow or other a definite shape rose out of the turmoil." To add to the delays, the Indians didn't show up when there was a dance or event at the Pueblo. Millicent, who was able to live in the partially completed site, would get up to find only the Spanish workers on-site. They explained to her that there was a fiesta or some other business at the Pueblo and usually in a day or so the Indian workers would come back at their own unhurried pace.

Millicent seems to have taken a cue from them. She wanted the house to be just the way she wanted it, no matter how many revisions were required. Her fellow perfectionist friend, Earl Stroh, commended her tenacity. "There was one door that led into what she called the Turtle Room," said Stroh. "I don't know how many times she had that door moved, a few inches one way, a foot another. She had the door, frame, and everything torn down and replaced until she found the proper place and it pleased her eye. She was always right."[18]

Millicent's bedroom, high-ceilinged with a window the whole width of one wall, was the first room ready to paint. There were other little "turtle rooms" at different levels and guest rooms but the other notably spacious room with high ceilings and vigas was the library. When a shaman was called in to bless the nearly completed job, he declared the placement of the master bedroom inauspicious. The room needed to be reshaped and moved six inches in order for Millicent to sight sacred Taos Mountain from her bed in the center of the room. She took in stride the modification, the costs and chaos it caused, and approved the changes. When the room was finished she discovered the gigantic plate glass window admitted sunlight too intense to bear, so the plate glass wall was replaced with windows with panes—cooler. She painted the walls deep Indian red and yellow. The vigas, typically left natural or stained brown, were a dark dull blue. In 1950 she shipped a beautiful "golden" bed, the gilded one Roald Dahl had slept in and written about to his mother, from Claremont to replace the mahogany four-poster she started out with.

The house was both Millicent's creative project and the opportunity to scavenge the country for the accessories she admired and wanted. She drove around collecting the old Spanish doors and window frames that are distinctive to the region. She was attentive to color, like the golden yellow she chose for the small living room that she appointed with a large Spanish crucifix, African masks, and her impressionist paintings. An enclosed square patio at the center of the house planted with roses lent a unique Oriental feeling.

When her house was not quite finished, Millicent threw a big open-air party to celebrate. The ceiling was not yet entirely closed. The unfinished patio was mounded with dirt. Millicent had it filled with the branches of cottonwood trees, stuck in the ground to mimic live tees. A big fire was lit and long wooden tables were set up for diners. At six when the invited guests began to arrive, Millicent was not present. Pots of food were delivered from the La Fonda hotel and two busloads of Indians arrived before the hostess, looking lovely and bewildered, came out to meet them. After dark, the bottles of whiskey set on the tables began to disappear with the Indians even though Coca-Cola had been provided expressly for them.

"The party in the firelight among the false trees assumed a joviality that became completely out of control," wrote Dorothy Brett both admiringly and full of wonder at the madness of providing hard liquor in such quantity to the Indians, who tried to dance, as Millicent had requested, but were too drunk. The Indians were coaxed back into the bus they'd come in only to run through it and scramble out the other door. The other guests decided to help by chasing them into the bus. The outlandish scene continued until the Indians eventually headed back to the Pueblo. Millicent seemed helpless but amused by the spectacle. Dorothy wrote in her account of the event in her memoirs that she thought Millicent had learned her lesson. At future parties the whiskey was hidden or carefully rationed.[19]

The locals began to talk about Millicent's "parties on the mesa" with big bonfires and Indian dancers. Bea Romero, who worked both for Millicent and the wife of the president of the First State Bank in

Taos, scoldingly told the latter, Dorothy Brandenburg, "I couldn't live like that." Romero quit working for Millicent and shook her head over the goings-on and "life out there."[20] Dick and Kay Dicus and his buddy Spud Johnson, a noted town figure, came to one big party Millicent gave. Dick and Spud liked to disappear into the bedroom of their hostess and put on her clothes, then return to the party in drag. As they cavorted on the snow in women's clothes, furs, and boas, bonfires blazing all around, Dick slipped on the ice and broke his rib. Kay Dicus was furious with him.[21] The Standard Oil heiress, with her penchant for living large, was making her mark on Taos.

CHAPTER TWENTY-TWO

Call of the Mountain

IN THE AUTUMN OF 1948 MILLICENT MADE A GRAND GESTURE TO her friend and designer Charles James. Despite her new focus on Taos and the continuing threat of poor health caused by overexertion, Millicent traveled to New York in November to present her gift of forty-five James gowns to the Brooklyn Museum for its "The Decade of Design" show, an homage to him. A hundred guests attended the opening, "the smartest and most unusual function in years," according to the New York *Daily News* on November 12, 1948. Dinner was served in the Great Gallery of the sculpture court, a fresh idea for a gala venue at the time. Frieda Lawrence, in an unexpected gesture of support and friendship, sent a telegram from Taos wishing Millicent success with the show.

Millicent presented the collection herself, wearing a James gown. It was the coup he had always dreamed of, seeing his designs (paid for by the client, Millicent, in this instance) enshrined in a design museum, in an event that burnished his reputation for design genuis. The sculptress Lillian Greneker, whose family foundation had underwritten the museum's costs, flew to Taos to sculpt a likeness of

Millicent's head for the show. Millicent's clothes were posed on mannequins against a backdrop of scarlet felt, lit by candlelight. The exhibition was such a success that the *Brooklyn Eagle* newspaper declared Millicent "the first patron of fashion designing the U.S. has ever had in a really big way." Millicent had done right by James and at the same time reaped a tax credit from her donation of his costly designs. This was no small matter; she was becoming more concerned about money.

Taxation and the stipulation that she could not borrow against the family trust limited her funds. The previous January she had looked toward a show of her jewelry designs at the Philbrook Art Center in Tulsa, Oklahoma, hoping that she would get a commission or sell selected pieces.

During a trip to Jamaica earlier in the year she wrote her mother that she intended to buy cotton shirts for Arturo, "but as money is scarce, I have to go easy." Money was becoming more of an issue—and a controlling tool—with her sons. Back in Taos she telegraphed Paul, who was traveling in Italy and had written her of his plans to extend his trip and asked for money. "Come home as arranged. Now don't be spoiled when asked to cooperate. Will send none until answered. Love, Mother." In her next message she admonished him to "come at once." She turned over their correspondence to her New York secretary Mathilde Seif who wrote to Paul at the Hotel Danieli in Venice. "Mother wants you to come home tomorrow as arranged." She expected him to travel on August 17, but on September 3 she telegraphed again on Millicent's behalf, saying, "Imperative you return New York. . . . Mother furious. Greetings, Seif."[1]

It was ironic that Millicent would resort to using funds to control her sons, much as had been done to her by her father. Sometimes it is hard to reconcile how freely Millicent spent money with the concern her correspondence expressed over the diminishment of her wealth and what was made public about the reduction of her fortune by taxes after her father's death. Her heirs believe that since her family fortune had at one time been almost unfathomable, she could never quite comprehend where money came from or how to manage it. It was just something that had always been there for her use. She shopped with total abandon. Not only did she seem unaware of the cost of things, she had a collector's mentality. The story of her ordering four dozen nearly identical blouses from Charles James was by this time well-known in fashion circles. He had called her a hoarder. Her maid had countered: "a collector." While she was in New York, Millicent received a telegram from Dick Dicus in Taos. Dicus was distressed to hear from townspeople that she owed them money. They didn't take any more kindly to her bill-paying practices, her once-a-year payment schedule, than her decorators had in Hollywood. He sent her a wire saying, "Sell the damn crown jewels and pay your bills."[2]

When she got back to Taos, she hired Dixie Yaple, a local woman whose family had owned a hardware store on Taos plaza. Dixie had also worked a few years in the movie industry before returning to Taos. Her local contacts and know-how suggested to Millicent that she could help her better manage her affairs. Yet Millicent's cavalier approach to bill-paying continued to dog her. Locals tried to dope it out. Clearly, she had the funds to pay them. Was it that she didn't like the act of handling money to distract, or cheapen her interaction with the personalities? Could she not understand what it was like for other people who lived a hand-to-mouth life? It was a mystery that frustrated a number of local merchants.

Millicent's newfound enthusiasm for Taos rubbed off when she returned to New York. She usually traveled with her fine paintings—the Manets, Monets, Renoirs, and van Goghs—when she changed locales for a few months. This time she also had a treasure chest of Indian silver, bracelets, necklaces, turquoise beads, conchos, and ketohs (the armbands that were worn by Indian men) that she fashioned for her own long wrists and cuffs. One of her first stops in Manhattan was Diana Vreeland's office at *Harper's Bazaar.* In the next issue she appeared, photographed by Louise Dahl-Wolfe, in a white linen Valentina shirt seated among four chairs, her arms beneath her puffy pushed-up sleeves covered in silver and turquoise ketohs and brace-lets, silver crosses dangling at the waist of a black Navajo-style skirt.

The photo is a textbook example of modeling technique. Though it is the iconic image of Rogers, it is also a classic example of how a model exhibits the clothes and accessories rather than projecting her-self. Her gaze is beautiful and wise, but withholding and knowing, indirect. It is the jewelry, abundantly worn and up front, that she is putting forward. As Harold Koda, curator of the Costume Institute of the Metropolitan Museum of Art, explains Millicent's keen sense of creative accessorizing: "Most women would have worn Van Cleef or Cartier, but her distinctive pairing of a James blouse and her own jewelry was a heartbeat ahead of her time. It wasn't the head-to-toe matching of that time, but a break from that. Most women didn't have the courage to emulate her style."3

Of course, she had added a distinctive counternote, the large and military-looking Russian Order of St. Catherine brooch that was loaned to her by Valentina, and while it was not at all Indian, the oversized pin helps create a mystifying eclectic look. A cowboy ker-chief of orchid silk added a flourish. With Millicent's inimitable stamp on it, Southwestern style was quietly launched in *Harper's Ba-zaar*. *Town & Country* soon followed with photos of her jewelry designs and news that she was "back from Taos!"

Koda is equally astute in his observation of Millicent's introduc-tion of Southwestern style to the fashion mainstream. "Southwestern style is such a specific way of dressing that it is diminished by bad representation of it. It is difficult to make it chic and there is the dan-ger of a Southwestern costume. But Millicent incorporated it into Amer-ican dress. It remained as a strong reference point into the design world in the 50s and 60s with the hippies." He breaks into open, unabashed admiration of the way Millicent captured whatever she touched with her style. "It is hard to wear a powerful iconic style without it being a costume. But it was not about the way she wore it. Her face, her coif, her attitude. It *became* Millicent. It was not so audacious, but such an imprint of herself! She muted the costume aspect and wore Southwestern style as her day clothes. It's all about attitude." In the end her service was to Southwestern style, rather than vice versa.

Vreeland's friend Polly Mellen registered the impact when she went with Vreeland to have an "enormous black cotton sateen skirt made. That year we all wore a black sateen skirt with ten petticoats," Mellen told Annette Tapert in her book about women who defined the art of living well, *The Power of Style*. Vreeland paid Millicent the utmost compliment, a bit backhandedly, by both copying her clothes and announcing, "I'm not interested in the dress, I'm interested in the woman inside the dress . . . her costumes would have been only that, if it hadn't been for her overwhelming personality—sensitive and vulnerable on the one hand, lusty and provocative on the other."[4]

Millicent was reenergized when she returned to New York. She appeared at some of her old New York haunts, El Morocco, the St. Regis, the Plaza, and the Ritz, but she was looking for newer, edgier venues. Rita Kip Marquand, a young society girl in her twenties, was working at *Harper's Bazaar* when Millicent came into the offices to see Vreeland. "She was simply extraordinary," Marquand said, remembering the impression Millicent made. Millicent, seemingly ageless, invited Marquand and several of the attractive and obviously well-bred—or at least well-mannered and polite—young women who flocked to such jobs at the fashion magazines to go out with her at night. She picked them up with her driver and took them down to the Bon Soir, a legendary Greenwich Village cabaret considered hip and a little beyond the boundary of polite society. The singer was Jimmie Daniels, an inordinately handsome black Harlem Renaissance vocalist Marquand compared to Sidney Poitier.

Millicent was "smashingly turned out" with lots of her Indian jewelry, a big squaw skirt, and her hair swept back. Marquand and her young colleague Dorinda Dixon, called "D.D.," watched Millicent invite Daniels to sit down with them at their table during his break. They studied her style, and concluded, as did almost everyone else, "she was just different from other people." They were surprised by her warmth and how she made them feel, that she was truly interested in what they thought and said. "She made you feel good and that these were happy times. It was all pretty swell," recalls Marquand.[5] Millicent did her own social organizing. She picked up the phone and made the call herself when she was inviting her younger guests to dinner. Marquand never saw Millicent out on the town with a woman friend; she was more likely to host a bevy of younger people, sometimes including one or more of her sons, to go where she wanted to go.

Arturo had fallen madly in love with a beautiful girl he had met that year in Jamaica, Mary Kitterman, nicknamed "Dusty." She had been crowned the Queen of Montego Bay in the island's annual festivity. Arturo phoned her every two hours and pressed his suit to the point of having Millicent invite her to tea in her apartment on East Sixty-eighth Street. Though Dusty would marry Arturo, at the time she wasn't as smitten as was he. "My son is in love with you," Millicent told her directly. "I'm not in love with him," Dusty replied.[6] Arturo at the time was in Argentina where he had been sent to represent the family at a relative's wedding. But Dusty was touched by Millicent's graciousness and kindness to her. As they chatted, it was the two of them who fell in love at that moment, in Dusty's opinion. Dusty thought Millicent looked "always perfect," and that day she was dressed simply but elegantly in a beautiful white blouse worn with a piece of Indian jewelry. Her two corgies and dachshunds were at her feet. She had been told by Arturo that Millicent was not well. She and Arturo would marry, much as Millicent had, in a courthouse wedding within the year. Millicent had Charles James make up dresses for her daughter-in-law, who continued to speak well of her after her marriage to Arturo failed. "She was delightful, a great friend to me, totally undemanding," remembers Dusty.

The East Coast trip dragged into the new year. At Thanksgiving Millicent wrote Brett that she would be spending it with "Paulie and my French underground friends," an interesting bit of evidence that her MSRC duties had involved more responsibility and expertise than mere everyday administration. Christmas was at Claremont. The longer she stayed away from Taos, the more she lamented it. "But I miss Taos and feel it in my heart. The mountain stands out clearly, through which one sees all the rest, and I feel I am protected by goodness, as though goodness was set over one. Hard to explain, but so glad a feeling."[7]

Back in Taos the following fall, Millicent decided to host Thanksgiving in her completed house and invited Mirandi to come up from Santa Fe. Mirandi explained she had already committed to her friend Ludovic Kennedy, a correspondent for the BBC, who was going out with the Hollywood actress and dancer Moira Shearer, newly of *The Red Shoes* movie fame; Shearer was doing a show up in Denver. Millicent expanded her invitation; they should all come to Taos for Thanksgiving. By this time Millicent's house was staffed with her black household employees from Claremont Manor. Besides her cook, she had two other women to help with the kitchen and the house. Her "darkies," she called them to Mirandi.

Mirandi and Shearer, twenty-four, were wide-eyed as they watched the black staff in white gloves and livery[8] serve Thanksgiving dinner at a long table set with silver and fine plates to the Indian guests, who chewed on their drumsticks rather than use cutlery, ate without napkins, and tossed their bones onto Millicent's beautiful rugs when they were finished. "It didn't bother Millicent. She was simply a marvelous hostess, so casual and unflustered. She took everything as it came and nothing surprised her. To her anything was just another incident in her life," said Mirandi. The only off-note that registered with Millicent came from Mabel Luhan's decision to hold court, pouting, it seemed, on the patio rather than joining into the larger affair. Millicent, bemused, ignored her. In an ironic twist of historical observance, the Indians were front and center in Millicent's Thanksgiving, whether she planned it that way or not. Indians, their life, their ways, and the things they made were becoming central to Millicent's life.

As Taos resident and historian Larry Torres explains, "What the Tahitians were to Gauguin, the Indians were to these Anglos."[9] It was the real or imagined aspects of Indian life, pure and one with the landscape, that captivated so many of Taos's newcomers. For Millicent the Indians had the added attraction of making things that appealed to her sensibilities and collector's heart. The Indians were her chief passion and interest.

Mabel Dodge's marriage to Tony Luhan had caused snickers and the predictable racial epithets from those who opposed or couldn't understand interracial mixing. Her marriage to an Indian suggested that she couldn't make the grade with her "own kind"—or that there was some male Indian sexual prowess—a handy explanation for her Anglo brethren—that she had fallen hostage to. Of course, neither was true. Mabel had been the controlling factor in her previous marriages. Whites, Anglos, Europeans, aristocrats, intellectuals, and refined New Yorkers had been at her feet. The fact was that women like Mabel, and now Millicent, had the freedom to pursue whoever turned their heads. They were equal to men in matters of pursuing their fancies and they weren't hostage to men and marriage for financial security or social betterment.

Of course, many contemporaries saw it differently. Bob Tenorio's grandfather, Maximilian, worked for Mabel as chauffeur. He explained such women to his grandson, Bob, who also filled in as a driver for Mabel. These women, Max told him, were "crazy easterners." In his community they were regarded as interlopers who fell in love with Taos, but wanted to make it more like the places they came from, with maids and chauffeurs, and the comforts of wealth.

Like Millicent, Mabel had a kennel's worth of exotic dogs during her years in Taos. The Tenorios remembered dalmations, basset hounds, a Pekingese, a Boston Bulldog, a Russian Wolfhound, and a Great Dane. The dogs were further evidence to Max that the women were all from the "crazy easterner" set. And there were sniggers from locals over the fact that Millicent had valet parking for parties at her house. Max explained to his grandson, "When you don't have money you're crazy, when you do have money you're eccentric." He categorized Mabel and Millicent as eccentric, though he considered Millicent to be regal, rather than haughty, and marveled at the aura around her. He described her "like someone walking on a cloud." He also shrugged at Mabel's marriage to Tony. Tony had begun as Mabel's gardener and was what Max Tenorio called a "Well set up buck, shirtless in the yard."[10] When the Millicents and Mabels of Taos were attracted to the men in their employ or yards they could do whatever circumstances allowed—and they wanted—and their critics be damned.

The other accusation often levied again them, usually nastily inferred rather than stated outright, was that they had inordinate sexual drives that could only be satisfied outside the "our kind" norm by savages or the specially endowed. It's unlikely that there was anything aberrant about Mabel, Millicent, and other wealthy women who fell for the primal maleness of the American Indian. Steeped in the myth of the hunter and the allure of nature, the Indian carried the romance of Western freedom, of natural mysteries, and of unbridled sexuality. Mabel, Millicent, Frieda Lawrence, and even Georgia O'Keeffe, whom Millicent had only yet crossed paths with, were to become emblematic of bohemian women in New Mexico, women who had already moved outside the world of prescribed social behavior for women of their time. Millicent and Mabel had each had three husbands. Frieda had left her first husband and three young children for D. H. and returned with an Italian lover to Taos after D. H.'s death. O'Keeffe, who settled in Abiquiu, New Mexico, was a loner and lived with a much younger companion, Juan Hamilton, well into her eighties.

Millicent unabashedly stated her admiration, with a dash of eros, for Indian men. In 1948 she wrote to Brett, "I do always wish white men had long hair, long black hair is wonderful. It gets me always in the middle of the tummy in a funny way. It has something so strong about it and male and powerful, it has some of the mountain [Taos Mountain] power about it."[11]

Indian men, tanned and muscular from outdoor work and life in the Pueblo, with their sleek black tresses worn loose or tied back in buns and braids, bristled with novelty and wild maleness. Their strong silent manner, born of their nature—or the language barrier—

smacked of force and mystery. Some, like Benito Suazo—who was in his twenties—a square-jawed and handsomely even-featured young nephew of Tony Luhan from the Pueblo, caught Millicent's eye. He was considered inordinately handsome and there was a troubled darkness to him. He had served in the army during the war and by some accounts returned to the Pueblo angry and violent. He was also thought to be an alcoholic. She hired him to work as her chauffeur, a coveted position in a community that lacked cars. Employment and transportation were both highly regarded on the Pueblo. Millicent could drive a car, but she generally chose not to, and her ability to navigate was limited according to her son Paul, who claimed she could not manage to put a standard shift into reverse.

Millicent was bewitched by the Indians almost from the moment she arrived in Taos. Her first visit to the Taos Pueblo where the mythic-looking four-story north pueblo adobe building, colored in rich earth brown tones but for the green and electric blue ("Taos blue") doors and window frames, standing against the mountain backdrop beneath the deep blue sky, intrigued her.

Shortly after her arrival she took Paul to watch an Indian dance on the Apache Indian Reservation near Dulce, New Mexico, five hours away by car. Tony Luhan and several Taos Pueblo Indians went along. The impression was indelible, and she wrote of it glowingly in a letter to Paul's former preparatory school teacher at Choate, John Joseph, who had been their recent guest.

Millicent had characteristically taken a true liking to Joseph, a near legendary boys' school teacher of the Mr. Chips variety who taught everything from classics to cooking to his adolescent charges and lastingly inspired them. He and Millicent bonded over her concern for Paul, who had been told he could not return to school due to his poor marks, as well as Joseph's eager appreciation for the history and Indian culture that Millicent was discovering.

She carried on a warm and often detailed correspondence with him about her new experiences in and around Taos. Her letters to him are the best record of the unmitigated joy she took in the Indians and their country. "We came back from Apache country where we spent two Winslow Homer-Renoir days of wild joy," she wrote him, tangentially taking a swipe at Mabel, who "Had tried to deter me from going. . . . Thank goodness we went." Millicent chafed at Mabel's criticism and discouragement of her Indian trips (probably because Tony often went along with the Taos Indian contingency. Millicent relied on him for help and entrée to the tribal lands she visited.) She commented disparagingly to Joseph about Mabel's Mexican journal after Mabel had asked her to read it and evaluate whether she thought it publishable. "I would have called it 'What I Ate for Three Months' or maybe, 'I, Mabel, Inc.'" quipped Millicent.

Mabel's displeasure with her aside, Millicent sounded most like a woman falling in love when she wrote, "In Rome, in Paris, in the east I have seen strange and lovely things that excited and delighted me, but never anything that reached down inside and belonged to me as that camp did through every minute of the time spent there. It was America, into the center and core and it was personally mine in a most curious, easy, at-home way."[12]

The Indians seemed intuitively to trust in Millicent's admiration of them and their craftsmanship. She quickly became known as a woman who bought in quantity and if she thought the asking price was fair, she didn't dicker, though occasionally she asked her son or a fellow shopper to do her bidding for her so that her interest didn't drive up the price. She thought nothing of stopping the Indians to buy jewelry off their backs, but as her reputation as a rich white woman traveled in advance of her appearances, she learned to let others do her bidding.

Taos Pueblo soon took note of her. She stood out, this tall blonde dressed in Indian clothes and moccasins. Tony Reyna, a handsome Indian who had returned a hero from the Bataan Death March, noticed her immediately, and she him. Reyna had spent enough time outside the Pueblo to be comfortable with Anglos, and he was destined to be active in its governance. He would become one of the elected governors. He also ran a jewelry concession, Tony

Reyna's Indian Shop, that sold wares from various Western Indian tribes.

Reyna remembers the day Millicent first came with her son Paul in their Ford station wagon to visit his Indian shop.[13] She had already adopted the Indian way of dressing and was wearing a Navajo skirt as she moved slowly among the Indians across the plaza. Admiring but tight-lipped about their friendship, he says that she was "always a lovely person" and that their friendship was chiefly about jewelry and the Indian things she collected. She consulted him about her purchases, their worth and value. He was along on several of her excursions onto other reservations. She wanted to learn all about the Indians, both their arts and their rituals.

Millicent's writing toward the end of her life suggests that she had adopted some of the Indians' spiritual outlook, but there is little question that the chief attraction of the Indian spectacles, dances, and rituals that she attended was their visual beauty. Her exposure to them may have expanded her intellectual and spiritual palette, but it didn't curb her penchant for buying what she wanted. She was not about to withdraw from the material world and her possessions. The jewelry, pots, and rugs she could bring home, but the scenes she witnessed made a deep impression on her.

She wrote toward the end of one of her most moving accounts of a trip taken into Indian territory, "It was like the pictures which one always longs to be in. AND THERE WE WERE IN IT," she thrilled.[14] She sounded more smitten than she had ever been. Arturo, less frequent on the Taos scene than his younger brother Paul, says, "I had never seen her happier" than she was in Taos. Hedda Hopper, with whom Millicent kept a correspondence after she left LA, noted in her "Looking at Hollywood" in 1948, a postscript of sorts on Millicent's departure from the Hollywood scene, "Millicent Rogers and her sons still are in Taos, N.M." and that they had ". . . fallen in love with the place." Millicent had, and like all falling in love it seemed to energize her outlook, her creativity, her relationship to others, her generosity, and her fervor for living—everything but her heart.

CHAPTER TWENTY-THREE

Taos

T SEEMS TO ME STRANGE SOMETIMES THAT I'VE ONLY BEEN IN Taos fifteen months for I feel so much 'of it.' As if my people had been buried in it's [sic] graveyards and my blood ties were in its earth. I feel so drawn to return when I'm away and so restless with the rest of the world because of it," Millicent wrote to Frieda Lawrence before her return to Taos in 1949.[1] It was the place where her longing for life and pursuit of beauty converged—and seemed to be satisfied. In the Northeast she wrote that she had wearied of being asked what it was about Taos that drew her or what she did there, and while it suited the fashion world and social observers to explain her devotion to Taos as merely another stage to conquer and to collect from, its effect on her was more profound.

Living in Taos required her to see her life from a fresh perspective. In letters, much as she had always scribbled in books and her girlhood diary, she explained her new standards for men, her appreciation for serenity and silence, her current attitude about money, religion, and the natural beauty that centered her heart and mind in Taos. The mountain and the outlook of the Indians were not a stage to pass through, she seemed to say, but a new grail. She embraced them wholeheartedly and shed the trappings and manners of her former life as best she could, as if their lessons were what was needed to complete her search for fulfillment and beauty.

Dressed in Indian clothes, living in a rustic yet unfinished house, answering to her own social interests, creating her own jewelry designs, eschewing outside standards for appropriate men, she determinedly set her own agenda for life and settled into Taos. Her mantra, had she one, may have been her closing to a letter to Frieda Lawrence: "Life goes too quickly when it is beautiful."[2]

Millicent's house in Taos was never finished in the way that Shulla House in Austria or Claremont Manor had been. It was lovely with all the added grace notes of Spanish adobe architecture, the windows she had acquired from the old Arroyo Hondo chapel up the road, and the little carved santos, Spanish saints, that she collected. Yet she seemed to hang on to a slight funkiness, delight in it even, as though its unfinished nature would prevent her life from being organized around any single, limiting principle. She was open to change and interpretation. There was no finality. The Indian rugs that she collected were seldom hung on the walls but arranged on floors, as the Indians used them. Visitors to her house remember that she had many Indian baskets on the floor, and ashtrays and books were scattered everywhere.

Her letters show that something deeper was working in Millicent during this time. Though she spent time and energy tending to her homes, wardrobe, and the vexing taxation that dogged her, a more profound philosophical shift, somewhat hidden, was talking place in her psyche.[3]

Though Millicent had had many friends in her life, her youthful friendships with Lela Emery, Cornelia Biddle, Rocky Shields Cooper, and her pal Margaret Mallory were relationships among social equals, birds of a feather, based on common experiences and culture. In Taos her friendships with Frieda Lawrence and Dorothy Brett were of a different nature, easier going and less predictable. They worked to bridge their differences. As they came to know each other, they stood little on social ceremony among themselves. Millicent would drift into the others' houses unannounced. A meal would be fixed on the spur of the moment. Brett knew Millicent was considered one of Frieda's intimates when "she was promoted to eating in the kitchen; perhaps of all places the most delightful for eating in." Millicent became a constant casual guest.

She seemed to delight in the impromptu social occasions. The others never knew when to expect her; she just came and sat down at the table, "telling her latest adventures of searching for old doors and windows, jewelry and santos. Shawls, she loved shawls. . . . How much fun she had with all of us!" Brett wrote. In her opinion, Frieda, a lusty and unbridled personality that all Taos seemed to delight in, invariably photographed with her hair askew and a cigarette dangling from her lips, most enjoyed "the times, when Millicent would drift in quietly and sit and gossip in her kitchen. And became entirely one of us." Millicent obviously enjoyed the acceptance enough to abandon one of her long-held prerogatives. She quit being late. Wrote Brett, "She learned to be on time because as amateur cooks we resented our suppers being spoiled by her unpunctuality." Millicent arrived on time for the "feasts" in Frieda's kitchen, Brett's friend Bob Davidson's omelettes, and Brett's steaks cooked in her fireplace.

Millicent was equally insouciant with Brett, who, while napping on her sofa would feel "someone tugging at my toes and I would open a resentful eye, and there would be Millicent smiling at me. She would come to see if I were doing anything exciting in the way of painting." Millicent bought Brett's much-admired paintings of the Buffalo Dance and Turtle Dance at the Pueblo, and Brett made her gifts of a few others as their friendship deepened. "I have nothing to give except my paintings, and she gave me so much," Brett explained. She expressed her devotion in a journal that she kept of her relationship with Millicent.[4] Though playful on occasion, Millicent generally showed more social reserve. At Mabel's, wrote Brett, she "floated gently in to the big dark living room. All her movements were quiet. She would sit looking strangely beautiful and untouchable and utterly impregnable. She was reserved, poised, self-controlled until her charming warm smile gave out a sudden unexpected intimacy."[5]

One evening Brett took Millicent with her to dinner at Bob Davidson's. Davidson, an Eastern transplant in his twenties who worked at various odd jobs trying to pay off his debts, lived in a dilapidated old adobe house in Tobacco Row up on the Loma, the hill west of the Taos town plaza that had once been a Spanish encampment.[6] Davidson cooked them a good meal on his smoky oil cooking stove, and seated them on hard chairs at his table. Brett called it one of the more primitive spots in Taos. Of Millicent she wrote, "She would come quietly in, all her movements were quiet. Slow rythmical. In her bunchy Navajo skirts, velvet tunic, and finely woven shawl and lovely jewelry she would walk in with her slow swinging walk. Her lovely shining fair hair shoulder length." Millicent seated herself happily among them. When she needed to use the bathroom, Davidson sent her to the outside privy with an oil lamp. "Nothing delighted Millicent more than going out armed with an oil lamp to the privy," remembered Brett, though tired of privies herself, she added.

As local wags observed, Brett sought out Millicent more when she was on the outs with Mabel and Frieda, but Millicent was completely accepting of her new friend's idiosyncracies. To some degree, Brett understood her best and wanted to protect her, especially from Mabel's capricious callousness toward the feelings of others. Millicent was more vulnerable than one might have imagined, unused as she was to someone like Mabel who played queen bee with her and cavalierly wounded others. Mabel and her coterie were deeply woven into the social tapestry of Taos when Millicent arrived. They were players in the intellectual and bohemian worlds they had helped to create, and they belonged in a way that Millicent would not. Her six years in Taos, though immensely satisfying personally, were a mere sideshow compared to the deep impact that Brett, Frieda, and, above all, Mabel Luhan made on 1940s Taos.

When Millicent had stayed at the The Tony House waiting for Turtlewalk to be habitable, it proved too close for comfort to Mabel, who according to Brett, "had her usual 'volte face,'" and "Millicent, without our experiences of Mabel's temperamental acrobats, was deeply hurt and puzzled. We, Mabel's friends of long standing, having been in and out of the dog kennel at regular intervals, let it run off our backs like [water] off a duck's back. But Millicent with her innate distrust of all human beings was astounded, angry, hurt, and bitter. So what could have been a very good friendship was terminated . . ." wrote Brett.[7]

The real difference between Mabel and Millicent, as Millicent's letters to Brett during one of her trips back East shows, was over Tony.[8] Millicent could not understand how Mabel "could have kept Tony away from the Pueblo—and it might be a little difficult to take him from his roots." She disliked Mabel meddling in her relations with the Indians, and huffily cut off Brett's defense of Mabel: "You can enjoy yourself feeling sorry for her. I don't, and never will." When Mabel commented negatively on the Indian labor Tony supplied for Millicent's house renovations, Millicent retorted to Brett: "If Mabel will keep her goddam claws out of it, it will be all right."[9] The two strong-willed women stayed at arm's length, and a rapprochement between them would come considerably later.

Mabel may have had cause to be threatened by Millicent's attention to Tony. Millicent, her letters suggest, had come some way from dismissing Tony as an "aging Indian" to Frank Waters. Two years after her arrival in Taos, he had become her standard for manhood, the antithesis for all she was coming to reject about white men and white society, and the model for the Indian approach to life that she now aspired to. She sent her regards to him in nearly all her correspondence to Brett and Frieda when she traveled away from Taos, and she strove to achieve his centered, disciplined reserve. "It would be good if like Tony I could put a blanket over my head and not be available—but are we not too white for that!" she wrote, frustrated by social commitments and travel delays in New York. She proudly asked Brett to tell Tony that she had kept her composure and not volunteered too much information about herself when she was taken to emergency after a taxi accident in which she was thrown into the rearview mirror and suffered a head injury. Tony had become her model for stoicism. With him in mind she claimed that she did not panic or flinch when a portion of her scalp was shaved and she was kept in the hospital.

Brett endeared herself to Millicent in many ways, but it was their shared appreciation of the Indians that was their strongest bond. Parties where the Indians danced were a common occurrence in Taos and a growing fascination for Millicent. Her house, with its narrow configuration of rooms, was not big enough for the dances, so Millicent lobbied Frieda to have a dance up at the Kiowa Ranch, the property she and D. H. had acquired from Mabel in the twenties. Millicent promised to supply the food and brought camping equipment for Arturo, his new wife Dusty, and Paul. They planned to stay overnight since such events typically stretched very late into the night.

Everyone crowded into the house for supper by the firelight in the living room until the Indians arrived. "In the rather small room, the throb of the drums, the clang of the bells on the legs of the Indians were hypnotic, they were so powerful and strong," Brett wrote later. "They danced as usual way into the night, until all of us were exhausted, with the sound, the swift movement, and the long days work of getting everything ready. At long last, the Indians went home and we all laid ourselves out on our cots. Every room was occupied. We had just overflowed."[10] Millicent was enthralled.

She wanted to go to Gallup, a major Indian trading post for the tribes of New Mexico and Arizona, and she invited Brett to come along. Afterward they would go camping in Hopi territory. The traveling party filled two cars and a station wagon driven by a nephew of Tony Luhan, along with three other Indians. It was equipped with tents, cots, bedrolls, and air mattresses. Brett's friend Howard Sherman drove Millicent's Chrysler for the passengers. They met up with Arturo and Dusty in Albuquerque and arrived late at the El Rancho

Hotel in Gallup, just in time for an evening performance of Indian dancing in the stadium there. Brett wrote of watching "The masses of Indians of all tribes, the handsome proud Navajos, the men slim, aloof, in their velvet tunics, silver bells and bracelets and tight blue jeans. The women in bright satin or velvet skirts, full-pleated, voluminous, their velvet tunics decorated with rows of small silver buttons down the front along the sleeves.

Millicent had walked into a fantastic world, to which her heart and soul belonged. She was, in her spirit, in her way of life, a part of this world, far more so than that other world of perfect clothes, social standing, and far too much money. Among the Indians she was at home; she was unknown, free, a human being among human beings. The Indians with their peculiar awareness knew this. Their response had the gift of understanding and sympathy, and her simplicity was as subtle as theirs. She was completely in her element."[11]

It was a conversion born of the anguish she suffered over Gable's rejection, as if that humbling loss and her newly felt vulnerability—coupled with the awareness of mortality that she had long understood—penetrated her deepest core and reset her eye and appreciation of beauty. This was a woman who had been exposed to, even collected, some of the world's finest art, furnishings, jewelry, clothes, and men, yet she now found fulfillment in mountain vistas, primitive pageants, and the company of people who communed with nature and believed the highest order of life was natural beauty and the mysterious workings of the universe. Now her aesthetic appreciation of unrefined elements, previously exhibited exclusively in her fashion style, flowered in combination with the spiritual aspects of the Indian world and gave her a newer and higher sense of beauty—not just of things, but of life. She had gone from thrilling over Fabergé's sparkling bejeweled eggs to being transported by glowing fireside dances in the most unexpected twist of her meteoric life.

In an uncustomary fit of insecurity, Brett was alarmed to learn that she would be sharing a room with Millicent at the hotel. "I thought of my ragged pyjamas, my inclination to snore as I looked indignantly at her exquisite nighty," Brett wrote. But when Millicent put her nightgown on, and it had a huge hole in the back, "That cheered me up enormously," she added. You can almost hear her chuckle as she fell fast asleep while Millicent finished her elaborate toilet for the night. Brett was first awake and looked at Millicent sleeping peacefully. At 9 A.M. Millicent waved a vague hand at her and ordered room service breakfast. Millicent hardly ever began her day before noon, as her doctors had suggested a slow start and lots of rest were good for her heart condition. It worried Brett who looked apprehensively at Millicent whenever she woke up, morning or night. Fascinated, Brett observed Millicent's routine of "Putting on her face" after she dressed. She watched her apply "her extraordinary subtle makeup. Then she would proceed to swallow a handful of assorted pills of all colours. After that she was ready and we would take off."

They headed for the Hopi mesas and the magical Walpi Pueblo, perched on a high rock mesa. "It seemed more like something out of one of Wagner's Rings, rather than the habitation of human beings," wrote the erudite Brett. They drove onto a second village where a dance was scheduled in a little plaza, up a steep incline. The question was whether Millicent would be physically able to manage the climb. She suggested the others go ahead and let her come at her own pace. Apprehensively, they did. Millicent shortly appeared, calm and unruffled, to stand in the hot sun during the dance. The Indians instructed the onlookers to be quiet and to understand the dance was a religious ceremony, but when the live snakes were set on the ground white women started scuffling and screaming. "The behavior of these tourists made one ashamed of ones race and colour," scoffed Brett.

When they got back to the station wagon, the driver had his head under the hood. The car had given them trouble all day so they pitched their tents where they were. After cooking over an open fire, their host and some Indians boys came with a drum and sat down to sing. Again, the faithful Brett recorded the scene: "Around the low fire, in a night full of stars, we sat listening to the voices of the Indians sailing out over the desert far below us, the steady soft thudding of the drum breaking against the rocks. Millicent sat in a dream, her full Navajo skirt billowing around her, the moon picking out in bright points the silver buttons on her tunic and silver belt, the firelight enriching the colors. Quiet and calm, she sat absorbed in the lovely night, the strange melody of the song, the rhythm of the drum; with her elbows on her knee, her chin on her hands, the fair hair falling softly on each side of her face. So fair and fragile she was, against the dark night and the dark Indian faces." Brett intervened with their host the next morning, explaining that Millicent's heart was too fragile to have to walk back up to the plaza to see the ceremony. With his help it was arranged that they could drive up and leave the car at the top all day. The drive up a narrow road still required traveling along a narrow overhang by foot. As they waited during the afternoon for the dancing to begin, Millicent befriended Indian boys on the scene who gladly showed her around. Then the Antelope men began to appear, singing softly. Again there were snakes. The old snake Chief came with an enormous bag of them. The scene was totally quiet. "No one moved and hardly breathed," wrote Brett. As the singing stopped the old snake men made a gentle hissing sound, like the fall of light rain on a roof, or the rustle of wind among leaves until it was taken up by the soft song of the Antelope men, a lullaby, a love song to the snakes, a gentle wooing of the snakes to bring them rain.[12] The Indian lands opened their splendor to them like a kaleidoscope of wonder after wonder. The next day they started out for Zuni lands at Mishongnovi.

The Zuni masked dances intrigued Millicent and her fellow travelers, but they got a strong sense that they were unwelcome observers, so they pressed on to Canyon de Chelly, the Navajo heartland poised on the floors and rims of three major canyons immortalized in the sepia photos of photo historian Edward S. Curtis. That night they drove up to the rim of the canyon and pitched their camp. They cooked steaks over a roaring fire and sat around to gaze at the multitude of stars that shone in the clear dark sky over them and the canyon below. They fell asleep listening to the beat of the Indian drums and the sound of Indians singing. Brett dreamed of weeping women, blood, and tragedy, after hearing the story of nearby Canyon del Muerto, where Navajo women and children had been massacred by Spaniards.

The next day they hired a guide to help them navigate through the sands and twists of the river valley and to find their way to the cliff dwellings left by the pre-Columbian people who had inhabited the valley before the Navajos. There was a flap when the car got stuck and Brett realized lunch had been left in the other car, but Millicent brushed the inconvenience aside. She pointed out that they had water and chocolate soda. Brett sometimes marveled at her equanimity. "Millicent, delicate as she was, could take a lot. She sat on the desert under her large shady hat, murmuring that someone would come along, and surely enough someone did." An old Navajo on a horse came by and promised to get them a tow. After a wait, a truck and two jeeps came to their rescue. Everyone was asked to pile into the jeep to make it heavy enough to tow with. "I can see Millicent, even now, with her smooth muscular movements climbing in and out of that truck. Finally sitting on the bench in that truck, her bunchy skirts spread out, the sun gleaming on the silver belt and silver buttons, on the deep red Corals and bright blue turquoises around her neck," Brett remembered. As Millicent was enchanted with the Indians, Brett was infatuated by Millicent.

No sooner had Millicent returned home than she began to plan her next expedition. She wanted to go to Apache land, to Horse Lake, for the fiesta in late fall that is known for the picturesque sight of tepees in a circle near the lake. Paul, Millicent, Brett, her handyman Trinidad and his wife Rufina arrived at sunset to find that only two Apache tents, and army tents at that, had been pitched. Only a little disappointed, they wandered down among the Apaches after cooking dinner at their campsite. A squaw dance went on through the night. It was late fall now, and cold after sundown. Dorothy was wakened by Millicent's laborious breathing during the night. She and Paul exchanged concerns over what they would do if Millicent had a sudden heart attack. They were fifty miles, at least, from a hospital, and that fear, wrote Brett, "lurked in the back of our minds, in spite of the pills that regulated the heart beat."

After two nights camping at Horse Lake, they headed back. Millicent wanted to return by Cumbres Pass, a winding route 10,022 feet up in Colorado's San Juan Mountains. Dorothy resisted what she considered "a horrifying mountain road that wiggles down the mountain in endless elbow turns, the sort of road that gives me hopeless vertigo. Millicent, calm, persuasive, smilingly persuaded me that all would be well." They stopped to buy a sheep, freshly slaughtered for them on the road, and packed it into the station wagon. Millicent fortified Brett with a cup of whiskey to help her endure the drive. Howard Sherman was driving, and kept the Chrysler in low gear in order to creep down the road, but Paul had taken the wheel of the station wagon and terrified the Indians riding with him by tearing down the mountain with tires screeching. At the bottom Millicent wanted to camp another night. The temperature dropped considerably overnight, and it was quite cold at breakfast time. The others waited, as usual, for Millicent to get up, put on her makeup, and take her pills. At noon, she was reluctantly ready to go home. The trip had involved an unusual amount of hardship and some daring, but the Standard Oil heiress, to the surprise of all concerned, madly loved it.[13]

Arturo was along on some of his mother's camping trips into Indian country and he remembers one outing with her, Brett, Tony Reyna, Trinidad Archuleta, Tony Luhan, and Benny Suazo into the Apache lands around the Jicarilla Apache lakes. On that trip, he recalls, Millicent wanted to try peyote, the Indian hallucinogen. She vomited it up on the first go and tried it again. She threw up again, but she was determined to experience its effect. The third time she managed to ingest it. In her Navajo costume she was invited to dance with the Apache Indian women and continued with the dance until she sank to the ground with exhaustion and had to go to bed. The next morning her fellow travelers waited for her to revive, a bit later than usual, and get started on the day.

On such a trip to the Gallup Inter-Tribal Ceremonial Millicent acquired a two-strand turquoise tab necklace by Zuni artist Leekya Deyuse. Paul's visiting tutor John Joseph was along with her when they passed an older man, his face creased and leathery, wearing an arrestingly large and beautiful necklace. Millicent immediately wanted it. "That's the most magnificent necklace I've ever seen," she said, flattering the wearer. The Indian explained that he had collected the several hundred pieces of turquoise over the course of his lifetime. He had polished the turquoise himself, he added. Millicent asked if it was for sale. No, he said, explaining, "Then I have only money." Millicent offered him a ride back to his village. Within three days, she had convinced him to sell the four-pound necklace. John Joseph did the bargaining.[14]

After the Horse Lake trip, winter began to close in on mountainous Taos with its quick storms, early snows, and sudden drops in temperature, yet Millicent continued to give open-air Indian dances on the mesa behind her house. They seemed to transport her, almost like a drug. She couldn't get enough. If a thunderstorm came up, the party would be transferred to Brett's studio on the north end of town. Millicent would bring the food in tubs, along with whiskey, and wine, beer, and colas and fruit juices for the Indians. Arranged around Brett's studio on cushions and chairs the guests watched the Indians dance, hypnotized by their own singing. Brett, eloquent in her own right, described the scene: "All the guests have arranged themselves around my messy gay studio. The brightly colored Indian paintings hang high up on the walls. Saws and hammers and all the paraphernalia of a work bench are pushed aside and people perch on the narrow table. In the bedroom the drum is beating softly. There is an occasional jangle of bells, as one of the Indians, ready dressed, begins to dance. We all sit and wait patiently. Millicent moves around, disappears into my box of a kitchen, and returns, with glasses of cocktails. The guests who have already eaten at her picnic on the mesa before the rain nibble cookies and sip their drinks. At last, impatient, Millicent taps on the bedroom door. It opens a crack. 'We ready now,' and in a few minutes the door opens and the blanketed singers come out and arrange themselves under the archway from the studio to the sun room and begin to beat the drums. The bedroom door re-opens. Out of it comes the line of feathered dancers. Slowly, gently, they dance into the room and become a circle of waving feathers, jangling bells. Some of the dancers have brought their little sons and the little boys dance earnestly. One of them, a very gay little four year old called Hermann, dances with such fervour and joy that his sunny gay character pervades everyone. As the evening goes on, the wine and beer provided for the Indians stimulates their dancing. They begin, as usual, to get caught up in the mesmerism of the drum and voices of the singers. Millicent sits on a low stool, quiet, absorbed as usual, her whole heart and soul hypnotized by the tremendous power of the song and the endless powerful beating of the drums. During the rests, she gets up to minister food and drink to all the guests, to the Indian guests, the singers, and to her own household, who have also come to the dance. She is untiring in her hospitality. Then at about midnight the dancers are tired. They bring the drum into the center of the room and the circle dance begins. This is a dance of friendship, and we can all take part in it. One of the dancers goes up to Millicent, takes her by the arm, and she dances slowly round with the rest of us. Between two feathered Indians she dances the curious half walk, half dance step round and round. Fatigue overtakes most of us. The circle dwindles and dwindles. The dancers return to the bedroom, take off their dancing clothes. To return to the circle, and round it goes. At last we all tire, the guests have been gradually slipping away, finally the Indians look at their tired sleepy children and decide to go, too. Everybody goes. . . . I fall into bed with the drum still beating in my head." When she wakes the next morning, the drum is still thudding in her head.[15]

Millicent by almost all accounts had found her new element in Taos. Yet no sooner had she found herself than fate, played in her case by a weak heart, began to stir restlessly in the background. She was lively, yet increasingly her heart curbed her energy and activities. Brett, who had become a studious observer of Millicent at this point, concluded, "She was enjoying every moment of her freedom from the life that her money had piled around her." What she lacked in physical energy she compensated for with presence. At the series of casual suppers given among friends, "She was always quiet, she was like moonlight drifting into a room, and spreading a glow of charm and beauty, and sadness amongst us. There was a deep sadness within her, and it lay around the lines of her lips." It seemed logical that the Indians, whose lives were governed by nature and their submission to forces they could not wholly understand or control, provided inspiration to Millicent.

The Indians offered her a model for living quietly and deliberately, without buzz and excess. "She'd seen so much artifice that the Indians seemed unspoiled and exotic to her," explains Larry Torres, both historian and friend of her son Paul. Tony Luhan was known to come to dinner and sit sometimes up to three hours in the presence of his hosts and guests, completely silent.

To Millicent the Indians offered a behavioral model and a philosophical alternative to the Western thought and practices that had governed her life so far. Hers was not merely a cliché case of "going native." She seems to have felt like Frank Waters, who wrote, "I loved the pueblo; it was so peaceful and quiet . . . for all its earthy homeyness somehow gave an otherworldly air of being oriented to the rhythms of sun, moon, and stars, and the forces of the earth and the waters around them, rather than the cash-register life of the town plaza. The people were poor, but seemed somehow enriched by inner self-assurance."[16] Janet Gaynor, after one particular visit to Millicent in New Mexico, remarked to her husband, "If Millicent lives five years longer she'll become a squaw."[17]

According to her son Paul, "MR," as he called her, "believed if you came from a privileged class, your duty and honor came from helping others . . . you have to give back."[18] She had watched her grandfather rebuild Fairhaven, emphasizing education and public works with his early fortune. She wanted to help others in some way, as her efforts with the medical and surgical relief agency demonstrated. In

Taos she asked as Christmas approached what she could give to the Pueblo. She hired an army transport car to take loads of blankets, boots, and bells to the Pueblo. The bells, intended for ceremonial uses and dancing, had been requested, as they were used in certain dances that the Tiwa, the proper name for the tribe that inhabited the Pueblo, had adopted from the Plains Indians. She located them in Vermont and ordered several hundred, their New England provenance no doubt causing a few Indian anthropologists to later scratch their heads in wonder.

Millicent was appalled to learn that the U.S. government kept track of the Indians by numbers rather than names, and she wanted to help rectify what she saw as the white man's injustice against them.[19] Arturo has claimed that she worked with Indian rights activist Oliver LaFarge, Lucius Beebe, and Frank Waters, traveling to Washington, D.C., to wage a campaign on their behalf, but there is no formal record of such a collaboration.[20] What she did do was underwrite the expense for a delegation of four Indians from Taos Pueblo to travel to Washington, D.C., by train. She was already on the East Coast and met them there, enabling the group to sit down with government officials and create the groundwork for the Indian Health Center on the Pueblo. Tony Reyna, her friend, was one member of the delegation. "She always wanted to help people," he remembers, and is admiring of how little recognition she expected in return. The Pueblo keeps no written records, and the two factors make it difficult to find documentation of Millicent's good works. Much as she declined the French offer of its Legion of Honor after the war, recognition was not the point with Millicent.

She also knew how to wage a campaign with charisma and flair as much as her pocketbook. She determinedly popularized Indian jewelry designs and native crafts to the fashion world by wearing them in fashion spreads and photos. By 1952 she had enlisted her mother's enthusiasm for popularizing American Indian art with the major museums of the Northeast and Europe. Mary, with her usual high-handedness, wrote the curator of the Metropolian Museum in New

York City expressing her disappointment over his refusal to feature an Indian Artist exhibition. She reasoned that such a show was under discussion in France, and "the French would appreciate these paintings of such artistic merit after the trash which has been sent over to them for so many years." These were women accustomed to getting their way.

Millicent's increasing affection and devotion to the Indians and the Pueblo were noticed by the Taos locals. Phoebe Cottam and her younger sister Shelly, daughters of one of Taos's leading families, were young girls when they rode their horses out to the Pueblo and watched Claude Anderson drive by with Millicent in his Pontiac convertible, headed to the Pueblo. Millicent was always dressed in her Navajo clothes and Phoebe heard her mother talk about Millicent. Mabel had told her mother that Millicent tried to outdo her with her parties and hospitality when she had stayed at the Tony House. Other than that, Phoebe concluded, "I don't think anyone paid any attention to Millicent really. She didn't socialize except with Brett and Claude Anderson."

Her biggest impact on Phoebe and her generation was fashion.[21] Phoebe knew the seamstress (the wife of the Navajo jewelry maker John Shorty) who had made a velvet blouse and skirt with lots of silver buttons for Millicent and asked her to make a similar blouse for her, too. It was Millicent's clothes and her blond hair that made her distinctive to a certain social segment of Taos. News of her supposed romantic involvement with a young Indian was of little interest. Phoebe Cottam's aunt, Barbara Cottam, had married a Navajo, and it wasn't unusual for Anglo newcomers to Taos, like Mabel and Millicent, to became enthralled—some romantically involved—with the Indians.

Gossip about Millicent went a different route. There were the inevitable potshots about her wealth and the inevitable, if wrong, conclusions about how she got it. "How did Millicent make her money?" one woman overheard her mother and her mother's friends talking. "Below the waist" was the reply.[22]

Sylvia Rodriguez, a professor of Anthropology at the University of New Mexico, was aware of Millicent's presence and role in Taos when she was growing up. From the perspective of a younger person and native of the community, Rodriguez says, "I always thought of her as being sort of a lost soul. She frequented Pueblo ceremonies draped in all that jewelry. She was sort of a poignant figure, really." She became a frequent enough visitor to be recognized by the Indian children when she arrived at the Pueblo. The young girls who saw her were as fascinated with her as she was with them, and they stained their lips with chokecherry juice to mimic her carefully drawn red lips and waved sticks for imaginary cigarettes like those she smoked from a long black holder. Juanita Marcus Turley, one of those girls, recalled they were simply "Playing Millicent." They watched her carefully when she rode out with her new young Indian chauffeur and rumored "boyfriend." She sat in the car parked at the edge of the Pueblo while Benito went inside the village to visit his family. Millicent reached out to her young admirers: "How are you doing in school?" There was cause at least for bemusement—if not for pity—that this woman at whose feet counts, princes, and handsome aristocrats of the Western world had fallen now waited outside in the car while her young Indian lover went inside without her.

She no longer set great store on appearances, as her stalking of Clark Gable had earlier shown. Benito's family, uneasy about the personal relationship between their son and the heiress, in keeping with Indian (and Yankee) convention, skirted the subject although they approved of his employment as her chauffeur. Such jobs were hard to come by in Taos and the money, which he contributed in part back to his family, was good.

While her Indian clothes seemed an affectation to some of the Anglos of Taos, the Indian women considered them to be respectful. She was properly dressed when she visited, not sporting the jeans and rough wear that were more customary for visitors. On one visit, wearing her broomstick skirt and Navajo blouse, she went down to the Rio Pueblo de Taos, the river that runs through the Pueblo, to wash dishes with the tribal women. On rare occasions around Taos and on the road trips that took her into back country Millicent wore jeans and heavy concho belts, but they were the exception to her Indian skirts and shirts. She often tied her hair back with a bandana, trailing down her back.

Millicent had indeed taken up with Benito "Benny" Suazo, Tony Luhan's handsome nephew, several decades her junior. Besides the initial attraction between them, their relationship seemed to develop around Millicent's attempts to teach Benny how to design and forge jewelry. She had a workbench set up in her bedroom where she did her own work and also instructed Benny in how to pour gold and silver and forge metals. Benny, as he was known, squired her to parties and social affairs and the distinction between being her driver or her escort was left to interpretation. She gave him a bedroom so he could live at the house. He told his brothers that she sleepwalked at night. When his half brother, Santiago, came to visit from the Pueblo, Millicent joined them in his room with an air of easy familiarity.

Benny was troubled, some said changed, when he returned from his wartime military service. "Drunk, broke, and angry," according to the locals. To Brett and observers he seemed bedevilled in his attempts to reconcile Indian life and the world he had experienced outside the Pueblo. He drank to excess, and while uncommonly handsome, his countenance was sober, grim even. Millicent had asked Tony to train Benny to drive for her because she didn't have a driver's license, and the practice among prosperous Anglos in Taos was to be chauffeured anyway, perhaps wise in light of the amount of drinking that was routine at parties. Millicent was fond of martinis, straight up with an olive, though she drank, as she ate, in moderation.

She was attentive to menu planning, table setting, and the hallmarks of gracious dining and service. Her luncheons often lasted for hours, but it was the social occasion and appearance of the table, serving, and display that she focused on. The nuts and bolts of cooking were left to her cook Ethel, who complained that there weren't enough pots in the kitchen. But Millicent's priority was elsewhere. She went to the church and contributed a thousand dollars, so long as it was understood that the priest would provide his Indian congregants to dance at her dinner.[23]

One Indian dance given during the Christmas season up at Dorothy Brett's had been an especially good time. Millicent's black help, the Indian women, dancers, and singers, might have carried on into the morning except that the guests began to leave after midnight. Benny had clearly had too much to drink and Millicent didn't want to ride in her car with him. Brett offered to give her a ride home. It was bitter cold weather. Benny got behind the wheel of Millicent's car and screeched onto the road back to town. Millicent followed shortly with Brett, and a mile or more down the road, they saw her Chrysler in a ditch. The car had hit a phone pole, which now lay across the top of the car and tangled it with wires. Benny sat inside, unconscious at the wheel. Passersby stopped to carry Benny into Brett's station wagon and she drove him, with Millicent seated at his side, to the hospital. Benny's injuries weren't serious. He suffered mostly broken ribs, but if Millicent had been traveling with him, she might have been killed by the pole that crashed into the passenger seat.

For the next several weeks Millicent asked Brett to drive her to the hospital every afternoon at four, and many evenings after supper. She told Brett that she had always wanted to be a doctor, but her health had prevented her from pursuing such an arduous course of study and profession. It seems an instance of grandiose dreaming on her part, but she had certainly been exposed to a parade of physicians during her life. While Brett nodded off in a chair in the hall, Millicent patiently sat with Benny, whom Brett increasingly regarded as a "difficult, strange boy, coming out of the war as so many did, bruised and hurt and morose."[24] Milllicent, with her kindness, was one of a long line who had attempted to rehabilitate him. For a while, there were no more dances.

If there was any question of Brett's enduring loyalty and affection for Millicent, Millicent's invitation to her to come to Jamaica in early 1950 closed the deal. In fact, it left her breathless with the childlike excitement she was known for. "I think of all the wonderful gifts she gave me, the trip to Jamaica was the high spot. I had never been to any tropical island, and I was all agog to go," Brett said, thrilled. Millicent planned to leave Taos soon after Christmas.[25]

CHAPTER TWENTY-FOUR

Travels with Millicent

BRETT, SO EAGER TO GO TO JAMAICA, GREW ANXIOUS WHEN Millicent postponed the trip for health reasons. "Millicent had a curious inhibition about starting anywhere. She would delay and delay for no apparent reason," Brett fretted. But the cause of Millicent's hesitation was real. Her energies had declined after the holidays and Dr. Hausner, her physician in Santa Fe, had advised her not to travel for at least another month. "I have no energy at all and my bones still ache," she explained in a letter to Paul. Yet she was determined to go, and she reassured him that she planned stops in Thomasville, Georgia, and Natchez, Mississippi, to break up the cross-country journey and to avoid the cold. "Jamaica will build me back again as it did before," she cheerily wrote.

Finances were also on her mind. Prospective buyers from Dallas had shown an interest in her jewelry designs, and she harbored the hope that her jewelry would sell enough to make a financial difference. "I hope the Texas people will really be interested in my work and want to see some of it . . . Johnny Schlumberger sold a lot when he went down. It's too bad I haven't some diamond bits to show them.

Diamonds always sell. But I haven't got any yet."[1] Heiress that she was, with no other marketable skills, she looked naively to small ways her own creative endeavors might make a difference when money felt tight.

At last she was well enough to travel, and their trip got under way in March. Millicent had decided to take along Trinidad and Benny, who was still wearing a brace after his accident. Millicent, Brett, and Benny rode in the Chrysler, driven by her foreman, Ralph. Her cook Ethel, the luggage, and the others went in a station wagon driven by an Indian boy named Lorenzo. Millicent's favorite dachshund, Fanny, was going along, too. Dixie Yaple, left behind to run things in Millicent's absence, chased their improbable caravan down the drive when she realized that the Indians had left their drum behind. And so they set out to make their way across the American South, a two-car caravan of three Indians, a Hispanic, a black woman, an American heiress, and a British aristocrat.

The first night they reached Dallas, where they had reservations at the Adolphus Hotel. The station wagon lost the other car in traffic and Millicent, Brett, Ralph, and Benito finally had to call the police to help find them. During the wait, Benito entered the lobby of the hotel and was ridiculed by several men for the shoulder length hair he was growing in true Indian fashion. "Why do you want to look like a girl?" one of the men drawled. Humiliated by such treatment, Benito dashed into a barber shop and got a crew cut. Straining matters further, Ethel, the black cook, was only permitted to stay in the hotel on a cot in Brett and Millicent's room. In other towns on the itinerary she would have to stay in "colored hotels." To prevent any further drama, Millicent ordered dinner to be served in their sitting room and everyone sat down to eat together.

In a motel in Arkansas it was the Indians who ran afoul of an innkeeper who told Lorenzo after Millicent and Brett had gone upstairs that if she'd known they were Indians she wouldn't have let them stay in her motel. Lorenzo was fuming the next morning when he related the story, sputtering, "Who does she think she is?" Brett, hoping for levity told him, "Go back and scalp her." Everyone burst into laughter.[2]

Their day, due to Millicent's practice of sleeping in, did not begin until almost noon. They took their time anyhow, and lingered a week in Thomasville, Georgia, where they stayed with Millicent's friend Placidia White. White was married to Henry Field, of the Marshall Field and Company dry goods family—and fortune—from Chicago. One night, Trinidad danced at the lakehouse of a friend of White's, where they fished by day and lounged in the hot and humid weather. Another evening Millicent threw her little dachshund, Fanny, across the room at Brett in frustration with the mosquitos that came through the screens and bit her. The upside, in Brett's opinion, was that the next morning they got an earlier start than usual because Millicent couldn't sleep. From Georgia they proceeded on to Miami with a stop on the way.

In Miami the number of rooms reserved for them proved inadequate, so extra beds were crammed into the rooms for Lorenzo and Benito. Ethel had stayed in Thomasville en route back to Claremont. The next day everyone flew to Montego Bay. It was the first time Dorothy and Trinidad had been on an airplane. Millicent disliked flying, but managed it. The real trouble came at customs in Montego Bay when Millicent was found to be carrying a small revolver. Though guns and knives weren't permitted, she wanted to have it with her and argued to keep it. In the end, she lost the quarrel and the gun was checked for her to collect when leaving Jamaica. Her insistence was rooted in an incident in Montego Bay several years earlier when she had wakened to discover a man under her bed who ran off with her purse full of money and jewels.

Brett had been carrying some of Millicent's jewels on the trip. She wore the pearl necklace and concluded that Millicent "thought no one looking like me would ever be suspected of wearing valuable pearls!" Through customs at last, they were met by native policemen and taxi drivers who knew Millicent and drove them the eight miles to Reading.

The low bungalow built of wood, with various small houses and gardens around it, was an old sugar mill close to the sea. Millicent's room had once been a separate storeroom, and the sea lapped at the concrete wall below her windows. The old cookhouse, the "cookem," would be appropriated for Brett's room and painting studio, but until it was ready she painted in the living room of the big house, fully appreciative of Millicent's patience and generosity in the matter of having her and her paints in the main living space.

"Thus began long lovely days," Brett wrote of the idyllic mornings when she and Trinidad sat and painted. "Millicent would come strolling out in her dressing gown, a thin silk wrap with stripes of many colours, wander around the garden, into my room to see what we were doing. She became fascinated by shells, and began collecting them." Benito, a sports fan, listened to the radio. In the afternoons they typically drove to the shore towns, where Millicent would buy shells from the fishermen at the shore. She also shopped in Falmouth to buy gaily patterned fabrics for shirts and dresses, but her chief occupation was looking at houses. "Millicent was indefatigable in her house hunting, her buying of mahogany beds and furniture," Brett observed.

Millicent clearly enjoyed herself immensely, writing to Paul (this time called "Paulous Pie") in great detail on notepaper in peacock blue ink about the "extraordinary country . . . the colours of sky and earth are brilliant, the sea changing all the time, a constant wind to cool one off. Every kind of fruit with exotic names." She wrote him of the "little wee lobsters . . . green crabs . . . the hidden green valleys and old houses falling to ruin—and the people so polite and good mannered . . . and they are every color from palest tan to blackest black. Everything busy in a leisurely way so instead of talking things get done, really done!!"[3] Millicent joined into the industry, shopping for all the family, inquiring about what kind of furniture Dusty and Arturo preferred, the heights of the ceilings, their disposition on eighteenth-century furniture and carved mahogany. She considered the cottons in Jamaica the best, and wanted to buy curtains for Peter to use in The Port.

"What do you hanker after?" she asked Paul, proposing a desk chair and "a nice strong shining black mahogany bed to fit in your room? A couple of bedside tables?" Millicent explained she was sending ashtrays to Arturo and would have cotton dresses made for Dusty and shirts for Arturo. "But as money is scarce I'll have to go easy. I can bring in $500 if I can wangle $500 from the accounts. Oh dear. How difficult it is!" The contradiction between her love of acquisition and the need for economy jumps out in the next line: "I wish someone would buy a jewel so I could go to town. In a small way well I can manage a little anyway. If you would like to fly down with me after school is out we can do it." She went on to say that she was sending him shirts. Her latest scheme for moneymaking was for Arturo and Peter to get a monopoly on siphon water for the United States and South America. Apparently as she wrote this, a lizard on the wall "just dropped a little kaka on my head—... that shows us a good idea!" Her upbeat tone was due in part over her improved health. "I'm getting a little fatter, thank goodness and feel better"—but she ended with regrets that she could not come up to New York. "I'm just not strong enough yet to come up into the cold north."

Brett recorded Millicent's nearly frenetic search for more Jamaican property to buy. "We investigated houses perched on hills, houses on the opposite shore near Kingston, beautiful old dilapidated houses, mostly without roofs partially destroyed by uprisings, desolate and deserted, yet still beautiful with mahogany staircases, floors, and paneling. The nights were filled with parties and invitations from Millicent's circle of friends. The two Indian boys, Millicent and I rarely missed a party." Benito got drunk at a number of them, and Millicent seemed helpless to stop him. Trinidad started performing Indian dances at the local nightclubs or on Millicent's lawn. Arturo, Dusty, and Paul came down to join them and spent hours swimming, snorkeling, and fishing at Doctor's Cove. Brett accepted invitations to go out sailing, but Millicent didn't go, declaring she wasn't a good sailor. Placidia White had taught them all to play canasta, ostensibly to give the young Indians some way to occupy themselves, and they played, almost frantically, every day.[4]

Brett was scheduled to go to New York where a one-man exhibition of her paintings was scheduled at the American British Art Gallery, but she struggled with the idea of leaving. Millicent offered to underwrite her travel costs, but Brett couldn't justify the expense "for two hours at a cocktail party at the gallery." She also worried about leaving Millicent, who still seemed frail, before her sons arrived. She decided not to go.

One event, which has stayed in the family lore, that Millicent's sons and grandchildren love to relate concerned a dinner invitation to the British governor's home in Jamaica. Millicent informed her host that she had several Taos Indians with her and she would like to bring them along with her. He was delighted to include the Indians as guests and she had her sons fit them in fine English suits, according to Arturo. But when it was time to leave for the evening, Arturo, barely able to hide his amazement, went to his mother's room. Millicent was primping in front of her vanity mirror as Arturo told her that the Indians had cut the crotch out of their suit pants, in keeping with the Indian tradition of not wearing closed trousers. Proper native male Indian dress comprises leggings and a loincloth or other wrap over a G-string. Millicent and Arturo howled with laughter, then wondered what to do. Millicent took the news with her usual aplomb and called the governor to explain the situation. Then they set off for the party as planned, with the Indians adding blankets to cover their custom alterations.[5]

Another minor problem had arisen with Benny, who had begun to pocket the tips that Millicent left in restaurants.[6] Gently, she instructed him to leave them on the table. Such infractions fuelled Brett's case against Benny. She disapproved of his relationship with Millicent, but Millicent did not want to hear Brett's complaints. Brett considered him to be "his own worst enemy. Psycopathics destroy not only themselves but those around them. B. should be under the care of a trained psycharist. [sic] ... one cannot protect him from his own character and behavior, that is impossible, and that is what M.A.R. has never understood..." she wrote in a letter to Paul in 1950. The differences between the two women on the topic remained. Millicent had adopted the philosophy that "white men have lost the core or filled it with dollar bills and whiskey and a white sort of democracy where only white skins go to heaven or inherit the earth," an ironic statement from one who had lived her whole life on the spoils of such ruthless pursuit. She mixed such contradictions with the same determined insouciance she had exuded in creating fashion from disparate design elements.

After visiting a number of dilapidated old houses for sale, Millicent settled on a large property, Orange Valley. Arturo, during their investigations of the premises, found a corpse in the cellar. Brett, who thought the place had a sinister feel even before the corpse was unearthed, was spooked by the discovery, but Millicent was undeterred. She bought the property anyway.

By late May the days in Jamaica were getting hot. Millicent spent hours being fitted by a series of dressmakers she had summoned, but at last she became restless with the heat. Brett found Millicent's patience with the Indians and her fellow travelers, including herself, quite remarkable. Brett had collected seashells with the animals still living in them, sticking them in the bushes below Millicent's room, yet she never heard a complaint when the odor from the rotting creatures wafted up to the windows. Nor did Millicent scowl over the bleating goat Brett had bought as a model for her painting. It threatened to wake her hostess every morning at six. "All the little things of everyday living left her unruffled and calm, but what never left her was her underlying distrust of the human race. That was a factor in her life, over which she seemingly had no control. She was an easy prey to the mischief-maker, to the whisperer, against that no friend of hers had any protection," wrote Brett, perhaps foretelling her own fate. What comes as a surprise is that Millicent, for all she had been through and despite how brazenly she had defied rules and flaunted social conventions most of her life, could still be stung by public opinion. She had stopped wearing the large pieces of jewelry she favored in Taos when she heard that people considered them extravagant and unseemly. She seemed hurt by their disapproval.

After their idyllic sojourn of several months the group's departure from Jamaica was chaotic. Minutes before their scheduled flight Millicent found one of her big pearl earrings missing. After searching frantically, she found it in the pocket of her dressing gown and the traveling party made it to the plane with barely a second to spare. Their twenty-seven pieces of luggage and the two dogs Millicent had bought in Jamaica were already waiting onboard. One, a Bullmastiff, had been sleeping in the "Cookem" with Brett after Millicent bought him to take back to Peter. Customs proved equally trying in Miami. After being detained for several hours, they were met by cars Millicent had ordered to take everyone on to the next stop: Claremont, Virginia.

Millicent had left what valuable jewelry she didn't want to take to Jamaica in a box in the bank in Thomasville, requiring a stop there on the way so she could retrieve it. The next day they arrived at Claremont. "How beautiful it was, set in its great flowering trees. The inside was as perfect as any house could be," Brett recounted. They were met by the Japanese butler and his wife, who ushered Brett to a room with Millicent's legendary gold bed, like something out of Louis XIV's court. Millicent had arrived with the notion of taking steps to sell the Claremont property, but she woke the next morning, clearly agitated over the decision. Dusty, Arturo, and Paul had arrived and settled into one of the guesthouses. Brett was asked to sit in the veranda and draw, for inventory reasons, all of Millicent's old silver cutlery. At last Arturo rescued her by photographing the pieces. Millicent flitted in and out in her gaily colored robe. Crates of shells and her purchases from Jamaica arrived. "Her capacity for buying was unlimited, an obsession with her," Brett concluded. Houseguests arrived just as the servants left for the weekend, so Arturo rose to the occasion as cook and made Béchamel eggs for everyone. The dearth of help annoyed Millicent, but she impressed the others by keeping calm. Her agitation was assuaged by planchette, a game played on a triangular spirit board that, like Ouija, promised to answer questions about the future. Everyone played until midnight.

In several days she and Brett would take the train to New York, where a house had been taken for her on Beekman Place. The Indians were put on a plane back to New Mexico because Millicent would be too busy to see to their welfare in the city.

Upon arriving in Manhattan, Millicent was disappointed with the small, cramped house with steep stairs up to her third-floor bedroom. Paul, who had left Claremont before them, was already asleep in the only other small bedroom, causing Brett to volunteer to stay elsewhere with friends. Millicent went about her business in the city, meeting Brett a few times to shop for her new passion, shells, and one night to take her to a "charming negro nightclub."[7] She also made time to visit with Peter, who was in the city with his former classmate and friend Tim Vreeland, Diana Vreeland's son. Tim, who remembered a more robust Millicent from the days she had swept into Groton like a movie star to see her son and awe his friends, found her changed. "She was more frail, otherworldly, as though she were halfway between this world and the other," he recalls.[8]

It was clear to those who knew her that she was not well. The same year, she resigned from the board of the Parsons School of Design, giving her illness as the reason. Van Day Truex took it hard, as she had been Parsons' most generous donor and an extremely close friend to him since their times in prewar Europe. His only piece of jewelry was a gold pinkie ring she had made for him that he wore as a talisman until he lost it in Italy, the same year as her resignation.[9]

It was almost July 1 when Brett took a taxi piled with luggage to Penn Station for the trip back to New Mexico. She and Millicent had been away for nearly four months. Millicent's maid followed in another taxi, also chock-full of luggage. Brett expected Millicent to arrive typically late, so she was surprised as her own taxi pulled into the station to see Millicent composed, perfectly dressed, waiting for her on the curb. She looked startlingly fragile. Everyone from the redcaps to the railway officers knew Millicent and scrambled to assist her, a reminder that her father, Harry Rogers, had been a railroad magnate. Paul arrived with the dachshund Fanny and her pup and smuggled them into their four-bunk train compartment. Millicent took the lower berth and the two women slept and rested almost the whole journey.

But Brett felt a difference had crept into their relationship. She couldn't explain what she described as "trouble." "I knew that trouble had been made, the deft shafts of suspicion put into her. That I knew, and by whom, as I had watched it being done. There is no defense against such people," she wrote cryptically. Was it family or guests who may have challenged the financial arrangement, to Brett's advantage, between the women? Had Brett, with her characteristic intenseness, offended her hostess? Or perhaps had their two-month trip in close proximity strained the bond of their friendship. Had Brett, of ambiguous sexual orientation, done something offensive? The "trouble" was not explained.

When their train pulled into Raton, New Mexico, Dixie and John Yaple were there to meet the women and drive them to Taos. "There ended for the time being, much of our close relationship," wrote Brett.[10]

CHAPTER TWENTY-FIVE

One with the Indians

I T SOON BECAME CLEAR THAT BRETT'S CAMPAIGN AGAINST BENITO Suazo accounted for most of the change in Millicent's disposition toward her friend. Brett had been so determined to undermine the relationship that she wrote Paul about Benito and also gossiped to the Taos community about the sleeping arrangements up at Turtlewalk. She went so far as to report that Benny had a "very pretty girlfriend" and to question why he wasn't married. All hell broke loose. Rather than put Millicent off Benny, Brett's criticism backfired and Millicent rose to his—and all the Indians'—defense. The attack unleashed Millicent's fury. Instead of cutting her friend out of her life, she set out in a spate of letters to convince Brett of her folly, and lecture her on the boundaries of friendship. In the letters, written from Claremont Manor and New York when Millicent was required to tend to business in those places, she ranted at Brett and used the occasion to vent about the plight of the Indians and the white-skinned people who had oppressed them. Beneath Millicent's fury lay the evidence of what the Indians had come to mean to her.

"You write about Benito to my Paulie and then you repeat it all over again to me. . . . The household and the spirit of the house was so upset all summer because of this enmity of yours. Servants, my negro servants, other servants, and neighbors were involved with whether or not people slept in their own beds! Most unpleasant, most unnecessary, most odious. I can't imagine that you have stopped to think long enough as to be aware of your implication in all of this tattle," raged Millicent. Then she got to the point: "Benito and his relation to me is not the affair of anyone at all but me and Benito. . . . You are simply trying to do him in because you do not like him." She took special offense when Brett called his relationship with her "Benny's great chance," as though she was an opportunity for an advancement that he did not want. She hearkened back to his attention to her during one of her bouts with sickness. . . . "When I was ill that time Benny took care of me. He did things for me then that no one but paid nurses have ever done, and then not with the heart in it—Benny is not bad, he's good. And I know it and no one but Benny can make me change my mind." When Brett mentioned his drinking, Millicent countered that her father and her own brother were alcoholics. She even stated Benny's right to a girlfriend and possibly marriage, if that was his choice. She implored, "Now Brett, it is high time you stopped all this nonsense about Benny. I do not like my children and their friends dragged into what is no concern of theirs at all."

Brett's intrusion provoked Millicent to denounce everything that had frustrated her, or restricted her life, so far. Millicent, in the full imperious voice that had always tended to dominate her correspondence, took her to task for saying " 'you should—you must.' My mother has said that to me all my life. There is a thing called love—not what Americans call love, not that little bloody fornication in a taxi. But a thing that grows trees and shakes mountains and moves the earth. . . . I know all white people think other people are queer, deficit, savage, etc., etc. . . . As for brown faces they are really in my heart the only kind I like. I don't trust white men. American men frighten me." And, she added, "They are tied to a paltry religion they call Christian." She was as certain of her convictions as she had always been.

She explained her appreciation of the Indians. She declared them ideal travel companions, their attitude "a sort of *lessez* [sic] *allez* which is good for nerves. I like their moods and silence and singing. They are reasonable people with whom I feel at home and strong, which I never do among white people. They give me something my heart needs. They are like being among the trees—or floating down a river. I like the way they look and act and *are*. I don't care whether they don't like to work. They were not created to work at white men's work. They have their own ways. The only thing I don't like is their food, that mess of Spanish-American glue that they concok [sic] is as far as I'm concerned vile." She backs down only a bit. "I know some very nice white people. I talk in generality—no reasons to name all the saints!!!" But she was not finished. White men, she said, had lost their ability "... to understand other men, can tread on others toes, and have everything their way. They have bored me ever since I can remember.... As I look at the average American man, I give up. (I'm as prejudiced as they are)." Then she caught herself and explained, "I'm just growing older and more pigheaded and uncooperative." One senses that the development thrilled her.

She rambled, but she always made her case in defense of the Indians. "The Indians were brought up by bad teachers, given only poorest kind of white ex-surplus, broken, put off their land. It's a wonder they are stubborn enough to survive." She returned to the personal. "Believe me Brett no one rushed into bed with me unless I want them there. And I haven't either wanted or known half the men who have claimed that privilege."

Once unleashed, she moved on to money and religion, even self-reflection. "Look in my mirror, it tells me nothing. Looking at my bank account is not my favorite pastime. Taking care of people who should be taking care of themselves if they ever had enough whatever it is to do so.... That famous 20,000,000 or is it 40,000,000. How it bores me. Oh dear, it bores other people so little." Then, getting back on message, she adds, "the mediocrity of the average white is frightening." She advocates that nonwhites "get together to stop the white man," and admires the Indians' economy with words. "... Tony,

Benny, all of them, me included, get better with few words. Words kill certain streams of contact and understanding that is wordless." Christianity she dismissed, saying that whites "most want to find a new sensation to talk about at a dinner table." Her diatribe seemed complete. "Yes, I'm bitter as hell about the Indians."

One new revelation in this spate of letters was her true affection for Tony Luhan. "I would have fallen for Tony had I come out sooner—he was altogether up my alley and my sort of man the 'sensitive soul.' I came too late, maybe three years, maybe five, maybe ten. Maybe 25. Too late is too late. . . . I understand Tony's way of life. I understand what Tony means without his words." When she learned that Mabel was selling items off from the Big House, she asked Brett: "if you ever stole anything for me steal now the picture in M's room of Tony going up the ladder when he was young. . . . and his big drum, nice glazed pottery, and santos on the mantel. I'll send you a check. *Don't* say for me." She underlined don't twice.

In her inimitable way she could put down the hatchet and segue mid-letter into shopping. Most of her letters to Brett that year were written from New York when she traveled East to tend to her business matters and address what to do with Claremont Manor. The trips depleted her physical energy and emphasized her longing to be back in Taos. In 1952, she wished Brett a Happy New Year from New York and said that she had been looking for boots for her, "like my old Lapland ones you like." She wrote that she'd heard Christmas Eve, a celebration with towering bonfires and a reenactment of the storming of the Church of San Geronimo on the Pueblo by the Spanish in 1684, was "heavenly at the pueblo," and lamented that she would miss the annual Christmas Day deer dance. "Next year," she wrote. Her outburst complete, she subsided. Her relationship with Brett became a patchwork of affection and dissension. No matter how pitched their arguments, their mutual appreciation of Taos's natural beauty and the Indians overcame their differences. In one letter Millicent closed, "Goodness, I will be glad to be home again and looking at the sky, the clouds and the mountains and listening to the silence." She had found what she was looking for.

CHAPTER TWENTY-SIX

With the Wide Sky

THE THREAT OF DEATH THAT HAD STALKED MILLICENT FOR most of her life slipped into Taos the winter of 1952, this time to stay. Her health took its final turn for the worse. She never completely recovered from a bout with strep throat that she had contracted the previous winter. She declined gradually, but evidence of her illness was unmistakable. Her features were sharper, haggard even, and she lacked the physical vitality to match her enthusiasm for pageants and people. She began to recede from the public and social arenas and no longer came into Taos Plaza for the fiestas that she had enthusiastically attended in previous years. Among townsfolk she became known for living quietly, often walking barefoot in her long skirts on her patio at Turtlewalk. There were no more big parties up on the mesa.

The bedroom facing Taos Mountain became a workshop and sitting room like the bedroom of her New York childhood, which had been made into a place for reading, drawing, and visitors to lift the spirits of the patient and be as different from a "sickroom" as possible. The floor was scattered with magazines and books, especially the detective stories that she loved. She kept handy the yellow paper for her sketches and designs and the lined paper that she preferred for writing letters. There was a jewelry design working area with her table and tools nearby. Her visitors were entertained. When she took to her bed during colds and brushes with pneumonia, she treated her guests to a display of the many bedjackets and lingerie that Charles James designed for her. Her physical energies waned, but her wit and spirits persisted. Her critical faculties and the urge to express herself were often sharpened. A certain prescience entered her correspondence.

In her most famous letter to her son Paul, written in January 1951, she turned thoughtfully spiritual and wrote:

> Did I ever tell you about the feeling I had a little while ago? We were driving with Dixie and John; suddenly passing Sandia Mountain I felt that I was part of the Earth, so that I felt the sun on my surface and the rain. I felt the stars and the growth of the moon, under me, rivers ran. And against me were the tides. The waters of rain sank into me. And I thought if I stretched out my hand they would be earth and green would grow from me. And I knew that there was no reason to be lonely that one *was* everything, and Death was so easy as the rising sun and as calm and natural—that to be infolded in Earth was not the end but part of oneself, part of every day and night that we lived, so that Being part of the Earth one was never alone. And all fear went out of me—with a great good stillness and strength.
>
> If anything should happen to me now, ever, just remember all this. I want to be buried in Taos with the wide sky. Life has been marvelous, all the experiences good and bad, and I have enjoyed even pain and illness because out of it so many things were discovered. One has so little time to be still, to lie still and look at the Earth and the changing colours and the tones—and the voices of people. And cloud and light on water, smells and sounds and music and the taste of woodsmoke in the air. Life is absolutely beautiful if one will disassociate oneself from noise and talk and live it

according to one's inner light. Don't fool yourself more than you can help. Do what you want—do what you want knowingly. Anger is a curtain that people pull down over life so that they only see through it dimly missing all the savor, the instincts, the delight— they feel safe only when they can down someone . . . and life is dimmed and flattened and blurred. . . . I've had a most lovely life to myself. I've enjoyed it as thoroughly as it could be enjoyed. And when my time comes no one is to feel that I have lost anything of it—or be too sorry. I've been in all of you, and you particularly will go on being to remember it peacefully—take all the good things that your [sic] life and put them in your eyes and they will be yours. . . .

Written on lined paper and scrawled in the margin, she signed, "Your friend, MR, with gladness to have been your friend."[1]

She hung on to levity at other times. In a letter to Paul and Peter, traveling together in Europe over the Fourth of July, she seemed in great form relating a story of one guest's silly reaction to his new surroundings up at Frieda's ranch. "Oh well, Taos does odd things to people!!" she nonchalantly concluded. Her appreciation of her friends and their foibles in Taos seems heightened as she wrote of Tony Luhan: "Tony is as funny as usual with his fine straight way of saying things and making jokes—Mabel would as usual kill me if she could."[2] She saw the world, and the Taos social scene, for what they were. "Nothing very exciting really here. The usual fierce fights between people . . . So it's been a good month so far!!!" When a man had driven his car into the ditch on the edge of her property and broken her fence, she merely sighed in a postscript scrawled vertically in the margins of her letter, "Poor man! Poor fence," without histrionics. She had become a woman who floated bemusedly while the sea of life flowed around her. "I'm O.K.," she added, as almost an aside, perhaps to assuage worry over her health. "Much love and kisses, Mummy."

With time on her hands, her letters increasingly went to whimsy.

During one convalescence, she wrote to "Paulie" that she had "found a formula for growing hair—listen carefully..." With Coogan hair tonic and Dr. Lazlo-Homeone hair oil and regular brushing she claimed she was "growing new hairs like mad—the front especially looks like a wooley dog. I have by mistake dyed it a dark and bedeviling looking red. So that for the week I look like an old Russian Madame—daughter of a Russian general." To Paul her hair tonic prescription rivaled in humor a letter she had written him during the war about George Washington. "I fear that all men did not love the father of our Country," she wrote after studying the painter John Trumbull's equestrian painting of Washington. "There is something familiar and impolite about that horses's posterior.... It dwarfs the portraiture. It is the foreground, It lingers in the memory.... It is the portrait of a horses behind—Mr. Washington is incidental.... too bad Mr. Roosevelt doesn't ride!!!! No!"[3]

News of Millicent's worsening condition began to travel. A few old friends like Charles James came to New Mexico for a visit. James was shocked by her wan appearance. Her hair, once so impeccably kept, was mussed and stringy, so he hired a hairdresser to do it for her, knowing it would cheer her up. Arturo Peralta-Ramos, and his second wife, Alice Rutherford, came to Taos to pay her a visit. Millicent and Arturo, though unable to live together, had remained friends. His durable debonair looks set locals like Celia Torres aflutter when she sold him a cigar from her family shop on Taos's plaza.

Millicent was still newsworthy. The *Los Angeles Examiner* reported that her mother was with her in New Mexico and that Millicent now took pills costing twenty-five dollars apiece every two hours to combat the infection in her heart valves. A telegram of inquiry and best wishes from Hedda Hopper to Millicent in February of 1952 was answered by Dixie Yaple, explaining that Millicent was in Santa Fe. Santa Fe was where her chief physician, Erich Hausner, practiced.

Her heart, its valves weakened, was laboring. As her circulation faltered she experienced discomfort and pain in her legs and arms, further slowing her deliberate movements. Rumors spread in Taos that she had fired the wife of a local physician from her household and nursing staff when the women's husband, Dr. Rosen, refused to extend her prescription for painkillers. She learned to slow her physical pace, though her spirit continued to be indomitable.

Her finances, strained by the added costs of her doctors and medications, made her querulous. Money matters crept into all her correspondence and she was ill-tempered with her sons, all nearly grown men. She balked at Paul's request to pay his rent: "I see no reason why you should expect me to do everything to help you when you do nothing in exchange." He received five hundred dollars in expenses from her monthly. "It would appear that I have great obligations to you and Arthur, but neither of you feel that you have any toward me." Paul's new hobby, car racing, vexed her. She grumbled that she had "paid your father's bills in that regard, but that is an extremely expensive hobby." They bickered, but made up. "My feelings are hurt. I have never accused you of being a spendthrift," she responded to one of his indignant parries.

The summer of 1952 was a period of financial and emotional retrenchment. Reluctantly Millicent sold Claremont Manor and began divesting its furnishings. The property caretaker, Jack Arnold, who said he'd spied her and Clark Gable together naked in the pool, drove her and some of her paintings and furnishings one last time to Taos.[4] Some things went to her boys, some into storage in Manhattan. Her East Coast secretary was entrusted with the task of making an inventory of all her things, the majority of them valuable collectibles. The brilliant gold bed, considered suitable for a king, that Brett had admired at Claremont was sent to Taos and moved into Millicent's spacious bedroom. As she had complained about money in Jamaica and then bought a piece of property, she looked ahead in the midst of this period of penny-pinching and ordered a six-thousand-dollar fur-trimmed cape from James for the following winter. She continued to struggle against taxes and at one point bleated in a letter to Brett: "I won't pay such taxes! . . . Everyone is getting after me at once." She went from defiance to worrying that she might have to sell even the Taos property.[5]

When she needed to be near her chief physician, Erich Hausner, who practiced in Santa Fe, the Yaples, Dixie and John, typically drove her back and forth. As her trips became more frequent, Millicent avoided hospitals and elected to stay in her own room at the Hotel La Fonda, the old landmark hotel on the plaza in Santa Fe. During one serious relapse, she was there for several weeks. Fearing the worst, her friends from Taos began to make pilgrimages south to her bedside. Mabel came to settle their differences and sat in her darkened room filled with flowers in pots and vases exchanging niceties, making peace. When Brett visited she was struck by how delicate Millicent looked. The veins shone blue through her thinned skin on both sides of her head, yet Millicent hung determinedly to life. According to Paul, massive doses of penicillin to fight her infections had damaged her inner ear and affected her balance.[6] Yet she broke into her wide smile for visitors and disdained her doctor's dire predictions. She was pleased when Rebecca James, one of Taos's self-styled characters, variously caustic or charming, brought one of the Colcha embroidery pieces she was becoming known for to Millicent as a gift. Millicent continued to look ahead.

Millicent talked to her friends about looking for a property in England, maybe even in Asia. Japan, with its clean, spare architectural style and sense of spiritual purity, caught her imagination. She told Arturo she was intrigued by the prospect of building in that architectural style, and Paul watched her begin to collect Japanese lacquer and prints by Hiroshige. She admired contemporary design, and it was as though the prospect of discovering and mastering a new design, as she had so often done, could save her. She was trying to fight off death with the best weapons she had: style and collecting. Defiantly, she ordered a full wardrobe for the spring from Charles James. Mary, convinced that the end was not yet at hand, went home to Boca Raton. Before leaving Santa Fe she wrote a line to Dorothy Brett, back in Taos, "Millicent is better. She sends her love," and explained that she herself was "much less anxious, trusting that there will be no *setbacks*."[7] Millicent managed to return home to Taos.

Her new interests were spiritual. Janet Gaynor, who kept in close touch by phone, suggested that she go to hear Ernest Holmes, the founder of the Religious Science movement, in his upcoming tour of New Mexico. Gaynor subscribed to his viewpoint on metaphysics and spiritual philosophy, and thought it would be of interest to Millicent, who now increasingly talked about religious matters, mostly as they related to the Indians. She seemed to have found her own hybrid religion.

Her style and level of thoughtfulness had matured far beyond the notes of upper-class asperity and condescension that had typified many of her letters. As always, she was led by her aesthetic sense, but now it was integrated into a deep feeling for life.

Her correspondence and phone calls to Janet Gaynor and Elizabeth de Bruniere toward the end of 1952 were a record of her tranquillity. The image she painted for them was of Indians keeping watch over her. Elizabeth de Bruniere got the impression that one stayed at the foot of the bed, as either a nurse or making incantations.[8] Benny continued studying the craft of jewelry making, often at the workbench by her bedside.

As winter approached, the signs of her decline were unmistakable. She began to walk with a stick and suffered dizzy spells. Her chief activity was wandering in the garden. Dorothy Brett spent time sitting with her in chairs placed in the sun on the west side of Turtlewalk. She fed a dozen cats at the back door, naming them for the days of the week they'd arrived until she had more than seven. To keep busy, Brett continued to contribute decorative flourishes to the house, still unfinished in places. Millicent continued to supervise, vested as always in "getting it right." Brett painted designs on the vigas over the patio. She brought over her maps of England for Millicent to study and they schemed about the house Millicent might buy in England.

At this point, Millicent's passage was neither operatic nor abrupt, but hushed. Brett, perched on scaffolding to paint overhead, watched her dear friend "swaying like a reed" as she walked through the rooms below. She noticed how frail Millicent's features had become, the soft frame of her ash blond hair around her face. The steps of one who had made grand entrances most of her life were now mincing, and she wobbled. Millicent did not like fooling herself. The week before Christmas she wrote to Paul, "I am tired of fighting."[9]

At Christmas her son Peter came with a friend. Peter, in college at Princeton until the previous spring, had spent less time in Taos than his younger half brothers. Arturo, and especially Paul, considered their mother's last relocation to the Southwest yet another adventure, but Peter was less smitten with the community so far, alien as it was from East Coast culture and Europe. They put up a Christmas tree in the corner of the room off Millicent's library and prepared to exchange gifts on Christmas Eve. A turkey dinner was served in Millicent's room, after which she managed to walk slowly over to a big armchair next to the tree. Her movements were labored, but Millicent had always loved presents, both the giving and receiving, and she rose to the occasion. To the satisfaction of her guests and family she carefully and gleefully unwrapped half of those for her before she was overcome with fatigue and returned to bed.[10]

The next day, Christmas, Brett drove Millicent out to the Pueblo to see the splendid pageant of the Deer Dance, an annual event at which the Indian dancers wear a full deer hide, the head and antlers eerily high above them, as they pay homage to the deer as a source of food and clothing by reenacting the hunt to the rhythmic chant of singing and drums. When Brett arrived at Turtlewalk to pick her up, Millicent was sitting in the bathroom with her woolly winter boots on, too weak to zip them up herself. But when they reached the Pueblo, to Brett's amazement, Millicent managed to walk unassisted across the outdoor plaza of the Pueblo and stand watching the ritualized dance underneath the wide winter sky, Taos Mountain as always bulking over them. Absorbed, she stayed until the end, after which Dorothy drove her to the house of an Indian friend where she could rest and warm herself before going home. Millicent seemed to know that she had seen her last dance and hearkened back to the camping trips she had made with Brett, telling her, "I think of all the dances, I love the Snake Dance the best." It made Brett wish she had taken her to a Navajo "Sing," a healing ceremony, for her heart. At the close of the afternoon she watched Millicent walk back into Turtlewalk. It was the last time she saw her.[11]

A local boy, Tom McCarthy, fifteen, was just learning to drive when his parents, merchants on Taos Plaza and unable to leave their store, asked him to drive the town priest, Father Hatch, up to Millicent's house a few days after Christmas. She had asked him to come to baptize her a Catholic. Tom sat outside in the old family Ford while Father Hatch performed the service. The old priest matter-of-factly returned to the car and asked Tom to drive him back to the parish.[12] The conversion allowed her to give instructions for her funeral in the Catholic Church. She asked to be buried in the cemetery out by the Pueblo, her head toward Taos Mountain. Her son Arturo, cynical about her conversion, confronted her for "hedging her bets." Their relationship remained nettlesome, he says, based in large part on his disapproval of her involvement with Benny. In the same old game that Millicent had learned from her experience with her father, she threatened to disinherit him unless he would take back his harsh criticism of her. In an act of cruelty (his term) that he lived to regret he refused to let her see her first born grandchild, his son Arturo Peralta-Ramos III, born in 1952. Yet he came to spar with her when she lay in La Fonda after one of her treatments, devoted in his way.

The cold that Millicent had suffered throughout the holidays developed into a strep infection that moved swiftly into her heart valves in her weakened state. It is likely that she had been having congenital heart failure for some time. Her pale and delicate countenance, noted by friends and visitors, was evidence that she was not properly oxygenating. Her heart was already greatly enlarged by the effort, more onerous at high altitude. While leaning down to dye clothes in her bathtub, as she commonly did to get the exact shade she wanted for her clothes, Millicent suffered a heart attack and fell, striking her head on a doorjamb. A hemorrhage began in her brain. On New Year's Eve she was rushed to St. Joseph's hospital in Albuquerque, one hundred miles away, for surgery to remove a brain clot. Her head was shaven, an indignity for Millicent that her sons would long remember, as well as the blackened eye from her fall. Her weakened system could not withstand the operation, and she suffered a massive brain hemorrhage at 7:15 in the evening. Paul arrived that night to watch as her oxygen source was removed and the attending physician pronounced her dead. Millicent was a month short of her fifty-first birthday. The arc of her life was ended. Her search was over. She had found beauty and passed on.

As she had specified, a funeral mass was held for her at The Guadalupe Catholic Church in the center of Taos five days later, delayed for the arrival of her mother from Boca Raton.

Her sons selected the Indian Chief blanket, rings, necklace, and concho belt for her burial in the Sierra Vista Ceremony, where her friends, family, and admirers, from Taos and as far as New York and Los Angeles, gathered to pay their final respects. They were startled by the number of Indians who quietly appeared, draped in their colorful blankets and customary silence. The attendance of the Indians, who believe that the journey of the dead is hindered by displays of grief or excessive memorials, was all the more noteworthy and indicated a true regard for her.

Millicent's interment, shorn of artifice, was a poignant mix of East Coast propriety and Western earnestness. Most of all, it was spontaneously beautiful—the bare location, the primitive purpose, the colorful clash, a hash of rustic elegance that Millicent would have loved. It was a strangely fitting end to all she had been and what she had become. Dorothy Brett was told by her friends at the Pueblo that a shrine had been made for Millicent on Indian land, but the location and dedication were kept secret. It was an honor Millicent would have appreciated.

Postscript

A FIGURE AS STRONG AND LEGENDARY AS MILLICENT Rogers was bound to cast a shadow in public and private long after her death. Millicent's enduring influence on the world of fashion goes beyond her inclusion in exhibits like the Metropolitan Museum's *High Style* and *American Woman*, shows that fascinate contemporary audiences with a look back at fashion history. Though her role as a trendsetter in fashion's Golden Age is assured, she continues to be mentioned as a current inspiration. Designer John Galliano unabashedly attributed his 2010 collection for Dior on the Paris runways to Millicent's inspiration. "Millicent Rogers had the attitude of a modern day woman before that attitude was really invented," says the designer, who professes admiration for her "fearless and fabulous style that still inspires today."[1] Anna Wintour described the cover photo of the October 2007 issue of *Vogue*, with actress Charlize Theron in a suede skirt and ruffled white shirt, as a "tribute to another great fashion original, Millicent Rogers." Hamish Bowles, European editor at large for *Vogue*, attributes her ongoing appeal to the seductiveness of "being fluid and not hidebound by life. She had a sense of the zeitgeist and stayed ahead of it. She broke so many barriers, surprising her contemporaries in the mid-century patrician world in which she was born into. She followed her own path and her style was highly personal. She exemplified fashion of the moment."[2]

While motherhood was never considered Millicent's strong suit during her life, she inescapably shaped the lives and personalities of her surviving children. Millicent's three sons each developed a markedly different relationship with their mother, and each of them has contributed a somewhat different image of her. They, and their heirs, have burnished the version of the mother whom they see their own reflection in, remaking her myth in something of their own image.

Peter, her eldest, was, according to his living half brother, intimidated by Millicent, and their relationship was perhaps more Oedipal. The French Countess de Ribes, who had a romance with Peter while Millicent was still alive, remembers how he constantly told her that she reminded him of his mother, obviously the model of womanhood in her son's mind. The highest flattery from her lover was that she reminded him of his mother.[3]

Peter was after all heir to European aristocracy, and while bedevilled by deciding on which side of the Atlantic he truly belonged, he was serious and conscientious, and bore the burden and blessing of having become his grandfather's largest heir when he was only eleven years old. To his classmates and peers, Peter seemed concerned about rising to the challenge of his heritage, husbanding the property in Southampton, continuing the beat drive traditions.[4] It came as no surprise when at age forty-five he married a European, German Baroness Wiltraud von Furstenberg. She claims that he never read his father's memoir, *My Dear Peter.* Written in old German, it posed a daunting translation task. If he did, he never mentioned it, further suggesting the distance in their mother-son relationship. "They had nothing in common," Wiltraud Salm, his widow, explains.

Arturo, her eldest child by Peralta-Ramos, suffered the usual dilemma of the middle son. His older brother was more of a model young man; his younger brother was the endearing baby. Arturo was caught in between. Less anchored to tradition than Peter by his lineage, Arturo was neglected by his own father, whom he sometimes did not see for many months at a stretch.[5] By his own account he was often quarrelsome with his mother, who noted early on in correspondence with her mother that he was no student and life would be his best teacher. He also has had the dubious privilege as Millicent's last living son of putting the most recent gloss on his mother's legend. He is overtly proud of her liberated sexuality and emphasizes his mother's promiscuity and her—and his—involvement in international intrigue, to a degree that is difficult for the biographer to evaluate. He is a self-described investment banker for military projects.

Paul, the youngest, was considered to be his mother's favorite during much of his life. Last to leave home and also a poor student, he was more dependent and often her companion during that part of her life when she explored new vistas and emotional territory in Taos. After her death he worked at establishing her legacy by creating the museum that is her namesake. He worked variously in the film and rare books businesses, but returned to Taos in 1980 until his death in 1997.

The truth about Millicent can be found in her sons' competing versions of her. Her essence is best expressed in the woman who would charm them, but in the end, leave their longing for her unrequited. Paul, on his own deathbed, more than forty years after her death, bared raw filial emotions untempered by time and unearthed by strain and illness. As his attending nurses asked him for necessary information for his chart, his psyche seemed frayed with suffering and longing. He burst out in a primal lament. "My mother died when I was twenty years old. What more do you want from me?"[6]

Millicent's estate, valued at $137,184, according to *The New York Times* on July 8, 1954, was left to her three sons. The interest she had in three trusts created by her father terminated at her death. The great Rogers fortune was gone. As written in a seven-page will that she had drawn up in January 1951, she left ten thousand dollars and all of her horses to Benito Suazo, except for a black-and-white pinto that she specified be given to her trusty foreman Ralph Vigil. She also willed Benito all the saddles and bridles on the ranch, an automobile, and her goldsmithing tools. With a collector's mentality to the end, she itemized her fine jewelry, artwork, and furnishings and specified which of her sons should receive them. Her property, the residuary estate, was divided between Paul and Arturo, she reasoned, because Peter was well provided for by her father.[7] She did not leave Roald Dahl the Renoir he had claimed she promised him during their affair. Nor did the party on the first anniversary of her death that Taoseños heard she had left funds to cover ever happen. Ralph Meyers, proprietor of the Taos Trading Post, claimed that she left a bill for a special jewelry order unpaid.

According to her heirs, an estate lawyer asked, "What are we going to do with all this junk," referring to several thousand pieces of the finest Navajo, Zuni, and Hopi silverwork and jewelry that Millicent had collected. That "junk" became the central collection of the Millicent Rogers Museum in Taos, New Mexico. The Peralta-Ramos brothers and Mary Rogers created a foundation in Millicent's name that by 1956 enabled the opening of a museum in a small adobe house on historic Ledoux Street in Taos. In 1968 it moved to its present location, a pueblo-style adobe house built in the 1940s on the northern outskirts of town where it has a sweeping view of Taos Mountain and the Pueblo lands to the east. Inside and out, it is a fine and continuing legacy to Millicent. Twenty thousand people visit annually, and the museum is widely considered to be a gem of the Southwest, a fine sampling of some of the best jewelry, pottery, rugs, Spanish Colonial furniture, and Hispanic devotional art. Over fifty-five hundred items are displayed in ten permanent exhibits. Its curators have managed to uphold Millicent's standards for excellence and "good eye" for acquisitions to add to the collection, which has doubled over fiftysome years. She is remembered there for her collector's prowess and impact on her family and community.

According to Federico Jimenez, jewelry maker and former member of the museum's board of directors, some years ago a young Indian man visited the museum and looked up at Millicent's photo on the wall. He seemed momentarily transfixed. "I know that lady," he said. "We have a picture of her in my house." Someone asked him to explain. "My grandmother told me this lady borrowed my grandfather for two years and that's why we have a picture of her," he said. Listening bystanders stifled their smiles.

The spirit of Rogers extends eerily to this day, especially in the galleries devoted to her personal collection and own designs, many with a background of some of the fine photos of her wearing and shopping for the articles on display. Her indomitable spirit radiates from the letters and drawings exhibited on the walls. Peering down from the famous life-sized photo of her taken by Louise Dahl-Wolfe that hangs in the first gallery, her image captured this author's imagination years ago. Who was this woman, I asked, and what was her life about?

Bibliography

Ballard, Bettina. *In My Fashion: An Intimate Memoir about the People, Places and Events That Make Up the World of High Fashion*. London: Secker & Warburg, 1960.

Bray, Elizabeth Irvine. *Paul Flato: Jeweler to the Stars*. Antique Collectors' Club Ltd., Woodbridge, Suffolk, U.K., 2010.

Burke, Flannery. *From Greenwich Village to Taos*. University Press of Kansas, 2008.

Collier, Peter, and David Horowitz. *The Rockefellers: An American Dynasty*. New York: Holt, Rinehart and Winston, 1976.

Coleman, Elizabeth Ann. *The Genius of Charles James*. New York: The Brooklyn Museum and Holt, Rinehart & Winston, 1982.

Conant, Jennet. *The Irregulars: Roald Dahl and the British Spy Ring in Wartime Washington*. New York: Simon & Schuster, 2008.

Dias, Earl J. *Henry Huttleston Rogers: Portrait of a Capitalist*. New Bedford, Massachusetts: Reynald-Walt Printing, Inc., 1974.

Dias, Earl J. *Mark Twain and Henry Huttleston Rogers: An Odd Couple*. Fairhaven, Massachusetts: The Millicent Library, 1985.

Dwight, Eleanor. *Diana Vreeland*. New York: William Morrow, 2002.

Fleming, Ann. *The Letters of Ann Fleming*. London: Collins Harville, 1985.

Garceau, Jean, and Inez Cocke. *Gable: A Pictorial Biography*. New York: Grosset & Dunlap, 1961.

Gordon-McCutchan, R. C. *The Taos Indians and the Battle for Blue Lake*. Santa Fe, New Mexico: Red Crane Books, 1991.

Goyen, William. *Goyen: Autobiographical Essays, Notebooks, Evocations, Interviews.* Austin: University of Texas Press, 2007.

Gregory, Eve S. *Claremont Manor: A History.* Richmond, Virginia: Plummer Printing Company, Inc., and Lewis Kirby, 1990.

Hahn, Emily. *A Biography of Mabel Dodge Luhan.* Boston: Houghton Mifflin Company, 1977.

Hoopes, Townsend, and Douglas Brinkley. *Driven Patriot: The Life and Times of James Forrestal.* Annapolis, Maryland: Blue Jacket Books and Naval Institute Press, 2000.

Leary, Lewis. *Mark Twain's Letters to Mary.* New York: Columbia University Press, 1961.

Lesley, Cole. *The Life of Noël Coward.* New York: Penguin Books, 1979.

Lewis, Adam. *Van Day Truex: The Man Who Defined Twentieth-Century Taste and Style.* New York: Viking Studio, 2001.

Luhan, Mabel Dodge. *Edge of Taos Desert: An Escape to Reality.* New York: Harcourt, Brace and Company, 1937.

Luhan, Mabel Dodge. *Winter in Taos.* Santa Fe, New Mexico: Las Palomas, 1982.

Lycett, Andrew. *Ian Fleming.* London: Phoenix, 1995.

Macintyre, Ben. *For Your Eyes Only: Ian Fleming + James Bond.* New York: Bloomsbury USA, 2008.

Morrill, Claire. *A Taos Mosaic: Portrait of a New Mexico Village.* Albuquerque, New Mexico: University of New Mexico Press, 1973.

Nichols, Charles Wilbur de Lyon. *The Ultra-Fashionable Peerage of America.* New York: George Harjes, 1904.

Obolensky, Serge. *One Man in His Time: The Memoirs of Serge Obolensky.* New York: McDowell, Obolensky Inc., 1958.

Porter, Dean, Ebie, Teresa Hayes, Campbell, Suzan, Thomas Gilcrease Institue of Art. *Taos Artists and Their Patrons 1898–1950.* Notre Dame, Indiana: Snite Museum of Art, University of Notre Dame, 1999.

Rasponi, Lanfranco. *The International Nomads.* New York: Putnam, 1966.

Rudnick, Lois Palken. *Mabel Dodge Luhan: New Woman, New Worlds.* Albuquerque, New Mexico: University of New Mexico Press, 1984.

Sherman, John. *Taos: A Pictorial History.* Santa Fe, New Mexico: William Gannon, 1990.

Tapert, Annette, and Diana Edkins. *The Power of Style.* New York: Crown Publishers, 1994.

Tarbell, Ida M. *The History of the Standard Oil Company.* Mineola, New York: Dover Publications, Inc., 1966.

Tisdale, Shelby J. *Fine Indian Jewelry of the Southwest: The Millicent Rogers Museum Collection.* Santa Fe, New Mexico: Museum of New Mexico Press, 2006.

Tornabene, Lyn. *Long Live the King: A Biography of Clark Gable.* New York: G. P. Putnam's Sons, 1976.

Vreeland, Diana. *D.V.* New York: Da Capo Press, 1984.

Waters, Frank. *Of Time and Change: A Memoir.* Denver: MacMurray & Beck, 1980.

Wayne, Jane Ellen. *Clark Gable: Portrait of a Misfit.* New York: St. Martin's Press, 1993.

West, Beverly. *More Than Petticoats: Remarkable New Mexico Women.* Guilford, Connecticut: Twodot, 2001.

Wood, Nancy. *Taos Pueblo.* New York: Alfred A. Knopf, 1989.

Woolman, Edna, and Ilka Chase. *Always in Vogue.* New York: Doubleday, 1954.

Yohanna, Kohle. *Valentina.* New York: Rizzoli, 2009.

Millicent Rogers in Taos, an unpublished manuscript from the Dorothy Brett/John Manchester Collection of letters in the Southwest Research Collection at the University of New Mexico in Albuquerque. Undated.

Unpublished material provided to Arthur J. Bachrach by Arturo Peralta-Ramos and Nita Murphy, the contents of which I am familiar with. Much of this material was contained in a lecture given by Nita Murphy at the Southern Methodist University's Fort Burgwin campus in Taos, New Mexico.

Notes

1: Farewell to an Heiress

1. William Goyen, *Goyen: Autobiographical Essays, Notebooks, Evocations, Interviews* (Austin: University of Texas Press, 2007), 29–32.

2: Fortune and Family

1. www.wikipedia.org/wiki/Abbie G. Rogers.
2. Peter Collier and David Horowitz, *The Rockefellers: An American Dynasty* (New York: Holt, Rinehart and Winston, 1976), 24.
3. Ibid., 38.
4. Earl J. Dias, *Mark Twain and Henry Huttleston Rogers: An Odd Couple* (Fairhaven, Massachusetts: The Millicent Library, 1984), 94.
5. Their correspondence, fond and humorous, is recorded in *Mark Twain's Correspondence with Henry Huttleston Rogers, 1893–1909*, edited by Lewis Leary (Berkeley and Los Angeles: University of California Press, 1969).
6. Earl J. Dias, *Henry Huttleston Rogers: Portrait of a "Capitalist"* (New Bedford, Massachusetts: Reynald-Walt Printing, Inc., 1974), 155.
7. Mark Twain's Angelfish Roster, www.twainquotes.com by Barbara Schmidt, from *Mark Twain's Aquarium: The Samuel Clemens's Angelfish Correspondence, 1905–1910* (University of Georgia Press, 1991).
8. *Mark Twain's Letters to Mary*, edited by Lewis Leary (New York: Columbia University Press, 1961).
9. Ibid.

3: RICH BEGINNINGS

1. *Mark Twain's Correspondence with Henry Huttleston Rogers, 1893–1909*, edited by Lewis Leary (Berkeley and Los Angeles: University of California Press, 1969), 600.
2. Edward J. Dias, *Mark Twain and Henry Huttleston Rogers: An Odd Couple*, 48.
3. Annette Tapert and Diana Edkins, *The Power of Style* (New York: Crown Publishers, 1994), 56.
4. Bunny Mellon, written response to my questions, May 20, 2010.
5. Sheila de Rochambeau, daughter of Lela Emery, interview with the author.
6. Charles Wilbur de Lyon Nicholls, *The Ultra-Fashionable Peerage of America* (New York: George Harjes, 1904).
7. Edward J. Dias, *Mark Twain and Henry Huttleston Rogers: An Odd Couple*, 171.
8. "H. H. Rogers Dead, Leaving $50,000,000," *The New York Times*, May 20, 1909.
9. Edward J. Dias, *Mark Twain and Henry Huttleston Rogers: An Odd Couple*, 169.
10. Christina Lucia Peralta-Ramos, granddaughter of Millicent Rogers, interview and public address at the Millicent Rogers Museum.
11. Diary of Millicent Rogers, 1917–1919 from the Archives of the Millicent Rogers Museum, Taos, New Mexico.
12. The Madeira school transcript spells the name this way, but expresses some uncertainty about it. Millicent's handwriting is also unclear. She often abbreviates the name "Mrs. Mc."
13. *The New York Times*, July 26, 1935.

4: COMING OUT

1. *Town Topics*, December 1919, 9.
2. Millicent's handwriting is sometimes hard to make out and she often abbreviated her nicknames for others.
3. Diary of Millicent Rogers, 1917–1919 from the Archives of the Millicent Rogers Museum, Taos, New Mexico, 109.
4. *Town Topics*, December 4, 1919.
5. Diary of Millicent Rogers, 1917–1919 from the Archives of the Millicent Rogers Museum, Taos, New Mexico.
6. "Mr. H. H. Rogers Announces End of Daughter's Engagement," *The New York Herald*, June 24, 1921.

5: THE GRAND TOUR

1. Arturo Peralta-Ramos III, Millicent's grandson, interview with the author.
2. *The Washington Post*, October 27, 1935, and October 25, 1936.
3. Charles Wilbur de Lyon Nichols, *The Ultra-Fashionable Peerage of America*, 81.
4. Shelby J. Tisdale, *Fine Indian Jewelry of the Southwest: The Millicent Rogers Museum Collection* (Santa Fe, New Mexico: Museum of New Mexico Press, 2006).

5. Serge Obolensky, *One Man in His Time: The Memoirs of Serge Obolensky* (New York: McDowell, Obolensky Inc., 1958).
6. Sheila de Rochambeau, interview with the author.
7. Letters from the Archives of the Millicent Rogers Museum, Taos, New Mexico.

6: BREAKING AWAY

1. Arturo Peralta-Ramos III, interview with the author.
2. Philip Peralta-Ramos and Arturo Peralta-Ramos, interviews with the author.
3. "Salm Blames Wife for Hasty Wedding," *The New York Times*, January 23, 1926.
4. Graf Ludwig Salm, *My Dear Peter: Confessions of a Father* (Linz, Austria: Port of Books, 2008), 77. Note: The details of Millicent's elopement and its denouement vary. The newspaper stories differ in small seemingly insignificant details. Did Colonel Rogers summon Millicent to travel alone to Paris or did he go to meet her? Did Rogers take his son to Oxford or send him alone? Did she return to the Ritz-Carlton at three or four o'clock, and so on. What is noteworthy is the account provided in Count Salm's self-published book, *My Dear Peter: Confessions of a Father.* He put his experiences down on paper in 1928 after his marriage to Millicent had ended and his battle for the affection of his son had begun. The book was not translated into English from its original Old German until 2008.
5. "Count, Who Married Heiress, May Have Lost Estate," *The Washington Post*, January 12, 1924.
6. Ibid.
7. "Salm Gives Berlin Story of His Love," *The New York Times*, July 28, 1929.
8. Graf Ludwig Salm, *My Dear Peter: Confessions of a Father.*
9. "Rogers Family Forgives Count and Heiress Bride," *The Washington Post*, January 11, 1924.
10. Graf Ludwig Salm, *My Dear Peter: Confessions of a Father*, 79.
11. Ibid.
12. "Count Salm Quits Hotel with Bride," *The New York Times*, January 13, 1924.
13. "Count Who Married Heiress, May Have Lost Estate," *The Washington Post*, January 12, 1924.
14. Ibid.
15. "Oil Heiress Hopes Absence May Soften Stern Parents," *The Washington Post*, January 27, 1924.

7: COUNTESS

1. Graf Ludwig Salm, *My Dear Peter: Confessions of a Father*, 95–102.
2. *Town Topics*, May 15, 1924.

3. The archives of Planting Fields Foundation; Family Collection; Series D—William Robertson Coe; Sub-Series 2—Correspondence, Family.

4. Ibid.

5. Joyce Mann, interview with the author.

6. "Rogers Countess Returning Home; Count to Vienna, *The Washington Post*, May 11, 1924.

7. Philip Peralta-Ramos, interview with the author.

8. "Rogers Countess Returning Home; Count to Vienna," *The Washington Post.*

9. "Doubt Count Salm Is Legally Divorced," *The Washington Post*, February 11, 1924.

10. Graf Ludwig Salm, *My Dear Peter: Confessions of a Father.*

11. "Col. Rogers Bent on Salm Separation," *The New York Times*, May 12, 1924.

12. "Col. Rogers Is Back with Daughter," *The New York Times*, May 17, 1924.

8: EXIT THE COUNT

1. *The New York Times*, July 1, 1924.

2. "Countess Salm Loses $2,500 Diamond Ring," *The Washington Post*, July 16, 1924.

3. Graf Ludwig Salm, *My Dear Peter: Confessions of a Father*, 111.

4. "Wife Footed Bills on Honeymoon, Says Count Salm," *The Washington Post*, December 9, 1926.

5. Graf Ludwig Salm, *My Dear Peter: Confessions of a Father*, 106–7.

6. Ibid.

7. "Son Born to Young Countess Salm," *The New York Times*, September 29, 1924.

8. Graf Ludwig Salm, *My Dear Peter: Confessions of a Father*, 131.

9. Ibid. 132–3.

10. Bettmann/Corbis, "Portrait of Millicent Rogers Salm," U104704P-A.

11. Associated Press, December 14, 1925.

12. "Salm's Visit to Son at Palm Beach Ends in an Angry Scene," *The New York Times*, February 15, 1926.

13. Sheila de Rochambeau, interview with the author.

14. "Salm's Visit to Son at Palm Beach Ends in an Angry Scene," *The New York Times*, February 15, 1926, and Graf Ludwig Salm, *My Dear Peter: Confessions of a Father*, 150.

15. Graf Ludwig Salm, *My Dear Peter: Confessions of a Father*, 161.

16. "Wife Footed Bills on Honeymoon, Says Count Salm," *The Washington Post*, December 9, 1926.

17. "Cash Payment to End Salm Separation Suit," *The Washington Post*, May 17, 1927.

18. Ibid.

19. "Married for Love Only, Declares Count," *The New York Times*, April 15, 1927.

9: ENTER THE ARGENTINE

1. "Countess Salm Denies Paying Marriage Tax," *The New York Times*, October 27, 1925.
2. AP news clipping, June 7, 1925, from scrapbooks at the Millicent Library in Fairhaven, Massachusetts.
3. From the family history provided by Arturo Peralta-Ramos III.
4. Philip Peralta-Ramos, interview with the author.
5. Anne Surchin and Gary Lawrence, *Houses of the Hamptons 1880–1930: The Architecture of Leisure* (New York: Acanthus Press, 2007); and Antonia Salm, interview with the author.
6. Adam Lewis, *Van Day Truex: The Man Who Defined Twentieth-Century Taste and Style* (New York: Viking Studio, 2001).
7. "Ramos to Wed Former Millicent Rogers, He Announces to His Friends in Paris," *The New York Times*, August 2, 1927.
8. "Ex Countess Salm Back with Father," *The New York Times*, July 6, 1927.
9. "Mrs. Rogers Leases Home," *The New York Times*, July 16, 1927.
10. "Mrs. Rogers Sails to Rejoin Her Son," *The New York Times*, July 17, 1927.
11. Mary Cummings, "Historic Hamptons Weddings," *Hamptons Country*, June 2000, Vol. 6, Issue 1.
12. "Talk of Remarriage of Countess Salm," *The New York Times*, May 20, 1927.
13. Arturo Peralta-Ramos II, interview with the author.
14. "Millicent Rogers' Betrothal Is Told," *The Washington Post*, August 2, 1927.
15. "Millicent Rogers Home with Fiance," *The New York Times*, August 24, 1927.
16. "Miss Rogers Is Bride at a Hasty Wedding," *The Washington Post*, November 8, 1927.
17. "Ramos and Bride Sail on Honeymoon," *The New York Times*, November 11, 1927.
18. "Ramos and Bride Happy," *The New York Times*, November 19, 1927.

10: AFTER THE HONEYMOON

1. "Ramos and Bride Back from Honeymoon Trip," *The New York Times*, March 1, 1928.
2. From Christina Lucia Peralta-Ramos, who intends to produce a cookbook of her grandmother's recipe collection.
3. "Mrs. H. H. Rogers Will Seek Paris Divorce," *The New York Times*, May 30, 1929.
4. *Time* magazine, July 22, 1929.
5. Adam Lewis, *Van Day Truex*.
6. Michael Coe, interview with the author.
7. Christina Lucia Peralta-Ramos, interview with the author.
8. Adam Lewis, *Van Day Truex*.

11: Making a Mark in Fashion

1. Lorna Koski, "Shock value: there was more to designer Elsa Schiaparelli than her wild whimsy . . ." *W* magazine, October 2002.
2. The Brooklyn Museum Archives.
3. Arnold Scaasi, interview with the author.
4. The Diana Vreeland papers at the New York Public Library.
5. Author's conversation with David Cooper from Cooper Technica, a vintage automobile restoration company in Chicago, Illinois, that is restoring the Delage. Millicent's son, Arturo Peralta-Ramos, and Cooper hope to correct earlier mistaken reports that Millicent had a Delahaye.
6. The Brooklyn Museum Archives.
7. Charles James, "Millicent Rogers," *The American Weekly*, March 22, 1953.
8. Elizabeth Ann Coleman, *The Genius of Charles James* (New York: The Brooklyn Museum and Holt, Rinehart and Winston, 1982).
9. Charles James letters to Millicent Rogers, from the Archives of the Millicent Rogers Museum, Taos, New Mexico.
10. Gary Alston, "Charles James: A Personal Memoir with Nancy James," www.houseofretro.com.
11. Archives of the Millicent Rogers Museum, Taos, New Mexico.
12. Ibid.
13. Ibid.

12: A Stylish Life

1. Philip Peralta-Ramos, interview with the author.
2. Christina Lucia Peralta-Ramos, interview with the author.
3. "H. H. Rogers, Financier, Dies at 56," *The New York Times*, July 25, 1935, and July 27, 1935.
4. "Rogers $15,000,00 Shared By Three," *The New York Times*, August 1, 1935.
5. "Family of Rogers Ready to Aid Him," *The New York Times*, September 13, 1935; *The World-Telegram*, October 14, 1936.
6. "Mrs. Ramos Is Wed to Ronald Balcom," *The New York Times*, February 27, 1936.
7. An off-the-record interview with author in May of 2010. She began the short reference with "Like my husband . . ."
8. Christina Lucia Peralta-Ramos, interview with the author.
9. "Wife Held Rogers Was Incompetent," *The New York Times*, July 2, 1936.
10. Ibid.
11. Ibid.
12. "Oil Magnate: Will Assailed by Widow," *The Washington Post*, July 2, 1936.
13. *The New York American*, June 9, 1936, from undated clippings in a scrapbook at the Millicent Library, Fairhaven, Massachusetts.
14. Ibid.

13: Will as Weapons

1. "H. H. Rogers to Wed Virginia Lincoln," *The New York Times*, July 1928.
2. "Will Battle," Arthur Mefford, *The Daily Mirror*, Millicent Library scrapbook, and www.wikipedia.org/wiki/Evelyn_Hoey.
3. "Family Reunion in Fight over Will Debt," *New York Journal and American*, February 8, 1937.
4. "Milestones," *Time* magazine, May 10, 1937.
5. "Count Salm Asks Guardian for Son," *New York Journal and American*, June 10, 1936, Millicent Library.
6. "Count Salm Loses Suit Against Ex-Wife," *The New York Times*, December 5, 1936.
7. "Millions at Stake in Salm Suit," *The Daily Mirror*, October, 30, 1935.
8. "2 Rogers Estates to Share Huge Tax," *The New York Times*, April 21, 1936; "H. H. Rogers Estate Taxed $13,138,000," *The New York Times*, May 24, 1936.

14: Expat Idyll

1. "Mrs. Ronald Balcom Goes Her Own Way," *Vogue*, January 1, 1939; *Harper's Bazaar*, 1939.
2. Annette Tapert and Diana Edkins, *The Power of Style* (New York: Crown Publishers, 1994), 64.
3. Babs Simpson, interview with the author.
4. Tim Vreeland, interview with the author.
5. Christina Lucia Peralta-Ramos, interview with the author.
6. Letters from the Archives of the Millicent Rogers Museum, Taos, New Mexico.
7. The tone of Millicent's letter to Allen suggests affection, but he is never mentioned again in her papers or by those who knew her and remains an unsolved mystery to the author.
8. Adam Lewis, *Van Day Truex*, 111.
9. Ibid.
10. Leonard Lyons, "The New Yorker," *The Washington Post*, May 27, 1940.
11. Arturo Peralta-Ramos II, interview with the author.
12. As told to Christina Lucia Peralta-Ramos.
13. "Father Loses Plea for Salm Allowance," *The New York Times*, May 26, 1939.
14. Sarah Horne, "The Glamorous Southampton Legacy of Millicent Rogers," *Dan's Hampton Style*, November 2006.
15. Arturo Peralta-Ramos II, interview with the author.

15: To the Manor

1. Eve S. Gregory, *Claremont Manor: A History* (Petersburg, Virginia: Plummer Printing Company, Inc., 1990), 6–7.
2. Annette Tapert and Diana Edkins, *The Power of Style*.

3. Letters from the Archives of the Millicent Rogers Museum, Taos, New Mexico.
4. Ibid.
5. Ibid.
6. Tricia Hurst, "Heiress Brings Lavish Lifestyle to Taos," *New Mexico Magazine*, November 1989.
7. Neil Letson, "A Woman of Some Importance," *Connoisseur*, June 1984.
8. Lucille Parsons Balcom, interview with the author.
9. Arturo Peralta-Ramos II, interview with the author.
10. Annette Tapert and Diana Edkins, *The Power of Style*, 46.
11. Christina Lucia Peralta-Ramos, interview with the author.
12. Adam Lewis, *Van Day Truex*, 136.
13. Letters from the Archives of the Millicent Rogers Museum, Taos, New Mexico.
14. Ibid.
15. Ibid.

16: WARTIME AND WASHINGTON

1. Hope Riding, "Capital Whirl," *The Washington Post*, February 27, 1941.
2. Townsend Hoopes and Douglas Brinkley, *Driven Patriot: The Life and Times of James Forrestal*, 132.
3. Oatsie Charles, interview with the author.
4. Archives of the Millicent Rogers Museum, Taos, New Mexico.
5. Michael Coe, interview with the author.
6. Arturo Peralta-Ramos II, interview with the author.
7. Archives of the Millicent Rogers Museum, Taos, New Mexico.
8. Ibid.
9. Ibid.
10. Jennet Conant, *The Irregulars: Roald Dahl and the British Spy Ring in Wartime Washington* (New York: Simon & Schuster, 2008).
11. Ann Fleming, *The Letters of Ann Fleming* (London: Collins Harville, 1985).
12. Archives of the Millicent Rogers Museum, Taos, New Mexico.
13. Ann Fleming, *The Letters of Ann Fleming*.
14. Millicent Library, scrapbooks, Fairhaven, Massachusetts.
15. Odette Terrel des Chênes, daughter of Millicent's friend Elizabeth de Bruniere, interview with the author.
16. Jennet Conant, *The Irregulars*, 112.
17. Ibid.
18. Donald Sturrock, *Storyteller: The Authorized Biography of Roald Dahl* (New York: Simon & Schuster, 2010).
19. Roald Dahl Museum and Story Center, Archives, Great Missenden, Buck-

inghamshire, England, Dahl's letter to his mother, #14/5/3/10, April 4, 1944.

20. Jennet Conant, *The Irregulars*, 112.
21. Roald Dahl Museum and Story Center, Archives, Great Missenden, Buckinghamshire, England, letters of May 1 and 11, 1944. [what are letter numbers?]
22. Ibid., August 5, 1944, letter #14/5/3/16.
23. Ibid., August, 25, 1944, letter #14/5/3/19.
24. Donald Sturrock, Roald Dahl's biographer, interview with the author.
25. Edward Landrigan, interview with the author.
26. Donald Sturrock, interview with the author.
27. Dahl seemed to think that her apartment was bugged. Archives of the Millicent Rogers Museum, Taos, New Mexico.
28. Donald Sturrock, interview with the author.

17: A CHANGED WORLD

1. "Rules Against Rogers Estate," *The New York Times*, December 7, 1943.
2. Archives of the Millicent Rogers Museum, Taos, New Mexico.
3. Ibid.
4. To avoid the distraction caused by her spelling and punctuation eccentricities, the excerpts to follow have been regularized by the author.
5. Letters from the Archives of the Millicent Rogers Museum, Taos, New Mexico.
6. Ibid.
7. Ibid.
8. A German word meaning warm, friendly, agreeable.
9. Antonia Salm, correspondence with the author, February 2, 2010.
10. Michael Coe, interview with the author.
11. Peter told this story to his friends Orsun and Patricia Munn, who shared it with the author.
12. Maria Janis, Gary Cooper's daughter, interview with the author.
13. Diana Vreeland, *D.V.* (New York: Da Capo Press, 1984), 142.
14. Warren Sinsheimer, Jerome's son, interview with the author.
15. Eve S. Gregory, author of *Claremont Manor: A History*, interview with the author.

18: BANGLES AND BAUBLES

1. "Rogers Heir Thinks Dress Poll Is Silly," *The Washington Post*, January 4, 1946.
2. Neil Letson, "A Woman of Some Importance," *Connoisseur*, June 1984.
3. In an interview with author Kohle Yohanna, Valentina's biographer, he explains that the designer loaned Millicent the brooch.
4. Shelby J. Tisdale, *Fine Indian Jewelry of the Southwest* (Santa Fe, New Mexico: Museum of New Mexico Press, 2006).

5. Penny Proddow and Marion Fasel, "Jewelry's Designing Women," *Art and Antiques*, October 1993.
6. Shelby J. Tisdale, *Fine Indian Jewelry of the Southwest*.
7. Robert Haskell in his review of the National Jewelry Institute's inaugural exhibition at the American Folk Art Museum in 2004 in *W* magazine, August 2004.
8. Annette Tapert and Diana Edkins, *The Power of Style*, 70.
9. Neil Letson, "A Woman of Some Importance," *Connoisseur*, June 1984.

19: A LEADING MAN

1. Hedda Hopper, "Looking at Hollywood," *The Los Angeles Times*, August 8, 1946.
2. Robin Adrian, Gilbert Adrian's son, interview with the author.
3. Christina Lucia Peralta-Ramos, interview with the author.
4. Jane Ellen Wayne, *Clark Gable: Portrait of a Misfit* (New York: St. Martin's Press, 1993).
5. Jean Garceau and Inez Cocke, *Gable: A Pictorial Biography* (New York: Grosset & Dunlap, 1961).
6. Ibid., 132.
7. Hutton Wilkinson, interview with the author.
8. Christina Lucia Peralta-Ramos, interview with the author.
9. Lyn Tornabene, *Long Live the King: A Biography of Clark Gable* (New York: G. P. Putnam's Sons, 1976), 334–5.

20: AFTER THE AFFAIR

1. Miranda Masocco Levy, interview with the author.
2. Mabel Dodge Luhan, *Winter in Taos* (Santa Fe, New Mexico: Las Palomas, 1982).

21: CHANGING THE SCENE

1. While there is no record that Millicent had actually been to Taos before this trip, there are snapshots of her on skis near Tres Ritas, north of Santa Fe, taken by the ski instructor Rene du Pasquer in 1940. She playfully poses topless from the back. Carson National Forest Service Archives.
2. R. C. Gordon-McCutchan, *The Taos Indians and the Battle for Blue Lake* (Santa Fe, New Mexico: Red Crane Books, 1991).
3. Mary Wheeler, Judge Kiker's daughter, interview with the author.
4. Lois Palken Rudnick, *Mabel Dodge Luhan: New Woman, New Worlds* (Albuquerque, New Mexico: University of New Mexico Press, 1984).
5. Christina Lucia Peralta-Ramos, interview with the author.
6. Susan Dicus, interview with the author.

7. Martha Reed, interview with the author.
8. Ibid.
9. Judy Anderson, interview with the author.
10. Lois Palken Rudnick, *Mabel Dodge Luhan: New Woman, New Worlds.*
11. Frank Waters, *Of Time and Change: A Memory* (Denver: MacMurray & Beck, 1998), 95.
12. Ibid.
13. Dalton Montgomery, interview with the author.
14. Norbert Vigil, Ralph's son, interview with the author.
15. Max Evans, interview with the author.
16. Letters from the Archives of the Millicent Rogers Museum, Taos, New Mexico.
17. Florence Bramante and Donna Montgomery, interview with Forrest Fenn and the author.
18. Tricia Hurst, "Heiress Brings Lavish Lifestyle to Taos," *New Mexico Magazine*, November 1989.
19. Center for Southwest Studies, University of New Mexico, Albuquerque.
20. Barbara Brenner, interview with the author.
21. Susan Dicus, interview with the author.

22: CALL OF THE MOUNTAIN

1. Archives of the Millicent Rogers Museum, Taos, New Mexico.
2. Susan Dicus, interview with the author.
3. Harold Koda, interview with the author.
4. Annette Tapert and Diana Edkins, *The Power of Style*, 64.
5. Rita Kip Marquand, interview with the author.
6. Dusty Kitterman Weiss, interview with the author.
7. Millicent Rogers letter to Dorothy Brett from New York in 1948, from the Dorothy Brett Papers, Harry Ransom Humanities Research Center, University of Texas at Austin.
8. Lois Palken Rudnick, *Mabel Dodge Luhan: New Woman, New Worlds* (Albuquerque, New Mexico: University of New Mexico Press, 1984), 328.
9. Larry Torres, historian and assistant professor at University of New Mexico, Taos, interview with the author.
10. Bob Tenorio, interview with the author.
11. Millicent Rogers letter to Dorothy Brett from New York in 1948, from the Dorothy Brett Papers, Harry Ransom Humanities Research Center, University of Texas at Austin.
12. Archives of the Millicent Rogers Museum, Taos, New Mexico.
13. Tony Reyna, interview with the author.
14. Ibid.

23: Taos

1. Millicent Rogers letter to Frieda Lawrence from New York, from the Harry Ransom Humanities Research Center, University of Texas at Austin.
2. Ibid.
3. Dorothy Brett Papers, from the Harry Ransom Humanities Research Center, University of Texas at Austin.
4. Dorothy Brett, "Millicent Rogers in Taos," from the Center for Southwest Research, University Libraries, University of New Mexico.
5. Ibid.
6. Bob Davidson's correspondence to Dorothy Brett, from the Harry Ransom Humanities Research Center, University of Texas at Austin.
7. Dorothy Brett, "Millicent Rogers in Taos."
8. Millicent Rogers letter to Dorothy Brett from New York in 1948, from the Dorothy Brett Papers, Harry Ransom Humanities Research Center, University of Texas at Austin.
9. Ibid.
10. Dorothy Brett, "Millicent Rogers in Taos."
11. Ibid.
12. Ibid.
13. Ibid.
14. Shelby J. Tisdale, *Fine Indian Jewelry of the Southwest*, 118.
15. Dorothy Brett, "Millicent Rogers in Taos."
16. R. C. Gordon-McCutchan, *The Taos Indians and the Battle for Blue Lake*, Introduction by Frank Waters (Santa Fe, New Mexico: Red Crane Books, 1991), viii.
17. Paul Gregory, Janet Gaynor's husband after Adrian, interview with the author.
18. Videotaped interview with Paul Peralta-Ramos by Larry Torres.
19. Arturo Peralta-Ramos II, interview with the author.
20. Millicent may have contributed money to enable the work of the Association on American Indian Affairs, but there is no documentation to support the claim that she traveled to Washington to lobby the government with LaFarge and Frank Waters, or with Lucius Beebe. Waters's widow, Barbara, never heard of such a trip and considers it unlikely since LaFarge and Waters didn't get along. Robert A. Hecht, author of *Oliver LaFarge and the American Indian* (Scarecrow Press, 1991), knows of no mention of Millicent Rogers in any of LaFarge's papers.
21. Phoebe Cottam, interview with the author.
22. Sylvia Rodriguez, interview with the author.
23. The Indians at Taos Pueblo had been converted to Catholicism after the conquistadors arrived in the late 1500s. In spite of their revolt in 1640 and abandoning the faith, over time "compatible threads of Catholicism were wound round and through their belief system," according to Nancy Wood, author of *Taos Pueblo* (Knopf, 1989). The Church of San Geronimo is on Taos Pueblo.

24. Dorothy Brett, "Millicent Rogers in Taos."
25. Ibid.

24: TRAVELS WITH MILLICENT

1. Archives of the Millicent Rogers Museum, Taos, New Mexico.
2. Dorothy Brett, "Millicent Rogers in Taos."
3. Archives of the Millicent Rogers Museum, Taos, New Mexico.
4. Dorothy Brett, "Millicent Rogers in Taos."
5. Arturo Peralta-Ramos, interview with the author.
6. Ernesto Luhan, interview with the author.
7. Dorothy Brett, "Millicent Rogers in Taos."
8. Tim Vreeland, interview with the author.
9. Adam Lewis, *Van Day Truex*, 170–1.
10. Dorothy Brett, "Millicent Rogers in Taos." The account of this Jamaica trip relies heavily on Brett's record of it.

26: WITH THE WIDE SKY

1. Ibid.
2. Archives of the Millicent Rogers Museum, Taos, New Mexico.
3. Ibid.
4. Eve S. Gregory, interview with the author.
5. Dorothy Brett Papers, from the Harry Ransom Humanities Research Center, University of Texas at Austin.
6. Videotaped interview with Paul Peralta-Ramos by Larry Torres.
7. Archives of the Millicent Rogers Museum, Taos, New Mexico.
8. Odette Terrel des Chênes, interview with the author.
9. Videotaped interview with Paul Peralta-Ramos by Larry Torres.
10. Dorothy Brett, "Millicent Rogers in Taos."
11. Ibid.
12. Tom McCarthy, interview with the author.

POSTSCRIPT

1. John Galliano, interview with the author.
2. Hamish Bowles, interview with the author.
3. Jacqueline de Ribes, interview with the author.
4. Tim Vreeland, interview with the author.
5. Arturo Peralta-Ramos, interview with the author.
6. Christina Lucia Peralta-Ramos, interview with the author.
7. Millicent's will from the Archives of the Millicent Rogers Museum, Taos, New Mexico.

Index

MR stands for Millicent Rogers. HHR stands for Henry Huttleston Rogers (Sr., Jr, and III). Kinship terms are in relation to MR. Women are listed under their maiden names, when known, e.g. Benjamin, Mary (mother) (Mrs. HHR, Jr.).